Network Security Auditing

Chris Jackson, CCIE No. 6256Cisco Press

Cisco Press

800 East 96th Street

Indianapolis, IN 46240

Network Security Auditing

Chris Jackson, CCIE No. 6256

Copyright © 2010 Cisco Systems, Inc.

Published by:

Cisco Press

800 East 96th Street

Indianapolis, IN 46240 USA

ISBN-13: 978-1-58705-352-8

ISBN-10: 1-58705-352-7

Printed in the United States of America

First Printing June 2010

Library of Congress Cataloging-in-Publication Data: Library of Congress Cataloging-in-Publication data is on file.

Warning and Disclaimer

This book is designed to provide information about Cisco network security. Every effort has been made to make this book as complete and as accurate as possible, but no warranty or fitness is implied.

The information is provided on an "as is" basis. The author, Cisco Press, and Cisco Systems, Inc. shall have neither liability nor responsibility to any person or entity with respect to any loss or damages arising from the information contained in this book or from the use of the discs or programs that may accompany it.

The opinions expressed in this book belong to the author and are not necessarily those of Cisco Systems, Inc.

Trademark Acknowledgments

All terms mentioned in this book that are known to be trademarks or service marks have been appropriately capitalized. Cisco Press or Cisco Systems, Inc. cannot attest to the accuracy of this information. Use of a term in this book should not be regarded as affecting the validity of any trademark or service mark.

Corporate and Government Sales

The publisher offers excellent discounts on this book when ordered in quantity for bulk purchases or special sales, which may include electronic versions and/or custom covers and content particular to your business, training goals, marketing focus, and branding interests. For more information, please contact: **U.S. Corporate and Government Sales** 1-800-382-3419 corpsales@pearsontechgroup.com

For sales outside the United States please contact: **International Sales** international@pearsoned.com

Feedback Information

At Cisco Press, our goal is to create in-depth technical books of the highest quality and value. Each book is crafted with care and precision, undergoing rigorous development that involves the unique expertise of members from the professional technical community.

Readers' feedback is a natural continuation of this process. If you have any comments regarding how we could improve the quality of this book, or otherwise alter it to better suit your needs, you can contact us through e-mail at feedback@ciscopress.com. Please make sure to include the book title and ISBN in your message.

We greatly appreciate your assistance.

Publisher: Paul Boger

Associate Publisher: Dave Dusthimer

Executive Editor: Brett Bartow

Managing Editor: Sandra Schroeder

Project Editor: Deadline Driven Publishing

Editorial Assistant: Vanessa Evans

Composition: Mark Shirar

Cisco Representative: Erik Ullanderson

Cisco Press Program Manager: Anand Sundaram

Technical Editors: Todd Reagan, Brian Sak

Senior Development Editor: Kimberley Debus

Copy Editor: Deadline Driven Publishing

Book Designer: Louisa Adair

Indexer: Ginny Munroe

CISCO

Americas Headquarters
Cisco Systems, Inc.
San Jose, CA

Asia Pacific Headquarters
Cisco Systems (USA) Pte. Ltd.
Singapore

Europe Headquarters
Cisco Systems International BV
Amsterdam, The Netherlands

Cisco has more than 200 offices worldwide. Addresses, phone numbers, and fax numbers are listed on the Cisco Website at **www.cisco.com/go/offices.**

CCDE, CCENT, Cisco Eos, Cisco HealthPresence, the Cisco logo, Cisco Lumin, Cisco Nexus, Cisco StadiumVision, Cisco TelePresence, Cisco WebEx, DCE, and Welcome to the Human Network are trademarks; Changing the Way We Work, Live, Play, and Learn and Cisco Store are service marks; and Access Registrar, Aironet, AsyncOS, Bringing the Meeting To You, Catalyst, CCDA, CCDP, CCIE, CCIP, CCNA, CCNP, CCSP, CCVP, Cisco, the Cisco Certified Internetwork Expert logo, Cisco IOS, Cisco Press, Cisco Systems, Cisco Systems Capital, the Cisco Systems logo, Cisco Unity, Collaboration Without Limitation, EtherFast, EtherSwitch, Event Center, Fast Step, Follow Me Browsing, FormShare, GigaDrive, HomeLink, Internet Quotient, IOS, iPhone, iQuick Study, IronPort, the IronPort logo, LightStream, Linksys, MediaTone, MeetingPlace, MeetingPlace Chime Sound, MGX, Networkers, Networking Academy, Network Registrar, PCNow, PIX, PowerPanels, ProConnect, ScriptShare, SenderBase, SMARTnet, Spectrum Expert, StackWise, The Fastest Way to Increase Your Internet Quotient, TransPath, WebEx, and the WebEx logo are registered trademarks of Cisco Systems, Inc. and/or its affiliates in the United States and certain other countries.

All other trademarks mentioned in this document or website are the property of their respective owners. The use of the word partner does not imply a partnership relationship between Cisco and any other company. (0812R)

Dedications

This book is dedicated to my beautiful wife Barbara, who also happens to be my best friend, and my two wonderful children Caleb and Sydney. Without your love and support, this book would not have been possible. I consider myself extremely lucky to have such a wonderful family in my life to share this journey with. You taught me the meaning of love and you make everything shiny and filled with joy.

About the Author

Christopher L. Jackson, CCIE No. 6256, is a security technical solutions architect in the U.S. Channels organization with Cisco and is focused on developing security consulting practices in the Cisco partner community. Throughout his career in internetworking, Chris has built secure networks that map to a strong security policy for a large number of organizations including UPS, GE, and Sprint. Chris is an active speaker on security for Cisco through TechwiseTV, conferences, and web casts. He has authored numerous whitepapers and is responsible for a number of Cisco initiatives to build stronger security partners through security practice building.

Chris is a highly certified individual with dual CCIEs (Routing and Switching & Security), CISSP, ISA, seven SANS GIAC certifications (GSNA, GCIH, GCFW, GCIA, GCUX, GCWN, and GSEC), and ITIL V3. Chris also holds a bachelors degree in business administration from McKendree College. Residing in Bradenton, Florida, Chris enjoys tinkering with his home automation system and playing with his ever-growing collection of electronic gadgets. His wife Barbara and two children Caleb and Sydney are the joy of his life and proof that not everything has to plug into a wall outlet to be fun.

About the Technical Reviewers

Todd Reagan, CCIE No. 20273, is a systems engineer for Cisco Systems where he focuses on security technologies. Todd has more than 12 years of experience in IP internetworking, including the design and implementation of global enterprise networks. His focus has been on the security considerations of Internet peering, MPLS, and VPNs. He holds a bachelors degree in computer science from Texas A&M University in College Station, Texas.

Brian Sak, CCIE 14441, CISSP, is a consulting systems engineer with Cisco Systems. He has more than 10 years of experience with network security. Prior to joining Cisco Systems, Brian provided consulting and assessment services for financial institutions, government agencies, and Fortune 500 companies.

Acknowledgments

Writing a book is not an easy task. Gene Fowler summed up the writing process with the following quote: "Writing is easy. All you do is stare at a blank sheet of paper until drops of blood form on your forehead."

There is simply no way this book would exist without the many people who have helped me along the way. Most of what I know about auditing and security comes from the fine people at the SANS institute, who provide the very best in vendor-neutral security training. Thanks to Tanya Baccam in particular for educating me about the art of auditing networks for fun and profit.

I am very lucky to have a strong support network at Cisco of the brightest and most talented engineers and hackers in the world. Todd Reagan helped with chapter 7, kept me straight on MPLS, and acted as a sounding board for my more insane concepts. Brian Sak played a major role in assisting with the writing of the wireless and password-hacking parts of the book. Victor Lam kept me sane and picked up the slack on my projects as I toiled away to get the book finished. You guys are incredible friends and words do not express how grateful I am for your support.

A big thank you to my managers Rob Learned, Chad Bullock, and Tony Bouvia. Over the past few years, they allowed me the time to work on this project and gave me encouragement and support along the way. You three truly care about the success of your people and represent the best qualities Cisco has to offer.

Thanks to Patrick Stark for being a fantastic friend and leader at Cisco. You always look out for us and help us get what we need. You are committed to our success and it shows.

Last, but definitely not least, I want to thank Brett Bartow, Kimberley Debus, Ginny Munroe, and all of the people at Cisco Press for working with me as I juggled my day job and this book. I started this project when dinosaurs roamed the land, and you stuck with me regardless of my elastic concept of time. I doubt there is a more professional bunch anywhere in the publishing business.

Contents at a Glance

Contents

Icons Used in This Book

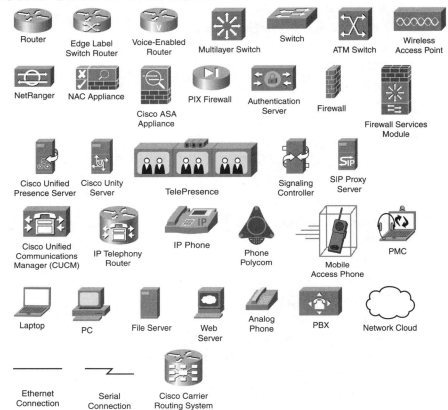

Command Syntax Conventions

The conventions used to present command syntax in this book are the same conventions used in the IOS Command Reference. The Command Reference describes these conventions as follows:

- Boldface indicates commands and keywords that are entered literally as shown. In actual configuration examples and output (not general command syntax), boldface indicates commands that are manually input by the user (such as a show command).

- Italic indicates arguments for which you supply actual values.

- Vertical bars (|) separate alternative, mutually exclusive elements.

- Square brackets ([ ]) indicate an optional element.

- Braces ({ }) indicate a required choice.

- Braces within brackets () indicate a required choice within an optional element.

Introduction

Mention the word audit to IT professionals and you will probably see their eyes glaze over as they imagine frightening visions of auditors with pointy tails, pitchforks, and checklists running around and pointing out all of the things they have done wrong to their manager. The purpose of a security audit is not to place blame or pick apart network design, but to ensure the integrity, effectiveness, and compliance of corporate security policies. Auditing provides the ability to test the assumptions companies have about how secure they think they are from threats and to gauge whether or not policies map to industry best practices and compliance laws. An organization's level of risk is quantified by placing a value on the assets of the business and analyzing what impact the exploitation of vulnerabilities can have to the business as a whole. Auditors find risk and check to see whether the appropriate controls are in place to mitigate exposure to that risk.

Auditing is not just about running a bunch of hacker tools in an attempt to break into the network. There are many types of audits, and the scope of an audit defines what the auditor inspects and how often. Many organizations require an annual audit of key systems by an outside firm (external audit), whereas others also mandate internal audits every six months or before and after any major IT project. If you are subject to PCI compliance requirements, you might need to have an audit preformed every quarter. The bottom line is if you aren't auditing today, you will be forced to through regulations or encouraged to by industry best practices. It simply makes good business sense to measure the effectiveness of your security investment.

The ultimate benefit of auditing is to continuously improve the processes, procedures, and controls put in place to secure valuable corporate assets. Businesses today have a responsibility to their customers to safe guard their confidential data. Numerous high-profile security failures have shattered that trust through carelessness while handling backup media and allowing millions of credit cards and financial records to fall into the hands of individuals determined to illegally profit at the expense of others. It takes only one major breach to appear in the news for a company to experience significant loss of shareholder value and sometimes even the total loss of the company itself. Having a policy and enforcing it are essential to protecting your business. Auditing that policy plays a key role in making sure that the policy actually accomplishes the goal of reducing risk and therefore protects key assets from loss. A large percentage of security failures can be minimized or prevented with a strong risk-based auditing program.

Goals

The goal of this book is not to be yet another hacker book devoted to the latest tools and techniques for breaking into networks. Those skills are useful, but are not the primary focus of a security audit. There have been many books devoted to that topic and they are typically out of date by the time they come to press because of the speed in which technology changes. This book is about measuring the deployment of Cisco security technologies to mitigate risk. Baseline technical testing is covered from a process standpoint, but the focus is not on penetration testing.

This book provides the reader with a practical guide to building an auditing and assessment program that factors in regulatory and industry security requirements, with real examples of how Cisco products can help address those needs. Recognizing that security is a system that relies on strong policy is the key principle. The value of the book lies in its ability to show real applications of Cisco security technology in the context of an auditing framework. Here are the key benefits of the book:

- Provides an overview of the auditing process and introduces important regulations and industry best practices.

- Demonstrates how to use commercial and open source tools to assist with the auditing process and validate security policy assumptions.

- Introduces IT governance frameworks such as Cobit, ITIL, and ISO 17799/27001 while providing guidance about how to leverage each with Cisco security products.

- Shows the reader how to segment security architectures into domains that provide a systems approach to auditing Cisco networks.

- Supplies a detailed auditing checklist after each domain for the reader to utilize in an auditing program.

- Provides design guidance for meeting auditing requirements and shows how complementary security solutions greatly increase the overall security posture of a company.

- Guides the reader to build an auditing program that utilizes the techniques presented in the book.

Who Should Read This Book?

This book is geared toward beginner to intermediate-level auditing and more specifically, auditing as it pertains to Cisco networks. The content is useful to anyone who wants to build a program to measure the effectiveness of Cisco security products. IT governance and auditing have common roots with financial auditing, and in many cases, it is ultimately the responsibility of the CFO in larger organizations. The language and procedures an IT auditor follows are similar to how a CPA might examine the books to certify that a business is keeping its records accurately and paying its taxes on time. Both disciplines keep there eyes open for fraud and try to anticipate how a system of controls can be circumvented. Every aspect of auditing, such as database auditing or web applications, is not covered as the focus of this book is on auditing the network. Numerous other books are dedicated to application and website auditing and would be better at providing a deeper understanding in those areas. If you are an IT auditor, security consultant, InfoSec manager, or someone who wants to assess his own network for good security deployment practices, then this book is for you.

How This Book Is Organized

The organization of this book breaks the material up into two major parts. The first part covers the principles of auditing and strives to teach the language and key components of the auditing process. This overview pulls together a number of techniques for identifying risk and shows how we must think like auditors in our network designs and device configurations. It also covers the major regulatory, industry compliance, and security framework initiatives. The section ends with a description of common auditing tools and techniques that can be used to assess and verify that the policy is enforced by technical controls.

The second part, consisting of Chapters 5 through 12, covers the major Cisco security solution domains, which break down Cisco security technologies into seven categories that enable the auditor to examine network security as a system of integrated components rather than individual products. Each chapter discusses the risks, threats, policies, procedures, and technical controls that can be deployed to defend each domain. Best practices on network security design and configuration are covered, too. The reader is also supplied with a checklist that can be used as a starting point or reference for auditing.

The following provides more detail on the contents of each chapter:

Part I, "Principles of Auditing"

Chapter 1, "Principles of Auditing": This chapter defines security fundamentals including policies, procedures, standards, and controls. The basics of risk management and the how, what, and why audits are performed. In addition, the auditing process is outlined with a six-step methodology that can be used in performing an audit.

Chapter 2, "Security and the Law": This chapter is about IT security laws and regulatory compliance with an overview of many of the major federal and state statutes governing IT Security. SOX, HIPAA, and GLBA are covered in addition to the PCI standard.

Chapter 3, "Security Governance, Frameworks, and Standards": Security governance frameworks such a COSO, Cobit, and ITIL help businesses coordinate people, process, and technology around security objectives. This chapter covers these frameworks, and also includes where to find source material that can be useful in building standards, procedures, and guidelines for security technology deployment.

Chapter 4, "Auditing Tools and Techniques": This chapter addresses the basics for evaluating security controls through technical testing. A combination of open source, commercial, and integrated Cisco testing tools are presented.

Part II, "Mapping Cisco Security Controls to Auditing Requirements"

Chapter 5, "Security Solutions Domains": Security solution domains are introduced in this chapter as a method for assessing network security as an interconnected system. This chapter also discusses building checklists for security audits.

Chapter 6, "Policy and Compliance": Policy and compliance is the first auditing domain and is focused on assessing security policies. This chapter provides an overview of key security policies that businesses should have and how they should be constructed.

Chapter 7, "Infrastructure Security": This chapter covers assessing baseline security features and configuration that should be implemented on Cisco routers, switches, and wireless devices.

Chapter 8, "Perimeter Intrusion Prevention": Assessing perimeter defenses is covered in this chapter, with a focus on firewalls and intrusion prevention systems.

Chapter 9, "Access Control": Access control technologies enable the enforcement of role-based access requirements that follow the principle of least privilege. This chapter describes how to assess identity-based networking solutions and network admission control.

Chapter 10, "Remote Access": This chapter covers how to assess VPN technologies including site-to-site and mobile-user VPNs. Best practices for deployment and testing methods are also discussed.

Chapter 11, "Endpoint Protection": Endpoint protection is about preventing and detecting attacks targeted at users and their network devices. This chapter discusses methods that can be used to assess policies, procedures, and controls to protect endpoints from web, email, malware, and data loss.

Chapter 12, "Unified Communications": This chapter addresses auditing Unified communications systems policies, procedures, and security controls used to maintain confidentiality and defend against fraud.

Chapter 1

The Principles of Auditing

Do you want to know a secret? Security isn't about hacking, nasty, malicious software, or the vulnerability of the day. Security is about maintaining a system and process that provide access to critical data without exposing your company or customers to excessive risk. Auditing is one of the most important aspects of maintaining that system, because it provides the opportunity to test assumptions about the security posture of networked systems and compare that posture with standards and regulations. Auditors ask the questions "How do you know that you are secure?" and "Can you prove that your security technology works?"

The purpose of this chapter is to introduce the key principles of auditing and to describe the auditing process.

Security Fundamentals: The Five Pillars

Auditing the security of a company requires that you have a good general understanding of what security is and what it is not. To understand security, it is critical that you realize that security is a process, not a product. Security is not a race with a finish line at the end, as you can never be 100 percent secure no matter how much money or time you spend on it. It's just not possible to anticipate every vector of attack; but, with the appropriate planning and protective strategies in place, high levels of security can be achieved. Cisco is, fortunately, in a unique position to help companies achieve their security goals by providing the tools necessary to embed security features into many aspects of the network. This means security can be leveraged as a system to better map to the policies, procedures, and more importantly, the business drivers that cause companies to want to safeguard their assets.

To understand security and to audit it as a system, you need to be able to identify how everything ties together conceptually. Security is a broad topic, and one of the few in information technology that literally touches all aspects of a business. From the data center to the break room, every function of a business has its own list of things that need to be protected from a certain level of risk. Managing risk is one of the most important factors in developing a strategy for protecting people, technology, and data. To focus security efforts and to make them manageable, it helps to break down the various aspects of security into the five pillars of security. Figure 1-1 shows the five pillars.

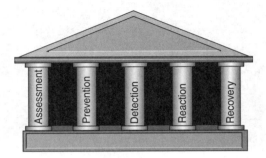

Figure 1-1   *Five Pillars of Security*

Assessment

The first step in protecting your company's assets is to assess the environment. Most people (thrill seekers excluded) wouldn't try to walk across a busy intersection with a blindfold on because not being able to see if the light is red or green could lead to a bad day. Understanding the business environment and direction helps identify the areas that the business deems most important and subsequently the most sensitive to disruption of services or theft. Much of what an auditor is asked to do in assessing risk requires sufficient knowledge of how the organization operates. Assessments document and identify potential threats, key assets, policies and procedures, and management's tolerance for risk.

The assessment process involves asking pointed questions. Just as if you were building a house, you would first start by surveying the land (available technology) to determine how suitable it is to build on. You would also need to know whether the area is prone to flooding (threats). How often does it flood (threat frequency)? Do you have the appropriate permits (laws and regulations)? What are the job site rules (policy and procedure)? What technology can you use to quickly and effectively build (technological components)? These questions and many more help the business plan a strategy for accomplishing its goals. Asking similar questions of the company's security enables you to examine various scenarios to identify weaknesses in defenses or procedures. What is the probability that you will be hacked tonight and have a "CNN moment" tomorrow? It's hard to say without a thorough assessment of the business and technology.

Assessments are not something that are done once and then forgotten. As the business needs change and new services and technologies are introduced, regularly scheduled reassessments should be conducted. Doing this gives you an opportunity to test policies and procedures to ensure that they are still relevant and appropriate.

Prevention

Many engineers focus on technology when they think of prevention. True prevention is more than a firewall or a security appliance: It encompasses administrative, operational, and technical controls. Prevention is not just accomplished through technology, but also policy, procedure, and awareness.

Policy must be documented and enforced with strict rules and consequences for violation. Documented procedures that utilize good security practices can help prevent misconfiguration, which is one of the most common methods that attackers use to compromise a system. Helping users understand what is and is not permissible, in addition to consistent and fair enforcement, goes a long way to lowering the overall risk to a company.

Too often, organizations fixate on trying to prevent bad things from happening when in reality, they simply can't stop everything. The magic box that Vendor X sells you can never anticipate all vectors of attack. This is where the concept of defense in depth comes into play. Defense in depth assumes that no control is perfect, so it helps to layer defenses so that you can compensate for known or unknown weaknesses in a technology or control. Technical security controls such as a firewall or intrusion prevention systems provide an important role in keeping a network secure, but they are not a silver bullet that you can plug in and expect to solve all of your security problems. Expect individual security controls to fail, but plan for the event by using multiple levels of prevention.

Detection

Your car's alarm system is one form of detection. Balancing your checkbook at the end of the month is another form of detection. Detection is how you identify whether or not you have a security breach or intrusion. Without adequate detection mechanisms, you run the risk of not knowing whether your network has been compromised. Dr. Eric Cole, author of *Network Security Bible*, said it best: "Prevention is important, but detection is a must." If you can't detect a compromise, then you run the risk of having a false sense of trust in your prevention techniques.

One example of the importance of detection can be seen in the 1996 disclosure by Ohio University of hackers who gained access to systems that resulted in the loss of over 137,000 Social Security numbers. These miscreants had total access and control for over a year! Obviously, detection mechanisms were either nonexistent or were not properly monitored. Of course, the worst example I have heard about that highlights poor detective controls is from the United States Department of Agriculture, who announced in 2007 that it exposed over 150,000 farmers' Social Security numbers because its database became live in 1981. Because no one can say for sure when it was actually connected to the Internet, over the 26 years it was active, it is estimated that the data was easily accessible for well over 10 years. Not a good thing!

Detective controls help to identify security incidents and provide visibility into activities on the network. It's important to detect an incident early so that you can formulate an appropriate reaction to recover services as quickly as possible.

Reaction

When prevention and detection are effective, reaction time is greatly reduced. No one wants to find out that they have a breach, but if you do have a compromise you need to do something about it now! Reaction is the aspect of security that is most concerned with time. The goal is to minimize the time from detection to response so that exposure to the incident is minimized. Fast reaction depends on prevention and detection to provide the data and context needed to recognize a security breach. Of course, just knowing about a compromise doesn't help if you haven't planned out in advance what to do. This planned and coordinated response is called *incident handling*. Some companies have a dedicated incident-handling team that can move in at a moments notice to reduce exposure time. Not everyone has the budget for these types of teams. Even if your company doesn't have a dedicated team, some forethought and planning can mean the difference between everyone falling all over themselves trying to figure out what to do next and restoring key services.

Automated response through technology is an important tool that reduces your reaction time to a security incident. But as good as automated response technologies are, you still need skilled people to handle the incident to ensure that the incident is real and not a hiccup on the wire. How quickly and efficiently incidents are handled is one of the most important tests to the effectiveness of a company's security program. When the alarms go off, how you react can make all the difference in the world!

Recovery

When your company has an eCommerce system that simply must be available to your customers or it processes hundreds of thousands of dollars in sales a minute, downtime is relatively easy to quantify. Recovery is where you play detective to determine what went wrong so that you can get the systems back on line without opening up the same vulnerability or condition that caused the problem in the first place. Do you patch the exploited vulnerability and recover the data from backup or do you have a bigger flaw in security controls that allowed the incident to occur? What was the reason that the system was compromised? How did the technical controls fail? Was there a misconfiguration? The recovery phase doesn't end with bringing the system back online. There is also the postmortem aspect that determines what changes need to be made to processes, procedures, and technologies to reduce the likelihood of this type of vulnerability in the future. As an auditor, you must ensure that the organizations you audit have a plan for recovery that addresses these issues.

Building a Security Program

Policies, procedures, and standards represent the foundation of a security program. These are the documents that detail the who, what, when, and how of protecting your business assets and resources. Yet, as important as these documents are, many organizations still don't have a formal policy and procedure set for information security. If you ask the average IT professional about his company's security policies and procedures, more often than not he will be hard pressed to answer your questions or produce a current copy. With regulatory compliance requirements such as SOX, GLBA, HIPAA, and PCI, this has started to change, but policy and procedure are still put low on the list of priorities. If they don't help the company sell more widgets, then why would the company do it? The reality is that policies and procedures are how you plan for and hopefully reduce the risk of bad things happening to your data. When you work on a car or an airplane, there is a set of procedures that you should follow to ensure that you are consistently performing the correct operations in the appropriate order. It is essential to have security procedures documented before hand, so that you reduce the risk of having those "extra" parts at the end of the job or worse (in the case of the airplane), a major problem that puts lives at risk.

An essential part of the auditor's job is to examine an organization's policies, procedures, and standards to ensure that they are complete, enforceable, and followed.

Policy

Policies are essential for all businesses regardless of size or industry. They act as a social contract between the company and its users that define acceptable behavior with corporate resources. Policies also provide guidance about how a company approaches security by defining why the security measure is in place, what is being protected, and to whom the policy is applicable. An organization should receive its guidance about the technologies and controls that need to be implemented based on the goals defined in the policy. Think of it as the blueprint for building the structure of the security program. Just as you wouldn't go to a lumberyard and build your house based on the wood and nails available, you should not implement security products and technology without a solid policy. At a minimum, a good security policy includes the following:

- **Purpose:** Why the policy exists. This section includes the reasoning behind the policy, potential ramifications to the company if the policy is not followed, and how it supports the corporate mission.

- **Scope:** To whom or what the policy applies. Is this a policy for contractors or full-time employees? The scope should use job titles or functions to identify the employees instead of an individual's name, so that the policy is unaffected as people change positions or go on vacation. Does the policy apply to development systems or key customer-facing servers? The scope section provides specifics about the assets and employees covered by the policy.

- **Policy statement:** The policy requirements. This is the meat of the policy document and includes specific details about what is permitted or prohibited. The wording should be clear and concise and not be open to interpretation. A policy should not include specific products or configurations, as these areas are covered in procedures and subject to change.

- **Enforcement:** Policy provides an enforcement point for discipline or prosecution in the event that an individual chooses not to play by the rules. Policy compliance is mandated through the disciplinary action statement. The enforcement section provides clear indication about the consequences of noncompliance with the policy and may include employment termination or other disciplinary actions.

■ **Terms and Definitions:** Clarification of terminology utilized in the policy statement, such as SPAM or malware.

■ **Revision History:** Summary of changes to the policy, with date of change, person or group that initiated the change, and a summary of what was changed.

The most important aspect of a good security policy is that the policy be clear, concise, and free of ambiguity. Providing examples helps to clarify the intent of the policy, but care must be taken to provide wording to cover areas that are not specifically mentioned. When writing policy, using imperative verbs such as will, shall, and must are essential to providing actionable direction. Trouble can arise when using subjective verbs such as should, may, and recommend because they represent an ideal state and do not imply a mandatory requirement or call to action. Many policies have been rendered ineffective and unenforceable by using subjective speech because the argument can be made that the policy is simply a recommendation and not a requirement. Telling an employee that he should follow the acceptable use policy is not the same as informing him that he *must* follow it.

Procedures

Procedures are detailed instruction about how a policy is to be implemented. These documents provide an operations manual that an administrator can use to address bringing a new system online, backing up critical data, firewall configuration, and so on. It is difficult to enforce consistency without a procedural checklist to follow. Each policy document should include a companion procedure document. This enables the organization to update technologies and leverage best practices, while writing down the process and techniques used so that they can be replicated and checked. Procedure documents can provide an auditor with insight into how closely the company under audit follows security processes and makes great checklist material for the audit itself. The following is a list of items found in most procedure documents:

■ **Purpose:** Explains why the procedure is in place and what the source policy is

■ **Scope:** Explains who is responsible for the execution of the procedure and what situation or technology to which it applies

■ **Warnings:** Includes safety or security warnings that must be followed to maintain integrity

■ **Procedure steps:** Detailed procedures that must be followed to configure or provision the technology covered by the procedure

■ **Revision history:** Summary of changes and when the procedure was last updated or reviewed

Standards

As a kid, you might have gone to an amusement park excited about getting on the latest rollercoaster only to find out you weren't quite tall enough to ride. This experience was a painful introduction to the definition of a standard. At the time, you might have thought that the cartoon character cutout that you didn't measure up to was put there to spoil your fun, but it served a purpose. That purpose was to enforce height standards for the safety mechanisms built into the ride.

Security standards serve the same purpose in that they dictate required controls or configurations that are considered best practices. Requiring alphanumeric passwords of 15 characters or more including special characters is an example of a strong password standard. Standards are the source material for the best practices that are used to create procedures. Fortunately, there are many well-documented standards available for use from standards bodies and Cisco. These standards and how to find them are covered in more detail in subsequent chapters. It is important to understand the reasoning behind a technology configuration or product selection choice that is used to address policy requirements. Cross-referencing procedures to standards documents such as the NIST 800 series or ISO27002 are great ways of justifying configuration and design decisions. With regulatory and industry requirements that mandate that companies exercise "due diligence" in securing their computing assets, it helps to be able to back up those claims through reputable third parties.

Security Controls

Security controls are the building blocks of a security program. They are the tools that you implement to protect the confidentiality, integrity, and availability of important assets and data. Much of the assessment work that an auditor conducts is centered on the many controls that a company has (or doesn't have) to reduce risk. Auditors are concerned with how effectively the controls accomplish the goals set forth by the security policy.

Controls are typically thought of in terms of technology. Firewalls or IPS systems come to mind, but there are many types of controls that can be used to protect your systems. The primary classification of controls can be accomplished by grouping them under three main categories: administrative, technical, and physical.

Administrative Controls

Administrative controls can consist of policies, such as Acceptable Use or security-awareness training. In addition, administrative controls can also consist of processes such as balancing the corporate books and security auditing. This type of control is typically focused on managing people, such as separation of duties, requirements for vacation, or any other rules that provide a deterrent to fraud or improper behavior.

Technical Controls

Technical controls consist of the technology that you implement to prevent or enforce behavior on the network or computing resources. They can include firewalls, Intrusion Prevention Systems (IPS), Host Intrusion Prevention Systems (HIPS), Role-Based Access Control (RBAC), or any other mechanism for enforcing policy.

Physical Controls

If you want to deter people from walking through your yard, put up a fence. Although this won't keep everyone out, it is an example of a useful physical control. In an office setting, physical controls include locked doors, key card access systems, video surveillance, guards, gates, and so on. This type of control is designed to restrict access to sensitive devices and areas.

Each of the primary control groups can be further broken out into specific types of actions the control can take. Although there are others, the standard set includes preventative, detective, corrective, and recovery.

Preventative Controls

Preventative controls enforce the confidentiality, integrity, and availability of data and assets. If the primary control is technical, then preventive controls are firewall rules, access control lists (ACL), or another technology used to block unauthorized access. Administrative preventative controls can include things like policies and warning banners. The primary category of controls (administrative, technical, and physical) gives context to how to implement the secondary controls.

Detective Controls

Detective controls are the alarm systems built into various parts of the business to detect if bad things are happening. These can be video surveillance, firewall logs, an IPS, or Security Incident Event Management (SIEM) system. This type of control also includes financial and security audits.

Corrective Controls

Corrective controls are reactionary in nature. An IPS blocking an attacking IP address is an automated corrective control that responds to the detection of malicious activity. A simpler example is a security guard double-checking that a door is locked when performing his nightly facilities check. A corrective control is a mechanism used to mitigate a security incident and is likely implemented after a detective control has discovered the problem.

Recovery Controls

Recovery controls are like parachutes on a plane. Hopefully, you won't need them, but they are there in case you do. Backup systems, redundant power supplies, and spare parts are all examples of recovery controls. Restoring services is the goal of these controls.

An auditor is responsible for determining whether or not the controls implemented are sufficient to protect the assets or meet the business requirements outlined in the policy documents. Do the controls adhere to best practice and are they in compliance with regulations and law? An auditor might also be asked to provide recommendations about how to improve the controls to better address current risks.

The interaction between the various controls discussed provides a nice view into whether or not a company under audit has addressed its controls in a thorough manner. Table 1-1 provides an example of how an auditor can logically group controls for a remote access (Virtual Private Network (VPN) solution to ensure it has been addressed.

Table 1-1   *Remote Access VPN Control Groupings*

	Administrative	Technical	Physical
Preventative	Remote access VPN policy	Firewall access rules, Secure Socket Layer (SSL) / IPSEC VPN, NAC posture assessment	Data center requires keycard, password recovery disabled on VPN appliance
Detective	VPN user access review	NAC Posture Assessment, intrusion prevention system (IPS), Mentoring Analysis and Response System (MARS) log review	Video surveillance, alarm sensor on door to equipment
Corrective	Access revocation procedures	NAC remediation	Auto locking doors, nightly security checks
Recovery	Recovery procedures documented	VPN cluster, modem pool	SMARTnet with HW replacement, Uninterruptible Power Supply (UPS)

Managing Risk

You manage risk every day of your life. When you get into a car, the real risk of getting into an accident on the way to your destination exists. This is a risk that everyone who drives realizes, so in order to mitigate the risk of something bad happening, you follow posted road signs, stop at stoplights, and signal before you change lanes. This can help to reduce the chances of something unpleasant happening, but it can't completely eliminate risk. There is always a person who drives aggressively or runs the red light. To reduce the impact of the event (pun intended)—in this case, a car wreck—you purchase vehicles with airbags, crumple zones, and antilock brakes. These technologies can help minimize potential damages (physical well being is the asset in this case) and hopefully give you enough time to react to the event so you can avoid it or walk away without any major harm.

Technology can help dramatically reduce risk, but only if applied in a manner that puts investments where they can do the most good. Airbags that go off 10 minutes after a wreck (or not at all) don't provide very much protection. An improperly installed IPS does not provide any meaningful data and can potentially degrade your ability to detect a real attack by generating unnecessary log data. Finding a real attack in this situation is like finding the proverbial needle in a haystack.

How much security is enough security? This is a question that plagues IT managers because there are no easy answers. Most organizations answer this question by implementing a risk-management program. SOX, GLBA, HIPAA, and PCI require a risk-management program because there is no one-size-fits-all approach to securing corporate assets and data. Organizations must understand the risks they face, and the only way to do that is through assessing risk.

Risk Assessment

There are many techniques used to assess risk. Some measure risk through numerical models, and others use experience and professional opinion to measure risk. No matter how good your models are or how extensive your research is, a portion of the equation always has a level of uncertainty. Risk by its very nature does not lend itself to a numeric value that is 100 percent accurate. Of course, if you can unerringly determine whether or not something is going to happen, I am sure you would move to Las Vegas and hang out at the casinos instead! To better understand the various models, it is necessary to define a few important terms:

- **Asset:** If you took an accounting class, you probably had the whole debits and credits thing drilled into your head. Putting a numeric value to an asset is easy for tangible items such as how much your routers cost or employee payroll, but the real challenge is in putting a value on the intangibles such as goodwill, opportunity cost, or loss of reputation. In summary, an asset is anything of value to your organization.

- **Threat:** A threat is any type of event that can cause loss and is usually measured in terms of probability or likelihood of occurrence. In the case of viruses, companies can see hundreds of infection attempts a month, so the threat of being exposed (though not necessarily infected) to a virus is close to 100 percent.

- **Vulnerability:** A vulnerability is a weakness that can result in a threat being able to compromise an asset. Hardware and software vulnerabilities are discovered on a daily basis, but the greatest number of vulnerabilities still comes from default configurations. One other thing to note is that just because a system is "vulnerable" does not mean that the vulnerability can be exploited. Hardening systems by removing unneeded services can help to reduce the potential vectors of attack by preventing access to vulnerable services.

- **Cost of exposure:** Cost of exposure refers to the total tangible and intangible cost associated with an asset being compromised. Many times the actual monetary value of an asset is a small portion of its total value to the organization. A $10,000 database server might have 1 million dollars worth of data on it. You have to understand the business processes and interconnections to assess the true cost of exposure. Interdependent systems can grind to a halt if a 25-cent part breaks.

The risk assessment process defined by NIST 800-30 provides an excellent guide to identifying risk to systems and processes. NIST 800-30 utilizes the following steps:

Step 1. **Characterize the system:** Understand the business processes and interdependency of the systems under review. Where does it fit into the organization and how is it used? What are the software and hardware versions deployed. How is it configured?

Step 2. **Identify threats:** Identify the threats to confidentiality, integrity, and availability. Extortion, corporate espionage, data theft, and disasters are all examples of potential threats.

Step 3. **Identify vulnerabilities:** Catalog the services and protocols used to generate a list of potential attack vectors. Software, hardware, and configuration can all have potential vulnerabilities. Automated software tools help, but experience and knowledge find the ones that scanning tools miss.

Step 4. **Analyze controls:** Identify whether or not the controls in place are sufficient when compared to the risks a successful compromise would have to the business. Each of the primary control categories—administrative, technical, and physical—must successfully address prevention, detection, correction, and recovery for the threats and vulnerabilities identified. This analysis finds which controls are missing or inadequate.

Step 5. **Determine the likelihood of an event:** Utilize the quantitative or qualitative approach to rank the likelihood of an event happening. The next section addresses a number of methods for doing this.

Step 6. **Analyze the impact of an event:** Attempt to put a monetary value on the impact a potential event can have to the company as a whole. Management understands the severity much better and is in a better position to allocate resources if it has an idea of how much money the event could cost the company.

Step 7. **Determine risks:** The values identified in previous steps are compiled to provide a snapshot of the risks the business faces. This step provides the prioritized list of security issues that need to be addressed.

Step 8. **Recommend controls:** A key part of an auditor's role is to recommend controls to reduce risk. These recommendations help the organization under audit better protect its assets.

Step 9.   **Document results:** Documenting the results of the risk assessment helps to show due care and due diligence. This step is also where the results of the process are presented to management.

Risk, as it relates to information security, can be defined quite simply as the probability or likelihood that a threat will exploit a vulnerability and cause damages. Although this definition might sound simple, there is some work that needs to be done to figure out the values you need to build your equations. There are two main approaches to risk analysis; one is quantitative and the other is qualitative.

The quantitative approach uses formulas to equate the frequency of a risk to a monetary value. These formulas themselves are not particularly complex, but the data used to feed the variables can be time-consuming and difficult to compile. Most of the data that exists is historical, and the rate of change that is seen in technology makes it difficult to maintain accurate values. In security, you don't have actuarial tables that give the average number of incidents per type of company or industry—similar to what is seen with insurance claim data—because most organizations simply do not track security incidents accurately or consistently. The most widely used source for this type of data generally comes for the yearly FBI/Computer Security Institute report on cyber crime. This report provides the number of reported incidents in various categories, such as data theft or security breaches; however, you are on your own to figure out what these events cost, as it is different per company and employee. You might have a worm infect a laptop, causing a user to be unable to work for a day. Calculating the technician time in reloading the machine might give you two hours at $60 per hour or $120 for that incident. What is often under reported is the total cost in productivity and lost data. You have the technician's time accounted for, but what about the individual who can't do his job because of the downed laptop? What about the lost report that took two weeks to complete and now must be rewritten because key files were corrupted? It's more difficult to quantify those types of losses. Still, many organizations have standardized on quantitative methods for risk analysis. Auditors must be aware of how these formulas work. Here are a few classic examples:

■   **Single Loss Expectancy (SLE) = Asset Value x Exposure Factor:** SLE is a formula that determines the expected cost of loss to an asset based on the exposure to the event that the asset incurs. The exposure factor represents how much damage there is as a percentage of loss to the asset. The percentage of loss ranges from 0 (no damage) to 100 percent (total loss). Unless there is complete destruction of the asset, the exposure factor is less than 100 percent. If a web server database worth $100,000 is corrupted during an attack, and the backup is able to recover only 70 percent of the data, then the exposure factor would be $30. A $100,000 asset x percent (EF) = $30,000 loss.

■   **Annual Loss Expectancy (ALE) = Single Loss Expectancy x Annual Rate of Occurrence:** The ALE calculation uses the output of the SLE formula and multiplies it by the expected number of occurrences of the event in a single year. If the web server is hit by an attack twice a year, then ARO would be 2. If you have never been hit but estimate that you will experience an attack sometime in 10 years, then ARO would be 0.1. After you determine the ARO, you can then multiple it by the SLE to determine the ALE:

$30,000(SLE) x 2(ARO) = $60,000(ALE)

- **Countermeasure Value = ALE Before – ALE After Annual Countermeasure Cost:** To determine how much you should spend on countermeasures to reduce the risk to assets, you can use the data generated by the previous functions to build a cost benefit analysis to help justify the purchase of a new countermeasure. During the post-incident analysis, it was determined that the attack could have been prevented through a combination of an IPS and better backup software for recovery. The total cost of the new countermeasures is $10,000. If you have $60,000 (Before ALE) – $20,000 (after ALE savings from the new countermeasure) – a $10,000 countermeasure cost, then you have added $30,000 of "value" to the organization by purchasing the countermeasure. This enables you to determine that purchasing this countermeasure is a good use of your security investment and saves the company $30,000.

- **Return on Security Investment (ROSI) = (ALE x Percent of risk mitigated) – Countermeasure cost) / Countermeasure cost:** The ROSI calculation is used to determine a return on investment value for a security countermeasure. You utilize ALE and multiply it by the percentage improvement in effectiveness of the new countermeasure and then subtract it by the cost of the countermeasure. Then you divide the total by the cost of the countermeasure, to determine the rate of return. To arrive at a Risk mitigation percentage, you should test the equipment in a lab or rely on a neutral testing organization to determine an appropriate effectiveness rate. Continuing with the DoS example, your $60,000 (ALE) x 80 percent (increase in risk mitigation based on testing) – $20,000 (cost of the countermeasure) you get $28,000, which would be how much you should save from the increased effectiveness of the countermeasure. If you divide $28,000 by $20,000 (the cost of the countermeasure) you can hope to realize a return on security investment of 140 percent. Not a bad deal!

Although none of the quantification techniques described are 100 percent accurate, there is still value in having a consistent and replicable way to determine how an organization invests in security. These are simple examples that require research and time to increase accuracy. Because a large number of companies don't have the time or inclination to do this level of number crunching, the qualitative methods for determining risk have become increasingly popular.

Qualitative risk analysis is less concerned with the numbers, and more interested in finding which assets are exposed to the greatest level of risk. The power of the qualitative approach is that it can provide a measurement tool that anyone can understand without majoring in statistical analysis. The results are actionable, and the rating system can be anything that the organization is comfortable with, such as high, medium, and low. The variables threat, vulnerability, and exposure are similar to the quantitative approach, but the ways in which we arrive at the values are quite different. The qualitative approach uses the following simple formula:

Risk = Threat x Vulnerability x Impact of Exposure

Assets are what you must try to protect, and those assets can be a database, business process, network access, or anything else that is an important part of how you do business. The easiest way to identify threats is to use the CIA triad of Confidentiality, Integrity, and Availability. These three areas represent the primary aspects that businesses attempt to protect, so if you measure your assets against CIA, you can determine potential threats to that asset. Confidentiality is keeping data private and out of unauthorized hands. Integrity is about ensuring that unauthorized parties do not tamper with data. Availability is concerned with keeping the service or system up and running.

After you determine your potential threats, you need to classify them based on the likelihood of an event happening. There are always potential threats out there, but some of them are just not practical. That's where the vulnerability aspect of the formula comes into play. A threat with no vulnerability is still a threat, but there is no risk to the asset because if any one of the variables is zero, then risk is zero. Risk depends on the presence of a threat and a vulnerability. Take, for example, the threat of a teardrop attack. The teardrop attack took advantage of a vulnerability in the IP stack where a maliciously crafted fragmented packet with overlapping offsets could cause a kernel panic or blue screen of death. In 1997 this was a real risk because the vulnerability was present in a large majority of Windows and Unix-derived IP stacks, and the threat of someone using this attack was great due to easily accessible exploit code. Unless you are running very old or devices that aren't patched, this is not something you would be concerned with today. The risk of this attack to modern operating systems is virtually nonexistent.

The last variable in the simplified risk equation looks at the impact to the organization if the threat is successful. If the threat is stealing customer credit card information, you can feel confident that the threat level is high because there is significant evidence that there are plenty of individuals with the skills, resources, and inclination to engage in this type of crime. If a company houses its customers' credit card information in a database that is connected to an Internet-accessible web server, then the potential for a vulnerability that could be exploited is also high. The impact of this event could be high, too, because customers do not forgive a company that experiences a breach like this. Based on this simple scenario, you can determine that the risk is high to this asset and it would be wise to focus your efforts on protecting the asset by providing controls and countermeasures that can reduce the risk of a compromise happening.

The point of all of this is to make sure that the organization that is being audited has addressed these issues in a manner that reduces the total risk to the organization. Auditors need to understand how to perform risk analysis to determine whether or not the controls are in place and appropriately address the level of risk to the asset. The auditor's role is also to provide recommendations for reducing risk, and that takes us to the next area of risk management: risk mitigation.

Risk Mitigation

After you have determined that there are legitimate risks to the company's assets, the next step is to figure out how to address those risks. The goal of most risk-management programs is to prove that the organization has preformed "due diligence" or "due care."

Due diligence and due care are legal terms that seek to determine whether a company or individual has been negligent in their duties. In the case of information, security organizations need to act (and document those actions) in a manner that secures business assets to a level that is prudent and reasonable given their value and risk. This prudent man rule is another aspect of law that comes up often when discussing risk mitigation. Directors and managers might be held personally liable for negligence of duty, if it is proven that they did not provide the necessary environment to protect the assets they have been charged with securing.

Note—It is important to involve legal council to ensure compliance with local and federal law. I am not a lawyer (I don't even know any good lawyer jokes), and this book isn't a substitute for good legal advice.

Mitigating risk is not simply about buying a product or writing a policy. Purchasing technology can be a component of addressing risk, but there are a number of options available. The following list details the choices a company must make when managing risk:

- **Accept the risk:** A company can choose to accept a risk for many reasons. If the probability of a threat successfully exploiting a system is unlikely or the cost to protect the system is so high that it would be cheaper to recover the system in house, then an organization might choose to accept this risk as part of doing business. The danger here is in underestimating the total cost of an exploit and not fully realizing the impact of the event to the business or customers.

- **Avoid the risk:** Sometimes in business, the reward is just not worth the risk. Companies might choose to not conduct business in a way that opens them up to risk. If you have a retail establishment and store credit card information on your Point of Sale (POS) systems as part of your processing of daily transactions, you run the risk of credit card information being stolen because you have this data scattered across all of your POS systems in all of your stores. You can avoid this risk by not storing the data on the POS system and simply running your credit card transaction through a headquarters-based clearinghouse with much higher levels of security.

- **Transfer or share the risk:** The simplest mechanism for transferring risk is to purchase an insurance policy. Other ways include outsourcing the risky service to a third party and building in strict service-level agreements (SLA) and contracts so that they are responsible for securing the data. Of course, regardless of who is "responsible" for an incident, there is still the damage to reputation that can occur with a data breach.

- **Reduce or mitigate the risk:** Implementing controls and countermeasures are how you can reduce or mitigate risk. You can avoid the risks on the Internet by simply unplugging external connections, but you lose all of the benefits that a global marketplace gives you. Purchasing countermeasures and implementing controls is a much less drastic response to protecting your systems.

■ **Ignore the risk:** This is the most dangerous of all options, because it can have dire consequences to shareholders and the organization as a whole. Ignoring risks does not make them go away and could cost your company everything in the end.

Risk in the Fourth Dimension

No, this isn't the section about Euclidean geometry or a discussion about Einstein's theory of relativity (I know you are disappointed!). Instead, the Fourth dimension as it applies to information security is about time. Time is important in security because it enables us to measure the effectiveness of countermeasures based on how long they are exposed to a particular event. When you think about the security of your data, how well do your countermeasures stand up to a sustained attack? When you want to purchase a safe, time is one of the most important factors in picking the correct one to do the job. If you go out and purchase a safe for your valuables, you have to decide what level of protection you need because no safe is impenetrable. Given enough time and the right resources someone can get into it. Safe manufacturers know this, so they rank their safes based on how long it takes an expert to break in. This is called Net Working Time and is displayed on a sticker or other label to indicate how well the safe did. If it is rated as a TL30, it should take an expert with grinding wheels, high-speed drills, saws, and hammers 30 minutes to get in. Of course, the time could be significantly less if you have a little C4, but you run the risk of an accident and destroying the items inside. A safe with TRL30 should withstand all of the hand tools and a gas-cutting and welding torch. The safe isn't designed to prevent someone from getting in forever, just long enough for you to detect that he is there and hopefully catch him before he makes off with your valuables.

The concept of using time as a measurement tool for security is not new. Many people have contributed to this concept, but Winn Schwartau was the first to write a book applying these techniques to information security. Schwartau's book, *Time Based Security*, details how to use time as a mechanism to determine whether or not the countermeasures are sufficient. This methodology—although not the only one to consider in risk assessment—gives us another tool that puts risk-management strategy into fairly simple terms that can help identify the areas that need the most attention. The following formula can be used to determine exposure time:

Exposure = Detection + Reaction

This technique uses detection and reaction as variables to measure potential exposure time to an incident. If you have a fire, the quicker you can detect it and react to it (put it out), the less damage you will have. Let's work through a quick example.

Let's say there is an organization selling vitamins on the Internet through an online shopping cart. The company operates its own web server and database and processes credit cards through its website. A new vulnerability in the web server is discovered and an exploit code is released that can enable an attacker to gain control of the server. On average the security analysts review vulnerability reports every 24 hours. After a vulnerability is detected, it takes about two hours to update the server and bring it back into operation. The formula to represent this scenario would look like this: Detection (24 hours) + Reaction (2 hours) = 26 hours. This means that there is an exposure time of roughly 26 hours. For those 26 hours, any customer placing an order can have his credit card information stolen, or the database itself can be siphoned off by the attacker. Many organizations do not have people dedicated to monitoring these types of events 24/7, so the detection time is drastically different. You can, however, easily see that you have a major problem that requires you to do something to tilt the equation back to the correct direction.

Prevention technologies can be used to decrease detection and reaction time, reducing exposure. An IPS appliance can decrease detection and also reaction time based on new signatures being deployed. If an IPS receives a new signature every 4 hours, then your exposure in the previous example would be cut by 22 hours. Using a web application firewall might completely prevent a successful attack of this nature in the first place, changing the organizations exposure time to zero.

Utilizing time-based security measurement provides a relatively simple method of determining how effective countermeasures are in real-world scenarios.

How, What, and Why You Audit

So far this chapter has spent a lot of time talking about the fundamentals of security, covering many areas that are essential knowledge for someone performing an audit. Auditing is most concerned with risk and how that risk is addressed. Are the controls put in place effective at protecting the assets? The only way to know is to test them. That is why the role of the auditor is so essential to good security. This section discusses the details of the audit process and provides an overview of the types of audits and key aspects that help make an audit successful.

Audit Charter

So what's the difference between a hacker and an auditor? Permission. The auditing, by nature, includes having access to sensitive data and systems. This function is defined by an audit charter, which is a document that defines the purpose, responsibility, authority, and accountability of the auditing program. This document helps to clearly define the requirement for performing audits and provides justification as to why the auditor should be given access to critical systems. An audit charter usually applies to an internal corporate auditing organization and will include the following:

- **Purpose of the auditing function**
    - Create a mission statement.
    - Set goal objectives.
    - Define the scope.
- **Authority**
    - Access rights to audited systems.
    - Obtain support of personnel to accomplish audit goals.

- Use technology to test auditing controls.

- Perform risk assessment.

- **Responsibility**

  - Develop an audit plan.

  - Maintain professional expertise.

  - Issue reports on results of audits.

  - Make recommendations for reducing risk.

  - Maintain integrity and professional standards.

- **Accountability**

  - Report deficiencies about control effectiveness to executives.

  - Provide reports about the current risk.

  - Ensure the organization complies with standards and legal requirements.

Engagement Letter

When an outside party performs an audit, an engagement letter must be obtained. This document functions in a similar manner to the audit charter, but is usually written per project. It includes many of the same items as the audit charter but is more specific about the deliverables of the current engagement. The engagement letter includes:

- **Authority**

  - Who contracted for the audit

  - Rights of access to systems

  - The signature of the company executive

- **Responsibility**

  - Scope of the audit

  - Specific deliverables

- **Accountability**

  - Who is to receive the final report

  - Agreed upon completion dates

Types of Audits

Audits can be broken down into a number of types, from the simple analysis of security architecture based on opinion, to a full-blown, end-to-end audit against a security framework such as ISO27001. The difference between types of audits is in what the auditor based the findings on and how detailed the audit's scope is.

Security Review

A security review is when you examine the security posture of an organization based on professional experience and opinion. Think of a security review as a site survey. In this type of examination, you look for issues that stand out as a way to help define the starting point for further activities. Running a vulnerability scanner such as Nessus would fall under this category. The tool generates a list of potential security issues, but the data must be analyzed further to determine on what needs to be acted on. This is the most basic form of security analysis and the primary output is in the form of an opinion. Examples include:

- Penetration test
- Vulnerability scan
- Architecture review
- Policy review
- Compliance review
- Risk analysis

Security Assessment

Security assessments utilize professional opinion and expertise, but they also analyze the output for relevancy and criticality to the organization. The analysis aspect of an assessment attempts to quantify the risk associated with the items discovered to determine the extent of the problem. If you have two servers with the same vulnerability, but one is your financial server, and the other operates as a print server a security assessment would rank the financial server as a high risk and the print server as a lower risk based on the severity and damage potential. The biggest differentiator between an assessment and a review is the depth to which the auditor examines the system and analyzes the results. Examples include:

- Vulnerability assessment
- Risk assessment
- Architecture assessment
- Policy assessment

Security Audit

A security Audit examines the organization's security posture against an industry standard (ISO27001 or COBIT) and/or regulatory compliance such as HIPAA or PCI. An audit includes review and assessment; it also conducts a gap analysis against standards to measure how well the organization complies. Audits take into account people, processes, and technologies, and it compares them to a benchmark in a standardized and repeatable way. Examples include:

- Compliance audit
- Policy audit
- Procedure audit
- Risk audit

The Role of the Auditor

The role of the auditor is to identify, measure, and report on risk. The auditor is not tasked to fix the problem, but to give a snapshot in time of the effectiveness of the security program. An auditor might be asked to make recommendations about what needs to be done to fix a deficiency in a control, but the objective of the auditor is to report on security weakness. Auditors ask the questions, test the controls, and determine whether the security policies are followed in a manner that protects the assets the controls are intended to secure by measuring the organization's activities versus its security best practices.

The auditor functions as an independent advisor and inspector. The auditor is responsible for planning and conducting audits in a manner that is fair and consistent to the people and processes that are examined. Auditors must have appropriate access and cooperation or the audit runs a risk of not being successful or worse, not identifying critical items that could jeopardize key systems. The auditing charter or engagement letter defines the conduct and responsibilities of an auditor.

Depending on how a company's auditing program is structured, ultimate accountability for the auditor is usually to senior management or the Board of Directors. The auditor must be independent of the business entity being audited or the impartiality of the audit can be called into question. Auditors are usually required to present a report to management about the findings of the audit and also make recommendations about how to reduce the risk identified.

Conflicts of interest can preclude an auditor from conducting an assessment of a particular system or organization. If you were the one that installed the firewall, it doesn't make sense for you to also be the one to audit it. Auditors are expected to excuse themselves from an audit if they feel that there is potential for a conflict to exist.

Places Where Audits Occur

Depending on the scope of the audit, an auditor can be asked to examine many different systems and processes. When defining the scope, the specific items to be audited fall under the category of policy, procedure, or control. Some audits are concerned only with policy review and nothing else, whereas other audits might assess all aspects of security by looking at all three areas. Regardless of how detailed the audit becomes, the three categories are not islands unto themselves. They represent interlocking components of the overall security strategy.

Policy Level

Auditing policy entails examining current policy to ascertain whether or not the policy meets the objectives of the business. It should be specific enough while not being so specific that you can't change your firewall rules without changing the policy. The policy itself should stay consistent regardless of how you accomplish executing the objectives of the policy. Of course an auditor might also find that the organization does not have a policy for a potentially risky business system, which would mean that the auditor would recommend the creation of a policy and give examples based on industry standards. Policy is the cornerstone of security, so care and attention need to be paid in the creation of these documents. Techniques for auditing policy include:

- Categorize policies into Administrative, Operational, and Technical.
- Ensure that the policy meets business objectives.
- Check for compliance to ensure the policy is being followed and enforced.
- Compare it against best practices (SANS, ISO, and COBIT).
- Identify gaps.

Procedure Level

Procedures represent how a company implements policy. Here is where all of the detail resides on how the company will go about protecting its assets. From an auditor's perspective, procedures provide a lot of information in creating checklists to measure how the business applies policy and controls. If a company has a policy that requires all systems to have a personal firewall installed, configured, and active at all times—but does not have a consistent procedure documenting how the firewall is to be configured—then the company will more than likely have a hard time enforcing this policy. These are the kinds of areas that auditors can help with by recognizing deficiencies in policy implementation and recommending solutions to improve security. Techniques for auditing procedures include:

- Compare procedures to policies to ensure that the procedures follow the spirit of the policies.

- Check for configuration compliance.

- Compare procedures with industry standard practices.

Control Level

Many audits and assessments are focused on the control level. Controls can be technical, administrative, or physical, and they can represent a key component in reducing risk. The auditor is concerned with whether or not the control provides a level of protection greater than the level of risk. Techniques for auditing controls include:

- Test control functionality.

- Inspect configuration.

- Inspect logs.

The Auditing Process

The auditing process can be easily broken down into a number of phases. Each phase builds on the last with the ultimate product being a report that documents the findings of the audit. Having a good framework to conduct an audit makes the process run smoothly and helps to eliminate opportunities for mistakes and inconsistencies that reduce the accuracy of the audit. The phases of an audit are:

- **Planning phase:** Audit the subject, objective, and scope.

- **Research phase:** Plan, audit procedures, and evaluate criteria.

- **Data gathering phase:** Gather checklists, tools, and evidence.

- **Data analysis phase:** Analyze, map, and recommend.

- **Audit report phase:** Write, present, and file the audit report.

- **Follow up phase:** Follow up, follow up, and follow up!

Planning Phase: Audit Subject, Objective, and Scope

The first and most important phase of auditing is in determining the overall strategy of the audit. What is the purpose of the audit? If the audit is in response to regulatory compliance requirements, the auditor must compare processes and procedures with those mandated by law. Alternatively, an audit of a newly installed firewall would have a different objective and be specific to one particular control. To figure out the degree and depth of the audit, there is a bit of work that needs to be done before sending the first test packet or stepping foot on site:

Step 1.   Identify the subject of the audit. Is the audit focused on people, process, or technology?

Step 2.   Determine the objective. What is the purpose of the audit?

Step 3.   Determine the scope. What systems, processes, or organizations are to be audited?

Step 4.   What is the timeframe of the audit?

Research Phase: Planning, Audit Procedures, and Evaluation Criteria

After you determine what the goal of the audit is, the next step is to formulate a plan for accomplishing the objectives of the audit. This phase will include:

- Identify the resources needed: skills and technologies.

- Identify the organizational structure, process, and data flow.

- Determine who in the organization under audit should be interviewed or involved.

- Identify logistics information, such as which facilities or locations need to be reviewed.

- The procedures used to test controls must also be identified, including what types of tools will be used.

- Measurement and evaluation criteria should be selected (for example, COBIT, ISO27001, or PCI technology standards).

- Review corporate policies and procedures.

- Build auditing checklists.

Data Gathering Phase: Checklists, Tools, and Evidence

Data gathering is the phase in which the auditor conducts the actual audit itself. The checklist that was created in the research phase is used to measure compliance with the standards and practices that were selected as benchmarks. The checklist acts as a guide that directs the auditor on where to look and what to expect. Many tools might be used to test the various controls to determine functionality and to generate the evidence that is used later in the analysis phase. The auditor looks to find "proof" or evidence of compliance with policy and standards. The auditor does the following:

- Examine system documentation.

- Conduct surveys on the effectiveness of policies and procedures.

- Conduct interviews of key personnel.

- Observation of systems and process in action.

- Review previous audits to look for trends.

- Review logs and reports.

- Inspect technical control configuration.

- Statistical sampling of data transaction.

- Run security analysis tools to verify technical control effectiveness.

Data Analysis Phase: Analyze, Map, and Recommend

After the auditor has gathered all of the evidence, the next phase involves analyzing what is discovered. This analysis requires an auditor's experience and professional knowledge to determine how to prioritize any deficiencies identified. If the audit is done in response to regulatory compliance requirements or industry standards, then the auditor should also map the observed controls to the applicable standard or law to identify if anything is missing or incomplete. Finally, most audits also have an opinion component where the auditor must state his professional opinion regarding the effectiveness of the organization's controls, and recommend solutions about how to improve the quality of the control to reduce risk. The actions in this phase are:

- Categorize and identify evidence gathered during the audit.

- Analyze policies and procedures for effectiveness.

- Prioritize risks and rank according to severity.

- Map identified controls to industry standards or regulatory compliance requirements.

- If required, make recommendations on policy, procedure, and technology improvements.

Audit Report Phase: Write, Present, and File the Audit Report

Authoring the audit report and presenting it to management is one of the most critical phases of the audit. Articulating the deficiencies found and recommendations about how to reduce risk are the primary reasons why the auditor is engaged in the first place. The report should include an executive summary and detailed findings about how the deficiencies discovered apply to the business. The report should not just be the output from a Nessus scan, but actually clarify why a particular vulnerability is determined to be critical or low risk. Recommendations about how to address each audit exception should also be included. The auditor shouldn't just drop off a stack of papers but also present the findings in a meeting between management, the auditor, and key stakeholders. This gives the auditor a chance to clarify findings and answer questions that might arise as the organization digests the audit report. After the report has been presented, the final work papers should be filed as proof of the audit. Auditing is not just about showing that you understand what needs to be done; it's also about proving it! This phase includes:

- Create a clear and concise report detailing risk.

- Write an executive summary that highlights critical items.

- Present the audit findings to management and key stakeholders.

- Develop solutions to address audit exceptions.

- Provide all documentation and evidence to be filed by the organization.

Follow-Up Phase: Follow up, Follow up, Follow up!

After the report is filed, that's it, right? Not quite. It is important to understand that an audit is a snapshot in time. The deficiencies found need to be addressed and should be remedied as soon as possible after the audit occurs. An auditor might be called back after the organization has had a chance to remediate the deficiencies so that the auditor can re-examine the new controls or process. This gives the auditor a chance to get feedback on the solutions chosen. To prevent a conflict of interest, auditors are not generally involved in fixing the deficiencies. This helps to keep the auditor neutral to the situation so that he can be objective and unbiased.

Summary

This chapter covered some of the fundamental aspects of auditing. Providing a risk-based auditing approach that leverages industry standards and best practices is an integral part of a company's IT Governance strategy. You can't protect what you don't know about. Auditing gives an organization the opportunity to test assumptions about how secure its assets and data are. In summary:

- The five pillars of security—assessment, prevention, detection, reaction, and recovery—define the process of security.

- The building blocks of a security strategy are policy, procedures, and standards. Policy is where security strategy is set, whereas procedures and standards provide guidance about how to accomplish the policies' objectives.

- Security controls are how an organization prevents, detects, corrects, and recovers from an incident. Many types of controls work together to build a defensive strategy. Building a control table can identify weaknesses in security posture.

- Risk management isn't just a recommended practice; SOX, HIPAA, and GLBA require it. Assessing risk provides the justification and prioritization necessary to invest time, money, and resources for the areas of security that are critical to the success of the business.

- Auditing is a process and has different degrees and depth. The scope of an audit defines whether or not you conduct a review, assessment, or full audit. The role of the auditor is to report on control deficiencies and risk.

References in This Chapter

Cole, Eric. *Network Security Bible*, First Edition. John Wiley & Sons, 2006.

Schneier, Bruce. *Secrets & Lies: Digital Security in a Networked World*. John Wiley & Sons, 2004.

Bejtlich, Richard. *The Tao of Network Security Monitoring Beyond Intrusion Detection*. Addison Wesley, 2004.

Landoll, Douglas J. *The Security Risk Assessment Handbook: A Guide for Performing Security Risk Assessments*. Auerbach Publications, 2006.

Peltier, Thomas R/Peltier, Justin. *Complete Guide to CISM Certification*. Auerbach Publications, 2007.

Slade, Robert M. *Information Security Management Handbook*, Fifth Edition, Vol 3. Auerbach Publications, 2006.

Schwartau, Winn. *Time-Based Security*. Interactive Press, 1999.

SANS Institute, The SANS Security Policy Project, http://www.sans.org/resources/policies/#question

Chapter 2

Information Security and the Law

Information security law is one of the key drivers of auditing in businesses today. Most companies agree that auditing security is a good idea, but actually doing it on a regular basis requires a commitment of resources and time that could easily be set aside for other projects. After a long string of high-impact security failures in business, security has shifted from a voluntary discipline to one that is required by law. Compliance to federal and state laws is enforced through fines, and, in some cases, jail time. In addition, the payment card industry created standards that address security requirements for anyone who processes credit cards as part of a business. If you don't comply, you can't accept credit cards and can face fines. For these reasons, auditors are tasked with identifying weaknesses in policy, procedure, and technology to determine whether a company meets the security requirements set forth by industry standards and law. To do this, auditors should have some knowledge of law as it pertains to information security and the penalties for noncompliance.

The purpose of this chapter is to present some common IT security laws and regulations that have an impact on network security. It is important to note that this chapter was written in 2010, and the laws and their interpretation may have changed drastically between the time this book was published and when you read it. This chapter is not meant to represent legal counsel in any way, and you are encouraged to check with an attorney for specific recommendations about laws that might apply to your company.

IT Security Laws

Technology and law sometimes have a hard time working together. Law is by its nature conservative because it strives to create a consistent basis for identifying right and wrong. The speed of technological advances makes it difficult for law and law makers to keep up. Many of the laws enacted over the past few years have been reactions to major events such as Enron, Choicepoint, or Heartland Payment Systems. These painful reminders of the impact of lax security have acted as a catalyst for law makers to take a tougher stance on computer-enabled crimes because of the significant monetary loss and potential consequences to the average person.

No one would argue that computers are used to commit crimes and our legal system and law enforcement professionals are dropped into the deep end of advanced technologies where hackers and criminals can hide behind the anonymity that the Internet affords. Awareness of the law can help ensure that a business follows the rules and builds controls in a way that provides law enforcement the evidence needed to detect crimes and prosecute criminals.

The term Cyberlaw has been coined as a means to describe law that pertains to the Internet and computer-related legal issues. This area of the law continues to change dramatically as lawmakers try to grapple with applying laws to protect people from criminals who have moved to the Internet in mass. To put the laws into perspective, it helps to understand the evolution of Cyberlaw.

Network computing in the early 1980s generally consisted of plugging your "blazing fast" 300-baud modem into the back of your Commodore Vic 20 and dialing out to your local bulletin board systems or Compuserve. The bulletin board system era of the 1980s helped to connect millions of individuals interested in computers. While legitimate computer enthusiasts ran most BBSs, others, of the less ethically constrained sort, formed the beginnings of the pirate software scene and created a place to go to share information and techniques about how to exploit other computers. Long-distance toll fraud was rampant, and law enforcement started to take a serious look at what to do with this new area of criminal activity. Of course, 1983 also brought us the movie *Wargames*, which not only introduced the world to the previously clandestine hacker community, but also showed a frightening scenario of what could happen if a "hacker" got access to a super secret government computer system. (I wonder how many IT security careers this movie started?)

Companies and government agencies were already feeling the effects of hackers on their systems, but with courts limited to using a set of statutes that were focused on physical loss of property and mail fraud, it was difficult to prosecute unauthorized computer access as a crime because nothing was technically "missing." In 1978, the state of Florida led the way with the first statute to assist in prosecuting computer theft and hacking, but unless you lived in or committed a computer crime in Florida, the law did not apply to you. In 1984, the United States Congress passed the first federal computer statute (18 U.S.C. § 1030), making it illegal to gain unlawful entry to a federal or financial institutions computer system. This statute was further amended in 1986 and became the Computer Fraud and Abuse Act, which criminalized unauthorized access, damage, fraud, or destruction of data belonging to others.

The global ubiquity of the Internet and the pervasive use of computers by companies to conduct business is why federal statues have such relevance to computer crimes. Congress has the right to create laws to regulate interstate and foreign commerce. 18 U.S.C § 1030 has provisions that identify a "protected computer" as a computer that "is used in interstate or foreign commerce or communication, including a computer located outside the United States that is used in a manner that affects interstate or foreign commerce or communication of the United States." "Used in interstate commerce" covers just about any computer connected to the Internet because you can use that computer to buy or sell goods and services across state lines. Today, there is a wide array of computer-related laws from a federal and individual state level, making them difficult to keep up with. There is simply no substitute for legal council in helping to navigate through them.

Hacking, Cracking, and Fraud Laws

Hacking, cracking, and fraud are areas of the law that attackers break when attempting to gain unauthorized access to the network. As mentioned in Chapter 1, "The Principles of Auditing," the only real difference between a hacker and an auditor is the permission afforded by the auditing charter or engagement letter. During the course of security testing, an auditor would be in violation of a number of these laws if he did not have authorization to conduct assessment activities. This section is intended to give an auditor a basic understanding of the laws that govern technical security testing to ensure that awareness of the importance of gaining permission before testing. Although an auditor is not law enforcement, he does have an obligation to report potentially illegal activities. This knowledge can help auditors identify questionable activities that they might uncover during an audit.

Computer Fraud and Abuse Act

The Computer Fraud and Abuse Act (18 U.S.C § 1030) has undergone many changes throughout the years as Congress struggles with the pace of technology proliferation and misuse. The Identity Theft Enforcement and Restitution Act of 2008 is the most recent modification to the provisions of this law. The CFAA is one of the more important statutes because it covers the "breaking-and-entering" aspect of computer criminal law. A digital intruder is identified by this law as someone who accesses an electronic system "without authorization." As an auditor, you can avoid violating the CFAA by making sure that you have full authorization, in writing, before conducting any type of auditing engagement.

The statute has seven primary provisions and covers a wide variety of computer crimes. Each of the seven provisions specifies access without authorization or escalation of privileges as a prerequisite and then includes specific instances of what an individual did while connected. Most criminal computer activity runs afoul of this law because it isn't just concerned with the breaking and entering of a computer system, but also the release of Malware (virus, worms, trojans, and so on), password cracking, and extortion through denial of service or theft. Section 1030 (a)(5)(B) provides the capability to prosecute for reckless and negligent behavior, which means that someone can't simply argue that he didn't understand what the blinking red "kill remote system" button on his hacking tool would do.

Table 2-1 provides a summary of the provisions of this law.

Table 2-1 *Summary of Computer Fraud and Abuse Act*

§ 1030 Offense	Description	Penalty
(a)(1)Obtaining National Security Information	Knowingly accessing a computer without authorization to obtain, transmit, or retain national security information that could harm the United States	Fine and/or 10 years 20 years second offense
(a)(2)Compromising the Confidentiality of a Computer	Intentionally hacking into a computer to stealing financial records from any protected computer	Fine and/or 1–5 years
(a)(3)Trespassing in a Government Computer	Intentionally hacking into a nonpublic U.S. computer without authorization	Fine and/or 1 year 10 years second offense
(a)(4)Accessing a Computer to Defraud & Obtain Value	Knowingly accessing a protected computer without authorization to commit fraud or obtain anything of value, including use of the computer greater than $5,000	Fine and/or 5 years 10 years second offense
(a)(5)(A)Knowingly Transmission of Code Program, Information, or Command and Cause Intentional Damage to Computer	Purposely breaking into a computer through automated or manual means resulting in loss	Fine and/or 10 years 20 years or life second offense
(a)(5)(B) Intentional Access Without Authorization and Caused Reckless Damage	Purposely breaking into a computer through automated or manual means and negligently causing damages resulting in loss of $5,000 or more during 1 year OR Modifying the medical care of a person OR Causing physical injury OR Threatening public health or safety OR damaging government computers OR Causing or attempting to cause death OR Causing damage to 10 or more computers in a year	Fine and/or 5 years 20 years second offense
(a)(5)(C)Intentional Access Without Authorization Causing Damage and Loss	Purposely breaking into a computer through automated or manual means without authorization and causing damage resulting in loss	Fine and/or 1 year 10 years second offense

continues

Table 2-1   *Summary of Computer Fraud and Abuse Act (continued)*

§ 1030 Offense	Description	Penalty
(a)(6)Trafficking in Passwords	Selling or exchanging passwords or other access information with the intent to defraud, affecting interstate or foreign commerce	Fine and/or 1 year 10 years second offense
(a)(7)(A)Extortion Involving Threats to Damage Computer	Attempting to extort money or anything else of value containing a threat to damage a protected computer system	Fine and/or 5 years 10 years second offense
(a)(7)(B)Stealing Confidentiality Information	Attempting to break into a computer-protected computer system to steal confidential information	Fine and/or 5 years 10 years second offense
(a)(7)(C)Extortion of Money for Not Damaging a Protected Computer	Demanding or requesting money or another thing of value in exchange for not damaging a protected computer	Fine and/or 5 years 10 years second offense

Access Device Statute

18 USC § 1029, the Access Device Statute (often referred to as the Credit Card statute), prohibits criminal activities relating to any identification mechanism that can be used to gain access to bank accounts, credit cards, or telecommunication services. This is a broad statute and covers ten individual activities ranging from the creation of fake credit cards to password cracking. Access devices defined by this law include "any card, plate, code, account number, electronic serial number, mobile identification number, personal identification number, or other telecommunications service, equipment, or instrument identifier, or other means of account access."

Credit card theft and the trafficking of credit card information is a big business for criminals. Phishing is one of the most common techniques used to get a victim to divulge credit card information, account numbers, and passwords through real and legitimate looking e-mails that redirect the user to fake websites that also look almost identical to the legitimate website they are imitating to harvest information. Many of these bogus websites act as proxies for the real banking site and silently record all of the information a person enters as he goes about online transactions. These are examples of crimes punishable under the Access Device Statute.

Auditors who are asked to assess password security typically run a cracking program to brute-force passwords. This activity can violate this statute. All password auditing should be approved and authorized before testing. The access device statute enables for prosecution of those who steal passwords or credit card numbers. Keystroke logging software and other password- or pin-stealing technology should be reported by the auditor as its presence might fall under this federal statute.

A summary of 18 USC § 1029 is shown in Table 2-2.

Table 2-2   *Summary of 18 USC 1029 Access Device Statute*

§ 1029 Offense	Description	Monetary Loss/Damages	Penalty
(a)(1)Counterfeit Access Devices	Knowingly and with the intent to defraud Produces, uses, or traffics in one or more counterfeit access devices Affecting interstate commerce	No loss required	Fine and/or 10 years Fine and/or 20 years for second offense
(a)(2)Unauthorized Access Devices	Knowingly and with intent to defraud Uses or traffics in one or more unauthorized access devices during any 1-year period Obtaining at least $1,000 in value during same 1-year period Affecting interstate or foreign commerce	Must obtain $1,000 or more in value during 1 year	Fine and/or 10 years Fine and/or 20 years for second offense
(a)(3)Possession of Access Device	Knowingly and with intent to defraud Uses or traffics in One or more unauthorized access device(s) During any 1-year period Affecting interstate or foreign commerce	No loss required	Fine and/or 10 years Fine and/or 20 years for second offense
(a)(4)Access Device Making Equipment	Knowingly and with intent to defraud Produces, traffics in, has control or custody of, or possesses Accessing device-making equipment Affecting interstate or foreign commerce	No loss required	Fine and/or 10 years Fine and/or 20 years for second offense

continues

Table 2-2 *Summary of 18 USC 1029 Access Device Statute*   *(continued)*

§ 1029 Offense	Description	Monetary Loss/Damages	Penalty
(a)(5)Misuse of Access Device Issued to Another	Knowingly and with intent to defraud Causing transactions to receive at least $1,000 of value During any 1-year period Using one or more access device(s) issued to another person Affecting interstate or foreign commerce	$1,000 or more loss in 1 year	Fine and/or 10 years Fine and/or 20 years for second offense
(a)(6)Solicitation to Offer or Sell Access Devices	Knowingly and with intent to defraud Soliciting a person for the purpose of offering an access device OR Soliciting a person for the purpose of selling information regarding an access device or applying to obtain an access device Without the authorization of the issuer of the access device	No loss required	Fine and/or 10 years Fine and/or 20 years for second offense
(a)(7)Modified or Altered Telecommunication Devices	Knowingly and with intent to defraud Uses, produces, traffics in, has control or custody of, or possesses a telecommunication instrument that has been modified or altered to obtain unauthorized use of telecommunication services Affecting interstate or foreign commerce	No loss required	Fine and/or 10 years Fine and/or 20 years for second offense
(a)(8)Scanning Receivers	Knowingly and with intent to defraud Uses, produces, traffics in, has control or custody of, or possesses a scanning receiver Affecting interstate or foreign commerce	No loss required	Fine and/or 15 years Fine and/or 20 years for second offense

continues

Table 2-2   *Summary of 18 USC 1029 Access Device Statute   (continued)*

§ 1029 Offense	Description	Monetary Loss/Damages	Penalty
(a)(9)Phone Phreaking	Knowingly and with intent to defraud Uses, produces, traffics in, has control or custody of, or possesses hardware or software configured to insert or modify telecommunication-identifying information so that the telecommunications instrument might be used to obtain unauthorized service Affecting interstate or foreign commerce	No loss required	Fine and/or 15 years Fine and/or 20 years for second offense

Electronic Communications Privacy Act

Mention the word wiretap, and memories of movies with government agents sitting in a nondescript delivery van with surveillance equipment listening in on telephone calls probably comes to mind. Of course, today, there are fiber optic cables delivering converged voice, video, and data at the equivalent of DS3 speeds to your house. That makes listening in on your conversation with grandma a lot harder than connecting a set of alligator clips to the telephone pole outside your house. The Wiretap Act, which first came into law in Title III of the Omnibus Crime Control and Safe Streets Act of 1968, was created to punish the unauthorized access of wire and oral communication. This law became less relevant as more and more communications became digitized, and the use of e-mail became widespread. In 1986, Congress enacted the Electronic Communications Privacy Act (ECPA) to broaden the reach of the Wiretap Act and to cover newer forms of electronic communications.

The ECPA consists of a series of statues that are broken down into three main sections (or titles). Title I: Wiretap Act covers the interception of wire, oral, and electronic communications while in transit, and it can be found in 18 USC §§ 2510-2522. Title II: Stored Communications Act protects communications stored electronically, such as e-mail or voicemail, and can be found in 18 USC §§ 2701-2712. Title III: Pen/Trap Statute, which is addressed in 18 USC §§ 3121-3127, regulates the use of pen register and trap/trace devices that are used to record phone numbers dialed, call routing, and signaling information that determines where a caller is or who it called.

Title I: Wiretap Act

The primary purpose of the Wiretap Act is to prohibit unauthorized individuals or law enforcement (without a warrant) from eavesdropping or disclosing oral or electronic communications. This applies to any communications, but specifically to computer networks, by making it illegal to install an unauthorized sniffer program. The key aspect of these statutes is to protect communications in transit or real-time communication, meaning that unless the communication is in motion (transmitted on the wire), it is not protected under this statute. The fact that the Wiretap Act was applicable only to real-time communications is why the Stored Communications Act was created (it is covered in the next section).

There are a significant number of exceptions to the prohibitions against eavesdropping, as outlined in the statutes that make up the Wiretap Act. The most relevant to network security are when one of the parties communicating consents to monitoring, where the service provider (the term service provider applies to business networks too) monitors the network to combat fraud and service theft, when monitoring computer trespassers, and when the system being accessed is a publicly available system (such as an Instant Message chat room). The following list summarizes the four primary exceptions to the Wiretap Act:

- **Consent exception:** This exception requires that one party has consented to communication interception. Login banners or terms of service that inform a user that his communications will be monitored should be displayed whenever possible. To help protect itself, a company must give notice to employees via a written electronic communications policy detailing that all communications are subject to monitoring. It is also highly encouraged to require a signed (physical or electronic) consent to monitoring document.

- **Provider exception:** The provider exception enables operators of communication services to monitor the use of their equipment in the course of conducting business for the purposes of protecting data and assets. This exception gives a company the capability to monitor communications on its networks via intrusion detection systems, packet capture tools, or other technologies that combat fraud and misuse.

- **Computer trespasser exception:** This exception is intended to enable victims of a computer crime to authorize law enforcement to monitor communications when under attack. The exception does not give someone the right to intercept third-party communications without being directed by or in conjunction with law enforcement. A company should never attempt to investigate a crime without engaging law enforcement authorities.

- **Accessible to the public exception:** Communications posted to open systems such as chat rooms, web forums, or blogs are not protected under the ECPA. If it is easily accessible to the public and nonprivate, then it may be monitored.

The Wiretap Act gives companies the legal authority to protect their assets by actively inspecting for fraud and abuse on their networks, making it perfectly legal to deploy full packet capture tools and IDS/IPS technologies. As auditors, it is important to ensure that a solid network inspection policy exists that is consistently enforced and all users are aware of it through login banners and documented, ongoing awareness training.

Table 2-3 provides a summary of 18 USC § 2511.

Table 2-3   *Summary of 18 USC 2511 Interception of Wire, Oral, or Electronic Communication Prohibited*

§ 2511 Offense	Description	Penalty
(1)(a)Illegal Wiretaps	Except as authorized (service provider, consent, or law enforcement with warrant) Intentionally intercepting, endeavoring to intercept, or procuring another to intercept or endeavor to intercept Any wire, oral, or electronic communication	Fine and/or 5 years
(1)(b)Illegal Wiretaps	Except as authorized (service provider, consent, or law enforcement with warrant) Intentionally using, endeavoring to use, or procuring another to use or endeavor to use any electronic, mechanical, or other device to intercept any oral communication If the device is affixed to or transmits signals through a wire communication connection; or, if the device transmits communications by radio or interferes with a radio transmission; or, if the device is reasonably known to have been sent through interstate or foreign commerce; or, if such device is used or endeavored to be used on the premises of a business whose operations affect interstate or foreign commerce; or, if such device obtains or is for the purpose of obtaining information relating to the operations of any business whose operations affect interstate or foreign commerce	Fine and/or 5 years
(1)(C)Disclosing Contents of Illegal Wiretap	Except as authorized within the statute (for example, service provider exception, consent exception, law enforcement Title III or Pen/Trap & Trace orders) Intentionally discloses or endeavors to disclose the contents of any wire, oral, or electronic communication Knowing or with reason to know that the information was unlawfully intercepted	Fine and/or 5 years

continues

Table 2-3 *Summary of 18 USC 2511 Interception of Wire, Oral, or Electronic Communication Prohibited (continued)*

§ 2511 Offense	Description	Penalty
(1)(D)Using Contents of an Illegal Wiretap	Except as authorized within the statute (for example, service provider exception, consent exception, law enforcement Title III or Pen/Trap & Trace orders) Intentionally uses or endeavors to use the contents of any wire, oral, or electronic communication Knowing or with reason to know that the information was unlawfully intercepted	Fine and/or 5 years
(1)(E)Disclosing Authorized Government Wiretap in Order to Obstruct Justice	Intentionally discloses or endeavors to disclose the contents of any wire, oral, or electronic communication Lawfully obtained by the government (for example, under Title III, FISA, and undercover operations) Intending to obstruct, impede, or interfere with an authorized criminal investigation, knowing that the information was obtained in a criminal investigation, and having received the information in connection with a criminal investigation	Fine and/or 5 years

Title II: Stored Communications Act

The Stored Communications Act was implemented to protect e-mail and voicemail from unlawful access. The Wiretap Act protects communications in transit, but does not protect the privacy of a message in storage or on a mail server waiting to be retrieved by the intended recipient. 18 USC § 2701 criminalizes illegally obtaining, altering, or preventing access to a communication in electronic storage. The law also provides felony charges for stealing communications to be used for commercial advantage, malicious destruction, or to further a criminal act. To be protected under this act, an electronic communication service that consists of voicemail or e-mail must be present, which means that a client's individual computer or home computer that received e-mail or voice mail does not apply because the client computer does not provide e-mail services to others.

There are several exceptions to the law:

■ **Service provider exception:** This law does not apply to "the person or entity providing a wire or electronic communication service: regardless of their motives in accessing stored communication". A business can inspect any e-mail or voicemail residing on systems and not violate the law. A written policy explaining that e-mail and voicemail can and will be monitored is also recommended.

- **Authorized use exception:** A user of the communications system can authorize others to access stored communications. This happens when employees go on vacation or have administrative assistants who handle scheduling and correspondence and are therefore excluded from this statute.

- **Court order exception:** There are numerous exceptions specifically mentioned in the statute about dealing with a court order to provide relevant evidence in the form of e-mail or voicemail. They are listed in section 2703, 2704, and 2518 (Wiretap Act).

Table 2-4 provides a summary of 18 USC § 2701-2712.

Table 2-4 *Summary of 18 USC 2701 Stored Wire and Electronic Communications and Transactional Records Access*

§ 2701 Offense	Description	Penalty
Accessing Voice Mail or E-mail	Obtaining, altering, or preventing authorized access to unopened voice mail and unopened e-mail by intentionally accessing without authorization a facility through which an electronic communication service is provided, or intentionally exceeding authorized access to that facility	2 years and fine for repeat offense under 2701, if committed for purposes of commercial advantage, malicious destruction or damage, or private commercial gain 1 year and fine for first offense, if committed for purposes of commercial advantage, malicious destruction or damage, or private commercial gain 6 months and fine if *not* committed for purposes of commercial advantage, malicious destruction or damage, or private commercial gain

Title III: Pen/Trap Statute

A *pen register* is a device that reads the routing information as a telephone dials a number, and a *trap and trace device* records incoming caller information. This statute was originally written to regulate monitoring telephone-calling information, but has been expanded to include additional applications in network communications. The Patriot Act modified much of the wording to include other methods of communication beyond just the telephone system.

Because the law was written to include "an instrument or facility from which a wire or electrical communication is transmitted," an enormous amount of network services are included. In fact the law includes protection for e-mail addresses, user accounts, instant messaging clients, and virtually any communication that has a source and destination. This includes many of the tools used by auditors to test security controls. Because an IP packet has both a source and destination address, a sniffer qualifies as a pen/trap device.

The primary purpose of this statute is to ensure that law enforcement has a court order before it puts these types of monitoring devices into use. The law also enables businesses to implement these types of tools at will without a court order under the following conditions:

- Any activity related to the operations and maintenance of the network services or to protect users from abuse or illegal activities

- Recording connection information (IP address, headers, and so on) to protect assets and users

- When consent is given for monitoring as part of an acceptable use policy or terms and conditions of service

Table 2-5 provides a summary of 18 USC § 3121-3127.

Table 2-5   *Summary of 18 USC 3121 Pen Registers and Trap and Trace Devices*

§ 3121 Offense	Description	Penalty
Prohibition on Pen Register and Trap and Trace Device Use	No person may install or use a pen register or a trap and trace device without first obtaining a court order.	Up to 1 year in prison and/or fine

Intellectual Property Laws

This section covers two of the most relevant intellectual property statutes that auditors can run into in the course of performing an audit. The Digital Millennium Copyright Act and Economic Espionage Act are laws that are intended to protect and criminalize the theft of intellectual property and prevent the circumvention of protection controls. As part of a security assessment, auditors might have to break protection controls and possibly discover incidents of proprietary information being removed by employees or unscrupulous business partners. Knowledge of these laws is valuable for auditors staying out of trouble and identifying potentially illegal activity.

Digital Millennium Copyright Act

Copyright protection has always been a challenge in the digital world. For many people, the theft of software, music, and movies doesn't seem as tangible as walking into a convenience store and stealing a gallon of milk. Use of the Internet and peer-to-peer file sharing forever changed the landscape of copyrighted content and control. To address the dangers of copyright infringement on the Internet, Congress approved the Digital Millennium Copyright Act as a means to combat online piracy, distribution of copyrighted works, and the circumvention of access controls.

When the Digital Millennium Copyright Act (17 U.S.C. § 1201, 1202, and 1204) was signed into law October 28, 1998, many felt that it was entirely too strict and stifled research and fair use of software. From a security researcher's standpoint, it seemed to be a signal to find another job, as much of what a security researcher does requires breaking access controls or other protection mechanisms in software. Fortunately, there have been a number of exemptions created to address these and a few other special case situations. Following are the exceptions most applicable to computer security professionals:

- **Software interoperability:** To get an application or piece of software to interoperate (exchange information) with existing software, it is permissible to circumvent access controls to portions of a program. The sole purpose for doing this must be for interoperability. The methods used to create interoperability can be shared as long as the information does not constitute copyright infringement or break any other laws.

- **Protection of personal information:** It is not illegal to disable spyware or other software that records personal information if the software does not allow someone to turn off those capabilities. Circumventing this type of activity is permissible as long as it does not affect any other function of the software application.

- **Encryption research:** Encryption research is defined as "activities necessary to identify and analyze flaws and vulnerabilities of encryption technologies applied to copyrighted works, if these activities are conducted to advance the state of knowledge in the field of encryption technologies or to assist in the development of encryption products." Under the DCMA, the researcher must purchase or lawfully obtain the encrypted copyrighted work—breaking the encryption is a necessary part of research, the researcher made a good faith attempt to get permission from the copyright owners, and breaking the encryption does not violate any other laws.

- **Security testing:** The DMCA defines security testing as "accessing a computer, computer system, or computer network, solely for the purpose of good faith testing, investigating, or correcting, a security flaw or vulnerability, with the authorization of the owner or operator of such computer, computer system, or computer network." The key to the exception is that the person conducting security testing is authorized to do so by the owner of the system under the test. This exception also allows for the release of technological tools to conduct these types of security tests as long as they do not utilize copyrighted information.

Table 2-6 provides a summary of the DMCA.

Table 2-6 *Summary of DMCA*

DMCA Offense	Description	Penalty
§ 1201 Circumvention of Copyright Protection Systems	A prohibition on circumventing access controls An access control circumvention device ban (sometimes called the "trafficking" ban) A copyright protection circumvention device ban	Commercial gain: The first offense is $500,000 and/or 5 years, and the second offense is a $1,000,000 fine and/or 10 years. Civil fines up to $2,500 or $25,000 per violation.
§ 1202 Integrity of Copyright Management Information	A prohibition on the removal of copyright management information	Commercial gain: The first offense is $500,000 and/or 5 years, and the second offense is a $1,000,000 fine and/or 10 years. Civil fines up to $2500 or $25,000 per violation.

Economic Espionage Act

The Economic Espionage Act of 1996 criminalizes the theft of commercial trade secrets. The law has two primary sections with 18 USC § 1831 focused on theft of trade secrets from U.S. companies for the benefit of foreign governments and 18 USC § 1832 focused on theft between companies in the United States. Both sections punish someone who steals proprietary information in any form. This theft can be physical or through making copies of files, memorizing formulas, taking pictures, uploading or downloading data, or any other method of getting information someone is not authorized to have or sell. A large majority of these cases seem to involve insiders who have tried to sell information from their companies or who took information to another company after leaving.

The area that is most important for auditors and computer security in general is that in order to prosecute someone under this law, the company must be able to show where it has followed "reasonable measures" to maintain the information's secrecy. Properly securing key assets and information should be a top priority for any organization. Information like the prototype for a new widget that is expected to make the company millions of dollars might not qualify as a trade secret if it is left in a folder on a file server that anyone in the company can access.

Table 2-7 provides a summary of the EEA.

Table 2-7 *Summary of Economic Espionage Act*

Offense	Description	Penalty
§ 1831 Electronic Espionage Act	Without authority takes, copies, or alters a trade secret, or fraudulently obtains a trade secret, or knowingly obtains a stolen or improperly obtained trade secret, or attempts or conspires to do the same Intending or knowing that a foreign government, foreign instrumentality, or foreign agent will thereby benefit	15 years and $500,000 For organizations, fine up to $10,000,000
§ 1832 Trade Secrets Act	Without authority, takes, copies, or alters a trade secret, or fraudulently obtains a trade secret, or knowingly obtains a stolen or improperly obtained trade secret, or attempts or conspires to do the same Intending or knowing that the trade secret owner will be injured With intent to convert a trade secret that is related to or included in a product produced for or placed in interstate or foreign commerce To the economic benefit of anyone other than the trade secret owner	10 years and fine For organizations, fine up to $5,000,000

CAN-SPAM Act of 2003

Leave it to those wacky members of Congress to think up a name like CAN-SPAM for the nation's first law restricting SPAM e-mail (and you thought politicians didn't have a sense of humor). CAN-SPAM stands for Controlling the Assault of Non-Solicited Pornography and Marketing Act, and although it doesn't prevent SPAM, it does put in place penalties for spammers and the businesses that advertise through SPAM messages. The law also charges the Federal Trade Commission (FTC) as the primary enforcement agency and allows for other federal and state agencies to assist if required.

There are five primary areas addressed by the CAN-SPAM Act:

- **Unauthorized access of a computer system:** Criminalizes hacking into a computer for the purposes of sending multiple SPAM messages through it.

- **Unauthorized use of e-mail relays:** A number of years ago, spammers would use the default settings of e-mail systems to forward e-mail they received and not just from the e-mail domain that they provided mail services for; system administrators have corrected this error, so spammers rely on malware that is used against vulnerable computers to allow a would-be spammer to utilize an infected PC to send spam and hide the spammer's identity.

- **Bans fake or misleading e-mail headers:** A common practice of spammers is to fake the e-mail source address to try to hide the source of the messages. The E-mail From field must properly identify the sender.

- **Bans creation of fake e-mail accounts and domain names for SPAM:** The law bans the creation of five or more e-mail addresses or two or more domain names using falsified registration data for the purposes of sending SPAM e-mail. It is also illegal to use scripts or other automated tools for mass registering for e-mail addresses.

- **Bans registering for IP addresses for sending SPAM:** Criminalizes registering for five or more IP addresses with false identification so that multiple SPAM messages can be sent.

Although the bulk of these provisions are intended to identify obvious spammers, it is important that businesses realize that they can be classified as a spammer if they don't follow the rules of the CAN-SPAM Act. Many companies use e-mail blasts or mass mailing as a marketing tool, which is perfectly legal, if the company adheres to the following requirements:

- Clearly identify that the message is a commercial advertisement or solicitation.

- Provide for an opt-out mechanism that gives the recipient the ability to decline any further e-mail messages. The sender has 10 days to remove the user from subsequent mailings.

- A valid postal address of the sender.

- Do not use tools that "harvest" or automatically gather e-mail addresses from websites or forums that have published notices that prevent this activity.

Table 2-8 provides a summary of the CAN-SPAM Act.

Table 2-8   *Summary of the CAN-SPAM Act*

Offense	Description	Penalty
§ 1037 CAN-SPAM Act	**(1)** Accesses a protected computer without authorization, and intentionally initiates the transmission of multiple commercial electronic mail messages from or through such computer, **(2)** Uses a protected computer to relay or retransmit multiple commercial electronic mail messages, with the intent to deceive or mislead recipients, or any Internet access service, as to the origin of such messages, **(3)** Materially falsifies header information in multiple commercial electronic mail messages and intentionally initiates the transmission of such messages, **(4)** Registers, using information that materially falsifies the identity of the actual registrant, for five or more electronic mail accounts or online user accounts or two or more domain names, and intentionally initiates the transmission of multiple commercial electronic mail messages from any combination of such accounts or domain names, or **(5)** Falsely represents oneself to be the registrant or the legitimate successor in interest to the registrant of five or more Internet Protocol addresses, and intentionally initiates the transmission of multiple commercial electronic mail messages from such addresses	Forfeiture of equipment used and/or money earned Fine and/or 1 year OR Fine and/or 3 years if: <ul><li>Unauthorized access to a computer to send spam</li><li>Involves 20 or more fake e-mail or account registrations or 10 or more fake domain name registrations</li><li>E-mail messages transmitted exceed 2,500 during any 24-hour period, 25,000 during any 30-day period, or 250,000 during any 1-year period;</li><li>Caused loss of $5,000 during 1-year period</li><li>Obtained anything of value of $5,000 or more during any 1-year period</li><li>Defendant was in a position of organizer or leader</li></ul>

State and Local Laws

Many of the federal laws that have been covered started at the state level. Although federal laws provide the greatest reach in prosecuting criminals, state laws can add extra penalties in areas not covered at the federal level. A significant portion of U.S. laws addressing current crimes and Internet annoyances are addressed by the states, as Internet crime and privacy have become a major topic for debate. The states are usually able to enact laws much quicker than Congress and can address the misuse of new technologies. For instance, 32 states have laws that ban computer-assisted, remote-controlled hunting over the Internet. Privacy and identity theft are the two issues most likely to be discussed, but the states are active in addressing many of the crimes committed on the Internet. Following is a list of some of the most recent state laws:

- **Cyber-stalking:** Forty-seven states have included laws against using electronic communications to threaten, harass, or stalk someone on the Internet.

- **Hacking and unauthorized access:** All 50 states have specific legislation criminalizing hacking, cracking, and unauthorized access to computer networks.

- **Virus laws:** Twenty-seven states have laws against releasing viruses, worms, or other malware with the intention of destroying, modifying, recording, or disrupting information stored on a computer system.

- **Electronic surveillance:** All 50 states (Vermont being the exception) include protection from unauthorized surveillance; 31 of the states specifically mention or have statues regarding interception of computer traffic.

- **Phishing:** Twenty-one states have laws against transmitting unsolicited e-mail messages pretending to be from legitimate companies or banks with the intent of tricking someone into divulging personal information.

- **Spyware:** Spyware is software that is loaded surreptitiously on a user's computer and is used to track a person's activity, collect personal information, or deliver popup messages advertising products. Anyone who has been on the Internet is well aware of this type of computer annoyance. Four states have enacted anti-adware and spyware legislation with limited success. The challenge is in defining what constitutes illegal spyware and adware, but the states are trying to make a difference.

- **Breach of information:** Although California gets credit for having the most widely known security breach notification law—Senate Bill 1386—45 other states have enacted laws requiring companies to notify customers in the event that the customers' personal information has been compromised.

Reporting a Crime

In the course of auditing a network, there is real potential for an auditor to uncover illegal activities. It is always important to work through management whenever something is uncovered that looks suspect, as most auditors are not trained law enforcement investigators. After a potential illegal act is identified, the auditor might be asked for advice about to do next. There is a lot of confusion about who to call, especially with crimes that might occur over the Internet where the criminal can be anywhere on the Earth.

Who to call depends on the scope of the crime and the dollar value of the incident. Six federal law enforcement agencies investigate Internet and computer-related crimes: the Federal Bureau of Investigations (FBI), the United States Secret Service, the Bureau of Alcohol Tobacco and Firearms (ATF), the United States Customs Services, the FTC, and the United States Postal Inspection Services.

The FBI and the Secret Service, however, are the two primary organizations from a federal perspective that are charged with investigating computer crime. As a general rule, the FBI and Secret Service tend to not investigate crimes under $1,000. It is important to identify damages when reporting a crime, such as the cost of lost service, employee labor costs, consultant time, and other directly related expenses because the severity of the crime directly impacts whether or not federal agencies can devote resources to investigate the incident.

Most people are familiar with the Secret Service's role as protection for the President and foreign dignitaries, but as a branch of the Department of the Treasury, the Secret Service also investigates financial crimes. The types of offenses investigated by the Secret Service include investigating counterfeiting of U.S. currency, forgery or theft of U.S. Treasury checks, securities fraud, identity theft, credit card fraud, money laundering, and computer fraud. In addition to its investigative responsibilities, the Secret Service created a national Electronic Crimes Task Force—by mandate of the Patriot Act—with the express purpose of co-operation between federal and state agencies to help protect the country's financial communications infrastructure.

The FBI's role in combating cybercrime is to stop individuals or groups that spread malicious software in the form of viruses and worms, identify and stop botnets, arrest those who traffic in or possess child pornography, stop individuals who prey on children in chat rooms or online, combat U.S. intellectual property theft, and hunt down organizations in the United States and internationally that engage in Internet fraud. With such a wide range of computer-related crimes that it must investigate, you can imagine that agents are busy. To help facilitate and triage computer crime complaints, the FBI and the National White Collar Crime Center set up the Internet Crime Complaint Center (IC3) to handle the high volume of calls for help. The IC3 provides a website where victims of Internet crimes can file a complaint. The IC3 website can be found at www.ic3.gov.

Table 2-9 provides a list of computer-related crimes and the federal government agency that can assist with investigations.

Table 2-9   *Agencies to Call by Category of Crime*

Category of Crime	Appropriate Agency
Computer Hacking	FBI, Secret Service, IC3
Password Trafficking	FBI, Secret Service, IC3
Child Pornography or Exploitation	FBI, U.S. Immigrations and Customs Enforcement (if brought in from outside the United States), IC3
Internet Fraud That Uses the Postal Services	United States Postal Inspection Services, IC3
Internet Fraud and SPAM	FBI, U.S. Secret Service, FTC, Securities and Exchange Commission (for investment-related span and fraud), IC3

continues

Table 2-9   *Agencies to Call by Category of Crime (continued)*

Category of Crime	Appropriate Agency
Internet Harassment or Extortion	FBI
Copyrighted Materials Piracy	FBI, U.S. Immigration and Customs Enforcement, IC3
Trademark Counterfeiting	FBI, Immigration and Customs Enforcement, IC3
Theft of Intellectual Property or Trade Secrets	FBI

If the crime occurs locally, the first place to start is with local state police. It can escalate the case if it turns out to be outside of the state's jurisdiction. If the crime is obviously federal in nature or international, then contacting either the FBI or Secret Service is the most appropriate first step. Regardless of the type of crime or what agency the crime is reported to, a good incident-reporting process should be in place to provide the information needed by law enforcement to properly investigate the crime. At a minimum, the auditor should see evidence that the business being audited is prepared to provide the following:

- **Key contacts:** A person assigned and trained to coordinate with law enforcement throughout the investigation. This should also be someone who knows the network and how things are configured.

- **Incident report:** This is a document that provides all the pertinent facts regarding the case—the who, what, when, and where of the incident. In addition, if it is known how the information was taken, it should be included in this report.

- **Configuration and documentation:** A topology map and technical details on the systems in question. Software versions, configuration files, system logs, and hardware types are all potentially relevant information.

Regulatory Compliance Laws

Compliance laws and industry regulations have been a major driving force for adoptions of IT security controls. Through the use of these regulations, businesses are required to have the appropriate level of protection to protect their capability to accurately report financials and ensure the security of customer information. This section provides an overview of the Sarbanes-Oxley Act (SOX), Health Insurance Portability and Accountability Act (HIPAA), Grahmm-Leach-Bliley Act (GLBA), and Payment Card Industry (PCI), which represent the four most common compliance areas that auditors are asked to measure security controls in the network against.

SOX

The Sarbanes-Oxley Act of 2002 is widely regarded as one of the most sweeping reforms of American corporate reporting since the 1934 creation of the Securities and Exchange Commission (SEC) by Franklin D. Roosevelt. SOX was enacted as a direct result of the dramatic accounting scandals perpetrated by Enron, WorldCom, and others. Millions of investors lost significant sums of money, and the public's trust in the accuracy of financial statements and reports was shattered. The primary purpose of SOX was to help restore that lost confidence in cooperate financial data, and to hold executives personally responsible for reporting accurately. Because practically all companies use computers to track and report financial and accounting information, SOX directly impacts IT departments.

Ask any CIO of a publicly traded company to tell you about SOX, and you will probably be in for an animated conversation on how much money it has cost and the disruption it has caused. The act itself is roughly 66 pages, segmented into 11 Titles with multiple sections in each Title. These sections detail everything from the creating of the Public Company Accounting Oversight Board (PCAOB), auditor independence, corporate responsibility, and criminal penalties. The sections that are most relevant to IT auditors are the following:

- **Section 302 Corporate Responsibility for Financial Reports:** This section requires that the CEO and CFO certify in quarterly or yearly filings with the SEC that they have reviewed the report being filed and it does not contain any untrue statements or is misleading in any way as to the financial state of the company. The signing officers are also required to establish internal controls that monitor the functionality and accuracy of the financial reporting system and have had those controls assessed 90 days prior to filing. Section 302 holds the CEO and CFO responsible for the accuracy of financial reports. The Department of Justice can also prosecute violations of 302 under mail and wire fraud.

- **Section 404 Management Assessment of Internal Controls:** Section 404 dictates that management is responsible for creating and maintaining internal controls over financial accounting that address potential risks that could result in inaccurate reporting. The effectiveness of the controls implemented by management is to be tested and certified by external auditors in a yearly report. Basically, anything that could jeopardize the accuracy or completeness of financial numbers must be documented and disclosed.

- **Section 409 Real Time Issuer Disclosures:** Real-time disclosure is defined in this section as "rapid and current." After a risk to reporting is uncovered, any changes to reported information must be made available to the public as soon as possible. This section speaks clearly to IT and has been used to justify automated risk management packages and numerous monitoring tools.

- **Section 802 Criminal Penalties for Altering Documents:** A strong records retention policy and procedures is critical to compliance with this section. It is required that all audit and work papers be saved for 5 years after the end of the fiscal year that the audit was preformed. This section also stipulates the retentions of any relevant audit documents, memos, correspondence, communications (including electronic records), and conclusions regarding the audit.

The brief summary of some of the highlights of SOX gives a glimpse at the complexity involved in complying with this law. The PCAOB has issued numerous auditing standards documents to help accountants and auditors tackle the complex set of requirements and nebulous mandates. As of July 25, 2007, Auditing Standard 5 was enacted to provide clearer guidance and hopefully reduce some of the ambiguity that exists in SOX that has cost companies millions of dollars in consulting and other fees associated with compliance. The goal is to help focus the internal control audit, mandated in section 404, on the most relevant portions of financial reporting process utilizing a risk-based, top-down approach. The changes also allow auditors to use previous years' audits where there were no changes to process, instead of having to reassess the same things. Auditors are permitted to use the work of others (consultants or internal corporate auditors) to help streamline the auditing process where applicable. It's important to note that in the 2007 guidance on SOX from the PCOAB that IT controls should only be part of a SOX assessment if they are directly part of or in support of addressing the risk of misstating earnings. This has helped to reduce the scope of SOX audits by focusing IT controls on auditing a much smaller subsection of IT governance. When SOX first came out, there was little guidance about what to audit, resulting in extensive IT audits that were not necessarily relevant. The following list highlights some of the areas that should be considered during a SOX audit:

- IT general controls identified by Cobit or COSO that support the security and operation of financial reporting.

- Any applications that are involved in the creation or processing of financial information.

- Segregation of duties through access controls for providing checks and balances for employees that can make changes to data or processing.

- Change management controls.

- Security monitoring of applications and controls used to protect financial data.

- Access controls for remote and local access to financial data.

- Employee access privileges to financials should be granted and reviewed based on employees who need to know.

- Financial e-mail messages, IM, and any other communications mechanism or systems used in processing financial records.

- End user controls for spreadsheets on computers used to generate accounting data.

Table 2-10 summarizes key points of SOX.

HIPAA

The Health Insurance Portability and Accountability Act of 1996 consists of two primary parts. Title I: Health Care Access, Portability, and Renewability is familiar to anyone who has changed or lost a job in which they took advantage of the ability to extend their

Table 2-10 *Summary of Sarbanes-Oxley Act of 2002*

SOX Offense	Description	Penalty
§302 Corporate Responsibility for Financial reports	Executive officers required to certify the accuracy of the data in quarterly and yearly reports filed by the company	Up to $5,000,000 in fines and/or 20 years in prison
§802 Alteration of Documents	Alteration or destruction of documents pertaining to financial data used before an investigation is performed	Fines and/or maximum of 10 years in prison
§903 Wire and Mail Fraud	Using computers or telecommunications devices to commit wire or mail fraud	Fines and/or maximum of 20 years in prison
§904 Employee Retirement Income Securities Act of 1974	Allows for prosecution under laws protecting fraud related to employee retirement plans	Fines up to $500,00 and 10 years in prison
§906 Failure of Corporate Officers to Certify Financial Reports	Details penalties for knowingly and willfully certifying inaccurate or misleading company financial reports	Up to $1,000,000 in fines and/or 10 years in prison for knowing violations Up to $5,000,000 and/or 20 years for willful violation
§ 1102 Tampering with a Record or Otherwise Impeding an Official Proceeding	Alteration, destruction, or mutilation of documents pertaining to financial data to impede an official investigation or proceeding	Fines and/or up to 20 years in prison

health care coverage. HIPAA provided amendments to COBRA (health care continuation coverage), preventing discrimination against pre-existing illnesses, minimal coverage requirements, and a host of other things that your friends in Human Resources are involved with on a daily basis. Title II: Preventing Health Care Fraud and Abuse; Administration Simplification; Medical Liability Reform is the part most auditors and IT administrators working with health care organizations need to pay close attention to.

Title II is intended to ensure the protection of all health care-related information, expedite access to health care data, reduce the chance for fraud, and ultimately allows health care providers the opportunity to streamline the processing required to receive payment for services rendered. The Department of Health and Human Services (HHS) Office for Civil Rights is responsible for providing guidance, investigation, and enforcing compliance with the Administrative Simplification portion of the law. To accomplish this goal, five standards were written to detail compliance requirements: Privacy Rule, Security Rule, Transactions and Code Sets Rule, Unique Identifiers Rule, and Enforcement Rule.

HIPAA is a well-documented federal law that also has clear penalties for violation. Violation of the HIPAA Security Rule could cost organizations up to $250,000, and individuals face a potential prison time of 10 years.

Two important terms used throughout the HIPAA law are Covered Entities and Business Associates. To understand HIPAA, you must understand who it applies to and to what degree it applies. These are:

- **Covered entities:** Covered entities consist of those businesses responsible for enacting the HIPAA regulations. If your business handles any type of protected healthcare information via a healthcare plan or benefits administration, it is more than likely a covered entity. HIPAA's three major categories of covered entities are:

  - **Health plans:** Health insurance plans, HMOs, or any other group or entity whose primary function is to pay for health care services.

  - **Healthcare providers:** Doctors, hospitals, or other providers of health care.

  - **Healthcare clearinghouse:** Any business or service that is involved in the processing, billing, or handling of health care information.

- **Business associates:** Business associates are identified as individuals or businesses that are involved in any aspect of handling protected health care information and are not a member or employee of a covered entity. The business associate is required to sign a contract that stipulates what they can and can't do with the information, and that they report to the covered entity any unauthorized use or disclosure. For example, a courier service that picks up and delivers lab samples from a physician group to a lab for testing is a business associate.

Privacy Rule

The privacy rule was written and put into effect in 2003 to protect a person's personally identifiable health care-related information in any "form or medium" from improper disclosure. It is a complex set of requirements for the handling of protected health care information (PHI) that defines who can handle health care information, what they can do with it, and penalties for improper disclosure or fraud.

The HIPAA privacy rule requires that a covered entity make reasonable effort to disclose the "minimum necessary" when handling protected health care information. The term "minimum necessary" has been controversial as it is vague in describing the amount of effort that should be expended to secure health care information. Generally speaking, it is required to adopt the following practices:

- Provide information to patients about their privacy rights.

- Adopt a clear privacy policy for employees.

- Provide training and continued education for privacy policy.

- Identify a privacy officer to monitor and assess compliance and initially investigate possible infractions.

- Define a security policy and set of procedures for handling protected health care information.

Security Rule

The HIPAA Security Rule is technology neutral and does not specifically require any security technology or devices to comply. It is a set of minimum best practices around information security that is specifically intended to keep electronic protected health care information (EPHI) and nonelectronic protected health care information secure. It doesn't address all risk possible, but it can be used as a component of an overall security governance program. The standards set forth by the security rule are divided into three categories:

- **Administrative:** These standards provide guidance for delegation of responsibilities, risk analysis, and creating a sustainable security program.

- **Physical:** These provide best practices for securing health care information systems from physical access, disaster, carelessness, and theft.

- **Technical:** These standards provide guidance for technical controls, such as access control, authentication, and encryption.

Each standard is further identified as required or addressable. Required items must be implemented to achieve compliance with the law. Addressable items, however, are up to the covered entity as to whether or not they are applicable to their organization. Flexibility is afforded to implement other technologies or solutions, but the organization's decision and reasoning must be documented thoroughly, based on security, risk, and financial analysis as to why they chose to deviate from the standard.

The security rule is not a step-by-step guide to compliance. Although it provides guidance and flexibility, there are some key areas that need to be addressed:

- A thorough risk analysis to determine how Electronic Protected Healthcare Information (EPHI) flows through a health care provider and the risks that data faces along the way

- Role-based access control to limit only authorized individuals within an health care provider to EPHI

- Monitoring tools and countermeasures to ensure the confidentiality, integrity, and availability of EPHI

- Keeping EPHI safe from unauthorized people and software (hacker tools and viruses or worms)

- Documented policies and procedures for access granting and revocation to EPHI

- Periodic audits and assessments to validate policy and procedures

For the complete text of the Security rule, go to
http://www.cms.hhs.gov/SecurityStandard/Downloads/securityfinalrule.pdf.

Transactions and Code Sets Standard Rule

The Transactions and Code Sets standard rule, which took effect in 2003, is important for overall HIPAA compliance and equally important as a requirement for health care organizations to get paid by insurance companies and Medicare or Medicaid. The bulk of this rule is focused on standardizing the codes used to identify procedures and services rendered based on the ANSI X12N standard. From an information security perspective, the electronic data interchange (EDI) aspects are worth noting. Most health care providers electronically file health care claims that use either the Internet or dialup as a transport mechanism. An auditor should be aware of the encryption strength and any potential protocol weakness in the systems submitting health care claims. These systems could be a tempting target for a would-be attacker.

Identifiers Rule

Before HIPAA's unique Identifiers rule, there was no standard way to identify a health care provider in the U.S. health care system. This caused significant delays in providers receiving payment for services. As part of the Healthcare Administration Simplification provisions in HIPAA, a national registry with unique National Provider Identifiers (NPI) was established in 2006.

Enforcement Rule

A law is not effective without penalties and enforcement. The HIPAA Enforcement rule, made effective in 2006, details a series of penalties for noncompliance, and also provides a framework to investigate violations of the law. The department of Health and Human Services (HHS) is responsible for enforcement and investigation of HIPAA violations. The HHS follows a mostly passive approach to detection of violations as it relies on individuals and organizations to submit complaints. This has been one of the biggest challenges with HIPAA compliance, because it relies on voluntary adherence to the law. The HHS does have the authority to conduct compliance reviews.

In 2009 the HITEC Act was passed, changing HIPAA penalties and enforcement significantly. What were previously considered light fines and consequences for noncompliance were changed to include stronger enforcement capabilities. The Enforcement rule allows for civil fines for the mishandling or unauthorized disclosure of PHI, if a complaint cannot be resolved informally. If a fine is assessed, the HHS can charge $100 per violation with a maximum fine of $1,500,000 in a calendar year for similar violations, depending on whether or not the organization was aware of the violation. This can be in addition to any criminal fines, which has resulted in a serious change to the effectiveness of HIPAA enforcement. In February 2009, for example, CVS Pharmacy was assessed, as of this writing, the largest fine in history for HIPAA violation totaling 2.25 million dollars. Table 2-11 shows the fines possible under the revised penalties for HIPAA violations.

HIPAA criminal enforcement is targeted at individuals who attempt to steal personal health care information. There have been numerous prosecutions of individuals under HIPAA.

Table 2-11 *Fines for Violation of HIPAA Provisions*

Violation Category of HIPAA Provisions	Fine for Each Violation	Maximum Fine for Violation of Identical Provisions in a Calendar Year
Did not know (and by exercising reasonable diligence would not have known) it violated HIPAA	$100–$50,000	$1,500,000
HIPAA violation due to reasonable cause and not willful neglect	$1,000–$50,000	$1,500,000
HIPAA violation due to willful neglect, but violation is corrected within the required time period	$10,000–$50,000	$1,500,000
HIPAA violation due to willful neglect and is not corrected in the required time period	$50,000	$1,500,000

Table 2-12 shows the criminal penalties for a HIPAA violation.

Table 2-12 *HIPAA Criminal Penalties*

Offense	Description	Penalty
Violation of HIPAA	Improper disclosure of individually identifiable health care information engaged in fraud	A person who knowingly obtains or discloses individually identifiable health information in violation of HIPAA faces a fine of up to $50,000 and up to 1-year imprisonment. Knowingly disclosing information under false pretenses raises the penalties to $100,000 and up to 5 years imprisonment. Willful disclosure with the intent to sell, transfer, or use individually identifiable health information for commercial advantage, personal gain, or malicious harm increases the penalties to $250,000 and up to 10 years imprisonment.

GLBA

The Grahmm-Leach-Bliley Act of 1999 (also known as the Financial Services Modernization Act) was enacted by Congress to address significant changes in the banking and financial services landscape that has occurred through the many mergers and acquisitions of the last 10 years. Although the bulk of GLBA was intended to allow banks to expand their service offerings through additional lines of business including insurance, stock brokerage, and investment services, the fact that the much larger and diversified banks would have unparalleled access to customers' private information, it became necessary to include privacy laws to help limit disclosure. The privacy provisions require these organizations to securely store private information, create policies, communicate to the consumer how private information is to be used, and to give the consumer the right to opt out of their information being shared to third parties.

The privacy protection laws are applied to financial institutions as defined by any organization "significantly involved in financial activities." These laws are broken into two titles and codified under Title I: Disclosure of Non-Public Personal Information §§6801-6809 and Title II: Fraudulent Access to Financial Information §§6821-6827. This definition encompasses a wide range of businesses including banks, credit unions, investment firms, real estate appraisers, insurance companies, vehicle leasing services, and retail establishments that offer credit cards. Financial institutions must be careful about how they handle and share nonpublic personal information (NPPI). NPPI is classified as any information that a consumer provides to obtain a loan, credit card, or other financial service that is not public knowledge.

There are three primary provisions of GLBA that organizations are required to comply with:

- **Financial Privacy Rule:** The privacy rule requires that institutions under GLBA must provide privacy notices to consumers that detail how the institution uses and under what conditions it might disclose private information. These privacy notices must be provided when financial services are started, and then annually, as long as those services continue. The consumer must be afforded the opportunity to opt out of information that is shared with third parties.

- **Safeguards Rule:** The safeguards rule mandates that a covered entity has a security policy and program in place that includes assigning an employee to coordinate and monitor the information security program. Additionally, GLBA requires that risk analysis be conducted to determine potential threats, design and deploy safeguards to secure data, and regularly test security controls (audit and assess).

- **Pretexting Protection:** The act of pretexting is criminalized under federal law in GLBA. *Pretexting* is a form of social engineering and is used to manipulate someone into divulging personal information through misrepresentation or a pretext. This technique is used in bank fraud to get balance information, transfer funds, or other activities, and it requires research to obtain Social Security numbers or a mother's maiden name to determine the identity of the caller. Financial institutions are instructed to secure customers' private information, and as such, they need to create policies and procedures to prevent unauthorized disclosure through this method. Employee training and awareness programs should be leveraged, too. Pretexting is permissible if it is used by authorized individuals to test the security safeguards of a financial institution.

Auditors examining an organization for GLBA compliance should pay attention to a few specific areas. GLBA, like SOX and HIPAA, does not dictate any technology or technical safeguards in particular, such as firewalls or IPS, but it does provide specific guidance about how the safeguards rule on the results that need to be achieved. Protection of customer information is the primary requirement and that can be accomplished in a number of ways. Here is a recommended list of specific areas to look at:

- Ensure the entity has a written information security policy and program.

- Conduct periodic independent security assessments with risk analysis for potential threats at least yearly.

- Ensure the organization identifies and ranks information assets (data and hardware) based on sensitivity and criticality.

- Implement role-based access controls to permit only authorized access to customer information.

- Ensure a change control mechanism is in place to monitor and approve configuration changes to key systems.

- Ensure the organization has a security monitoring system to detect attacks or unauthorized access.

- Ensure the organization has a documented incident-handling program and response in the event of a data breach.

- Assess service providers (anyone providing a service for the financial institution) to ensure adherence to privacy safeguard requirements.

Table 2-13 provides a summary of the Criminal and Civil offenses for GLBA.

PCI DSS

Practically everyone today has a credit card (or multiple cards) and it is tough to buy or sell anything in which a credit card is not involved. The ubiquity of the credit card makes it an incredibly enticing target for criminals all over the world. To help address uniformly securing credit card account information through industry best practices, Visa and MasterCard joined forces to develop the Payment Card Industry Data Security Standard (usually shortened to PCI DSS). The PCI standard has been endorsed by most of the major card issuers, including American Express, Discover, and JCB. Unlike the many laws discussed so far in this chapter, PCI is not a federal or state statute. Instead, PCI relies on a series of contractual obligations between the merchants and the credit card issuers so that anyone who processes, stores, or transmits credit card data must provide a minimum level of security to ensure the confidentiality and integrity of the cardholder data. If an organization wants to continue accepting and processing credit cards, it must adhere to the rules. PCI doesn't provide penalties because the individual credit card issuers that follow PCI handle that aspect.

Table 2-13 *Summary of Grahmm-Leach-Bliley Act of 1999*

GLBA Offense	Description	Penalty
Noncompliance with GLBA Privacy	Noncompliance with §§6801-6809	Financial institutions fined up to $100,000 per violation Officers and directors personally liable up $10,000 per violation Prison sentence up to 5 years.
§6821 Privacy Protection for Customer Information of Financial Institutions (Pretexting)	It shall be a violation of this subchapter for any person to obtain or attempt to obtain, or cause to be disclosed or attempt to cause to be disclosed to any person, customer information of a financial institution relating to another person— (1) by making a false, fictitious, or fraudulent statement or representation to an officer, employee, or agent of a financial institution; (2) by making a false, fictitious, or fraudulent statement or representation to a customer of a financial institution; or (3) by providing any document to an officer, employee, or agent of a financial institution, knowing that the document is forged, counterfeit, lost, or stolen, was fraudulently obtained, or contains a false, fictitious, or fraudulent statement or representation.	Fines for individuals up to $250,000 or maximum imprisonment of 5 years Fines for organizations up to $500,000 Aggravated penalty involving more than $100,000 in loss in 1 year, three times the amount of fines found in 18 U.S.C. § 3571 and a maximum of 10 years in prison

The PCI Security Council was created to maintain and update the data security standard. PCI DSS 1.2.1 is the most recent version of the standard and became effective August 2009. The PCI DSS provides detailed information about required security practices for protecting storage and transmission of cardholder information, and is divided into six main categories with 12 control objectives. PCI provides guidance about configuration of security controls, wireless, and all other aspects of technology that are used in processing credit cards. Following are the PCI DSS 1.2.1 required controls:

- **Build and maintain a secure network:**

    - Install and maintain a firewall configuration to protect data.

    - Do not use vendor-supplied defaults for system passwords and other security parameters.

- **Protect cardholder data:**

    - Protect stored data.

    - Encrypt the transmission of cardholder data and sensitive information across public networks.

- **Maintain a vulnerability management program:**

    - Use and regularly update antivirus software.

    - Develop and maintain secure systems and applications.

- **Implement strong access control measures:**

    - Restrict access to data by a business on a need-to-know basis.

    - Assign a unique ID to each person with computer access.

    - Restrict physical access to cardholder data.

- **Regularly monitor and test networks:**

    - Track and monitor all access to network resources and cardholder data.

    - Regularly test security systems and processes.

- **Maintain an information security policy:** Maintain a policy that addresses information security.

The PCI standard is the agreed upon baseline for securing cardholder data, and based on the volume of credit card transactions processed per year, merchants are required to undergo specific validation requirements for compliance. In the case of Visa and MasterCard, both use similar methodologies for determining what a merchant or service provider should do to be in compliance. Visa Cardholder Information Security Program (CISP) and MasterCard's Site Data Protection (SDA) have common criteria for identifying the risk level and validation requirements. Other credit card issuers don't have the same commonality about requirements, so it is important that you read about the specifics for each issuer.

Visa and MasterCard identify four levels of merchants and three levels of service providers:

- **Merchant levels:**
    - Level 1 merchants have total yearly transactions greater than six million, and any merchant, regardless of size, that has had a cardholder data breach or is determined to be of significant risk. These merchants are required to conduct an annual onsite audit by a Qualified Security Assessor (QSA), and conduct a quarterly network security scan by an Approved Scanning Vendor (ASV).
    - Level 2 merchants have between one million and six million transactions a year. These merchants must submit an annual PCI DSS self-assessment questionnaire and conduct quarterly network scans with an approved ASV. MasterCard announced that it would require level 2 merchants to have an annual onsite security assessment by a QSA before December 31, 2010.
    - Level 3 merchants have 20,000 to one million e-commerce transactions per year. These merchants must submit an annual PCI DSS self-assessment questionnaire and conduct quarterly network scans with an approved ASV.
    - Level 4 merchants have less than 20,000 e-commerce transactions per year. This level also includes all other merchants that have less than one million transactions a year. These merchants must submit an annual PCI DSS self-assessment questionnaire and conduct quarterly network scans with an approved ASV.
- **Service provider levels:**
    - Level 1 service providers consist of all VisaNet processors and all payment gateways. This class of provider processes, stores, or transmits payment transactions for merchants also known as a third-party processor. Validation requirements include annual onsite audits through a QSA and conduct a quarterly network security scan by an ASV.
    - Level 2 service providers are not a VisaNet processor or payment gateway and store, process, or transmit more than one million accounts/transactions a year. Validation requirements include annual onsite audit through a QSA and conduct a quarterly network security scan by an ASV.
    - Level 3 service providers are not a VisaNet processor or payment gateway and store, process, or transmit less than one million accounts/transactions a year. Validation requirements include an annual self-assessment and conduct a quarterly network security scan by an ASV.

Auditing Level 1 merchants or level 1-2 service providers for PCI compliance requires that you work for a QSA. QSAs are security-consulting firms certified by the PCI Security Council to conduct audits. The process for getting certified requires training, testing, and signing a business agreement adhering to the requirement and code of conduct with the PCI Security Council. There are a number of QSAs across the globe, with a complete list available on the PCI Security Standards Council website (www.pcisecuritystandards.org).

ASVs are companies that are authorized to conduct the remote penetration and vulnerability scanning required to be conducted quarterly by the various merchant and service provider levels. To become an ASV, a security solutions provider must pass a live remote scan test conducted by the PCI Security Standards Council. This test examines the capabilities of the security firm in conducting scans, finding vulnerabilities in networks and web applications, and the quality of the scan reports presented to the customer. After the PCI SSC has approved the vendor, it is then added to the list of ASVs and can be used by merchants and service providers. A complete list of ASVs can be found on the PCI Council's website at www.pcisecuritystandards.org.

The vast majority of merchants that must comply with PCI are required to file a PCI DSS self-assessment questionnaire. This document acts as a checklist to certify that the 12 requirements of the PCI standard are met, and questions are answered with a simple yes, no, or not applicable. If any portion of the checklist is answered with a no, the merchant or service provider is considered noncompliant and must fix lacking areas.

The key for auditors reviewing PCI requirements is identifying what is in scope from a PCI perspective. Network segmentation is essential to reducing the number of devices and parts of the network that need to be assessed. PCI considers devices in scope if they have any potential to interact with the logical flow of cardholder information as it is transmitted and processed. Segmenting the network properly prevents unrelated devices such as printers and user workstations from being part of the compliance equation. All businesses can benefit from the documentation, excellent checklist for compliance, and general security controls PCI provides.

Summary

This chapter provides information about several key federal and state laws that directly impact information security practices. Auditors must be aware of how laws influence the design and implementation of security systems and controls and the penalties for ignoring the laws. In summary:

■ Most of the hacking laws classify hacking as access without authorization. Make sure that you have permission for any security testing you might do while auditing networks and hosts.

■ Packet capture and monitoring networks for fraud and abuse in a corporate environment are perfectly legal. All organizations should have a well-defined monitoring policy that employees are aware of, and it is recommended to have them sign off of written policies.

■ Make sure that you attain professional legal advice when building corporate information security policies. Many of the laws are tricky and constantly changing.

■ Developing a strong information security strategy that leverages best practices can help to comply with multiple regulations.

References in This Chapter

Harris, Shon, et. All. *Gray Hat Hacking: The Ethical Hackers Handbook.* McGraw-Hill Osborne, 2005.

Wright, Benjamin. *Business Law & Computer Security.* SANS Institute, 2004.

Federal Hacking Laws

United States Department of Justice: Computer Crime and Intellectual Property Section, http://www.cybercrime.gov

Prosecuting Computer Crimes, http://www.cybercrime.gov/ccmanual/index.html

Prosecuting Intellectual Crimes Manual, http://www.cybercrime.gov/ipmanual/index.html

Robinson, Steven, U.S. Information Security Law Part1-4, www.SecurityFocus.com

Alabama infraguard Computer crime summary, http://www.infragard-mo.net/Computer_Crimes_Statute_Summary.htm

Federal Bureau of Investigations: Cybercrime Division, http://www.fbi.gov/cyberinvest/cyberhome.htm

United States Secret Service: Electronic Crimes Task Force, http://www.secretservice.gov/ectf.shtml

State Laws

National Conference of State Legislatures, http://www.ncsl.org/IssuesResearch/TelecommunicationsInformationTechnolgy/ComputerHackingandUnauthorizedAccessLaws/tabid/13494/Default.aspx

SOX, http://en.wikipedia.org/wiki/Sarbanes%E2%80%93Oxley_Act

PCAOB, http://pcaobus.org/Pages/default.aspx

HIPAA, http://www.hhs.gov/ocr/privacy/

GLBA, http://www.ftc.gov/privacy/privacyinitiatives/glbact.html and http://en.wikipedia.org/wiki/Gramm%E2%80%93Leach%E2%80%93Bliley_Act

PCI standards, https://www.pcisecuritystandards.org/index.shtml

Chapter 3

Information Security Governance, Frameworks, and Standards

To audit a process, procedure, or technology, you must first measure the current state against the desired state; this enables you to identify the gaps. The terms "best practice" and "standards" are used to describe how a company should configure or manage its security controls, but if you put two security professionals in a room and asked them to describe the best way to accomplish a particular company's goals, you would likely get a slew of different answers. With all of these best practices floating around, it becomes difficult to pick the "better" practice and it comes down to determining what fits the organization as a whole and that is where understanding information security governance becomes so important. Governance drives the organization to institute best practices and measures its performance. A best practice doesn't become a standard until the organization adopts it and decides to comply with it. Auditors need to be aware of various best practices and industry standards available today to better tailor audits to the companies for which they are conducting them. This chapter introduces key concepts of information security governance and a few of the most common frameworks and standards that can be used to build a checklist to audit networks in a manageable and measurable fashion.

Understanding Information Security Governance

Information security governance is a part of an overall IT governance strategy that is focused on reducing risk and providing value back to the organization in the form of protecting assets and aligning to business needs. Governance is about assigning responsibility for the use and protection of corporate assets to the managers and employees entrusted with their care in addition to measuring the results of their actions. Data has become one of the most valuable assets a company possesses, and its proper protection is no longer best effort but required by law and shareholders. Scanning through laws like HIPAA, GLBA, and SOX, you will find that each one identifies either the board of directors or executive management as being ultimately responsible for securing corporate data. To adhere to the law and to provide due care in managing the business data, organizations must build a sustainable security program that addresses these requirements.

A security governance strategy provides the blueprint to direct and control the security program with clearly defined goals and objectives. Figure 3-1 shows how information security governance provides the glue to coordinate the efforts of people, processes, and technologies to better secure the key assets of a company.

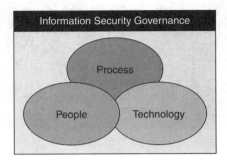

Figure 3-1   *Information Security Governance Infrastructure*

When a business builds a security governance strategy, it can rely on frameworks, standards, and guidelines to address specific controls and processes that are part of the security program. Looking at the various standards documents, it is clear that there is overlap between them. No one standard addresses all of the needs of a security program, though some, such as COBIT, get close; most successful programs leverage some pieces from each. By grouping the standards into the categories of people, process, and technology, it is easier to see how they can be used together to shore up the weaknesses and leverage the strengths of each. Figure 3-2 shows how some of the key standards and frameworks overlap while also highlighting where they are the strongest.

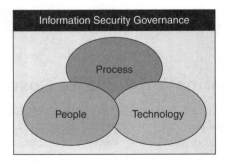

Figure 3-2   *Overlapping Standards and Frameworks Provide Strength*

Although the governance strategy is different depending on a company's tolerance for risk, size, and regulatory requirements, there are a number of common elements that all companies should address. Some of the objectives and deliverables of an information security governance program are as follows:

- Alignment of information security with the business's strategy and objectives

- Effective management and utilization of resources (people and technologies) with a clearly defined organizational structure

- Risk management to reduce the potential impact of events on information systems assets

- Security policies to address business requirements and regulatory compliance

- Security standards for each policy so that procedures and guidelines are defined

- Performance management through measurement, monitoring, and reporting to track attainment of organizational security objectives

- Assessment of security processes and procedures to measure effectiveness and compliance

- A review and update process for security policies, standards, and procedures

- A process for the evaluation of new threats and risks to the organization

- Optimized usage of security investments

- Integration of security into all aspects of the business

- Security awareness training

Analyzing a security governance program requires that the auditor have detailed information about how the organization conducts itself. No two companies are exactly alike in this respect; however, there are five main areas that auditors should focus attention on to determine the effectiveness of the security program.

The first area starts at the senior management level. Senior management sets the tone and culture for the organization, the priorities, and strategy. If the organization has poor support from management or management doesn't seem to take security seriously enough, then all other areas of the security program will suffer. Many executives still think of security as being an IT or technology problem and would rather spend money on controls than tackle the larger job of changing the organization's approach to security. If the security group finds it difficult to get the appropriate tools or make changes when risk is identified, there is a strong possibility that the biggest threat to the organization might ultimately be the organization itself. Auditors should look for these types of issues by talking to employees and administrators to identify these issues. More than likely, auditors will find that the security governance strategy is weak and can make recommendations about how to better articulate and report on risks to the organization.

The second area that should be examined is the specifics of the security program. This starts by examining the goals and objectives of the security program to determine if the goals are attainable, measurable, and realistic given the organization's risk profile and business model. Looking at the policies in place and controls identified to enforce the policies will provide a view of the security architecture. If policies are in place but they are either not enforced or adhered to inconsistently, it is difficult to manage these policies. After the security architecture is identified, the auditor can start planning for how to test the effectiveness of policy and architecture and relevancy to the goals of the program.

The third area is how the organization measures its successes and failures in execution of the security program. Measurement is critical to any process operating successfully, and analyzing how a company measures itself can be telling for an auditor. Identifying performance goals, program maturity levels, and success criteria can show how the business sets priorities for security. Audit and assessment is the execution of security management and a critical component of management of the program.

The fourth area is the risk-management program. Risk management drives security architecture development and deployment. Knowing how the business selects and identifies controls is an important part of managing risk. Buying products before risk is quantified is like "putting the cart before the horse." Doing this can lead to placing technology into the network without necessarily adding real value.

The final area concerns how the business addresses continuous improvement of its security program. One of the quickest ways to see whether a company is improving its security posture is to look at past audits to determine whether the same deficiencies are being identified audit after audit. This indicates quite clearly that the company didn't have an effective improvement process for security. Auditors should also determine whether the organization has a process for updating policies and procedures as new technologies and risks are identified. Stale policies and outdated procedures do not lend themselves to being effective tools, requiring individuals to modify or augment the procedures to accomplish their jobs. This type of adaptation means inconsistent deployments and increases the risk of opening up vulnerabilities.

Security governance is successful only if it is sponsored and managed from the top. Executives must make it a component of measuring business success.

People: Roles and Responsibilities

In the not so distant past, the responsibilities of a company's security administrator primarily consisted of adding, removing, and resetting user accounts and passwords. As the role of IT in business has evolved, so have the requirements and responsibilities of the information security functions of most corporations. Companies have hired CIOs and Chief Information Security Officers (CISO), and numerous organizational structures have been implemented to get a handle on the complexities associated with managing and protecting data. Regardless of how the teams are divided, the goal is to ensure a clear reporting structure that requires accountability at every level.

Information Security Governance Organizational Structure

Figure 3-3 shows a sample information security governance organizational structure.

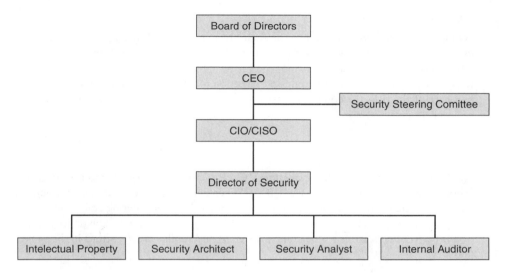

Figure 3-3   *Information Security Governance Organizational Structure*

Information security governance begins at the top with the Board of Directors and CEO enforcing accountability for adherence to standards and commissioning the development of security architectures that address the security requirements of the business as a whole. The auditing function might be its own group (or outsourced to a third party) and might report to the CEO or directly to the Board of Directors to maintain its independence.

Board of Directors

The Board of Directors is responsible for protecting the interests of the shareholders of the corporation. This duty of care (fiduciary responsibility) requires that it understand the risk to the business and its data. The Board of Directors is responsible for approving the appropriate resources necessary to safeguard data. It also needs to be kept aware of how the security program is performing.

Security Steering Committee

The Security Steering Committee has an important role in security governance; this group is responsible for setting the tactical and strategic direction for the organization as a whole. The group generally consists of the CEO, CFO, CIO/CISO, and the internal auditing function (or oversight if it is outsourced to a third party). Other business functions might also be present, such as Human Resources and business operational leaders, depending on the size and organizational complexity of the business. This team reviews audit results, risk assessment, and current program performance data. The committee also provides approval for any major policy or security strategy changes.

CEO or Executive Management

Senior management must answer to the Board of Directors and shareholders of a company. Furthermore, if the company is publicly traded, the CEO and CFO must personally attest to the accuracy and integrity of the financial reports the company issues. Executive management sets the tone and direction for the rest of the company and must be aware of the risks the company faces for the confidentiality, integrity, and availability of sensitive data.

CIO/CISO

The CIO/CISO is responsible for aligning the information security program strategy and vision to business requirements. The CIO/CISO ensures that the correct resources are in place to adhere to the policies and procedures set forth by the steering committee. This role generally reports to the CEO and Board of Directors and reports how the organization is performing relative to the company's goals and similar organizations in the same industry.

Security Director

The security director's role is to coordinate the efforts for securing corporate assets. The responsibilities include reporting on the progress of initiatives to executive management and building the teams and resources to address the various tasks necessary for information security. This role also acts as a liaison to other aspects of the business to articulate security requirements throughout the company. The security director manages the teams in developing corporate data security policies, standards, procedures, and guidelines.

Security Analyst

A security analyst builds the policies, analyzes risk, and identifies new threats to the business. Business continuity and disaster recovery planning are important functions performed by the analyst to prepare the company for the unexpected. The analyst is also responsible for creating reports about the performance of the organization's security systems.

Security Architect

A security architect defines the procedures, guidelines, and standards used by the company. Architects help to select the controls used to protect the company's data and they make sure that the controls are sufficient for addressing the risk and complying with policy. This role is also responsible for testing security products and making recommendations about what will best serve the needs of the company.

Security Engineer

A security engineer implements the controls selected by the security architect. Security engineers are responsible for the maintenance of firewalls, IPS, and other tools. This includes upgrades, testing, patching, and overall maintenance of the security systems. This role might also be responsible for testing the functionality of equipment to make sure that it operates as expected.

Systems Administrator

A systems administrator is responsible for monitoring and maintaining the servers, printers, and workstations a company uses. In addition, administrators add and/or remove user accounts as necessary, control access to shared resources, and maintain company-wide antivirus software.

Database Administrator

The Database Administrator (DBA) has an important job in most companies. The DBA is responsible for designing and maintaining corporate databases and also securing access to the data to ensure its integrity. The ramifications of lax security in this role can be severe, especially considering the reporting requirements mandated by SOX.

IS Auditor

An auditor's role in security governance is to assess the effectiveness in meeting the requirements set forth by policy and management direction. The auditor is tasked to identify risk and report on how the organization performs to upper management. The auditor provides an impartial review of projects and technologies to identify weaknesses that could result in loss to the company.

End User

End users have a critical role in security governance that is often overlooked. They must be aware of the impact their actions can have on the security of the company and be able to safeguard confidential information. They are responsible for complying with policies and procedures and following safe computing practices, such as not opening attachments without antimalware software running or loading unauthorized software. A solid user security awareness program can help promote safe computing habits.

Spotting Weaknesses in the People Aspect of Security

There are many different roles involved in securing the assets and a data of a company. An auditor should be on the lookout for areas that might represent opportunities to improve how a company instills security as part of corporate culture. Confusion and lack of direction are often signs of weakness in management's commitment to protecting assets. Some things to be on the lookout for are:

- Lack of management commitment to security

- Key assets not identified and inventoried

- Poor adherence to processes and procedures

- No follow-up on issues identified

- Apathy toward security

- Lack of segregation of duties in key roles

- Inconsistent application of policy

- Poor communication between roles

- Unclear job descriptions or roles

- Poor documentation

Process: Security Governance Frameworks

Security governance frameworks represent solutions to the question of how to manage security effectively. The manner in which a company builds a governance structure is a reflection of the organization of the company and the laws and business environment in which it finds itself. Auditing the security governance practices of a company requires understanding how the organization manages the processes and procedures that make up its security program and compare those aspects to recognized governance frameworks. Luckily, there are many sources that an auditor can use to identify best practices in building a manageable, measurable, and effective security governance program. The frameworks mentioned in this text are not a complete list, and significant research is constantly being conducted in this area. What follow are three of the most frequently found frameworks, and should get you started in understanding how they can be applied to the organizations you audit.

COSO

The Foreign Corrupt Practices Act of 1977 (FCPA) is a law that requires any publicly traded company to accurately document any transactions or monetary exchanges it is involved in (to prevent off-the-books money transfers). Additionally, the law requires that a publicly traded company also have a system of internal accounting controls to monitor fraud and abuse and test them through compliance auditing. This law had little guidance from the Securities and Exchange Commission (SEC), and in response to this, a consortium of private organizations created the Treadway Commission to figure out what companies needed to do to comply with this law. The Committee of Sponsoring Organizations of the Treadway Commission (COSO) was formed in 1985 to improve the accuracy of financial reports and to standardize on internal control methods to reduce fraudulent reporting. COSO studied the problem and issued guidance about how to create an internal controls framework that complies with the FCPA. The resulting document, called "Internal Controls: Integrated Framework," was published in 1994 and provided common language, definitions, and assessment methodologies for a company's internal accounting controls. This COSO report is considered the standard by which accounting auditors assess companies to ensure compliance with the FCPA and SOX section 404.

The COSO report lists a few main concepts that guided the development of the COSO framework and define what internal controls can and cannot do for an organization. These concepts show the relationship between people and processes in respect to the effectiveness of controls, and they define the principles with which to implement them:

■ Internal control is a process and not a one-time activity.

■ Internal control is affected by people; it must be adopted through the organization and is not simply a policy document that gets filed away.

■ An internal control can provide only reasonable assurance, not absolute assurance, to the management and board of a business. A control cannot ensure success.

■ Internal controls are designed for the achievement of business objectives.

The COSO internal controls framework consists of five main control components as seen in Figure 3-4. These controls are the foundation of the COSO framework and provide a means for auditors to assess a company's control efficiency, effectiveness, reliability of financial reporting, and compliance with the law.

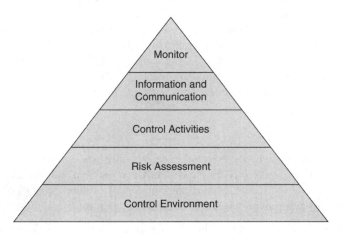

Figure 3-4   *COSO Internal Controls Framework*

Control Environment

The control environment defines how an organization builds its internal governance program and affects the company as a whole. The CEO, Board of Directors, and executive management are most involved at this level, creating the ethics environment and organizational structure and defining the roles and responsibilities. The control environment consists of the people, culture, and ethics of the business.

Risk Assessment

Solid risk assessment methodologies are important to any successful governance program. COSO identifies this area as critical to all control development activities and for identifying business objectives. You can't protect what you don't know about, so a thorough risk assessment provides the data to help a company design controls to protect its assets and achieve its strategic goals.

Control Activities

This section covers the controls that COSO recommends to help mitigate risk. The main categories for controls in COSO are operational, financial reporting, and compliance. The controls identified are broad in nature and cover some IT-related issues, but COSO doesn't address this area as well for IT as it does the accounting side. It does highlight the various activities that should be controlled, but leaves it up to management to figure out how to do it.

Information and Communication

Having an organization in which information and communication are free to flow between all aspects of the business is addressed in this component of COSO. Information, according to COSO, is the data used to run the business, whereas communication is defined as the method used to disseminate information to the appropriate individuals. People cannot do their jobs efficiently and effectively if they are not provided with the necessary information. Without the appropriate lines of communication and timely action, problems can turn into catastrophes. Communication is the mechanism that drives the other four components of the COSO framework.

Monitoring

Auditing and measurement are essential in determining how controls perform. Monitoring can be the alarm system that identifies a problem and provides valuable data for fixing issues for the future. Monitoring can consist of periodic reports, audits, or testing mechanisms that provide the status of individual controls.

COSO is one of the more widely adopted internal control frameworks for large companies due in no small part to the mandates set forth through SOX 404. In response to criticism that the framework was impractical for smaller organizations, the committee published "Internal Control over Financial Reporting for Small Public Companies" in 2006.

The COSO framework represents the grandfather of internal controls and though it was designed primarily for accounting controls, it still provides value for companies building out a security governance strategy. From an IT perspective, the five main components are entirely relevant to securing information, but the actual controls themselves don't go to the same level of depth as other frameworks such as Control Objects for Information and related Technologies (COBIT).

COBIT

The COBIT framework was created by the Information Systems Audit and Control Association (ISACA) and IT Governance Institute (ITGI) as a response to the needs of the IT community for a less generalized and more actionable set of controls for securing information systems. The ITGI is a nonprofit organization that leads the development of COBIT through committees consisting of experts from universities, governments, and auditors from across the globe. The COBIT framework is a series of manuals and implementation guidelines for creating a full IT governance, auditing, and service delivery program for any organization.

COBIT is not a replacement but an augmentation to COSO, and maps directly to COSO from an IT perspective. Although COSO covers the whole enterprise from an accounting perspective, it does so by providing high-level objectives that require the business to figure out how to accomplish them. COBIT on the other hand, works with COSO by fully detailing the necessary controls required and how to measure and audit them. The built-in auditable nature of COBIT is why it has become one of the leading IT governance frameworks as it gets as close as can be expected to a turnkey governance program. COBIT does not dig down into the actual tasks and procedures however, which necessitates using other sources to develop standards and procedures for implementing the controls. In other words, COBIT won't tell you the best way to configure AES encryption for your wireless infrastructure, but it will provide you with a mechanism for identifying where and why you need to apply it based on risk.

The role of COBIT in IT governance is to provide a model that takes the guesswork out of how to bridge the gap between business goals and IT goals. COBIT considers business the customer of IT services. Business requirements (needs) ultimately drive the investment in IT resources, which in turn need processes that can deliver enterprise information back to the business. The cyclical nature of business needing information and IT delivering information services are the foundation of COBIT. Information is what IT provides to the business and COBIT defines the following seven control areas as business requirements for information:

- **Effectiveness:** Information should be delivered in a timely, correct, consistent, and usable manner.

- **Efficiency:** Information is delivered in the most cost effective way.

- **Confidentiality:** Data is protected from unauthorized disclosure.

- **Integrity:** The business is protected from unauthorized manipulation or destruction of data.

- **Availability:** Data should be accessible when the business needs it.

- **Compliance:** There is adherence to laws, regulations, and contractual agreements.

- **Reliability of information:** Data correctly represents the state of the business and transactions.

IT resources in COBIT are the components of information delivery and represent the technology, people, and procedures used to meet business goals. Resources are divided into four areas:

- **Applications:** Information processing systems and procedures
- **Information:** The data as used by the business
- **Infrastructure:** Technology and systems used for data delivery and processing
- **People:** The human talent needed to keep everything operating

IT processes (or activities) are the planned utilization of resources and divided into four interrelated domains. Each process has its own controls that govern how the process is to be accomplished and measured. There are 34 high-level processes and hundreds of individual controls. The domains and processes are:

- **Plan and Organize (PO):** Defines strategy and guides the creation of a service and solutions delivery organization. The high-level process for this domain is as follows:
  - PO1 Define a strategic IT plan.
  - PO2 Define the information architecture.
  - PO3 Determine technological direction.
  - PO4 Define the IT processes, organization, and relationships.
  - PO5 Manage the IT investment.
  - PO6 Communicate management aims and direction.
  - PO7 Manage IT Human Resources.
  - PO8 Manage quality.
  - PO9 Assess and manage IT risks.
  - PO10 Manage projects.
- **Acquire and Implement (AI):** Builds IT solutions and creates services. The high-level process for this domain is as follows:
  - AI1 Identify automated solutions.
  - AI2 Acquire and maintain application software.
  - AI3 Acquire and maintain technology infrastructure.
  - AI4 Enable operation and use.
  - AI5 Procure IT resources.

- AI6 Manage changes.

- AI7 Install and accredit solutions and changes.

- **Deliver and Support (DS):** User facing delivery of services and solutions. The high-level process for this domain is as follows:

    - DS1 Define and manage service levels.

    - DS2 Manage third-party services.

    - DS3 Manage performance and capacity.

    - DS4 Ensure continuous service.

    - DS5 Ensure systems security.

    - DS6 Identify and allocate costs.

    - DS7 Educate and train users.

    - DS8 Manage service desk and incidents.

    - DS9 Manage the configuration.

    - DS10 Manage problems.

    - DS11 Manage data.

    - DS12 Manage the physical environment.

    - DS13 Manage operations.

- **Monitor and Evaluate (ME):** Monitors IT processes to ensure synergy between business requirements. The high-level process for this domain is as follows:

    - ME1 Monitor and evaluate IT performance.

    - ME2 Monitor and evaluate internal control.

    - ME3 Ensure compliance with external requirements.

    - ME4 Provide IT governance.

Each of the processes in COBIT is written for managers, users, and auditors by addressing each group's needs. Each process control objective is built using a template that includes:

- A general statement that provides answers to why management needs the control and were it fits

- The key business requirements that the control addresses

- How the controls are achieved

- Control goals and metrics

- Who is responsible for each individual control activity

■   How the controls can be measured

■   Clear descriptions of measuring how mature the organization is in accomplishing the control using a detailed 0–5 scale Maturity Model

Measurement of each process and controls is accomplished through a Maturity Model. The COBIT Maturity Model is based on the Capabilities Maturity Model pioneered by Carnegie Mellon's Software Engineering Institute (SEI). The Capabilities Maturity Model was designed as a tool for ensuring quality software development. COBIT has modified the model to deliver a measurement and tracking tool that identifies the current state of adoption (maturity level) for each process so as to compare an organization execution with industry averages and business targets. This helps management identify where the company's performance is in relations to its peers and provides a path to improve with specific and prescriptive steps used to get there.

The COBIT Maturity Model scale provides the following measurements, as illustrated in Table 3-1.

Table 3-1   *COBIT Maturity Scale*

0	Nonexistent	Not performed
1	Initial/Ad hoc	Process is chaotic, not standardized, and done case by case.
2	Repeatable but intuitive	Relies on individual knowledge, no formal training, and no process management.
3	Defined process	Standardized and documented processes; formal training to communicate standards.
4	Managed and measurable	Processes are monitored and checked for compliance by management; processes are reviewed for improvement; limited automation.
5	Optimized	Processes are refined and compared with others based on maturity; processes are automated through workflow tools to improve quality and effectiveness.

Using COBIT requires customization to better align with the company implementing it. COBIT is not designed as a governance strategy in a box, but as a reference for building a process-focused system utilizing international standards and good practices. Companies still need to determine a risk management methodology and build out a technical infrastructure to automate the various COBIT processes indentified. COBIT's real value is in providing the management, measurement, and organizational glue to tie these functions together.

IT auditors love to use COBIT mainly because it creates a well documented set of processes and controls that can be assessed along with the metrics and requirements for each control. COBIT's usefulness is also apparent when the organization under audit does not use COBIT as a governance framework because an auditor can build checklists and plan audits based on COBIT to ensure that all aspects of the IT process are preformed. COBIT is also an invaluable resource when writing the audit report because it allows the auditor to justify and compare his findings to a well-respected standard.

ITIL

The Information Technology Infrastructure Library (ITIL) provides documentations for best practices for IT Service Management. ITIL was created in the late 1980s by Great Britain's Office of Government Commerce to standardize Britain's government agencies and to follow security best practices. A study was conducted and generated a significant amount of information (roughly 40 books) that became known as ITIL. The books were revised and consolidated in 2004 and became a series of eight books focused on IT services management. This version 2 of ITIL became popular among organizations looking for an internationally-recognized, proactive framework for managing IT services, reducing cost, and improving quality. Version 3 of ITIL was released in June 2007 to refresh the core service and support delivery material that many companies have implemented, and to move the ITIL framework towards a life cycle model that includes management of all life-cycle services provided by IT. The five books that make up version 3 are:

- **Service Strategy:** This book is the foundation for the others by defining business to IT alignment, value to business, services strategy, and service portfolio management.

- **Service Design:** Focused on the design of IT processes, policies, and architectures. Includes service-level, management, capacity management, information security management, and availability management.

- **Service Transition:** Covers moving from the design phase to production business services and change management. Also includes service asset and configuration management, service validation and testing, evaluation, and knowledge management.

- **Service Operation:** Provides information on the day-to-day support of production systems. This includes service delivery and services support, service desk design, application management, problem management, and technical management.

- **Continual Service Improvement:** This book covers service improvements and service retirement strategies.

ITIL is primarily about delivering IT as a service and the lifecycle of service development, implementation, operation, and management. ITIL is used by companies for overall management of IT and also for managing security processes as well. Auditing an ITIL shop requires that the auditor understand the basics of ITIL to speak the same language. ITIL also works well with COBIT as a means for fleshing out the service delivery of each process. The ITGI even creates a mapping between COBIT and ITIL for organizations that want to utilize the two standards. ITIL also meets the criteria for ISO 20000, which means that it can be used to achieve international certification. Whether a company chooses to go for certification or not, ITIL gives guidance about how to move from a reactive to a proactive approach to managing IT and security as a service.

Technology: Standards Procedures and Guidelines

Knowing what processes and controls need to be in place is half the job; the other half is implementing the technology and procedures that allow the control to work as intended. Most auditors focus their efforts on testing and validating controls to ensure that they are functional and dependable. Penetration testing, configuration review, and architecture review are all part of this type of assessment, so auditors needs to know where to go to find guidance, templates, and sample designs that have been proven to work through consensus and extensive testing. The best security programs don't provide much benefit if the execution of those programs relies on poor control choices. The following standards and best practices can help the auditor distinguish good security designs from bad and provide reference architectures to compare against.

ISO 27000 Series of Standards

The ISO 27000 series are internationally recognized security control standards for the creation and operations of an Information Security Management System (ISMS). Previously known as ISO 17799 and originating from British Standard 7799, the ISO 27000 series is one of the most widely used and cited documents in information security today. All the major governance frameworks reference ISO when discussing key controls, and it is a great resource to address a wide range of security needs from data-handling standards, to physical security, to policy. ISO 27000 is broad and covers a great deal of content that is broken into seven published standards documents with ten more currently in preparation. This overview is centered on the first two standards: ISO 27001 and 27002.

The first ISO standard is ISO 27001:2005 Information Technology Techniques-Information Security Management Systems. It provides the requirements for a security management system in accordance with ISO 27002 best practices. ISO 27001 identifies generic technological controls and processes that must be in place if a business wants to be certified as compliant with the ISO standard.

The contents of ISO 27001 are:

- **ISMS:** Establish the ISM, implement and operate, monitor and review, and maintain and improve documentation requirements, control of documents, and control of records.

- **Management responsibility:** Involves commitment, provision of resources, and training for awareness and competence.

- **Internal audits:** These are the requirements for conducting audits.

- **ISMS improvements:** These are the corrective and preventative actions.

- **Annex A:** Controls objectives and controls, and controls the objects checklist.

- **Annex B:** Organization for economic cooperation, development principles, and this international standard.

- **Annex C:** Correspondence between ISO 9001, SIO 14001, and this standard.

A key concept used in 27001 is the Deming Cycle process improvement approach: Plan, Do, Check, and Act. This continuous improvement cycle was made famous by Dr. W. Edwards Deming whose quality control techniques methodology is a way to show that a process can be continually improved by learning from mistakes and monitoring the things done correctly to further refine the capabilities of the system. The Deming Cycle is simple yet powerful, and ISO 27001 applies it to security management in the following manner:

Step 1.   **Plan:** Establish the ISM according to the policies, processes, and objectives of the organization to manage risk.

Step 2.   **Do:** Implement and operate the ISM.

Step 3.   **Check:** Audit, assess, and review the ISM against policies, objectives, and experiences.

Step 4.   **Act:** Take action to correct deficiencies identified for continuous improvement.

ISO 27001 provides guidance for setting up an ISMS and an excellent checklist for assessing compliance with the standard by specifying what controls need to be in place. An organization can be certified through an approved assessment and registration organization as being in compliance with 27001. There are over 3,000 companies certified against ISO 27001. Many companies choose certification as a mechanism to "prove" their competence in building an information security program, but also because certification provides proof for SOX and other legal compliance frameworks that the company has met the requirements of those laws. The other benefit of ISO 27001 is its global acceptance as an accepted standard that is required for conducting business with some companies, which can provide a unique business opportunity for a company that goes down the path of certification.

The second ISO standard is ISO 27002:2005 Security Techniques Code of Practice, which consists of international best practices for securing systems. This standard provides best practice information about everything from Human Resources security needs to physical security and it represents the detailed implementation requirements for ISO 27001. ISO 27002 is full of good high-level information that can be used as a source document for any generalized audit or assessment. It consists of security controls across all forms of data communication, including electronic, paper, and voice (notes tied to pigeons are not included).

The 12 areas covered in ISO 27002:2005 are:

- Intro to information security management
- Risk assessment and treatment
- Security policy
- Organization of information security
- Asset management
- Human Resources security
- Physical security

- Communications and ops management
- Access control
- Information systems acquisition, development, and maintenance
- Information security incident management
- Business continuity
- Compliance

The ISO standards define a solid benchmark for assessing a company's information security practices, but as with most high-level control documents, it doesn't give the auditor details about security architecture or implementation guidance. 27002 is a great internationally recognized standard to refer back to for control requirements in an audit report or findings document and makes excellent source material for an auditor's checklist.

NIST

The National Institute of Standards and Technologies (NIST) is a federal agency of the United States government, tasked with helping commerce in the U.S. by providing weights and measurements, materials references, and technology standards. If you have configured your computer to use an atomic clock source from the Internet to synchronize time to, then you have used a NIST service. NIST also provides reference samples of over 1,300 items, including cesium 137, peanut butter, and even oysters. The division within NIST that is most interesting from an information security standpoint is the Computer Security Resource Center (CSRC), which is the division tasked with creating information security standards.

The CSRC is currently directed by the United States Congress to create standards for information security in response to laws such as the Information Technology Reform Act of 1996, the Federal Information Security Management Act of 2002 (FISMA), and HIPAA. Although FISMA is a federal law and not enforceable in the private sector, private companies can reap the benefits of the many excellent documents NIST has created for FISMA compliance.

Federal Information Processing Standards Publications (FIPS) standards are a series of standards that government agencies must follow by law according to FISMA. FIPS standards include encryption standards, information categorization, and other requirements. FIPS also mandates standards for technology through a certification program. Hardware and software involved in encrypting data via AES for example, must be FIPS 140-2 (level 2) compliant to be used by the federal government. Many Cisco products meet these requirements; for a complete list of all vendors tested, go to http://csrc.nist.gov/groups/STM/cavp/validation.html.

The NIST Special Publications (800 series documents) are a treasure trove of good information for auditors, systems administrators, and security practitioners of any size company. These documents give guidance and provide specific recommendations about how to address a wide range of security requirements. These documents are created by academic researchers, security consultants, and government scientists. They are reviewed by the security community through a draft process that allows anyone to provide comments and feedback on the documents before they are made standards. The documents are also revised on a regular basis as new technologies become adopted.

Table 3-2 provides a list of some of the most widely used NIST 800 series documents. This list is not exhaustive, and there are new documents added all of the time, so check the NIST website on a regular basis for updates and new drafts.

Table 3-2   *NIST 800 Series Documents*

SP 800-14	*Generally Accepted Principles and Practices for Security Information Technology Systems*
SP 800-18	*Guide for Developing Security Plans for Information Technology Systems*
SP 800-27	*Engineering Principles for Information Technology Security (A Baseline for Achieving Security)*
SP 800-30	*Risk Management Guide for Information Technology*
SP 800-34	*Contingency Planning Guide for Information Technology Systems*
SP 800-37	*Guidelines for Security Certification and Accreditation of IS Systems*
SP 800-47	*Security Guide for Interconnecting Information Technology Systems*
SP 800-50	*Building an Information Technology Security Awareness and Training Program*
SP 800-53	*Recommended Security Controls for Federal Information Systems*
SP 800-53A	*Techniques and Procedures for Verification of Security Controls in Federal Information Technology Systems*
SP 800-54	*BGP Security*
SP 800-55	*Security Metrics Guide for Information Technology Systems*
SP 800-58	*Security Considerations for VOIP Systems*
SP 800-60	*Guide for Mapping Types of Information and Information Systems to Security Categories (2 Volumes)*
SP 800-61	*Computer Security Incident-Handling Guide*
SP 800-66	*An Introductory Resource Guide for Implementing the Health Insurance Portability and Accountability Act (HIPAA) Security Rule*
SP 800-77	*Guide to IPSEC VPNs*
SP 800-88	*Guidelines for Media Sanitization*
SP 800-92	*Guide to Computer Security Log Management*
SP 800-95	*Guide to Security Web Services*
SP 800-97	*Establishing Wireless Robust Security Networks: A Guide to IEEE 802.11i*
SP 800-100	*Information Security Handbook: A Guide for Managers*

The Cyber Security Research and Development Act of 2002 requires that NIST develop checklists to help minimize the security risks of hardware and software used by the federal government. These checklists show detailed configurations of many hardware and software platforms including Cisco. SP 800-70 outlines the format, goals, and objectives of the checklists, and how to submit a checklist if you build one that you would like to share. NIST provides these checklists in Security Content Automation Protocol (SCAP) format and can be loaded into a SCAP-validated scanner for automated auditing. There are a number of scanning vendors that support SCAP such as Qualys and Tennable (Nessuse Scanner). For a complete list of scanning vendors and downloadable checklists, visit http://checklists.nist.gov.

Center for Internet Security

The Center for Internet Security (CIS) is a not-for-profit group dedicated to creating security best practices and configuration guidance for companies to help reduce the risk of inadequately securing corporate systems. CIS provides peer-reviewed configuration guides and templates that administrators and auditors can follow when securing or testing the security of a target system. These guides are well written and provide a sufficient level of detail down to the actual configuration level to use as a checklist while also explaining why the particular configuration option needs to be implemented.

CIS refers to its best practice documents as benchmarks and has two categories:

- **Level 1 benchmarks** consist of the minimum level of security that needs to be configured that any skilled administrator can implement.

- **Level 2 benchmarks** focus on particular applications of security based on the type of system or manner in which the system is used. Proper security depends on understanding risk, which determines at what level you need to protect an asset. Laptops, for example, have a different risk profile than servers, which are explored in the Level 2 benchmark section in detail.

The CIS benchmarks are often used for configuration-level auditing of technology for proper implementation of security features and good defensive practices. Many compliance laws dictate high-level controls, but never go into the details of how to actually perform the tasks necessary. These benchmarks developed by CIS help to fill in the blanks when auditing for compliance through consensus-validated device configuration recommendations. CIS also makes available automated assessment tools that leverage these benchmarks. CIS benchmarks can be found at www.cisecurity.org.

NSA

The National Security Agency (NSA) has been responsible for securing information and information assurance since it began in 1952. As a component of the U.S. Department of Defense, the NSA is typically known for its cryptology research and cryptanalysis of encrypted communications. The NSA created the DES encryption standard that was (and still used in the form of 3DES) the most commonly deployed encryption technique, until it was replaced by AES.

Although the NSA's mission is to keep government communications private, it has also shared a significant amount of computer security research in the form of configuration guides on hardening computer systems and network infrastructure equipment. Through research conducted by the Information Assurance Department of the NSA, a series of security configuration guides have been posted to help the public better secure computers and networks.

These guides cover:

- Applications

- Database servers

- Operating systems

- Routers

- Supporting documents

- Switches

- VoIP and IP telephony

- Vulnerability reports

- Web servers and browsers

- Wireless

Auditors are free to use these configuration guidelines when examining security controls. They make a great resource and are updated as new technologies and applications are studied. You can find the guides at http://www.nsa.gov/ia/index.cfm.

DISA

The Defense Information Security Agency (DISA) is a component of the U.S. Department of Defense that is charged with protecting military networks and creating configuration standards for military network deployments. DISA provides a number of useful configuration checklists for a wide variety of information system technologies. Security Technical Implementation Guides (STIG) are great source material for security configuration assessments and highly recommended as a tool for any auditor looking for vetted configuration recommendations. While STIGs are written with military auditors in mind, they are easy to read and include justification for the configuration requirements and what threats are mitigated. You can access the current list of STIGs at http://iase.disa.mil/stigs/stig/index.html.

SANS

The SANS (SysAdmin, Audit, Network, Security) Institute is by far one of the best sources of free security information available on the Internet today. Established in 1989 as a security research and education organization, it has become a source of training and knowledge that shares information about security for hundreds of thousands of individuals across the globe. The SANS website has something for everyone involved in information security, from the CIO to the hard-core security technologists and researchers.

SANS is in the business of security education and delivers training events, conferences, and webcasts. It offers an extensive array of technical security and management tracks covering everything from incident handling and hacking to creating security policies. SANS security training conferences are the most common venue for a student attending these courses, but many are also offered through on-demand web training and self-study. Each of these courses also offers an opportunity to test for certification through the GIAC organization (a separate entity that governs the certification and testing process for SANS). For those students who want a more traditional education process, SANS is accredited in the state of Maryland to grant master's degrees in information assurance and management.

Although SANS focuses on training, it also provides a wealth of free security information as part of its mission to use knowledge and expertise to give back to the Internet community. SANS offers the following free services and resources that are perfect for auditors and security professionals to use to gain insight into new issues and understanding technical security controls:

- **SANS reading room:** The reading room consists of over 1,600 computer security whitepapers from vendors and research projects written by SANS students going for GIAC Gold certification. There are a wide range of topic categories, ensuring you will find something relevant to what you are looking for from best practices to configuration guidance.

- **SANS Top 20:** SANS Top 20 is a list of the top 20 vulnerabilities in operating systems and applications that hackers attack. This information is updated yearly by a large panel of security experts, and it provides auditors and security practitioners with a good list of high-risk areas they need to ensure are addressed. Although this list is good, it doesn't cover the latest threats, so it should not be used as a checklist, but rather as a tool to focus your efforts.

- **SANS security policy samples:** If you are looking for sample security policies, this resource is a goldmine. All of the policies represented are free for use, and in some cases, you can simply insert the business's name. These policy templates cover a wide range of security functional areas and are added to on a regular basis. It is important to note that security policies are a serious documents and require that legal departments and HR departments be involved in their adoptions.

- **SANS newsletters:** SANS provides a number of newsletters available as e-mails or RSS feeds that you can subscribe to. Many topics are present, including one focused on auditing (SANS AuditBits).

- **Internet Storm Center:** The Internet Storm Center is a group of volunteer incident handlers who analyze suspicious Internet traffic from across the globe. They look at packet traces to determine if a new virus, worm, or other attack vectors have popped up in the wild. The ISC also compiles attack trend data and the most frequently attacked ports. Incident handlers are always "on duty," and you can read their notes as they go about analyzing attacks.

- **SCORE:** SCORE is a joint project with the CIS to create minimum standards of configuration for security devices connected to the Internet. These checklists are available for free and provide sound guidance about necessary technical controls.

- **Intrusion Detection FAQ:** The Intrusion Detection FAQ is a fantastic resource for better understanding how to identify an attack on your network. FAQs cover the basics of intrusion detection, details about tools to use, and a detailed analysis of sample attacks.

The SANS website should be considered mandatory reading for auditors who want to better understand the tools and techniques attackers use to break into systems. Having all of this knowledge in a single place is useful as auditors tailor their checklists and audit criteria to address current events and attacks.

ISACA

If you are involved in security auditing to any degree, you undoubtedly have heard of the Information Systems Audit and Control Association (ISACA). ISACA is the largest association of IT auditors in existence with over 65,000 members across the world. Many of the auditing techniques and security governance processes used to audit IT today have been compiled and standardized by ISACA. Over 50,000 people have earned the Certified Information Systems Auditor certification (CISA), demonstrating knowledge in auditing. The Certified information Systems Manager (CISM) is also offered to test IT governance and management expertise.

ISACA is more than just a certification-granting organization. In addition to founding the IT Governance Institute and developing COBIT, they have created the de-facto standards guide for assessing and auditing IT controls. The IS standards, guidelines, and procedures for auditing and control professionals are regularly updated and reviewed to provide the auditing community with standards, guidelines, and procedures for conducting audits. The auditing guide includes:

- **Standards of IS Auditing:** This section includes Code of Conduct for professional auditors, auditing process from planning to follow-up, and various other standards for performing audits.

- **Auditing G:** This section provides information on how to conduct audits while following the standards of IS auditing.

- **Auditing Procedures:** How to audit various types of systems and processes is detailed in this section, providing a sample approach to testing controls such as firewalls and intrusion detection systems.

The IT Assurance Guide to using COBIT is another excellent resource for how to conduct an audit using COBIT as the governance framework. Regardless of whether or not the company being audited uses COBIT, the guide describes how to leverage the controls identified by COBIT and apply those to the audit process. This enables an auditor to follow a well documented framework to ensure that no major areas are missed.

Cisco Security Best Practices

The Cisco website is a primary resource for anyone configuring or maintaining Cisco gear, as Cisco provides a wealth of guidance for configuration and design of security systems. Cisco believes in pervasive security throughout its product lines, so it should come as no surprise that security design guides and best practices are available for all Cisco products.

Cisco takes an architectural approach to security that focuses on security as a system. A firewall is an important security component, but by itself does not address all of the security needs of a diverse organization. To better align to defense in depth and security solution architectures, Cisco has created a best practices repository that encompasses all types of network designs with security embedded. The two areas that are most relevant to auditors looking for best practices are the Design Zone and Cisco Validated Designs program.

The Design Zone's main objective is to take the guesswork out of building a scalable and manageable network solution that maps to business requirements. These design guides cover a wide range of solutions and best practices for configuring and developing architectures for places in the network, such as the branch office or campus and vertical industries such as retail and health care. Security practices are integrated into each solution, and there is a dedicated section covered in the Design Zone for security. The Design Zone for security provides fundamental protection strategies for the network as a whole and is built on the principles introduced by SAFE. The Design Zone for security categories are:

- **Network Foundation Protection:** Core network security design fundamentals

- **Secure Branch:** Branch office security designs

- **Enterprise Campus Security:** Campus network security design guidance for the network core

- **Secure WAN:** Security services for wide area network connectivity

- **Secure Data Center:** Security for critical data and applications

- **Threat Control:** Security solutions that protect against attacks and intrusions from the core of the network to the end points

Following are solution-specific design guides that auditors might find useful:

- **Secure Unified Communications:** Designing and securing voice services and applications

- **Network Virtualization:** Network path isolation and access control techniques for delivering secure network services on demand

- **Secure Wireless:** Security concerns and solutions for mobile devices and applications

- **Secure Industry Solutions:** Solutions focused on particular industries such as healthcare, government, and retail

- **Security Product Implementation Guidance:** Individual product installation guides and examples

The Cisco Validated Designs (CVD) program was created to provide not just design guidance in the form of a whitepaper, but to provide solutions that are tested and documented to work together. All of the designs placed in the Design Zone have been through the CVD process to provide reference designs with recommended configuration and code versions. Each CVD is built in a lab environment that closely represents a customer deployment scenario. There are three types of deliverables created for CVDs:

- **System Assurance Guides:** Guides that provide the results from testing and give system and solution recommendations for network deployment.

- **Design Guides:** Full architectural design, technical deployment, and implementation guides for the solution

- **Application Deployment Guides:** Interoperability guidance for third-party applications that have been tested with Cisco solutions

Cisco also has technical papers and other references such as hardware and software matrices for CVDs when applicable. Auditors can find more information about the Cisco Design Zone and CVD program at www.cisco.com/go/designzone and www.cisco.com/go/cvd.

Summary

This chapter delivers an overview of IT security governance and some of the key governance frameworks, standards, best practices, and guidelines that can be used to assess a security program. Although no one framework or standard addresses every aspect of a security program, the controls and best practices they represent can be used as building blocks for a cohesive security governance strategy. In summary:

- Security governance is the coordination of people, process, and technologies to meet business objectives and reduce risk.

- Clearly defined roles and responsibilities with the appropriate measurement are essential to successful security service delivery.

- COSO, COBIT, and the ISO 27000 series provide high-level strategies and controls for managing information security and the ability to audit against them.

- Technology best practices are available from a wide variety of sources, including NIST, NSA, DISA, SANS, ISACA, CIS, and Cisco. Each provides detailed configuration and design guidance that explains how to design and set up network security countermeasures.

References in This Chapter

Peltier, Thomas and Justin Peltier. *Complete Guide to CISM Certification*. Auerbach, 2006.

—*Information Security Governance: Guidance for Boards of Directors and Executive Management*, Second Edition. IT Governance Institute.

—ISO 27001:2005 (27001 and 27002)

—COBIT 4.1 Executive Summary and Framework. ISACA.

—*ITIL V3 Foundation Coursebook*. Pink Elephant, 2008.

Web Resources

www.coso.org

www.iso.org/iso/home.htm

www.nist.gov

www.coso.org

www.wikipedia.org

www.isaca.org

www.sans.org

www.cisecurity.org

www.Cisco.com/go/cvd

www.cisco.com/go/safe

www.cisco.com/go/designzone

Chapter 4

Auditing Tools and Techniques

Assessing security controls involves more than simply scanning a firewall to see what ports are open and then running off to a quiet room to generate a report. It is natural for security engineers to gravitate toward technology and focus on technical security control testing (otherwise known as penetration testing), because it is likely the "fun" part of security for most engineers. Conducting a penetration test is like throwing down the gauntlet to security professionals, and it gives them an opportunity to flex their hacker skills. Testing security as a system, however, involves significantly more than launching carefully crafted evil packets at the network to see what happens. This chapter discusses software tools and techniques auditors can use to test network security controls.

It is important to note that this is not a chapter about hacking. You will not learn all of the techniques and tools available today for breaking into networks. Do a search at your favorite online bookseller for the terms hacking, hacker, or penetration testing and you will find a slew of books devoted to the topics. Security testing as a process is covered, but the focus is on gathering the evidence useful for an audit. Thoroughly assessing security controls serves a vital part in determining whether or not a business is compliant with its policies, procedures, and standards. Through security controls testing, you can determine whether the organization meets its goals for reducing risk and keeping evildoers out of the network and away from critical systems.

Evaluating Security Controls

Security controls are the safeguards that a business uses to reduce risk and protect assets. Policy determines what security controls are needed, and those controls are selected by identifying a risk and choosing the appropriate countermeasure that reduces the impact of an undesirable event (such as a customer database being stolen). The evaluation of security controls in its simplest form validates whether or not the control adequately addresses policy, best practice, and law. Testing security controls for effectiveness and measuring them against standards are of the best ways to help an organization meet its obligations to shareholders and regulatory responsibilities.

As discussed in Chapter 1, "The Principles of Auditing," the main security control types are administrative, technical, and physical. Under each category, the specific controls that can be implemented are preventative, detective, corrective, or recovery. These control types work together, and in general, you must provide controls from each category to effectively protect an asset. When testing controls, make sure that each functional category is addressed and all controls are implemented in a way that doesn't allow someone easy circumvention. You can have the most advanced firewall in the world as a preventative control, but without monitoring its effectiveness through detective controls, such as log reviews and IPS, you would never know for sure if it enforced policy. These missing pieces are typically what hackers exploit to break into systems, and it's the auditor's job to identify and report on weaknesses in the system.

When evaluating security effectiveness, you need to examine three primary facets for every control. All security incidents, from break-ins to lost customer records, can usually be traced back to a deficiency that can be attributed to people, process, or technology. Testing these areas enables you to analyze security from a big picture perspective, gives you a better understanding of how an organization performs today, and recommends improvements for tomorrow. Following are the three facets to examine:

- People are users, administrators, data owners, and managers of the organization with varying levels of skills, attitudes, and agendas. If users are not following security policies, there might be a need for stronger administrative controls such as security awareness training or penalties for noncompliance (this is the "up to and including getting fired" clause that HR puts in the employee manual). An organization can also implement a detective/corrective control to enforce policies such as having the latest antivirus updates or operating system patches before the user is allowed on the network. People also represent the organizational structure and policies that drive security.

- Process represents how the organization delivers the service of IT. These are the procedures and standards that are put into place to protect assets. Processes must be up to date, consistent, and follow best practices to be effective. Process is one of the most important areas to test, because most attacks that result in significant loss have a component in which process has failed. Take, for example user account creation and decommission. Someone is hired, and a request is put into IT to create the appropriate accounts the new hire. Who is allowed to send the request? Is it any hiring manager or does it have to be one from Human Resources? How is the request validated as legitimate? Without strong process and the appropriate controls in place to prevent, detect, and correct, anyone can call and impersonate a hiring manager and request an account be created. This is significantly easier (and quicker) than trying to run a brute force, password-cracking tool against a server.

- Technology represents the facilities, equipment, computer hardware, and software that automate a business. Technology enables people to accomplish repetitive jobs faster and with less error. Of course, technology also enables someone to do stupid things just as efficiently (and faster). Misconfigurations and poorly implemented software can take a mistake and multiply its impact exponentially. Imagine leaving the door unlocked on a room that houses hardcopy files. Someone could potentially walk into the room and take files, but it would take a long time (not to mention effort) to hand carry those documents out to a car. Now, imagine misconfiguring a server in the DMZ to allow for access from the Internet to a key database server. Someone could download the entire database and not even leave a trace that they were there. This is why it is so important for a business to standardize on best practices and configurations that are known to work. Best practices tend to anticipate many of these scenarios.

Evaluating security controls requires the auditor to look at a system with the eyes of a hacker and anticipate how things could be exploited to gain unauthorized access. Just because something "shouldn't" be exploitable, doesn't mean that it isn't. The only way to know is to test the system and the individuals who are tasked with monitoring and maintaining it should do the testing.

Auditing Security Practices

The first step for evaluating security controls is to examine the organization's policies, security governance structure, and security objectives because these three areas encompass the business practices of security. Security controls are selected and implemented because of security policies or security requirements mandated by law. Security is a service provided by IT to the business, so measuring it as such enables you to see many of the connections to the various functions of the business. As discussed in Chapter 3, "Information Security Governance, Frameworks, and Standards," there are standards, laws, and benchmarks that you can use as your baseline to compare against. Normally, you include content from multiple areas, as businesses may have more than one regulation with which they must comply. It is easiest to start with the organization's policies and build your security auditing plan from there. Some criteria you can use to compare the service of security against are:

- Evaluation against the organization's own security policy and security baselines

- Regulatory/industry compliance—Health Insurance Portability and Accountability Act (HIPAA), Sarbanes-Oxley Act (SOX), Grahmm-Leach-Bliley Act (GLBA), and Payment Card Industry (PCI)

- Evaluation against standards such as NIST 800 or ISO 27002

- Governance frameworks such as COBIT or Coso

After you have identified the security audit criteria that the organization needs to comply with, the next phase is to perform assessments to determine how well they achieve their goals. A number of assessments are usually required to determine appropriate means for referring back to the scope, which defines the boundaries of the audit. The following are types of assessments that might be preformed to test security controls:

- **Risk assessments:** This type of assessment examines potential threats to the organization by listing areas that could be sources of loss such as corporate espionage, service outages, disasters, and data theft. Each is prioritized by severity, matched to the identified vulnerabilities, and used to determine whether the organization has adequate controls to minimize the impact.

■ **Policy assessment:** This assessment reviews policy to determine whether the policy meets best practices, is unambiguous, and accomplishes the business objectives of the organization.

■ **Social engineering:** This involves penetration testing against people to identify whether security awareness training, physical security, and facilities are properly protected.

■ **Security design review:** The security design review is conducted to assess the deployment of technology for compliance with policy and best practices. These types of tests involve reviewing network architecture and design and monitoring and alerting capabilities.

■ **Security process review:** The security process review identifies weaknesses in the execution of security procedures and activities. All security activities should have written processes that are communicated and consistently followed. The two most common methods for assessing security processes are through interviews and observation:

  ■ **Interviews:** Talking to the actual people responsible for maintaining security, from users to systems administrators, provides a wealth of evidence about the people aspect of security. How do they feel about corporate security methods? Can they answer basic security policy questions? Do they feel that security is effective? The kind of information gathered helps identify any weakness in training and the organization's commitment to adhering to policy.

  ■ **Observation:** Physical security can be tested by walking around the office and observing how employees conduct themselves from a security perspective. Do they walk away without locking their workstations or have sensitive documents sitting on their desks? Do they leave the data center door propped open, or do they not have a sign-out procedure for taking equipment out of the building? It is amazing what a stroll through the cubicles of a company can reveal about the security posture of an organization.

■ **Document review:** Checking the effectiveness and compliance of the policy, procedure, and standards documents is one of the primary ways an auditor can gather evidence. Checking logs, incident reports, and trouble tickets can also provide data about how IT operates on a daily basis.

■ **Technical review:** This is where penetration testing and technical vulnerability testing come into play. One of the most important services an auditor offers is to evaluate the competence and effectiveness of the technologies relied upon to protect a corporation's assets.

This section covered evaluation techniques for auditing security practices within an organization. Many of the security practices used to protect a company are process- and policy-focused. They represent the primary drivers for technology purchases and deployment. Technology can automate many of these processes and policies and needs a different approach to testing effectiveness. The remainder of this chapter covers tools that can be used to test security technologies.

Testing Security Technology

There are many terms used to describe the technical review of security controls. Ethical hacking, penetration test, and security testing are often used interchangeably to describe a process that attempts to validate security configuration and vulnerabilities by exploiting them in a controlled manner to gain access to computer systems and networks. There are various ways that security testing can be conducted, and the choice of methods used ultimately comes down to the degree to which the test examines security as a system. There are generally two distinct levels of security testing commonly performed today:

- **Vulnerability assessment:** This technical assessment is intended to identify as many potential weaknesses in a host, application, or entire network as possible based on the scope of the engagement. Configurations, policies, and best practices are all used to identify potential weaknesses in the deployment or design of the entity being tested. These types of assessments are notorious for finding an enormous amount of potential problems that require a security expert to prioritize and validate real issues that need to be addressed. Running vulnerability scanning software can result in hundreds of pages of items being flagged as vulnerable when in reality they are not exploitable.

- **Penetration test:** The penetration test is intended to assess the prevention, detection, and correction controls of a network by attempting to exploit vulnerabilities and gain control of systems and services. Penetration testers (also known as pentesters) scan for vulnerabilities as part of the process just like a vulnerability assessment, but the primary difference between the two is that a pentester also attempts to exploit those vulnerabilities as a method of validating that there is an exploitable weakness. Successfully taking over a system does not show all possible vectors of entry into the network, but can identify where key controls fail. If someone is able to exploit a device without triggering any alarms, then detective controls need to be strengthened so that the organization can better monitor for anomalies.

Security control testing is an art form in addition to a technical security discipline. It takes a certain type of individual and mindset to figure out new vulnerabilities and exploits. Penetration testers usually fit this mold, and they must constantly research new attack techniques and tools. Auditors, on the other hand, might not test to that degree and will more than likely work with a penetration tester or team if a significant level of detailed knowledge in required for the audit. When performing these types of engagements, four classes of penetration tests can be conducted and are differentiated by how much prior knowledge the penetration tester has about the system. The four types are:

- **Whitebox:** Whitebox testing is where the tester has complete information about the design, configuration, addressing, and even source code of the systems under test.

This type of test is generally used to simulate a worst-possible scenario of an attacker who has intimate knowledge of the network and systems.

- **Blackbox:** Blackbox testing is the classical penetration test in which the tester simulates an external hacker and is given no information about the subject under test, other than what he can glean from the testing methods. The concept of this type of test is to identify weaknesses that can be exploited based on publicly available information.

- **Graybox:** This is a test that falls in the middle of the other two types in that some information is disclosed to the tester to "get him started." Intended to simulate the insider threat, the penetration tester might be provided network diagrams, IP addressing, and user-level access to systems.

- **Red Team/Blue Team assessment:** The terms Red and Blue Team come from the military where combat teams are tested to determine operational readiness. In the computer world, a Red and Blue Team assessment is like a war game, where the organization being tested is put to the test in as real a scenario as possible. Red Team assessments are intended to show all of the various methods an attacker can use to gain entry. It is the most comprehensive of all security tests. This assessment method tests policy and procedures, detection, incident handling, physical security, security awareness, and other areas that can be exploited. Every vector of attack is fair game in this type of assessment.

Auditors should have a base knowledge of testing tools and techniques. Using testing frameworks is a useful way to develop a technical testing planning. The next section introduces a couple of well known testing frameworks.

Security Testing Frameworks

There are numerous security testing methodologies being used today by security auditors for technical control assessment. Four of the most common are as follows:

- Open Source Security Testing Methodology Manual (OSSTMM)

- Information Systems Security Assessment Framework (ISSAF)

- NIST 800-115

- Open Web Application Security Project (OWASP)

All of these frameworks provide a detailed, process-oriented manner in which to conduct a security test, and each has its particular strengths and weaknesses. Most auditors and penetration testers use these frameworks as a starting point to create their own testing process, and they find a lot of value in referencing them.

OSSTMM

OSSTMM was developed under the Creative Commons License as a free methodology to conduct security testing in a thorough and repeatable manner. The current released version 2.2 of the manual highlights the systems approach to security testing by dividing assessment areas into six interconnected modules:

- **Information Security:** Competitive intelligence, data leakage, and privacy review

- **Process Security:** Access granting processes and social engineering testing

- **Internet Technologies Security:** Network mapping, port scanning, service and operating system (OS) identification, vulnerability scanning, Internet app testing, router/firewall testing, IDS testing, malicious code detection, password cracking, denial of service, and policy review

- **Communications Security:** Private branch exchange (PBX)/phone fraud, voicemail, fax, and modem

- **Wireless Security:** 802.11, Bluetooth, handheld scanning, surveillance, radio frequency identification (RFID), and infrared

- **Physical Security:** Perimeter, monitoring, access control, alarm systems, and environment

The OSSTMM has a strong following in the community and provides a good reference for what areas need to be examined and what types of results to expect. It is not a "click here, do that" type of document; rather, it requires a level of knowledge of various tools and techniques to accomplish the goals of the tests. Version 3.0 of the OSSTMM is a significant update that is still a work in progress. As of this writing, it is in beta with no timeline announced for release. Becoming a member of the project will provide access to the current beta draft and other documents such as templates and spreadsheets that can be used in conducting an audit with this methodology.

ISSAF

The ISSAF is one of the largest free-assessment methodologies available. Weighing in at 1200 pages, it provides a level of detail that is staggering. The authors believe that is it better to provide all of the information possible that an auditor might need than to limit it to high-level objectives. Each control test has detailed instruction for operating testing tools and what results to look for. It is split into two primary documents. One is focused on the business aspect of security, and the other is designed as a penetration test framework. The framework has not been updated in sometime (file date is 2006), but it is still useful as source material for controls testing and as a full-assessment methodology. The level of detailed explanation of services, security tools to use, and potential exploits is high and can help an experienced security auditor and someone getting started in auditing.

NIST 800-115

The NIST 800-115, Technical Guide to Information Security Testing, provides guidance and a methodology for reviewing security that is required for the U.S. government's various departments to follow. Like all NIST-created documents, 800-115 is free for use in the private sector. It includes templates, techniques, and tools that can be used for assessing many types of systems and scenarios. It is not as detailed as the ISSAF or OSSTMM, but it does provide a repeatable process for the conduction of security reviews. The document includes guidance on the following:

- Security testing policies
- Management's role in security testing
- Testing methods
- Security review techniques
- Identification and analysis of systems
- Scanning and vulnerability assessments
- Vulnerability validation (pentesting)
- Information security test planning
- Security test execution
- Post-test activities

OWASAP

The OWASP testing guide was created to assist web developers and security practitioners to better secure web applications. A proliferation of poorly written and executed web applications has resulted in numerous, easily exploitable vulnerabilities that put the Internet community at risk to malware, identity theft, and other attacks. As a nonprofit organization, OWASP has created a number of tools, guides, and testing methodologies that are free for anyone to use. The OWASP testing guide has become the standard for web application testing. Version 3 was released in December of 2008 and has helped increase the awareness of security issues in web applications through testing and better coding practices.

The OWASP testing methodology is split as follows:

- Information gathering
- Configuration management
- Authentication testing
- Session management
- Authorization testing

- Business logic testing

- Data validation testing

- Denial of service testing

- Denial of service testing

- Web services testing

- AJAX testing

Each test provides a summary of the issues, tools that can be used to assess the service, and examples of expected results. The information and examples given are thorough, and reference materials on the tools used or issues discussed are included at the end of each of the individual tests. The OWASP project also has a subproject called WEBGOAT that enables you to load a vulnerable website in a controlled environment to test these techniques against a live system.

Whatever your approach is to testing security controls, you must ensure that it is consistent, repeatable, and based on best practices. Your audits will be more thorough and you will be less likely to miss major issues that might slip by if you are "winging" your tests. Leverage the great resources that are available free from the security community and feel free to contribute your own ideas, so that everyone can benefit.

Security Auditing Tools

One thing is certain about security auditing tools: The power and sophistication of tools that auditors have at their disposal increase exponentially every year. Not only are the authors of these tools truly brilliant individuals (and some scary ones, too), they have also helped the security community significantly through the automation of advanced testing techniques.

If you attend Blackhat, DefCon, or other security conferences, you can see the latest and greatest additions to this growing list of powerful applications. Fyodor, the author of NMAP, has conducted a yearly survey of the members of his mailing list (over 4,000 high-energy security professionals) to rank the top 100 security tools. This list includes a number of the tools discussed in this section. There are many books written from the security tool perspective, with indepth discussions of the various uses, switches, and techniques to implement these programs. Consider this an introduction to the uses of these tools, and auditors are encouraged to read *Security Power Tools* from O'Reilly Press for a fantastic discussion of security tools and their many configuration options. There are also a number of free whitepapers and guides on the Internet. The following sections discuss a few commercial and open source assessment tools that can be used to effectively audit Cisco networks.

Service Mapping Tools

Service mapping tools are used to identify systems, remote services, and open ports. These types of tools can be used to test a firewall rule base or response given different real or crafted IP packets.

Nmap

Nmap is the network and service scanning tool of choice for most security professionals. It is a free, open source application available on all UNIX and Windows operating systems. The tool is command-line based, but there are a number of graphical frontends for those who want a point-and-click experience.

Nmap can be used to scan for service ports, perform operating system detection, and ping sweeps. Nmap uses an "operating systems normal" response to a valid connection request or "tear down" response to determine whether a port is open (listening and responding) or if it is not enabled. A typical TCP connection follows a three-way hand-shake to set up communications.

Step 1.   Computer A sends a Syn packet to computer B to initiate communication-Syn.

Step 2.   Computer B replies to computer A with an acknowledgement packet-Ack.

Step 3.   Computer A sends a Syn acknowledgement packet to computer B to start the session-Syn Ack.

Step 4.   A connection is established and data communications can begin.

Auditors can use Nmap to get a quick idea of what hosts and services are available on a network. It can be used to scan a single subnet or much larger networks. Nmap performs a ping sweep to identify hosts that are active on the network and then proceed to identify what services respond. You can also check the configuration of firewalls and access policies for critical systems.

Before using Nmap on UNIX type systems (LINUX, BSD, and Mac OS X), you need to obtain root privileges via SUDO to use any features that cause Nmap to create custom packets. Nmap can be run without administrative privileges, but some of the advanced scanning techniques such as SYN scanning and anything that needs to access the raw IP stack will fail.

If you execute Nmap with its default settings, and assuming you have root privileges, Nmap performs a SYN scan:

```
nmap 192.168.1.3
```

Nmap sends a SYN to all of the ports listed in its services file (over 1,000 ports) and looks for a SYN/ACK response. If it gets a response, it assumes that the port is open and immediately sends a RST (reset) to close the connection and then move on to the next port to be tested. If there is no response, Nmap assumes that the port is closed. The SYN scanning process is simple and is why Nmap can scan a host so quickly.

```
Starting Nmap 5.21 ( http://insecure.org )
```

```
Interesting ports on 172.16.1.3:
Not shown: 1707 closed ports
PORT      STATE SERVICE
135/tcp   open  msrpc
139/tcp   open  netbios-ssn
445/tcp   open  microsoft-ds
3389/tcp open   ms-term-serv
MAC Address: 00:1A:92:0A:62:B1 (Asustek Computer)

Nmap done: 1 IP address (1 host up) scanned in 2.226 seconds
```

Scanning for UDP ports is handled differently. Because UDP doesn't have a handshake process like TCP, the UDP packet must be crafted in a manner that causes the operating system to respond back. If you send a UDP packet to a closed port on a server, the TCP/IP stack is supposed to send an ICMP port unreachable message back. If a host does not send this response, it is assumed that the port is open. Obviously, a firewall can wreak havoc with a UDP scan, so it is a major limitation of searching for open UDP ports with tools like Nmap.

```
sudo nmap -sU 172.16.1.3
Starting Nmap 5.21 ( http://insecure.org )
Interesting ports on 172.16.1.3:
Not shown: 1481 closed ports
PORT       STATE          SERVICE
123/udp   open¦filtered ntp
137/udp   open¦filtered netbios-ns
138/udp   open¦filtered netbios-dgm
500/udp   open¦filtered isakmp
1434/udp open¦filtered ms-sql-m
1900/udp open¦filtered UPnP
4500/udp open¦filtered sae-urn
MAC Address: 00:1A:92:0A:62:B1 (Asustek Computer)

Nmap done: 1 IP address (1 host up) scanned in 62.419 seconds
```

Utilizing the OS detection and versioning features of Nmap is also useful for identifying the type of OS and versions of services that run on a remote system. Nmap enables you to perform versioning (-sV) and OS detections (-O) separately or together as a combined command (-A):

```
nmap -A 127.0.0.1
Starting Nmap 5.21 ( http://insecure.org )
Interesting ports on 172.16.1.253:
Not shown: 1707 closed ports
PORT     STATE SERVICE VERSION
22/tcp  open  ssh     Cisco SSH 1.25 (protocol 1.99)
23/tcp  open  telnet  Cisco router
```

```
80/tcp   open   http     Cisco IOS administrative httpd
443/tcp open   https?
MAC Address: 00:19:E8:3C:EE:40 (Cisco Systems)
Device type: switch
Running: Cisco IOS 12.X
OS details: Cisco Catalyst C2950 or 3750G switch (IOS 12.1 - 12.2)
Network Distance: 1 hop
Service Info: OS: IOS; Device: router
Nmap done: 1 IP address (1 host up) scanned in 18.877 seconds
```

Nmap provides several ways to mask your identity when scanning. One of the more popular mechanisms is through an idle scan. This is a clever technique that utilizes unique identifiers for every IP communication stream (IPIDS). Some operating systems simply increment the IPID every time a new connection is made. If you can find a host that is not being used, you can use it to bounce scans off of and make the remote system think the scan is coming from the idle host. To pull this off, you have to first find a host with incremental IPIDs.

```
nmap -sT -O -v 172.16.1.3
Starting Nmap 5.21 ( http://insecure.org )
Initiating ARP Ping Scan at 17:28
Scanning 172.16.1.3 [1 port]
Completed ARP Ping Scan at 17:28, 0.01s elapsed (1 total hosts)
Initiating Parallel DNS resolution of 1 host. at 17:28
Completed Parallel DNS resolution of 1 host. at 17:28, 0.05s elapsed
Initiating Connect Scan at 17:28
Scanning 172.16.1.3 [1711 ports]
Discovered open port 3389/tcp on 172.16.1.3
Discovered open port 135/tcp on 172.16.1.3
Discovered open port 139/tcp on 172.16.1.3
Discovered open port 445/tcp on 172.16.1.3
Completed Connect Scan at 17:28, 1.62s elapsed (1711 total ports)
Initiating OS detection (try #1) against 172.16.1.3
Host 172.16.1.3 appears to be up ... good.
Interesting ports on 172.16.1.3:
Not shown: 1707 closed ports
PORT      STATE SERVICE
135/tcp   open   msrpc
139/tcp   open   netbios-ssn
445/tcp   open   microsoft-ds
3389/tcp open   ms-term-serv
MAC Address: 00:1A:92:0A:62:B1 (Asustek Computer)
Device type: general purpose
Running: Microsoft Windows Vista
OS details: Microsoft Windows Vista
```

```
Uptime: 0.926 days (since Fri Jan  4 19:15:18 2008)
Network Distance: 1 hop
TCP Sequence Prediction: Difficulty=260 (Good luck!)
IP ID Sequence Generation: Incremental
Read data files from: /opt/local/share/Nmap
OS detection performed. Please report any incorrect results at
http://insecure.org/Nmap/submit/ .
Nmap done: 1 IP address (1 host up) scanned in 2.802 seconds
          Raw packets sent: 17 (1460B) ¦ Rcvd: 17 (1408B)
```

Now that you have found a host that can be used for stealth scanning, you simply need to use one of the TCP services to bounce off of. In this example, port 445 (Microsoft directory services) is used. It is important to disable the initial ping that Nmap sends by default (-P0) to see whether a host is up before scanning to prevent any packets from your computer being sent to the destination system you are trying to scan.

```
nmap -P0 -sI 172.16.1.3:445  172.16.1.253
Starting Nmap 5.21 ( http://insecure.org )
Idle scan using zombie 172.16.1.3 (172.16.1.3:445); Class: Incremental
Interesting ports on 172.16.1.253:
Not shown: 1707 closed¦filtered ports
PORT     STATE SERVICE
22/tcp   open  ssh
23/tcp   open  telnet
80/tcp   open  http
443/tcp  open  https
MAC Address: 00:19:E8:3C:EE:40 (Cisco Systems)
Nmap done: 1 IP address (1 host up) scanned in 17.770 seconds
```

Going through the hundreds of ways an auditor can use Nmap is beyond the scope of this book. Suffice it to say, you should read the manual pages of Nmap carefully if you intend to fully exploit its capabilities. There is an excellent Nmap tutorial that can be read for free at http://nmap.org/bennieston-tutorial/. For a more thorough Nmap exploration, read *NMAP Network Scanning*, written by the tools creator Gordon "Fyodor" Lyon. Some examples of useful Nmap commands for auditors are included in Table 4-1.

Table 4-1 *Useful Nmap Commands*

Nmap Command Example	Description
nmap –sP 192.168.1.0/24	Ping the entire 192.168.1.0 subnet to see which hosts respond.
nmap –P0 192.168.1.5-11	Scan IP hosts at .5–11. Assume hosts are available for scanning, don't ping to check and perform a SYN scan. (By default, Nmap doesn't scan a host if it doesn't receive a ping response.)

continues

Table 4-1   *Useful Nmap Commands*   *(continued)*

Nmap Command Example	Description
nmap −A 192.168.1.4	Scan host and attempt identification of services running on ports and the OS.
nmap −O 172.16.2.3	Scan host and attempt to identify what OS it runs.
nmap −p22,23,25 10.10.1.1	Scan a host to see whether ports 22, 23, and 25 are available.
nmap −sT −A −v 192.12.1.24	Scan a host with full a TCP connect and perform OS and service version detection with verbose reporting.

Hping

Hping is a tool that expands on basic ping functionality by providing the capability to create custom IP packets for the auditing and testing of security controls. Hping enables the sending of arbitrary packets, the manipulation of IP options and fields, and basic port-scanning capabilities. Not only does Hping send packets, but it also enables the auditor to set up a listening mode that displays any packets that return matching a certain pattern. This can be useful when testing security controls such as firewalls or intrusion detection system (IDS) and intrusion prevention system (IPS).

> **Note**—Hping2 is the version used in this book, but it is also worth checking out Hping3, which is written in TCL for integrated scripting support and sports an interactive command-line interface. Hping3 is command-compatible with Hping2.

Some of the uses of Hping are:

- **Port scanning:** Hping provides basic port-scanning capabilities including an incremental option (++ before the port number) that enables an auditor to scan a range of ports with custom packets and TCP options. This tool doesn't replace Nmap, but provides a high level of control about exactly what packets get sent on the wire.

- **Network protocol testing:** Hping can create practically any packet you want to manufacture to test how a system responds to malformed communications.

- **Access control and firewall testing:** Hping can be used to test firewall and IDS rules to ensure they work as expected. Hping can accept input from a text file to create payload data that can be packaged and sent to a remote system (like exploit code). This feature can be used to verify IPS signatures and monitoring systems.

The following example shows Hping scanning ports from 134 to 140. Notice the SA flags in the response denoting a SYN ACK response on the live ports, and RA flags or Reset Ack on closed ports:

```
hping2 172.16.1.3 −S -p ++134
HPING 172.16.1.3 (en1 172.16.1.3): S set, 40 headers + 0 data bytes
```

```
len=46 ip=172.16.1.3 ttl=128 DF id=4802 sport=134 flags=RA seq=0 win=0 rtt=0.6 ms
len=46 ip=172.16.1.3 ttl=128 DF id=4803 sport=135 flags=SA seq=1 win=8192 rtt=0.8 ms
len=46 ip=172.16.1.3 ttl=128 DF id=4804 sport=136 flags=RA seq=2 win=0 rtt=0.8 ms
len=46 ip=172.16.1.3 ttl=128 DF id=4805 sport=137 flags=RA seq=3 win=0 rtt=0.9 ms
len=46 ip=172.16.1.3 ttl=128 DF id=4806 sport=138 flags=RA seq=4 win=0 rtt=0.8 ms
len=46 ip=172.16.1.3 ttl=128 DF id=4807 sport=139 flags=SA seq=5 win=8192
rtt=0.8 ms
len=46 ip=172.16.1.3 ttl=128 DF id=4808 sport=140 flags=RA seq=6 win=0 rtt=0.8 ms
....Truncated for brevity
```

Some useful Hping commands are included in Table 4-2.

Table 4-2 *Useful Hping2 Commands*

hping2 Command Example	Description
hping2 172.16.1.4 –p 80	Sends a TCP Null packet to port 80 on host 172.16.1.4. Most systems respond with a Reset/Ack flag if they are up and not firewalled.
hping2 192.168.1.4 –p 80 –S	Sends a SYN connect packet to host 192.168.1.4 at port 80. If the port is open, you will see a SYN/ACK response.
hping2 172.16.1.10 –S –p ++22	Sends a SYN connect packet to host 172.16.1.10 port 22 and increments the port number by 1 after each packet sent. Open ports respond with SA flags and closed ports respond with RA flags. It is useful for mapping ports sequentially.

Vulnerability Assessment Tools

There are many vulnerability assessment tools available today, from commercial applications to well-known open source tools. A vulnerability scanner's purpose is to map known vulnerabilities in products and present a report of potential vulnerabilities. This type of tool is great for automating the assessment of multiple hosts and usually provides nice severity categorization and output for reports. Obviously, you need to be careful when performing vulnerability tests on business systems because some of the assessment mechanisms these tools use to find vulnerabilities can crash services or cause an outage. Auditors should have a plan in place for restoring service in the event of a problem and perform testing outside of peak utilization times. Taking down the accounting server in the middle of processing payroll will not win you any friends and could be a career-limiting move. The following sections discuss vulnerability assessment tools that are good examples of the types of applications auditors can use to find control weaknesses.

Nessus

Nessus is a popular vulnerability scanner that looks for known vulnerabilities in operating systems, networking gear, and applications. Currently at version 4, Nesus has expanded its functionality significantly since it was introduced as an open source project more than

10 years ago. With the release of Version 4, Nessus has become a closed source product owned by Tennable Network Security. While the scanner is still free for home use to scan your personal devices, if you use it in any other capacity outside of the home, a professional feed license is required. The professional feed provides access to the latest updates and advanced features such as compliance checks (PCI NIST or CIS), SCAP protocol support, the ability to load it as virtual appliance, and product support from Tenable. The yearly professional license fee for Nessus is around $1,200.

Nessus is only as good as its latest vulnerability database update so it is imperative that you keep it up to date. If your organization conducts vulnerability assessments on a regular basis, opting for the commercial plugin feed adds support and access to the latest updates (often many times a day). The free plugin feed lags the commercial by seven days and does not include the auditing plugins that can be used to look for policy violations and specific types of data that don't belong on an end users' systems (such as credit card information).

Nessus is available for Windows, Linux, and Mac OS X. The only differences between the versions are cosmetic for the most part, but network-scanning performance is better on Linux-based systems. A well-written installation guide and videos are available on Tennable's website. These walk you through the process for getting Nessus up and running on your operating system.

Scanning a system with Nessus is straightforward and doesn't require a whole lot of effort to do. The first thing to do after logging in to the web interface for Nessus is configure the policies you will use to assess the network. This section is where you configure scanning preferences and the plugins that you assess the network against. Plugins are at the heart of the Nessus engine and provide the assessment intelligence used to find vulnerabilities and compliance violations. Thousands of plugins can be used during a scan, but it is recommended you enable only plugins for the devices you are assessing to greatly speed up the process. If you scan routers and switches, it doesn't make sense to turn on nonapplicable plugins like AIX security checks (unless you truly like watching the digital equivalent of paint drying).

Optionally, you can input login credentials and SNMP strings for databases and windows domain credentials to get a more thorough scan of operating system files and networking equipment settings. Figure 4-1 shows the plugin selection process used to configure scanning policies.

After scanning policies have been configured, select the device IP addresses that will be assessed. To start a scan, simply provide target addresses to scan, and then the scan policy that you want to use. You can select individual IPs, entire subnets, or you can import a text file with all of the addresses for the entire organization. After your targets are selected, select launch scan and Nessus will start its vulnerability analysis. Figure 4-2 shows the scan selection and launch process.

After the scan has been launched, Nessus performs all of the hard work gathering vulnerability information in the background. Depending on the complexity and depth of your scan, it can take a few minutes or a number of hours. After Nessus has finished, you will have a nice list of items it discovered that you can browse by severity level. Nessus ranks

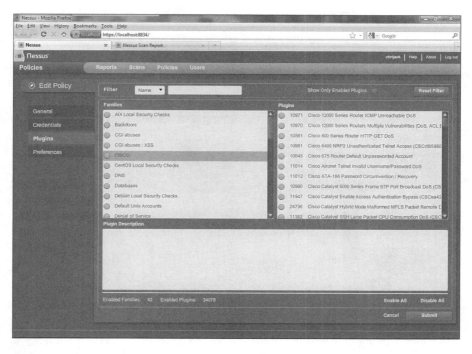

Figure 4-1   *Selecting Plugins in Nessus*

Figure 4-2   *Starting a Scan with Nessus*

vulnerabilities by severity using a high, medium, and low scale. Low severity is most commonly found and usually represents difficult-to-exploit weaknesses, information disclosure, or other potential security issues to be aware of that are not cause for alarm. Medium and high levels are the ones to be most concerned with and represent major vulnerabilities with known exploits that should be patched immediately. Figure 4-3 shows a Nessus scan summary with severity ranking of vulnerabilities found.

Figure 4-3   *Nessus Scan Vulnerability Ranking*

Detailed explanations of each vulnerability can be seen by clicking on the vulnerability and reviewing the informative description provided. There are also recommended solutions to address the problem and links to technical documents that analyze the vulnerability to a greater degree. Common Vulnerability Scoring System (CVSS) ranking is also applied to each vulnerability as a standard way to categorize the vulnerability. The complete report can be downloaded in a wide range of formats to incorporate the vulnerability information into an auditor's report. Figure 4-4 shows the detailed view of a medium-ranked vulnerability identified during scanning.

While basic Nessus scans are relatively simple, there are numerous advanced configuration options that serious auditors must become familiar with to get the most value out of their vulnerability scans. Auditors should not just launch Nessus against the entire organization's address range without a plan and expect to get anything of significant value. These types of shotgun approaches can cause a lot of trouble, especially because some of the plugins are potentially disruptive to servers and networking gear. There's nothing like taking down the company database or WAN links to win friends and influence management's opinion of your value to the organization.

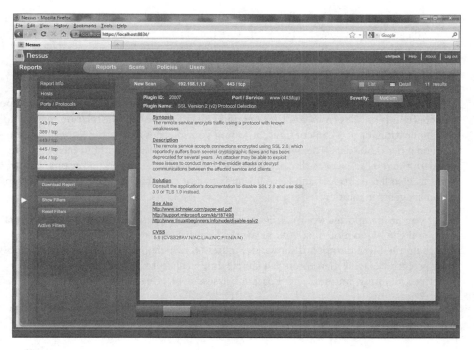

Figure 4-4 *Detailed Vulnerability Analysis*

For more information on using Nessus, the book *Nessus Security Auditing*, written by Mark Carey, is a great reference that can help an auditor learn the nuances of using Nessus. Check out the video demos on Tennable's website to see the product in action: http://www.tenablesecurity.com/demos/index.php?view=demo_videos.

RedSeal SRM

RedSeal Security Risk Manager (SRM) is a commercial risk management and threat identification application that eases the burden of analyzing a network to find vulnerabilities in configurations and visualizes the severity of what could happen if network security controls are compromised. The power of this application is that it enables an auditor to identify, prioritize, and report on the risk an organization faces at every point in the network. SRM builds a model of the network by importing configurations from network devices, vulnerability data from scanners, and the applications that are present. It performs Network Configuration Checks (NCC) that compare device configurations against standards and that identify vulnerabilities leveraging the National Vulnerability Database hosted by NIST. The NCCs ferret out any misconfiguration in access lists and identify unneeded services and potential policy violations. SRM also analyzes network configurations for compliance with corporate policy and PCI standards. These checks are continuously updated in the form of RedSeal's Threat Reference Library (TRL) files, which are imported into the application.

SRM comes in two flavors: an appliance version that you can install in a network and use as a dedicated risk analysis tool or a software-only install that can be loaded on a Windows laptop, desktop, or server that meets the minimum hardware requirements. The architecture of both versions is client-server, where interaction with the application requires loading a Java-based client.

After it is installed, SRM needs to be fed data about your network. You can either import the configuration files from your devices and vulnerability scan information directly to the application, or you can configure it to poll your devices and retrieve configuration data on a periodic basis. The ability to import the data "offline" without having to inter-act with the remote devices directly is a benefit for auditors and organizations that don't want to install the product and leave it running all of the time or would prefer a portable risk-management solution.

After you have imported your configuration files and vulnerability assessment informa-tion, you can begin modeling your networks security posture. Launching the client brings up the SRM dashboard shown in Figure 4-5, which gives the user a quick glance at the current risks identified through a simple graphical representation that shows best practice violations, warning, and a pass/fail assessment of network policy.

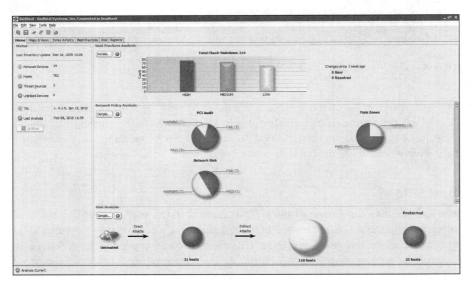

Figure 4-5 *SRM Home Tab*

The Maps and views tab enables an auditor to examine the network topology for access vulnerabilities by simply clicking on any one of the network devices represented on the map. The detail viewer at the bottom of the screen shows where packets generated from computers behind the device selected would be able to reach on the network. When an auditor assesses policy compliance, this one feature can reduce the amount of work the auditor has to do to assess access lists and other security controls in the network. This network path exploration function can easily show what types of traffic are allowed between segments and what threats different areas of the network pose to critical services. Figure 4-6 shows what parts of the network are accessible by Internet users and the protocols that are allowed through.

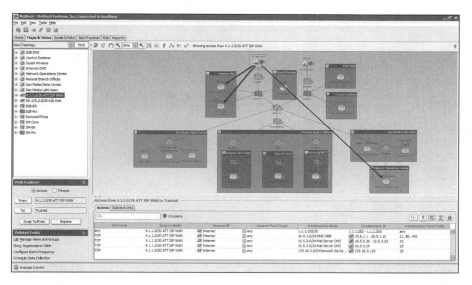

Figure 4-6   *SRM Maps & Views*

The Zones and Policy tab gives the auditor a compliance view of the network that assesses topology against corporate policy and regulatory requirements. The SRM has built-in rules for PCI DSS standards and the capability to add custom business policies that can be used for analysis of the network. Figure 4-7 shows the Zones and Policy tab and a PCI compliance assessment.

SRM can also automatically generate a PCI compliance report that can be used for ensuring that the appropriate controls are in place to meet the PCI DSS standard. Figure 4-8 shows a sample PCI report.

Configuration comparison of network devices against NIST security best practices is accomplished from the Best Practices tab. This is a quick way to identify misconfigured devices that represent poor security implementation. Figure 4-9 shows best practice configuration compliance failures found by SRM.

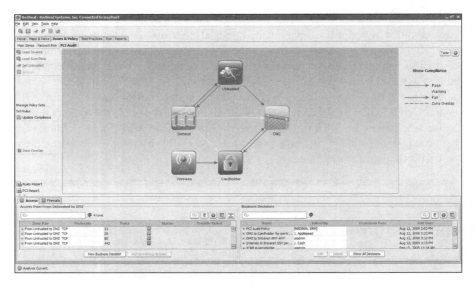

Figure 4-7   *SRM Zones and Policies*

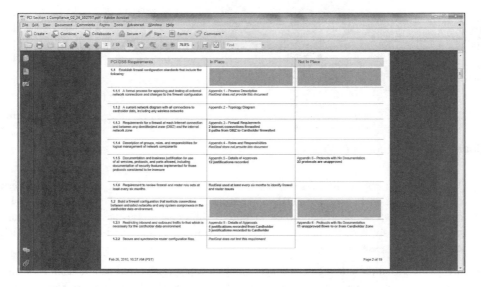

Figure 4-8   *SRM PCI Report*

Selecting the Risk tab takes you to the risk map, as shown in Figure 4-10, which shows risk in a graphical display by protocol, host, vulnerability, and mitigation priority. You can also export the data from this screen to a jpeg or as a text file for inclusion in a report.

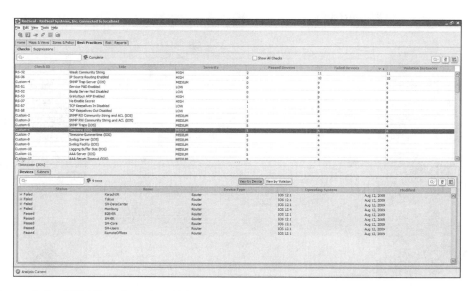

Figure 4-9   *SRM Best Practices Tab*

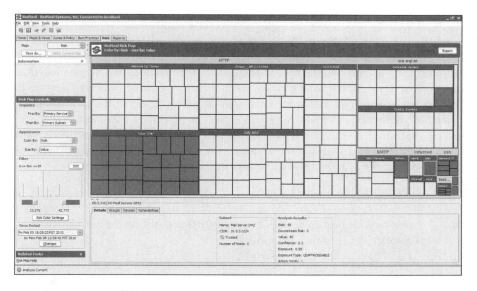

Figure 4-10   *SRM Risk Tab*

The last tab is the Reporting tab. It houses the various built-in reports that SRM provides. The reports can be run on the fly and saved to PDF for archiving. Figure 4-11 shows a consolidated security posture report that provides an overview of key findings. Running historical reports can also be helpful to show how risk is reduced over time as identified risks are mitigated. Many organizations use this information as a performance indicator for the success of their security programs.

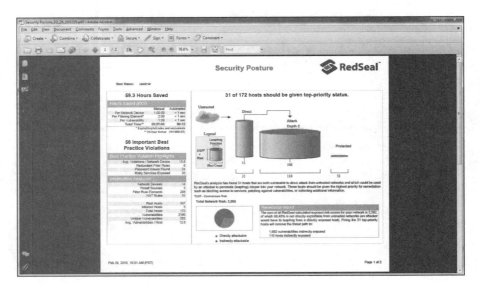

Figure 4-11   *SRM Reporting Tab*

RedSeal Security Risk Manager is a useful tool for visualizing and reporting on risk. Auditors can use it to aide in identifying whether a network is configured according to best practices, but also as a means to interpret business risk by assigning asset values and automatically quantifying the risk. Most auditors use a number of discrete tools that pull portions of this data, but having the ability to identify potential vulnerabilities and then extrapolate downstream attack potential is a compelling aspect of this product. For example, you may wonder whether a web server can be compromised and how much access the current configuration affords that web server to the internal network. Simply click on the Threats To tab and see visually what could potentially happen. Threat modeling is a powerful way to increase the security posture of the network.

Some of the other uses for SRM are:

- Prioritizing what host or devices to remediate first based on the overall risk and downstream threat to the organization

- Modeling a potential perimeter breach to determine what types of compensating technologies or controls need to be in place to reduce the risk of leapfrogging from one system to another

- As a measuring tool for management to correlate the changes in risk over time and as systems are remediated

- As new vulnerabilities are identified in applications, quickly modeling the impact of those vulnerabilities to the network as a whole

- As new services or business-to-business connections are brought online, modeling the risk to connected systems

- The ability to conduct a best-practices audit per device with the click of a button

Packet Capture Tools

Validation and testing of security controls are the most important aspects of conducting an audit. Auditors shouldn't just assume a firewall or IPS will enforce policy; they must test it and gather evidence abour how well those controls do their jobs. Packet capture tools are familiar to anyone who has had to troubleshoot a challenging network redesign or configuration. Packet capture tools are also extremely valuable when testing firewall rules, IPS signatures, and practically any other scenario where you need to see exactly what is going across the wire. Tcpdump and Wireshark are two free tools that should be in every auditor's repertoire.

Tcpdump

Tcpdump is a free packet capture program that operates as a simple command-line based "sniffer". It has been compiled for practically every operating system and leverages the UNIX Libpcap library (Winpcap on Windows) to copy traffic from the wire and display it on the screen or save it to a file. This simple packet sniffer provides a detailed view into the actual bits and bytes flowing on a network. Tcpdump is a simple application that doesn't have a graphical interface that abstracts the details of the packet capture process to automatically detect problems. It is left to the auditor to use his knowledge and experience to identify anomalies or issues. That doesn't mean that Tcpdump doesn't decode traffic; it just doesn't perform higher-level interpretation like Wireshark.

The other benefit of Tcpdump is that it can be used to grab the raw communications off of the wire in a format that a slew of other analysis tools can use. Tcpdump data files can be used as input into Snort, PDF, Wireshark, and may other packet-analysis applications. Tcpdump's capability to load on virtually any computing platform provides a portability that makes it the de facto standard for security testing.

Tcpdump is an easy tool to get started using. Simply open a command prompt, type in the command Tcpdump, and it happily starts displaying all of the packets seen by the first interface it finds on the machine. To be more specific about the interface you use (wireless or wired), you can type:

```
tcpdump -D
1.en0
2.fw0
3.en1
4.lo0
```

Tcpdump lists the interfaces available on your computer so that you can then select by number which one you want to use. This is especially useful on the Windows version (Windump) because Windows stores device information in the registry and assigns a cryptic address to your interfaces. After you have the appropriate interface, in this case Ethernet0 (en0), you can begin capturing traffic by issuing the command tcpdump –i 1 (or tcpdump –I en0):

```
tcpdump -i 1
tcpdump: verbose output suppressed, use -v or -vv for full protocol decode
listing on en0, link-type EN10MB (Ethernet), capture size 68 bytes
17:16:15.684181 arp who-has dhcp-10-90-9-126.cisco.com tell dhcp-10-90-9-
126.cisco.com
17:16:15.746744 00:1a:a1:a7:8c:d9 (oui Unknown) > 01:00:0c:cc:cc:cd (oui Unknown)
 SNAP Unnumbered, ui, Flags [Command], length 50
```

Using the default capture parameters, Tcpdump captures only the first 68 bytes of any packet it sees and will not decode any packets. This mode is useful for a cursory glance of traffic data, but doesn't provide the level of detail necessary for testing security. To increase the amount of data captured, you can modify the snaplen (snapshot length) with the **–s** option. For any Ethernet segment, the max length is typically 1514, so issuing the command **tcpdump –s 1514** copies every bit of data your interface receives.

Not all data is interesting or necessary to see when testing devices. Tcpdump has a simple, yet powerful filtering system that can be employed to sort through all of the noise on the wire to get to the traffic you are looking for. There are four basic filter options to help fine-tune your search.

- **Net:** Display all traffic to/or from a selected network; for example:

    ```
    tcpdump net 172.16.1.0/24,tcpdump net 192.168.0.0/16
    ```

- **Host:** Display packets to/or from a single host; for example:

    ```
    tcpdump host 192.168.32.2
    ```

- **Protocol:** Select IP protocol to capture (TCP, UDO, or icmp); for example:

    ```
    tcpdump udp 172.16.23.2
    ```

- **Source/Destination port:** Display traffic from a specific port; for example:

    ```
    tcpdump dst port 80
    tcpdump src port 22
    ```

You can add advanced filtering logic by stringing together the basic filter options with AND, OR, and NOT to get exactly the traffic you want to see. For example, if you want to see all UDP traffic from a host with the IP address 10.2.3.1 with a source and destination port of 53 (DNS,) you would use:

```
tcpdump host 10.2.3.1 and udp dst port 53
```

Another example would be if you wanted to see any nonSSH traffic from a user's subnet to a firewall management address at 192.168.23.1.

```
tcpdump dst 192.168.23.1 and not tcp port 22
```

Beyond the simple filters, Tcpdump can also allow someone who understands how the TCP/IP headers are formed to specify combinations of bits to examine. This is done through advanced options that require you to know what bits equal what flags in the TCP headers. You can find a good reference for the TCP/IP headers and fields created by the SANS institute at http://www.sans.org/resources/tcpip.pdf.

If you want to display all of the TCP packets captured that have both a SYN and a FIN flag set in the same packet (obviously a crafted packet), you would need to have a Tcpdump key on the flag fields you were looking for, and it would help to consult a chart that shows the offset in the TCP header and the bits you wanted to test against.

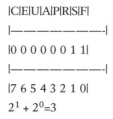

```
|C|E|U|A|P|R|S|F|
|————————-|
|0 0 0 0 0 0 1 1|
|————————-|
|7 6 5 4 3 2 1 0|
```
$2^1 + 2^0 = 3$

This provides a binary representation of 3 to check for SYN and FIN being present in the TCP flags. Consulting the TCPIP table, you can see that the TCP flags start at hex offset 13, which gives you a filter that looks like the following:

```
tcpdump -i eth0 (tcp[13] & 0x03)=3
```

Filtering can be complex, and if you make a mistake with the filters when capturing, you can miss the data stream you are looking for. It is usually best to do a raw capture, write it to a file, and then run your filters and other tools on the captured data file. Doing this enables you to examine the traffic in many different ways.

Writing a Tcpdump data file named capture.dmp:

```
Tcpdump -s 1514 -w capture.dmp
```

Reading a Tcpdump data file named capture.dmp:

```
Tcpdump -s 1514 -r capture.dmp
```

Table 4-3 lists useful Tcpdump commands.

Table 4-3 *Useful Tcpdump Commands*

Tcpdump Command Example	Description
tcpdump –r file_name –s 1514 -vv	Read the capture file name with a snaplen of 1514 and decode of very verbose.
tcpdump –w file_name –s 1514 -e	Write capture to file_name with a snaplen of 1514.
tcpdump –I eth0 –s 1514 –vv -e	Capture packets from interface Ethernet 0, decode very verbose, and include Ethernet header information.
tcpdump host 10.2.3.1 and udp dst port 53	Capture packets from host 10.2.3.1 that are UDP going to port 53 (DNS).
tcpdump –i 3 (tcp[13] & 0x03)=3	Capture and display packets on interface 3 with SYN and FIN bits set in TCP header.

Wireshark/Tshark

For those looking for a more full-featured GUI-based sniffer, you would be hard pressed to find a better one than the open source project known as Wireshark. Wireshark started life as Ethereal, written by Gerald Combs in 1998. Due to a trademark issue with the name Ethereal being owned by his former employer, the project was renamed in 2006 to Wireshark. Wireshark has become one of the most widely used and arguably the best packet capture application available. Best of all, it is completely free to use and actively developed by a team of over 500 volunteers.

Wireshark operates very much like Tcpdump in that it captures live traffic from the wire, reads traffic from a captured file, and decodes hundreds of protocols. Where Tcpdump has a simpler decode mechanism, Wireshark supports vastly more protocols and has a protocol decode framework that allows for the creation of custom packet decoders in the form of plugins. The display capabilities and advanced features such as stream following and packet marking make it easy to see what you want very quickly.

The filtering capabilities in Wireshark also allow for highly granular display and capture filters that follow the Tcpdump filter creation syntax. So, if you know Tcpdump, you will feel at home using Wireshark. Of course, Wireshark also has its own more detailed filtering language that can use specific keywords to search for fields of interest that don't require you to figure out what the offset is and what bits are required.

Using Wireshark is simple. After launching the application, select an interface to capture on, select start, and you will see captured traffic streaming from your interface. If you select an option before start, you will be presented with a screen, as shown in Figure 4-12, that allows you to limit the types of traffic you want through capture filters and a slew of other settings to finetune Wireshark's behavior.

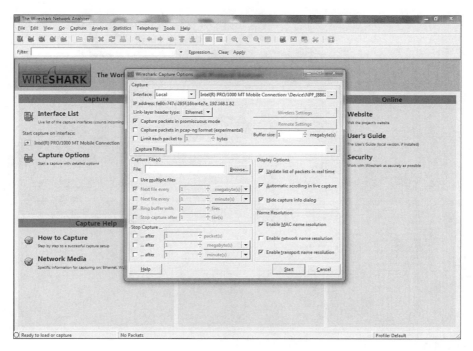

Figure 4-12   *Wireshark Capture Options*

The Wireshark GUI display provides a great way to visualize communications. All of the information you would see scrolling by on the command line can be viewed on screen. If you select a packet that interests you, you can drill down into the details of that packet by simply clicking the portion of the packet you want to see. In the example shown in Figure 4-13, we have selected an SSL version 3 packet. Wireshark decodes the packet and shows in HEX and Ascii what is in the payload. Looks like SSLv3 encryption does work!

One of the most valuable features of a packet-capture application for auditors is the capability to save and load captures. Wireshark supports many different file formats including commercial sniffing products and Tcpdump. By saving it in Tcpdump format, you ensure that the captures are able to be read by the widest variety of analysis tools. It is common for auditors to capture packets on a network and then use the capture files with other security tools for later analysis, such the open source intrusion detection tool Snort. Captures can also be replayed through the network interface of an auditor's laptop for security device testing purposes.

Tshark is the command-line equivalent of Wireshark, and uses the same major commands and options. Decodes provide the same level of detail as the GUI, but without the display flexibility or point and click operation. Tshark reads and writes capture files and is compatible with Tcpdump.

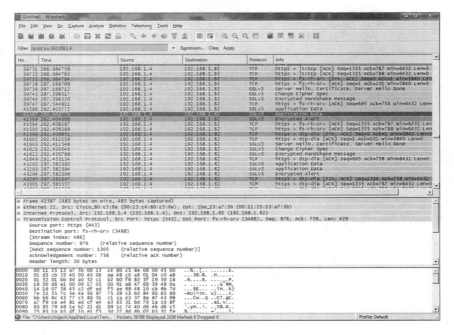

Figure 4-13   *Wireshark Protocol Decode*

Penetration Testing Tools

Auditors can leverage high-quality penetration testing tools to make auditing security controls significantly easier. Most professional penetration testers use a combination of general purpose exploit frameworks such as Core Impact and Metasploit in addition to their own custom scripts and applications. Not everyone in security is an uber hacker or has the time to build their own tools to test for exploitable services. These two applications are powerful and represent the best of the commercial and open source penetration testing tools available.

Core Impact

In the world of penetration tools, Core Impact is widely considered the best commercial product available. Developed by Core Security Technologies, this software package is a comprehensive penetration testing suite with the latest commercial grade exploits and a drag-and-drop graphical interface that can make anyone look like a security penetration testing pro. Writing exploit code and delivering it to a remote system is not a trivial task, but Core Impact makes it look easy. The framework Core has developed provides a modular platform to create custom exploits and making the tool appropriate for even the most advanced penetration test. Core Impact boasts a significant array of tools to test security controls. This product identifies vulnerabilities and automatically selects the appropriate exploits to gain control of remote systems (no way to have a false positive here). It does this without having to worry about tweaking and manipulating multiple tools and by including all of the functionality you need built right into the application itself.

Remotely exploitable network vulnerabilities are the Holy Grail of the security world, but Core Impact doesn't just rely on those types of exploits. It also provides client-side attacks designed to test how well the users follow security policy. You can embed Trojans into Excel files or other applications and email them to a user to see if they are following policy. If the user opens the suspicious file against policy, then Core Impact gains control of the computer and takes a screenshot of the desktop (suitable for framing!). There are also phishing capabilities that allow you to gather e-mail addresses and other information (useful for social engineering) off of the corporate website. This information can be used to target specific users and test their response, just like the bad guys do.

Core Impact also includes web application penetration testing features to test web security controls. Cross-site scripting and SQL injection attacks can be launched from the tool providing a complete penetration testing suite.

The Core Impact dashboard shown in Figure 4-14 is the first screen you see when launching this product and includes general information about the number and types of exploits available, and what operating systems are exploitable via the tool. There is also a link to update the exploits to download the latest attacks and modules.

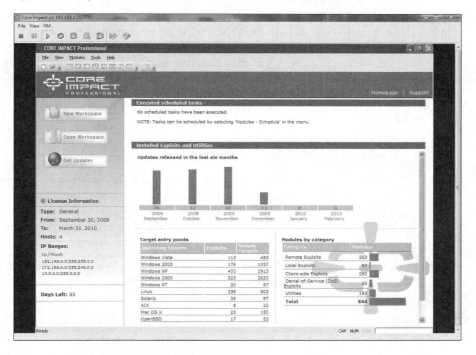

Figure 4-14 *Core Impact Dashboard*

In Core Impact, you can define workspaces to segment individual assessment engagements. Each workspace is password-protected and encrypted on the system to prevent sensitive data from falling into the wrong hands. These workspaces store a complete record of all of the activities and modules run during the penetration test.

After you have created a workspace or loaded an existing workspace, you are presented with the main console. This is where you decide what types of modules and exploits you are going to initiate. Core divides the exploits into the following categories:

- **Remote exploit:** These are attacks that can be initiated from a remote system usually in the form of a buffer overflow against a vulnerable service.

- **Local exploit:** These are privilege escalation attacks (gaining administrative access) that take advantage of weaknesses in applications or running processes on a system.

- **Client-side exploit:** Client-side exploits are designed to trick a user into executing code, surfing to a website, or launching malicious e-mail attachments. These types of exploits include phishing, Trojans, Keyloggers, and similar tools that target users.

- **Tools:** These are various components that can be used to assist with the exploitation process of a client, such as injecting an agent into a virtual machine.

Knowing what exploit to run against a system is the part that makes penetration testing a challenge. It requires playing detective to figure out what services are available and what versions, which usually necessitates using various tools such as Nmap and Nessus. Finding these vulnerabilities and matching them to the appropriate exploit is where Core Impact shines. Core Impact uses a wizard-based interface labeled RPT, which means Rapid Penetration Test; it follows a six-step penetration testing process for network and client tests. The web penetration testing wizard has a six-step process and all three are described in the following step lists.

The six-step network penetration test consists of:

Step 1.   **Network information gathering:** Runs Nmap and Portscan against common services to identify operating systems and patch levels.

Step 2.   **Network attack and penetration:** Uses the vulnerability information gathered in the first step to select possible exploits to use based on operating system type and services available. Sends real exploits and attempts to gain access to load an agent kit, which is a piece of code loaded into the memory of the remote system, enabling Core Impact to interact with the compromised computer.

Step 3.   **Local information gathering:** Leverages the agent kit loaded to identify applications loaded, software patch levels, directory lists, and screen shots of the desktop. This can be used to prove that remote access was achieved.

Step 4.   **Privilege escalation:** Some exploits work against user level processes only and do not give you complete control of the operating system at the kernel level. This wizard is used to upgrade access to root or administrative privileges by exploiting user level access processes.

Step 5.   **Cleanup:** Removes all traces of the agent kits and cleans up logs on the compromised systems.

Step 6.   **Network report generation:** Generates a report that details all of the activities the penetration tester engaged in and all of the vulnerabilities and exploits successfully used. This also provides an audit trail of the test.

The six-step client-side penetration test wizard consists of:

Step 1.   **Client-side information gathering:** Searches websites, search engines, DNS, and WHOIS to harvest e-mail addresses to target specific users through social engineering. You can also import addresses from raw text files.

Step 2.   **Client-side attack and penetration:** This wizard walks you through the process of crafting an e-mail to send to a user to try to entice them to load an attached Trojan or mail client exploit. You can also exploit web browsers by e-mailing links to exploits served by the Core Impact tools built in web server. The goal is to load an agent kit that will provide access to the system.

Step 3.   **Local information gathering:** Same as with the network wizards, this wizard gathers information on the remote system.

Step 4.   **Privilege escalation:** Uses subsequent vulnerabilities to gain admin or root level access to the system.

Step 5.   **Cleanup:** Removes all agent kits and traces of access.

Step 6.   **Client-side report generation:** Repots are created on which users "fell" for the attacks and what vulnerabilities were used and exploited.

The four-step Web Penetration test wizard consists of:

Step 1.   **WebApps information gathering:** This process analyzes the website's structure and gathers information on the type of webserver software and code levels in use.

Step 2.   **WebApps attack and penetration:** The Web Attack and Penetration Wizard sniffs out vulnerabilities in the web applications and attempts to exploit them. It performs cross-site scripting, SQL injection, and PHP attacks.

Step 3.   **WebApps browser attack and penetration:** Cross-site scripting is used to exploit a user's web browser in this wizard. E-mail addresses are gathered for the target organization, and links are sent to get the user to click on and download an agent kit.

Step 4.   **WebApps report generation:** Reports are generated for the web exploit process including all of the activities the penetration tester performed and which systems were compromised.

Figure 4-15 shows the Core Impact tool in action.

A remote computer at IP address 192.168.1.61 was compromised using a buffer overflow vulnerability in the Microsoft RPC service, and a Core Impact Agent was loaded in memory. After this occurs, the penetration tester has full control of the remote machine and can use the remote computer to attack other machines, sniff information off of the local

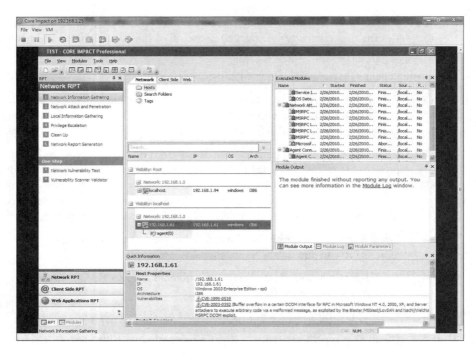

Figure 4-15   *Core Impact Vulnerability Exploit*

network, or a wide range of other attacks. Figure 4-16 shows a remote shell that was opened on the compromised computer, giving the auditor direct command-line access. As the old saying goes, "A picture is worth a thousand words."

Auditing requires the testing of controls and sometimes requires sending exploits to remote systems and testing the response of controls such as firewall, IPS, or HIPS products. This information can be exported into a variety of formats for reporting and correlating with vulnerability findings. With all of the advanced exploit techniques and reporting capabilities in Core Impact, it can be one of the best tools an auditor has in assessing security device capabilities and validating whether or not a vulnerability is actually exploitable.

Metasploit

The Metasploit project is responsible for providing the security community with one of the most important and useful security tools available today. Originally conceived and written by H.D. Moore in 2003 to assist with the development and testing of security vulnerabilities and exploits, the project has developed a life of its own through the contributions of many of the brightest security researchers today. The Metasploit Framework takes many of the aspects of security testing from reconnaissance, exploit development, payload packaging, and delivery of exploits to vulnerable systems and wraps them into a single application. The power of the framework comes from its open nature and extensibility. If you want to add a feature or integrate it into other tools, you can add support

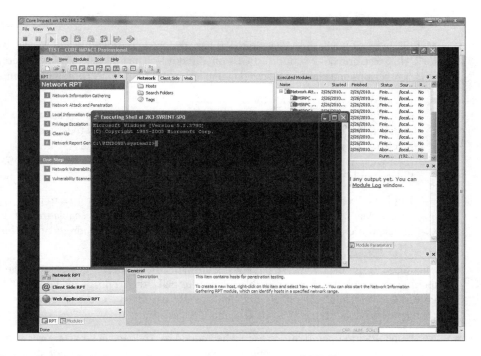

Figure 4-16   *Core Impact Opening a Remote Command Shell*

via new modules. Written in the Ruby programming language, Metasploit is available for all of the major operating systems: Windows, UNIX, Linux, and Mac OSX. The project is located at www.metasploit.com.

Unlike commercial products like Core Impact, there isn't the same level of polish or features designed for less experienced security professionals. There are no reporting capabilities or the simple wizard-based GUIs; this tool is designed for those security professionals who want to directly control every aspect of a penetration test. The current version 3.3 has improved dramatically and includes four choices for the user interface.

- **Msfconsole:** This is the primary console. It provides access to all of Metasploits exploits, payloads, and auxiliary modules through an intuitive command driven interface. Every portion of the interface has help features either through the command **help** or **–h.** You can easily find exploits and payloads by issuing the search command.

- **Msfcli:** This is a **-ine** interface executed from a UNIX or Windows command prompt that provides access to Metasploit. Designed to provide quick access to a known exploit or auxiliary module, it is also useful for scripting.

- **Msfweb:** MSFweb provides control of Metasploit through an interactive web interface. By default, it uses the built-in web brick web server and binds to the loopback address at port 55555. You can, however, select a real IP address and access the Metasploit from another computer's web browser. Firefox, Internet Explorer, and

Safari are all supported.

- **Msfgui:** In version 3.3, the Metasploit GUI has advanced considerably and is available for UNIX platforms (3.2 supports a GUI on Windows). The interface has integrated search functions and status and session connection information to exploited systems:

  - **Payloads:** Payloads provide the commands to add users, execute commands, copy files, launch a VNC session, or just initiate a command shell back to the attacker. Payloads are what are sent with the exploit to provide the attack a mechanism to interact with the exploited system. These payloads are available for a wide number of operating systems, including BSD, UNIX, Windows, OSX, Solaris, and PHP web environments.

  - **Exploits:** Exploits are the code and commands that Metasploit uses to gain access. Many of these are in the form of buffer overflows that enable the remote attacker to execute payloads (arbitrary software). There are hundreds of exploits for Windows, UNIX, and even a few for the Apple iPhone.

- **Encoders:** Buffer overflows are targeted against specific processor types and architectures. Metasploit's encoders enable the user to make the payloads readable for PowerPC, SParc, and X86 processors. You can also modify the encoder settings to change the payload to try to evade IDS and IPS signatures.

- **NOPS:** NOPS (no operation) are used when added to payloads in a buffer overflow because the exact location in memory of where the overflow occurs is not always known. NOPS allows there to be a margin of error in the coding of an exploit, because when the processor sees a NOP, it ignores it and moves on to the next bit of code in the buffer. After it reaches the payload, it executes the hacker's commands. Most IDS/IPS trigger on a string of NOPS (known as a NOP sled). These modules in Metasploit allow for the customization of the NOP sled to try to evade IDS/IPS systems.

- **Auxiliary:** The Auxiliary modules in Metasploit provide many useful tools including wireless attacks, denial of service, reconnaissance scanners, and SIP VoIP attacks.

After you install Metasploit, you have a choice about how you interact with it by picking the appropriate interface. Using Metasploit from the interactive console allows direct access to the most powerful components of the framework. However, if you want a point-and-click experience, the new GUI or web interface is available. Figure 4-17 shows the Metasploit console and commands displayed for help.

To launch the GUI, enter the command **msfgui** or click the icon under the Metasploit installation menu. The interface loads and you are presented with a simple interface that lists the different modules and a session list and module output window. Figure 4-18 shows the GUI under Linux.

Figure 4-17   *Metasploit Console and Commands*

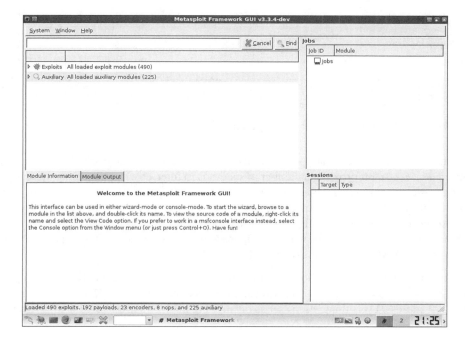

Figure 4-18   *Metasploit GUI*

In this example, the remote system is a Windows 2003 Server we are attempting to exploit. The easiest way to find exploits for a particular operating system is to use the built-in search function of the GUI. Entering **windows 2003** in the search window displays a list of modules where Windows 2003 is listed in the description of the module as being applicable. Scrolling through the list and selecting the RPC DCOM buffer overflow that gave us worms like Blaster, the interface presents a four-step process for configuring the exploit, which is illustrated in Figure 4-19.

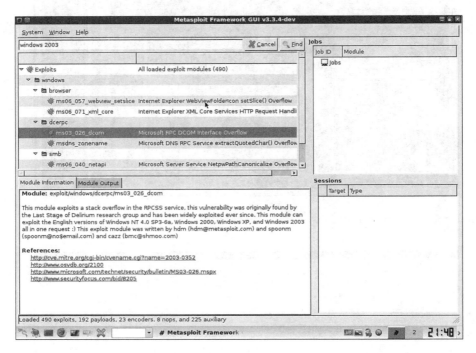

Figure 4-19 *Selecting an Exploit for Metasploit*

First, define the payload that you would like to use to execute code on the remote machine. Metasploit provides a number of methods to interact with the remote system after it is compromised. Grabbing a command shell or even using the Meterpreter to launch attacks on other systems through this compromised machine is possible. One of the slickest payloads available injects a VNC process into memory and gains access through remote control of the machine. Figure 4-20 shows the selection of a payload that will create a VNC terminal session with the target.

Next, enter configuration options and runtime parameters for executing the attack. LHOST is the local IP address you will use to connect back to, and RHOST is the target's IP address. Everything else is set as default. Figure 4-21 shows how the attack is configured.

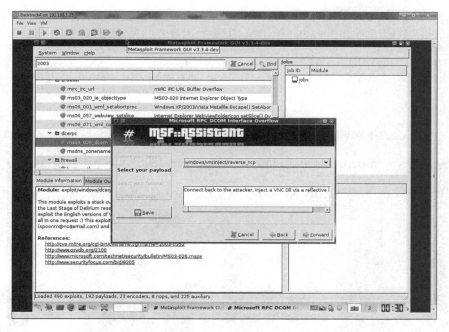

Figure 4-20   *Selecting VNC dll Injection*

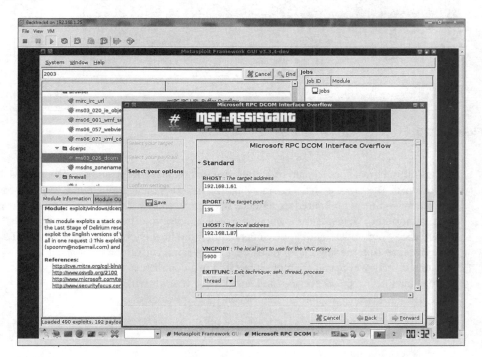

Figure 4-21   *Configuring Metasploit Attack Parameters*

After selecting forward, you are presented with a screen that shows the selected options and your settings for the exploit. After you have approved the configuration, you can launch the exploit. Metasploit sends the buffer overflow and payload to the remote system and list a connection coming back from the exploited host. If the attack works, then VNC Viewer automatically loads and you have full control of the remote host. Figure 4-22 shows a VNC session that was created from the exploit sent to the Windows 2003 server. Metasploit is even kind enough to launch a "courtesy" command for you.

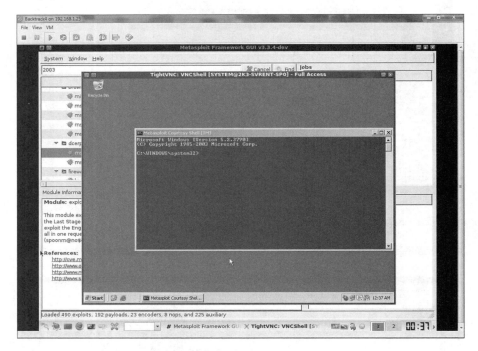

Figure 4-22   *VNC Session from Remote Computer*

Metasploit is a great tool for auditors, the price is right (as in free), and the capabilities are powerful. The biggest challenge in using Metasploit is the learning curve required for the average auditor with limited experience with host or network attacks. From an educational standpoint, Metasploit is a wonderful tool to hone your penetration-testing skills and enhance your understanding of vulnerabilities and how hackers exploit them. As a penetration-testing framework for research and development of new exploits, it is unmatched. If, however you are more interested in a commercial grade product with a vendor's technical support services and easy-to-use wizards with excellent reporting capabilities, tools such as Core Impact become a compelling choice.

BackTrack

BackTrack is a Linux live CD distribution built on Slackware Linux that doesn't require any installation and can be run from practically any PC with a CD ROM. You can also configure BackTrack to boot off of a USB memory stick making it an extremely portable, easily available security-testing environment. BackTrack4 is one of the most complete suites of security assessment tools ever assembled, saving security professionals count-less hours of finding, installing, and compiling hundreds of different security applica-tions. There are other security-focused distributions available, but none are as widely regarded and supported as BackTrack.

BackTrack is offered as a free distribution from www.remote-exploit.org and is available for download directly from the website or Bit-torrent network. Once downloaded, you can use it from a CD, USB memory stick, or load it into VmWare. The benefit of loading to a read/writeable format is obvious in that you can store settings, update packages, and customize the environment. Regardless of your preferred method of use, the tools includ-ed are extensive and are organized by the Open Source Security Testing Methodology. The categories are:

- **Information gathering:** DNS mapping, Whois, Finger, and mail scanning

- **Network mapping:** Port and services mapping, OS fingerprinting, and VPN discovery

- **Vulnerability identification:** Tools to identify service, SQL, VoIP, and HTTP vulnera-bilities

- **Web application analysis:** Web application hacking tools for the frontend services (XSS, PHP) and the backend database (SQL injection)

- **Radio network analysis:** Wireless sniffers, scanners, and cracking tools

- **Penetration:** Tools to exploit vulnerabilities and compromise systems (Metasploit is the primary application.)

- **Privilege escalation:** LAN sniffers, password sniffers, and spoofing tools

- **Maintaining access:** Backdoors, rootkits, and tunneling applications for retaining access after exploiting

- **Digital forensics:** Disk editors, file system dump tools, and hex editors for recover-ing evidence from deleted and hidden files

- **Reverse engineering:** Malware analysis tools, application debug tools, and hex and assembly tools

- **Voice over IP:** VoIP cracking and recording tools

- **Miscellaneous:** Tools that don't fit in any other category that can assist with penetra-tion testing

Summary

This chapter introduced security testing methodologies and some of the tools used to conduct those tests. It is not an exhaustive list of all potentially useful security testing tools, but should give a sampling of some of the most popular that any auditor can find useful. If you are interested in learning more about penetration testing or want to take a class with hands on practice, the SANS Institute offers a fantastic class called Security 560: Network Penetration Testing and Ethical Hacking.

In summary:

- Evaluating security controls requires testing three elements: people, process, and technology. If one area is weak, it can leave an organization vulnerable to attack.

- Penetration testing is a discipline that requires a structured and repeatable methodology. Without one, you are simply launching exploits and hoping to get in.

- Commercial tools such as Core Impact and open source tools such as Metasploit assist with testing security controls. Which one you choose depends on your budget, skill level, and desired reportability.

- The easiest way to get access to many of the tools discussed in this chapter is to download and launch Backtrack3. Not only does it save you many hours of setup, but it also gives you a powerful suite of tools with strong community support.

References in This Chapter

Security Testing Frameworks

Information Systems Security Assessment Framework, http://www.oissg.org/

Open Source Security Testing Methodology Manual, http://www.isecom.org/osstmm/

NIST 800-115: Technical Guide to Information Security Testing and Assessment, http://csrc.nist.gov/publications/nistpubs/800-115/SP800-115.pdf

Open Web Application Security Project, http://www.owasp.org/index.php/Main_Page

Security Testing Tools

NMAP, http://nmap.org

Hping, http://hping.org

Nessus, http://nessus.org

RedSeal SRM, http://www.redseal.net

TcpDump, http://sourceforge.net/projects/tcpdump/

Wireshark, http://www.wireshark.org/

Core Impact, http://www.coresecurity.com/

Metasploit Project, http://www.metasploit.com/

Backtrack, http://www.backtrack-linux.org/

Chapter 5

Auditing Cisco Security Solutions

Cisco offers an extensive security technology portfolio that encompasses every aspect of network communications. Auditing this wide range of devices requires an approach that analyzes the network as a system of controls and not just as individual devices. This chapter's purpose is to define security services that are enabled through logical groupings of Cisco products. These security services deliver business solutions through security controls that cover people, process, and technology. The introduction of these auditing domains provides a roadmap for how the remainder of this book is organized and also puts into context how each domain is used to address the security needs of a business. The process of defining auditable items for each domain using control frameworks and recommendations for building auditing checklists through the use of good security practices are also discussed.

Auditors and Technology

As information technology and its usages increase, companies have become more reliant on computers to automate business processes. The depth of IT audits and the skills required of auditors has increased dramatically as a result. In the early days of assessing security, auditors typically focused on identifying the presence or location of specific technologies, such as firewalls and routers, and less on how well these technical controls were integrated into the business processes or their effectiveness. The mere presence of a security device did not indicate that it was adequately protecting the digital assets of the organization or mitigating risk, but it was a required control and that was good enough. Much of this disconnect over the effectiveness of security controls had to do with the fact that auditors in general were not technologically inclined, having most often come from the financial world. This lack of understanding technology would lend itself to interesting and often heated conversations during which system administrators had to defend their use of a particular technology because it was not on the auditor's checklist, and the auditor simply did not understand how it worked.

Luckily, information security auditors are now much more knowledgeable about the role of technology and how security controls operate. The sheer number of technologies implemented in business today, such as video, voice, instant messaging, and web applications, has and continues to challenge an auditor's technical skills. There is also an ever-changing list of new threats that face the organization as these new technologies and protocols are introduced. Security used to be focused on the perimeter of the network as a means to determine what was considered trusted or not trusted. Now, the border of the network no longer stops at the firewall, and it's not uncommon to have the edge of your network be at a coffee shop or a hotel halfway across the world through an SSL VPN connection. Factor in the business side of security, with the need to manage the growing risks, regulatory compliance, and the desire to use technology to enable new and more profitable business ventures, and it becomes plain to see what a challenging task it is to audit today's IT systems. Auditors must understand the technology to spot risk, and without that knowledge, the quality and effectiveness of their assessments are greatly diminished.

Security as a System

Effective auditors think of security as a system, where the alignment of people, process, and technology to the goals of the business determine the success or failure of a security program. Security is a system of moving parts in much the same way that a car is. It's a good idea to have your mechanic inspect your car before going on a long trip. You would hope that he would do more than simply check that the doors lock or that the engine runs. To properly inspect a vehicle, there are numerous checks that must be performed to evaluate many individual components that make up independent, yet cooperative systems within the vehicle, such as the engine, drive train, instrument cluster, steering, braking, and safety features. Spot checking does not tell you if you can anticipate any problems on your trip; a more thorough operations test is required. Of course, a mechanic won't inspect every single wire, knob, or button in the car, but he should check the areas that have the highest risk of leaving you stranded on the side of the road. Inspecting the security controls of a business is a similar process; as the auditor, you inspect the organization's security controls based on identified risk, compliance to policy, and the law.

The auditor's inspection is key to the health of an organization's security program. The auditor's primary deliverable back to the organization is a risk assessment report, which details the impact those risks could potentially pose to the confidentiality, integrity, and availability of the business assets. The auditor is also responsible for identifying weaknesses in controls, which are determined through the review of records, logs, and actually testing the functionality of those controls. Additionally, an auditor must also identify weaknesses in process, which can be one of the biggest areas of risk an organization faces. If a backup tape storing hundreds of thousands of credit card numbers turns up missing, this clearly is not a technology problem, but one of process in the handling and protection of sensitive media.

Another important aspect of the auditor's job is to recommend new or updated controls to address deficiencies found during the audit process. These recommendations address the risks found and might even include specific technologies or solutions that can better protect assets found to be vulnerable. Recommendations that are focused on best practices and industry standards also help to address process areas in need of improvement or that can be better preformed through technology. Most audit reports have a prioritized list of deficiencies found and usually include recommendations on what can be done to address those deficiencies.

Cisco Security Auditing Domains

One of the first questions new auditors typically ask is, "Where do you start when assessing security?" It can be intimidating when you think about it, looking at all the different aspects of the business to determine whether or not those processes, procedures, and technologies protect the assets they are intended to protect. If you had armies of people that you could send throughout the organization, it would be easy to conduct a comprehensive audit, but unfortunately, the reality of budget constraints and the need to do more with less forces businesses to be a bit more judicious in the allocation of resources. The next best and more realistic way to audit security is to divide security into manageable domains that are focused on business requirements and take into account the operational aspect of security. This approach is also used to manage the audit process by creating logical divisions that represent how companies actually use security products.

Defining the scope of an audit is one of the most critical parts to get right from the beginning in an auditing engagement. Audits can be conducted from the top down at the organizational level or from the bottom up at the technology or process level. Tailoring the audit to the organization's requirements ensures that the auditor meets expectations and can properly manage the audit process. The scope of an audit can be differentiated by what level of the business is being analyzed. In general, there are four high-level business-focused audit categories:

- **Auditing an organization:** This level of auditing is typically focused on the governance aspect of security and touches all aspects of the business. Organizational auditing is often done in conjunction with certification or accreditation (such as ISO 27001) and can be involved from a resource and time standpoint.

- **Auditing a domain:** Domains are IT services offered to the business and at this level, the auditor groups interconnected processes, technologies, and business functions to assess them as one unit. These domains encompass all of the people, processes, and technologies associated with security service areas such as remote access, perimeter intrusion prevention, and access control. This level is primarily focused on service delivery, architecture, and meeting the security requirements of the business.

- **Auditing a function:** At this level, the auditor assesses a functional aspect of the business that includes multiple processes and technologies used to secure the business service. Business functions represent business services such as HR, finance, and manufacturing. An auditor reviews the function-specific security controls, technologies, and processes used by the business function.

■ **Auditing a process:** The lowest level of auditing and most specific is to assess a security process. A *process* is defined as the steps performed to accomplish a specific task, for example, to create new user access to the network. The auditor reviews and observes all of the steps from process initiation to completion for policy compliance and good security practices.

Auditors might be asked to audit at any of these four levels, but auditing at the domain level most represents assessing security as a system. With Cisco products, security features and capabilities are integrated into every device, so the concept of multiple functions, processes, and controls being in the same device must be considered. A router can be a firewall, IPS, and phone system all at the same time, which means that the auditor must logically separate out the services offered by the device when testing. Each domain identifies multiple layers of defense in depth and the policies and procedures that are applicable. Individual security devices and technologies can reside in multiple domains, which highlights their multifunctional role.

The seven auditing domains, as described briefly, are the foundation for the organization of the rest of this book and build upon each other for auditing network security. We focus on each of these domains in more detail in subsequent chapters of this book. It's important to note that the domains covered are focused on Cisco network security and are not indicative of all aspects of security; for example, physical security and disaster recovery are not included in this list. Although these domains are important for organizations to address, they are outside of the scope of this book. The following list shows the seven auditing domains:

■ Policy, compliance, and management

■ Infrastructure security

■ Perimeter intrusion prevention

■ Access control

■ Secure remote access

■ Endpoint protection

■ Unified Communication

Policy, Compliance, and Management

Policy, compliance, and management are the foundations of all security programs, so it is fitting that the first domain focuses on these aspects from which security controls are born. This domain is where policy is reviewed to identify whether or not the appropriate policies are in place to guide the organization and address regulatory compliance. Management and monitoring of policy and compliance can be automated through Cisco management technologies and are assessed in this domain, too.

■ Processes and functions assessed:

■ Key policies are instituted.

- Controls and countermeasures are defined.

- Standards are identified.

- Assets are identified and assessed.

- Risks are identified.

- Vulnerabilities are determined.

- Security governance programs are created.

- Auditing is conducted.

- Law and industry compliance requirements are identified.

- Cisco technologies assessed:

- Cisco Security Manager

- Monitoring Analysis and Response System (MARS)

- Network Compliance Manager

Infrastructure Security

The infrastructure security domain concerns itself with auditing routers, switches, and wireless for best practice to properly secure critical services. Regardless of the vector of entry into the network, be it wired or wireless, care should be taken to ensure the confidentiality, integrity, and availability of services being offered. Infrastructure security should be considered a minimum for properly securing an organization's access to computing resources. Much of this domain utilizes best practices, Cisco SAFE, and Cisco Validated Designs as the foundations for configuring the many security features that exist on routers and switches.

- Processes and functions assessed:

- Configuration of best practices

- Change control

- Router baseline security

- Switch baseline security

- Wireless baseline security

- Cisco technologies assessed:

- Router

- Switches

- Wireless

Perimeter Intrusion Prevention

The perimeter intrusion prevention domain assesses how well an organization detects, prevents, and responds to attacks against corporate assets. Intrusion prevention is usually considered the first line of defense in most organizations. Firewall and router access control lists help reduce the amount of services exposed and log key information on connections made, including the IP addresses of the devices that connect to services. Intrusion prevention systems allow for the automated decoding of packet information to find out what's going on inside the data packet being sent. This domain doesn't just examine intrusion prevention systems or firewalls, but also the processes for detecting attacks and automated responses to those attacks.

- Processes and functions assessed:
  - Network edge configuration best practices
  - Firewall configuration and rule base
  - Intrusion-prevention system configuration
  - Routers as security devices
  - Host intrusion prevention systems
  - Threat and attack monitoring
  - Incident-handling capabilities
- Cisco technologies assessed:
  - MARS
  - Firewall appliance
  - Router-based firewalls
  - Intrusion prevention systems
  - Cisco Security Agent

Access Control

The goal of the access control domain is to address user access restrictions and policy enforcement. One of the most effective mechanisms to lower an organization's overall security risk is to give users the minimum access they need to perform their particular roles. Access control allows an organization to follow the concepts of least privilege for user access and provides a mechanism through technologies such as 802.1x and NAC Appliance to assess the posture of the client to determine access. This domain also covers administrative access, passwords, and methods for assessing network access control technologies.

- Processes and functions assessed:
    - Role access requirement modeling
    - Network admission control
    - Identity-based networking services (802.1x)
    - User accounts administration
    - Endpoint posture assessment
    - Acceptable use policy enforcement
    - Guest access and services
- Cisco technologies assessed:
    - Access Control Server
    - MARS
    - Routers
    - Switches
    - Firewall
    - CSA
    - NAC
    - IBNS

Secure Remote Access

The secure remote access domain assesses how an organization secures the confidentiality of information in transit across public networks. This includes user remote VPN services, site-to-site VPNs, business-to-business connectivity, and internal network data services that require encryption technologies. Properly assessing the policy, procedures, and technologies associated with VPNs is critical for maintaining the integrity of an organization's security.

- Processes and functions assessed:
    - Remote user access policy and configuration
    - Branch office connectivity over VPN
    - VPN authentication methods
    - VPN portals and tunneling
    - Endpoint posture assessment and policy enforcement

- Cisco technologies assessed:

    - MARS

    - ASA

    - Routers

    - IPS

    - NAC

    - CSA

Endpoint Protection

Secure applications and hosts assess the technological controls to protect the confidentially, integrity, and availability of the data, operating systems, applications, and information contained on servers, workstations, and other devices utilizing services available on the network. Protection from malware such as viruses and worms is an important aspect of securing a user's system; however, policy enforcement and user awareness training are equally critical security functions that are addressed here. This domain also addresses acceptable use enforcement and data loss prevention.

- Process and functions assessed:

    - Client protection

    - Application and service hardening

    - User policy enforcement

    - User security awareness education

    - Policy compliance monitoring

    - Threat awareness

    - Email policy enforcement

    - Web policy enforcement

    - Data loss prevention

    - Malware prevention

- Cisco technologies assessed:

    - Ironport Email Security Appliance (ESA)

    - Ironport Web Security Appliance (WSA)

    - Mars

    - NAC

    - CSA

- Routers

- IPS

- ASA

Unified Communications

This domain identifies key areas that are necessary for securing a unified communications installation. IP telephony is an application, and as with all applications, it needs to be deployed securely and assessed for potential vulnerabilities. Toll fraud, eavesdropping, and denial of service are all potential threats to an organization's phone system. Auditing unified communication installations against best practices and recommended security configurations help identify areas of improvement as well as opportunities to mitigate risk. There are numerous security features available in the Cisco Unified Communications suite of products that should be utilized.

- Process and functions assessed:

  - IP telephony configuration best practices

  - Call control protection

  - Toll fraud prevention

  - Encrypted telephony

  - Monitoring telephony threats

- Cisco technologies assessed:

  - Cisco Unified Call Manager

  - Cisco Unified Call Manager Express

  - MARS

  - CSA

  - Firewall

  - Routers

  - Switches

  - IPS

Defining the Audit Scope of a Domain

The first step in auditing is to define the scope of what it is you are assessing. Properly scoping an audit ensures that you're testing the right aspects of security and the appropriate assets and technologies. The scope also determines to what degree or depth to which you are going to test them.

Using the auditing domains can help you stay focused on the systems that are interconnected based on the security service they represent. You might end up using multiple domains in a single audit, as they are designed in a modular fashion to be flexible. Selecting which domain comes down to determining what technology or aspect of security the organization wants you to inspect. Firewalls would fall under the intrusion prevention domain, and protecting endpoints from viruses and worms would fall under the endpoint protection domain. After you have identified the security domains to be used in the audit, perform a little research to determine "the lay of the land" from a technological and security standpoint. Some things that you will need to look for are:

- The critical assets and where they are located
- The security controls currently in place
- Any recent changes
- Results of previous audits
- Current documentation and network diagrams

After you have identified what controls are in place and what assets are where, conduct a risk assessment on the domain that you're going to audit. This risk assessment helps to better highlight the areas that need the most attention because of their criticality to the organization. When conducting the risk assessment, do the following:

- Rank critical assets.
- Rank potential threats.
- Rank potential vulnerabilities.
- Determine the likelihood of an identified risk.
- Determine the potential impact of the risk.

This exercise provides clear direction about the most important systems to audit.

Audits are typically preformed against assets, technology, physical location, compliance, or applications. Regardless of what is tested, the auditor must examine how the security of the service is affected by people, process, and technology. This is where the auditing domains come in to play as they address security from a systems approach as opposed to individual technologies. If you perform an audit against a firewall, for example, you might find that it completely adheres to best practice and is configured properly based on the risks and assets it is being used to protect. The reason that the firewall is there in the first place is to protect a critical service, such as a web server tied to a database. If you are conducting only a firewall audit, the web application itself is probably outside of the scope of your audit. If something happens after the audit, such as customer records are compromised because of an unseen vulnerability in the web server that was not identified, it's not because of the firewalls that there was a breach. The firewall did its job;

however, based on the audit itself not being appropriately scoped by domain, vulnerabilities in a critical system were not identified. If Goldilocks was an auditor, she would tell you that the breadth of an audit should not be too wide or too narrow, and that risk ultimately identifies to what depth and what systems need to be inspected.

Identifying Security Controls to Assess

Selecting what controls to use when designing a security program involves understanding the risks and security objectives of the organization. Policy provides the mandate and direction, and controls exist to realize the security goals by reducing risk. You can't simply choose a bunch of controls, throw them down on paper, and expect that the security program will have any coherence. Unfortunately, many organizations have made control decisions based heavily on technological recommendations and not in support of a larger security architecture. Luckily, there are numerous control frameworks that take into account the interrelated nature of security and address mitigating risk around people, process, and technology.

There are three well-known and respected sources that an auditor can use to identify necessary security controls, and what should therefore be assessed in a business: COBIT, ISO 27002, and NIST 800-53. The frameworks of these controls (introduced in Chapter 3, "Information Security Governance, Frameworks, and Standards") address different parts of the organization from governance to the tactical delivery of security. They work together and can be used for assessing a business from the top to the actual implementation of security. COBIT provides high-level managerial controls designed to manage IT governance as a whole from a lifecycle perspective for the entire organization, not just security. ISO 27002, on the other hand, provides strategic high-level controls for information security management and operations. NIST 800-53 is a much more tactical, operationally focused set of controls and best practices for the implementation of security technologies.

COBIT is a full IT governance framework that is built as a tool for management to better identify the value delivered by information technology. COBIT addresses everything from the management of third-party services (outsourcing), new systems acquisition, problem management, and budgeting. COBIT identifies four main categories of controls: planning and organization, acquisition and implementation, delivery and support, and monitoring. The category that is most directly related to auditing networks is the delivery and support section, which describes 11 control objectives geared specifically to information security. There are many good practices to be leveraged from COBIT, and because it was created by ISACA and ITGI, auditing and measurement of each control is clearly detailed in each section.

Table 5-1 lists COBIT process areas and their relationship to people, process, and technology.

ISO 27002 is an international standard directly focused on information security and is considered a benchmark for implementing security management. While COBIT is more focused on the process of delivering information technology services, ISO highlights var-

Table 5-1   *COBIT Processes Mapped to People, Process, and Technology*

People	Process	Technology
Define and Manage Service Levels	Manage Performance and Capacity	Ensure Systems Security
Manage Third-party Services	Ensure Continuous Service	Manage the Configuration
Identify and Allocate Costs	Manage Service Desk and Incidents	Manage Problems
Educate and Train Users	Manage Physical Environment	Manage Data
	Manage Operations	

ious control objectives necessary for securing information assets. In fact, COBIT is actually built on ISO 27002, and it references the controls outlined in ISO as ways of accomplishing process goals.

The codes of practice identified in the 132 security controls addressed by the ISO 27002 standard represent many of the common security mechanisms organizations need. The goal of ISO is to address the objectives of security and doesn't tell you how to implement the objectives, so you won't see specific requirements for types of technology or configuration parameters. Those details are left up to the organization to choose and standardize upon.

Table 5-2 shows the ISO 27002 objectives mapped to people, process, and technology.

Table 5-2   *ISO 27002 Controls Mapped to People, Process, and Technology*

People	Process	Technology
Access Controls	Communications and Operations Manager	Network
Organizing Information Security	Compliance	Database
Human Resources Security	Business Continuity Manager	Systems
	Security Incident Management	Endpoints
	Asset Management	Application Infrastructure
	Physical and Environmental Security	Messaging and Content
	Information Systems Acquisition, Development, and Maintenance	Data
	Security Policy	

NIST is a set of tactical controls that delves much more deeply into implementation. The great thing about NIST 800-53 is that it details security control requirements in a template format. NIST 800-53 uses a simple ranking system of low, medium, and high to determine the controls necessary to meet the protection objectives.

The NIST standards are used for securing U.S. government systems, and are thought out and practical for most organizations to adopt. Auditors performing more technical audits and assessments will find NIST useful for developing checklists.

Table 5-3 maps NIST control objectives to people, process, and technology.

Table 5-3   *NIST 800-53 Controls Mapped to People, Process, and Technology*

People	Process	Technology
Risk Assessment	Personnel Security	Identification and Authentication
Planning	Physical and Environmental Protection	Access Control
System and Services Acquisition	Contingency Planning	Audit and Accountability
Certification, Accreditation, and Security Assessments	Configuration Management	Systems and Communications Protection
	Maintenance	
	System and Information Integrity	
	Media Protection	
	Incident Response	
	Awareness and Training	

Mapping Security Controls to Cisco Solutions

Cisco provides the broadest range of security controls available from any vendor. Every product Cisco sells has integrated security features designed to help automate the security functions of an organization. This broad array of products and technologies maps quite nicely to industry standards and control frameworks. The real challenge for auditors is to identify how best to configure and implement the solutions Cisco provides, so that they can assess how well an organization protects its resources and assets. The seven domains introduced earlier in this chapter give the auditor a way to approach Cisco security technologies with a security services approach.

Controls are simply security objectives and they operate as guidance on what must be accomplished to protect an asset. If you look at the controls laid out in the ISO standard, you will see hundreds of potential controls that an organization can implement. If you are not going for certification to the ISO standard, you have the option of choosing only those controls from the list that are relevant to the business and objectives of the organization. A thorough risk assessment can determine which controls must be implemented and the extent to which technologies for mitigation should be deployed.

Of course, risk is subjective and depends upon who you are talking to in the organization. If you examine the threats against a print server, for example, you might find that there are numerous vulnerabilities that could allow a hacker to take a print server offline or reconfigure it to point to a queue that the hacker can use to view the print jobs. The potential loss of data and confidential information is real in this instance, but for the most part there is a relatively low potential for this to happen. Most organizations do not have an intrusion prevention system deployed to protect a print server, because the risk is not worth the cost of mitigation. A print server is not a particularly high-value asset nor operationally critical system, but if your CEO wants to print something and that print server is offline because of an attack, the criticality from a subjective standpoint is probably going to increase exponentially. This is an example of how every business application is critical to someone, but the selection of controls and the level of mitigation should always be determined based on the risk to the organization.

Mapping the controls an organization decides to implement to Cisco technologies is made easier by logically grouping controls that work together. This logical grouping of complementary technologies is how the seven security domains were created. Each domain addresses people, process, and technology, but does it in a way that highlights the interconnected nature of the many control objectives found in best practices. Because this book is focused on assessing Cisco technologies, the bulk of the items addressed will be from a technical perspective. As an auditor, you cannot lose sight of the importance of people and process in providing strong security.

Table 5-4 maps key ISO control objectives to Cisco auditing domains. Each of these domains encompasses specific technologies that enable the automation and monitoring of the security objectives specific to that domain. Many of the same technologies are used throughout the domains, but each is configured in a way that addresses different control objectives. Each domain has its own dedicated chapter in this book, which provides much more detail about the controls and provides guidance for assessing each system.

The Audit Checklist

The auditing checklist acts as the blueprint for the entire auditing process. This step is critical to ensuring the success of the audit and achieving the objectives set forth by the organization. When an auditor builds a checklist, it should be constructed to ensure complete coverage of the assessment objectives given the scope of the audit engagement for each item to be inspected. The checklist itself provides areas to be audited, control objective, assessment methods, and results (evidence) expected to prove compliance.

Table 5-4 *ISO 27002 Control Objectives Mapped to Auditing Domains*

ISO 27002 Control Objectives		Policy, Compliance, and Management	Infrastructure Security	Perimeter Intrusion Prevention	Access Control	Secure Remote Access	Endpoint Protection	Unified Communication
5	Security Policy	x	x	x	x	x	x	x
6	Organization of Information Security	x						
7	Asset Management	x					x	
8	Human Resource Security	x			x	x		
9	Physical and Environmental Security	x						
10.1.1	Document Operating Procedures	x						
10.1.2	Change Management	x						
10.1.3	Segregation of Duties	x					x	
10.1.4	Separation of Development, Test, and Operational Facilities	x	x	x	x			
10.3.1	Capacity Management	x						
10.4.1	Controls Against Malicious Code	x		x	x		x	
10.4.2	Controls Against Mobile Code	x		x	x		x	

(*continues*)

Table 5-4   *ISO 27002 Control Objectives Mapped to Auditing Domains (continued)*

ISO 27002 Control Objectives		Policy, Compliance, and Management	Infrastructure Security	Perimeter Intrusion Prevention	Access Control	Secure Remote Access	Endpoint Protection	Unified Communication
10.6.1	Network Controls	x	x	x	x	x	x	x
10.8.1	Information Exchange Policies and Procedures	x	x	x				
10.8.4	Electronic Messaging	x		x	x		x	
10.9.2	Online Transactions	x		x		x	x	
10.10.1	Audit Logging	x	x	x	x	x	x	x
10.10.2	Monitoring System Use	x	x	x	x	x	x	x
10.10.3	Protection of Log Information	x					x	
10.10.4	Administrator and Operator Logs	x						
10.10.5	Fault Logging	x						
10.10.6	Clock Synchroni-zation	x	x	x	x	x	x	x
11.1.1	Access Control Policy	x						
11.2.1	User Registration	x			x	x		
11.2.2	Privilege Management	x					x	

(*continues*)

Table 5-4   *ISO 27002 Control Objectives Mapped to Auditing Domains (continued)*

ISO 27002 Control Objectives		Policy, Compliance, and Management	Infrastructure Security	Perimeter Intrusion Prevention	Access Control	Secure Remote Access	Endpoint Protection	Unified Communication
11.2.3	User Password Management	x						
11.3.2	Unattended User Equipment	x					x	
11.4.1	Policy on Use of Network Services	x			x	x	x	
11.4.2	User Authentication for External Connections	x			x	x		
11.4.3	Equipment Identification Networks	x			x	x	x	
11.4.4	Remote Diagnostic and Configuration Port Protection		x	x	x	x	x	
11.4.5	Segregation in Networks		x		x	x	x	x
11.4.6	Network Connection Control	x	x		x	x	x	
11.4.7	Network Routing Control	x	x	x				
11.5.1	Secure Log-on Procedures				x	x	x	

(continues)

Table 5-4   *ISO 27002 Control Objectives Mapped to Auditing Domains (continued)*

ISO 27002 Control Objectives	Policy, Compliance, and Management	Infrastructure Security	Perimeter Intrusion Prevention	Access Control	Secure Remote Access	Endpoint Protection	Unified Communication
11.5.2 User Identification and Authentication	x	x		x	x	x	x
11.5.3 Password Management Systems	x					x	
11.5.4 Use of System Utilities	x		x			x	
11.5.5 Session Time-Out	x			x	x		
11.6.2 Sensitive System Isolation		x	x	x	x		
11.7.1 Mobile Computing and Communications	x	x	x	x	x	x	x
11.7.2 Teleworking	x	x	x	x	x	x	x

The more detailed a checklist is, the easier it is for others to follow, which enables an auditor to enlist the organization's systems administrators and other support staff to help in gathering evidence. No one will know the systems better than those who work on them on a day-to-day basis, which should accelerate the speed of gathering audit evidence.

Creating a good checklist for the audit requires that all of the preparatory work has been completed, that the scope is accurately identified, and key assets and threats to the organization have been catalogued. After the prep work has been completed, the auditor now has the information required to start building the auditing checklist.

Many auditors have prebuilt checklists for various systems and technologies that they have previously been asked to assess. These can be used as a starting point and generally will save a considerable amount of time when auditing similar technologies or systems. However, just as no two organizations are the same, few audits are exactly alike. This means that a certain amount of customization of the checklist is expected so that it can more accurately fit the needs of the organization being audited. There are many places to find sample checklists; a quick search on Google identifies a number of sites that you can use to download examples. The sans.org website provides a good list of checklists by technology that can be easily incorporated. You can also find examples from ISACA at www.ISACA.org.

Many times, an auditor finds that he must create a checklist from scratch because he is assessing a new technology or system and doesn't have a pre-canned checklist that applies to the scope of the audit. Creating the checklist is not that difficult because there are so many great sources of best practices and standards on which to base a checklist. The secret to writing a good checklist is the selection of applicable controls and processes, given the scope of the audit. You should have checks that examine the three primary control areas of people, process, and technology. Incorporating all three ensures that your checklist addresses all of the dimensions of security.

In general, a good checklist includes the following:

- **Auditor's name and date:** Be sure to include the auditor's name and any other auditing team members. The date the audit was completed is also useful for building a timeline showing improvement.

- **Description of audit objectives:** The description of audit objectives provides a quick and concise overview of the scope and systems that will be assessed. An example description that can be used: "The assessment of intrusion prevention controls for corporate DMZ against Cisco CVD and CIS benchmark level 1."

- **Mapping to best practices and standards:** Standards such as ISO 27002 or NIST 800-53 provide lists of controls that are considered essential to properly securing systems. These lists of controls make a good source material for the checks that are conducted during an assessment. Good checklists can reduce subjectivity by referencing each question or task to a particular best practice or standard.

- **Mapping to policies:** The items on the checklist might also include specific policies that the organization utilizes and would like to have checked for compliance.

- **Mapping to regulations:** Practically every company in the world has specific laws or regulations with which they must comply. Most laws or regulations have requirements for proving that organizations have conducted assessments, so referencing areas that are applicable on the checklist can help an organization to show compliance.

- **What to assess:** Control objectives should be clearly articulated, so that the auditor understands the goal of the security function being tested. A control's objective should not be vague, as in "protect web servers from attack." It should identify specific requirements such as "protect the web servers from cross-site scripting." In the second example, the objective is much more in line with current threats, and it clearly states something that is actionable.

- **Why to assess:** Sometimes during an audit, the organization questions why a particular control is being inspected. Adding this section provides the justification and identifies the potential risk that the control being assessed is intended to mitigate.

- **How to assess:** The assessment methods an auditor chooses depend on the scope of the audit itself and the specific control being assessed. For the most part, though, there are three main categories of assessment methods an auditor typically employs in gathering evidence. These methods consist of an examination of pertinent documents, the interview of those responsible for security, and the actual testing of specific controls and processes. The assessment method should be outlined in the checklist with detailed instructions on what tools or scripts are to be used, tests performed, commands to be entered, questions asked, and documents reviewed. It is not uncommon to use multiple assessment methods to test a control. For each method used, you should provide enough information so that consistency and repeatability are easily attained. Consider this a scientific process in which the steps taken are just as important as the results obtained.

- **Results expected:** The results expected from testing should be clearly described, preferably with examples to minimize any potential subjectivity. The closer you get to determining whether or not the control objects are met, the better the checklist. This area acts as guidance for the auditor conducting the assessment.

- **Results observed:** This section is where the auditor can document pass/fail and any pertinent information that should be added to the final report. This is not the area where the auditor copies and pastes pages of scanner data; however, it does allow the summarization of key deficiencies or places where the organization excels in executing the control objective.

Chapters 6–12 provide sample checklists that can be used as is or customized for your organization's assessments.

Summary

Auditing today's networks is not easy and requires a methodical approach to ensure that all facets of security are properly assessed. In summary:

- This chapter highlighted the requirements for auditing security as a system and introduced the auditing domains as a mechanism for assessing complex security controls.

- The importance of defining the scope of the audit is key to creating an appropriate checklist, testing the right aspects to the right depth and providing the expected deliverables.

■ Mapping Cisco technologies to industry standards like ISO 27002, COBIT, or NIST enables the auditor to translate technologies into technical controls that can be measured.

■ Development of a solid checklist or audit plan helps the auditor stay focused on testing security from the people, process, and technology perspective.

■ The auditing checklist provides a roadmap for conducting the audit and a record of the results obtained, and the more detailed the checklist, the easier it is for others to follow and reproduce the results.

Chapter 6

Policy, Compliance, and Management

A security policy is a document that provides the high-level direction and goals that a business utilizes to control and protect its assets and information. The security policy should be the foundation for which all security decisions are measured against and consulted before any product or technology is put into place. In general, a security policy tells you what activities are acceptable, required, or forbidden when interacting with business-owned resources. For the auditor, ensuring that a security policy meets the objectives of securing the business's assets and compliance requirements requires assessing policy documents and comparing them against best practices. An auditor also interviews and observes how well employees follow policies and indentifies any areas of improvement.

This chapter provides an overview of what to look for when assessing an organization's information security policies for compliance with law and industry regulations.

Do You Know Where Your Policy Is?

Be honest with yourself: When was the last time you actually read your company's security policies? Was it sometime shortly after you completed your new hire paperwork? Old, dusty policies sitting in a binder somewhere or visiting a website cannot help guide the security direction of an organization. Security policies should be easily accessible and posted preferably on an intranet site that is available to anyone who has a question about what is permissible network conduct.

It's important to note that security policies are not just "nice-to-have" exercises in documentation; they are essential guides for all security-related activities. Having a set of current security policies is also required by a number of laws and industry regulations. Some example compliance requirements for policies are:

- **Payment Card Industry Data Security Standard (PCI):** Requirement 12 of PCI instructs organizations to "maintain a security policy that addresses information security."

- **Federal Information Security Management Act of 2002 (FISMA):** Relies on guidance from the NIST series of documents, specifically NIST 800-53 that requires the creation, review, and dissemination of a security policy.

- **Health Insurance Portability and Accountability Act (HIPAA):** Section 4.2 of HIPAA requires the identification of someone responsible for security and the point of contact for security policy, implementation, and monitoring.

- **Sarbanes Oxley Act (SOX):** Requires adequate security control structure in which the Public Company Accounting Oversight Board (PCAOB) has determined a standards-based control framework such as ISO 27001 or COBIT, which both require security policies endorsed by upper management.

Strong, clear, and enforceable policies are needed for organizations of all sizes. Just as you would never build a house without a blueprint, you should never design security controls without policies to back them up.

Auditing Security Policies

The purpose of the security policy is to document the business requirements for security and define the goals of the organization for protecting its intellectual property and assets. A security policy is not supposed to make it impossible to do your job or create a police that requires high levels of bureaucracy to maintain. The policy should be simply worded and provide easily understood guidance for conducting business in a safe manner. The policy also helps reduce risky behavior by explaining why a user should not engage in activities such as downloading unapproved applications and loading them on their corporate-owned laptops. Part of the auditor's job is to make sure that the policy balances the goals of easy network access and strict security and does not tip too far in either direction.

Understanding an organization's corporate culture also plays an important part in assessing policies. Support from upper management plays a key role in determining whether or not a policy is enforced or ignored. This means that part of a policy assessment should include interviews and conversations with employees to determine how they feel about corporate policies. Many users couldn't even tell you where a specific policy is or even who to ask to find out about it. Culture is a factor in employee policy compliance, and ultimately in the execution of security in general. If employees think of security policy as just one more inhibitor to being able to perform their jobs, they will attempt to circumvent or ignore it. Educating users about the importance of policy in protecting the business is a continual process that must be preformed.

The policy should be written to require compliance by the business and employees. This is why it is important to have management support and sign off on the policy. Policies also need to be reviewed by the company's Human Resources and legal departments to ensure that the requirements are within the law and employment practices.

Policies are controls for people, and they need to balance access with security. If a policy is too restrictive, productivity can be adversely affected. This can also result in users finding ways around the policy. Many organizations banned wireless access points from deployment because they were not comfortable with the technology from a security perspective. Although IT would not install an access point, many users simply went to their neighborhood electronics store, purchased home grade wireless APs, and installed them on their own. In this scenario, the risk was made even worse because of the policy being too restrictive, resulting in users deploying them in an unsecure manner.

Policies without consequences are not worth the paper (or electrons) they are written on and cannot help achieve the desired security behavior in the user community. Lax polices that have little or no consequences are viewed as recommendations. Of course, consistent enforcement is also essential because if one employee is allowed to get away with risky behavior, it sets a precedence that says the policy is not enforceable for other employees.

It is important you separate a policy from procedures and standards because while the governance directives of a security policy might remain static, the procedures and standards can change based on technological or operational requirements. A policy should list only general security goals, as in "All company data transiting the Internet between branch offices and headquarters will be encrypted based on corporate encryption standards." The previous statement does not tell what type of product or encryption methods are used because they can change rapidly based on technology or new product purchases. Standards are used to identify specific technologies, products, and even configurations that an organization uses to accomplish policy goals. An example of corporate standard might be to provide AES256 bit-level encryption utilizing Dynamic Multipoint VPN tunnels between all remote offices for data and voice traffic. The procedure document in this case details the configuration, software version, and operation of the routers running the service. Considering the amount of effort and consultation with other parts of the organization required to enact a new policy, it makes much more sense to try to keep the policy consistent and let procedures and standards deal with the specifics of how to accomplish the goal.

Chapter 1, "The Principles of Auditing," includes a section that details the differences between security policies, procedures, and guidelines. To review, the minimum required policy items include:

- **Purpose:** Why the policy exists. This section includes the reasoning behind the policy, potential ramifications to the company if the policy is not followed, and how it supports the corporate mission.

- **Scope:** Who or what the policy applies to. Is this a policy for contractors or full-time employees? The scope should use job titles or functions to identify the employees instead of an individual's name, so that the policy is unaffected as people change positions or go on vacation. Does the policy apply to development systems or key customer-facing servers? The scope section provides specifics about the assets and employees covered by the policy.

- **Policy statement:** The policy requirements. This is the meat of the policy document and includes specific details about what is permitted or prohibited. The wording should be clear and concise and not open to interpretation. A policy should not include specific products or configurations because these areas are covered in procedures and subject to change.

- **Enforcement:** Disciplinary action statement. The enforcement section provides a clear indication about the consequences of noncompliance with the policy.

- **Terms and definitions:** Clarification of terminology utilized in the policy statement, such as SPAM or malware.

- **Revision history:** A summary of changes to the policy that includes the date of change, the person or group who initiated the change, and a summary of what has changed.

Assessing the effectiveness of a policy requires the auditor to look at the policy from the viewpoint of those who will interpret its meaning. A well intentioned policy might recommend a particular course of action, but unless specific actions are *required*, there is little one can expect the policy to actually accomplish to help protect the organization from risky behavior. When assessing a policy in this light, you need to examine it against certain key criteria:

- **Is the policy implementable?** There are limits to technology and the lengths to which a business will go to secure its assets. It can be impossible to comply with poorly written policies.

- **Is the policy enforceable?** If you don't intend to enforce a policy, then why does it exist in the first place? Policy enforcement must be consistent, fair, and follow employment laws.

- **Is the policy easy to understand?** Policies written by technical people can be overly detailed and contain technical jargon that is not widely known. A well-written policy is clear to anyone regardless of technical aptitude.

- **Is the policy based on risk?** Policies should always be based on reducing risk to the organization. A solid risk-management program identifies areas that are potential soft spots to the security of the organization. Policies should then be developed to reduce that risk.

- **Is the policy in line with business objectives?** Furthering business goals and objectives is the only reason policies are written in the first place. Security policies should always support business objectives by helping to reduce risk.

- **Is the policy cost effective?** Requiring expensive safeguards for a low-value asset is not a good use of resources. Security policies should always be measured against the potential loss an organization can experience versus the cost of securing the asset. Loss is not just a monetary metric, but also includes customer goodwill.

- **Is the policy balanced between security and access?** Policies that are too strict can cause employees to develop workarounds to get their jobs done. Security is a balancing act where reducing risk must be weighed against productivity requirements.

- **Does the policy accomplish its intended purpose?** Policies that don't accomplish their goals are common. This is because of interpretation or politics that weaken a policy to the point of ineffectiveness. Always compare the policy against its desired goals to ensure it meets its objectives.

- **Is the policy current?** Revision dates tell you a lot about management's commitment to security and whether or not the policy is actively used. Some policies are well written and broad enough to stand for a number of years, but if there is not a formal review cycle, policies can become ineffective due to changes in threat landscape. Policy reviews should be conducted periodically in conjunction with risk assessments. This allows a policy to stay relevant and maintain its value.

- **Does management support the policy?** Having management sign off on the policy is critical to enforcement and builds a security culture.

- **Is the policy effectively communicated?** Having a policy is one thing; actively communicating the policy and training users to identify potentially risky behavior is another thing.

Measuring how well security policies are implemented in the company is an important part of a security policy assessment. Utilizing a maturity model is a great way to gauge where an organization is in its evolution toward fully integrating security into business processes. One framework that provides a nice measurement system for security policies is the Federal Information Security Assessment Framework the NIST organization created. The framework provides a maturity model that measures policy integration on a 1 to 5 scale. A 0 reflects an organization with no security policies whatsoever, and a 5 reflects a business that has security policies and procedures integrated into all aspects of business processes.

Table 6-1 shows the levels of measurement in the maturity model.

Table 6-1 *Federal Information Technology Security Assessment Framework Maturity Model*

Level of Policy Integration	Description
0	There are no security policies.
1	Policies are written.
2	Detailed procedures and standards for implementing the policies exist.
3	Implementing the procedures and standards exists.
4	Testing the compliance and effectiveness of the procedures and standards exists.
5	Policies and procedures are fully integrated into the organization.

Measuring against a maturity model is a great way to provide guidance for improving an organization's policies and procedures. An auditor providing benchmark measurements that can be used to compare execution of security policies adds significant value to the assessment process. After all, the purpose of assessments is to help the organization improve its overall security posture.

Standard Policies

Information security policies differ widely between organizations, depending on the industry and specific business models followed. However, although the policies might have different names, the intent is similar. All policies should be created based on a solid risk assessment that takes into account the business goals and specific threats facing the organization. The examples in the following sections provide a basis for comparing the policies that an organization has implemented against a baseline of common policy types. This is not an exhaustive list, and it is the auditor's job to identify any missing policies that are unique to the organization.

Acceptable Use

The acceptable use policy is one of the most important policies to implement in an organization. This policy sets the stage for security and establishes acceptable behavior when utilizing business networks. Companies provide network connectivity and computing devices to further their business goals, and they expect employees to exercise proper judgment and adhere to corporate requirements for protecting sensitive data and assets. This policy specifically states that security is the responsibility of, and applies to, everyone in the organization. It also includes specific guidelines about acceptable behavior, required behavior, and prohibited behavior. This policy should have strong enforcement requirements that must be approved by Human Resources, as the violation of this policy can result in termination of employment or disciplinary action.

Minimum Access

The purpose of this policy is to require adherence to corporate standards (usually referenced in more detail in a separate standards document) regarding patch level, security software, and configuration of networked devices. These devices can be desktops, printers, routers, mobile devices, or anything else that would communicate on the network. This policy requires that any device connecting to the network follows security standards or is subject to removal or quarantine if it is out of compliance.

Network Access

The network access policy is intended to minimize risk to the organization by establishing criteria for granting local-area network (LAN) and wireless access to the organization's network. This policy generally dictates what class of devices can be connected to the network and prohibits self-provisioning of networking equipment such as switches, routers, and wireless access devices. Many organizations also reference adherence to other policies such as monitoring and logging, remote access, guest access, mobile computing, desktop, and minimum acceptable policies. Although this policy might seem like a placeholder, it is important to specify the access requirement that the organization wishes to enforce before access is granted.

Remote Access

Remote access connections extend the edge of the corporate network to anywhere in the world with an IP connection. Not surprisingly, this also dramatically increases the risk of unauthorized breaches. The intent of this policy is to reduce that risk by requiring that specific conditions be met before more access is granted. This policy is typically designed around internal employees who need remote access; third parties, such as vendors or business-to-business connections would be covered under a separate policy focused on extranet-type connections. References to the minimum access standards and specific technology standards to protect a VPN connection should be addressed here.

Internet Access

Internet access policy is designed to provide guidance for employees to understand what permissible Internet-related activities are. This includes types of websites that are prohibited, such as gambling sites or pornography sites, and whether or not nonbusiness surfing of the Internet is permissible. This particular policy can exist as part of the acceptable use policy, but some organizations find it necessary to identify this policy separately because of how important the Internet is in conducting business today.

User Account Management

Managing the requirements for the creation, decommissioning, and auditing of user accounts is addressed in this policy. It is important for an organization to have a strong set of processes and procedures for the creation of accounts on systems and the decommissioning, which is typically initiated by a user's supervisor when there is a job change or termination. The support personnel required to follow the procedures also need to be formally trained in what is required and how to ensure that this policy is followed. To ensure compliance with this policy, audits of user rights should also be conducted on a regular basis.

Data Classification

Not all data is created equal, and some organizational data is valuable not only to the organization itself but also to competitors. Identifying and classifying different data types and how they are to be protected in the organization are the purpose of this policy.

These classifications enable the creation of specific controls to protect the data based on its importance to the organization. The business component that creates the data should be responsible for its classification based on the organization's classification structure. An example classification structure is:

- **Public:** Information might be disclosed to anyone inside or outside of the organization. Any outwardly facing document or webpage should be part of this data classification.

- **Confidential:** This type of information is the default classification for any company or employee-created documents, e-mail, or presentations that are used in the organization for conducting business. Any employee with a business need to access this type of information should be authorized; however, specific permission and possibly nondisclosure agreements must be signed to disclose the information to a third party.

- **Highly confidential:** These documents represent sensitive information that only select individuals in the organization, based on job function and role, should be able to access. This information, as a general rule, is not to be shared externally without specific approval of the data owner. Some examples are personnel information, strategic plans, product designs, and nonpublic financial data.

- **Private:** This classification is for sensitive information that is usually restricted to officers and those individuals specifically named to have access. Disclosure of this information can cause significant harm to the organization and must be protected at all costs. Examples of this classification are merger and acquisition plans, corporate sales forecasting, and pre-patent research and development data.

Change Management

Poor change management practices are attributed to more outages and down time than from evil hackers by a large margin. The objective of this policy is to reduce the risk of uncontrolled device configuration changes by mandating adherence to good change control techniques. Identifying a formal service management program such as ITIL can help build the framework for change control across the organization. Good change management practices include standardized configurations, approval of all changes, and a rollback process if the change causes unforeseen problems. This policy is applicable to all technology services.

Server Security

A server security policy mandates baseline configuration, and it assigns server owners with the responsibility to conform with corporate standard and best practices around installing, configuring, and operating business services and systems. Limiting active services to only those necessary for running the applications required, configuration backups, and security requirements are outlined in this policy. Monitoring and auditing requirements might also exist in this policy to ensure that the system is configured and patched appropriately.

Mobile Devices

Laptops and other mobile-computing platforms have a significantly higher risk of theft, potential loss of company data, and contact with malicious software. This higher risk necessitates having specific rules that address the greater precautions that need to be followed to mitigate and limit the businesses exposure. Hard disk encryption, anti-malware, and the types of data are allowed to be present on laptops are all addressed by this policy. Physical security requirements, such as where to report lost or stolen devices, should be discussed here, too.

Guest Access

Providing guest access is a challenge for many companies. Allowing uncontrolled devices access to the LAN is not a good security practice. This policy defines the conditions and processes that should be in place to protect the organization, while allowing the company to be a good host to guests and other third parties. Conference room and wireless access are addressed in this document. Requiring guests to read and agree with acceptable use policies is also addressed. Some companies have guests sign a document and then provide a code for temporary access, whereas others utilize technology to automate much of this. The policy's intent is to enforce the company standards and identify the procedures for allowing guest users use of the network.

Physical Security

Physical security policies help control access to network infrastructure and systems. Gaining physical access can greatly increase the risk of successfully compromising a critical information asset. This policy lists required precautions to minimize outages caused by theft, power, fire, and cooling while also enforcing control of devices that can be brought in or taken out of sensitive facilities.

Password Policy

Enforcing strong passwords and good password practices are detailed in this policy. The enforcement of password strength at creation and password protection procedures should be identified, including procedures such as not using the "remember password" functions in browsers. Rules prohibiting transmitting passwords in e-mail or sharing passwords between employees are included in this policy.

Malware Protection

Addressing protection from malware (any type of malicious software) sent in e-mail attachments, downloaded from the Internet, or just "picked up" while surfing websites is a significant portion of a security administrator's workload. This policy creates the framework for preventing, detecting, and cleaning up malware. Specific versions of security software and patch update schedules are handled in subsequent standards and procedure documents.

Incident Handling

When strange things happen, the incident handling policy is there to guide the organization in initiating and reporting the issue to the appropriate groups and individuals. When an attack is underway or a key system is offline, it is not the best time to try and figure out what to do next. Incident handling from a security perspective is a discipline of its own. This policy sets up the working structure for incident handling and the communication methods to initiate the process.

Audit Policy

The audit policy provides the authorization for auditors to request access to systems that need to be assessed and tested. The auditing department might be required to have system-level or root access to any device on the corporate network that is within the scope of an audit being conducted. The auditing team also needs access to log data, traffic records, and documentation, and it will be granted the right to inspection by this policy.

Software Licensing

Businesses using unlicensed shareware or more licenses than they purchased are at risk of fines and lawsuits from the software companies that make those products. Therefore, the tracking of licenses is an important aspect of compliance, and a policy is written to set up the requirement for license metering, application inventories, and formal software purchasing processes. Formally prohibiting activities, such as downloading and installing unapproved software applications, is a major part of this policy.

Electronic Monitoring and Privacy

Businesses have the right and the duty to monitor communications traversing company-provided equipment and resources. This policy is intended to state what types of systems are subject to monitoring and the data that will be collected. The idea is not to create a "Big Brother is watching you" environment, but to ensure that malicious behavior is detected as early and accurately as possible. Electronic monitoring requirements might differ between countries, so always seek legal counsel.

Policies for Regulatory and Industry Compliance

Every organization, regardless of size or industry, has to comply with the law and industry-compliance requirements. Auditors should have a general working knowledge of some of the key laws and regulations with which businesses must comply. Because policies dictate how the organization is going to structure security controls, those policies must take into consideration compliance. All businesses should be encouraged to seek legal counsel whenever questions of law arise from a policy review, because unless the auditor is also a practicing lawyer, he should never attempt to provide legal advice.

Assessing policies for compliance requires you to identify what laws or industry requirements are applicable to the business. If the business accepts credit cards as a form of payment, then it definitely falls under PCI and must plan for how it will protect and limit the potential loss of cardholder data. Having an online shopping cart also requires compliance with PCI and privacy regulations. If children can potentially purchase items or come to the business's website, then the business also has to comply with the Child Online Protection Act. Marketing efforts conducted through e-mail would fall under the CAN-SPAM Act and must have an opt-out mechanism in place for those people who don't want advertisements. These examples show how practically any commercial venture that uses technology has to adhere to a wide range of laws. Auditors should also understand what the penalties for violation of these laws would be. In some cases, it is a monetary fine; others such as PCI can issue a fine or even suspend the business's capability to take credit cards as payment. Noncompliance with SOX can result in prison sentences for executives. The most important aspect of auditing for compliance is for the auditor to understand the business and the way in which the organization operates to ensure that the policies and security controls are compliant and address the risks that the company faces.

Chapter 2, "Information Security and the Law," includes an overview of specific regulations and how they apply to information security. Table 6-2 provides a list of some of the most common regulations and the areas that security policies and procedures need to address for each.

Table 6-2 *Security Policies and Procedures Dictated by Regulatory Bodies*

PCI	GLBA	HIPAA	SOX	SB1386
Firewall configuration and change control	Elevate the written security policy to the board of directors for approval.	Authentication and access control	Confidentiality	Confidentiality
Antivirus and malware	Complete periodic vulnerability assessments to identify foreseeable internal or external threats.	Application and data security	Security continuity	Integrity of data at rest and in transit
Strong authentication	Implement a network-monitoring system to detect attempted attacks on or unauthorized intrusions into customer information.	Data security at rest and in transit	Secure information access	Policy and procedures to protect against attack
Vendor-supplied default passwords	Establish an incident-response program.	Auditing capability	Policy control and enforcement	Security monitoring
Credit card storage		Patient and data confidentiality	Establish an internal controls framework such as Coso or COBIT	Security auditing
Data encryption			Periodic auditing	
Security auditing				
Security testing and vulnerability scanning				
Security monitoring				
Application development				
Policy review and dissemination				

Cisco Policy Management and Monitoring Tools

Cisco offers a number of applications that can be used for management, monitoring, and policy enforcement. Management of policy should be automated to ensure standardization and adherence to procedures and workflow. The following sections include examples of products that can be used during an audit for quick reporting of compliance. They can add value to the security program of any organization.

Cisco MARS

Cisco Monitoring Analysis and Response System (MARS) is a security event management product designed to make sense of all of the data generated by network security appliances and applications. MARS takes the guesswork out of identifying threats and attacks to the corporate network by supplying context to the many events created on a daily basis. While the primary purpose of MARS is to deal with real-time threats, it is also a repository for security logging information, which makes it a wonderful tool for gathering evidence during an audit. MARS comes with hundreds of built-in reports, many of which address the specific needs of regulatory and industry compliance. Some of MARS features include:

- Creating a topology map of the network

- Learning the behavior and configuration of devices in the network

- Automatically downloading IPS signatures from cisco.com to identify the latest threats to the network

- Utilizing Netflow to detect traffic anomalies that could be zero-day attacks

- Over 150 compliance-specific reports that can be customized to an organization's needs

- The ability to visualize attacks and the paths that traffic flowed through the network

- Integration of Cisco Security Manager (CSM) to map security events with firewall rules and intrusion prevention system signatures

- Monitoring for Cisco products and support for third-party security appliances, such as Checkpoint and Snort (MARS also has the capability to import events from other nonnative supported devices with MARS custom event parsers.)

- Support for historic event archival for audit and trend reporting

Because MARS acts as a repository for all security events in the network, it can be useful for an auditor to get a sense of what types of security issues are being seen, and more importantly, what the business does with the information MARS provides. MARS has built-in compliance reports that enable an auditor to quickly hone in on the specific areas that he wants to inspect. MARS groups reports by compliance area to make it easier to get the right information for compliance assessment purposes. Table 6-3 lists pertinent compliance report groupings in version.

Figure 6-1 shows a MARS PCI report detailing attacks detected by device.

Table 6-3 *MARS Compliance Report Groupings*

Compliance Report Group	Description
COBIT DS3.3: Monitoring and Reporting	Reports on device operational and capacity reporting for COBIT.
COBIT DS5.10: Security Violations	Details reports about security incidents for COBIT.
COBIT DS5.19: Malicious Software	Reports identify viruses, spyware, and trojans detected on the network.
COBIT DS5.20: Firewall Control	Reports detail traffic permitted, denied, and top destinations.
COBIT DS5.2: Authentication and Access	Reports cover user and administrator logins to key systems.
COBIT DS5.4: User Account Changes	Reports cover database and host user account changes.
COBIT DS5.7: Security Surveillance	Reports cover top events and attacks identified.
COBIT DS9.4: Configuration Control	Reports cover database object, network device, server, and registry changes identified.
COBIT DS9.5: Unauthorized Software	Reports cover unapproved software such as spyware, chat, and peer-to-peer.
FISMA Compliance Reports	Reports address specific requirements of the Federal Information Security Management Act.
GLBA Compliance Reports	Reports address specific requirements of the Gramm-Leach-Bliley Act.
HIPAA Compliance Reports	Reports address specific requirements of the Health Insurance Portability and Accountability Act.
PCI DSS Reports	Reports address the Payment Card Industry Data Security Standard.
SOX 302(a)(4)(A)	Sarbanes Oxley reports on database and host admin login attempts specific to 302(a)(4)(A).
SOX 302(a)(4)(D)	Sarbanes Oxley reports on database changes and server changes specific to 302(a)(4)(D).
SOX Compliance Reports	Reports on SOX compliance.

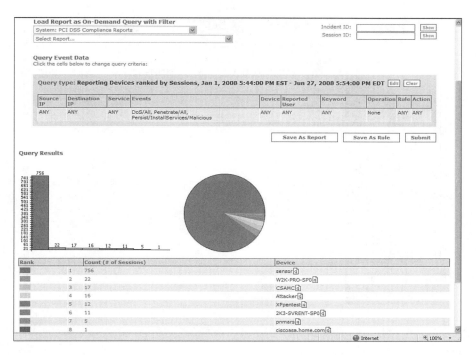

Figure 6-1 *MARS PCI Report*

Cisco Configuration Professional

Cisco Configuration Professional (CCP) is a full-featured security device configuration application for Cisco routers. Cisco Configuration Professional Express is a web-based security configuration tool loaded on all new routers and used to configure only security features and basic connectivity. CCP enables the configuration of all Cisco router features, including voice and wireless. The security configuration capabilities are extensive, with wizard-based tools and monitoring features that auditors can use to gather information on the security posture of IOS devices. The CCP auditing tool, shown in Figure 6-2, compares the current configuration against Cisco-recommended best practices for securing.

CCP also provides the capability to use the auditing feature to fix any potential vulnerability discovered. It has an easy, wizard-based remediation function. Figure 6-3 shows an example assessment conducted against a router.

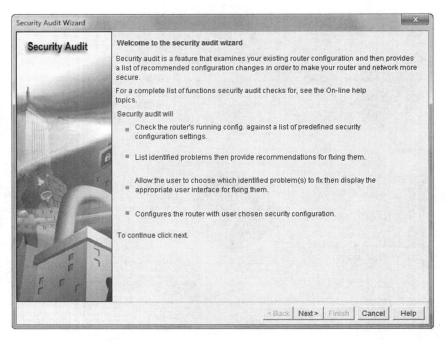

Figure 6-2 *CCP Security Best Practices Audit*

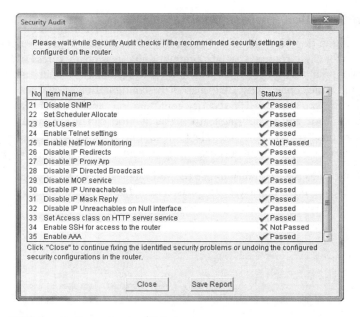

Figure 6-3 *CCP Router Security Audit Report*

Cisco Security Manager

CSM provides advanced management capabilities for Cisco security technologies that reside in Cisco firewalls, routers, and switches. Althoug the embedded device management and CCP are perfectly capable of managing smaller networks of less than ten devices, as you start to move above that level or have more complex departmental separations of duties (security operations and network operations), having a role-based application that can manage all aspects of security device configuration is a worthwhile investment.

As mentioned earlier, having workflow and configuration change control is essential to maintaining a strong security posture and preventing down time from configuration errors. CSM provides multiple levels of operational control to automate the change approval and validation process. Every change is documented and archived with before and after configurations for easy rollback if a problem is encountered. The workflow process requires approval from supervisors or technical leads, too. Figure 6-4 show how the approval process in CSM works.

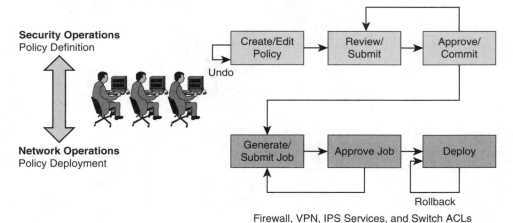

Figure 6-4   *CSM Workflow and Approval Process*

As a network becomes larger and the number of devices increases, the need for consistent configurations and adherence to corporate standards and policies can become time-consuming to enforce. CSM utilizes policy inheritance to ensure that a device has policy-compliant configurations while still allowing for the flexibility of local, per-device unique configuration. Auditors can examine the default policies, and then drill down on specific devices to review the deployed configurations. Figure 6-5 shows how inheritance can accomplish baseline security standards and local policies.

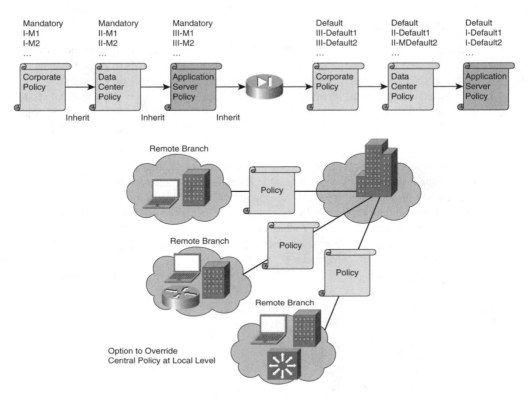

Figure 6-5 *Policy Inheritance of Mandatory and Device-Specific Policies*

There are many policy- and compliance-related functions present in CSM. Auditing networks that utilize CSM is much easier because it acts as a centralized repository for configuration across the organization. Some of the key CSM features for compliance auditing are:

- Evidence of documented and consistent security policy implementation across all firewalls, routers, and switches

- Exportable reports of who configured what, when, where, and why for change-management process validation

- The ability to detect any device configuration changes implemented outside of CSM (bypassing the approval and workflow process)

- Role-Based Access Control (RBAC) for support personnel and network administration to limit access to specific commands or configuration capability based on the user's job role

- A fully documented and configurable workflow process for recording approval, documenting changes, deploying changes to devices, and rolling back changes if necessary

Cisco Network Compliance Manager

Cisco Network Compliance Manager (NCM) is a product that addresses an organization's need to automate network compliance, configuration, and change management. NCM is primarily designed to enforce secure configuration baselines and centralized logging of all changes to networking devices. Additionally, NCM can automate compliance checking and auditing by providing a solution that conducts assessments in real time against networking equipment. NCM is a multivendor platform, which enables the integration of most third-party networking gear. Based on the HP Opsware platform, NCM can be part of a larger enterprise-wide assessment solution that also addresses application and database compliance requirements.

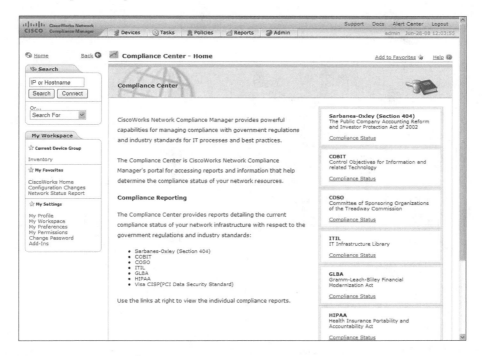

Figure 6-6   *NCM Compliance Center*

NCM can help when conducting audits by reducing the time needed to gather information and compare it with standards. The built-in compliance center (see Figure 6-6) enables auditors to compare current network device configurations against regulatory and industry requirements. The current list of supported compliance checks are:

- **Sarbanes Oxley (Section 404):** The Public Company Accounting Reform and Investor Protection Act of 2002

- **COBIT:** Control Objectives for Information and Related Technology

- **COSO:** Committee of Sponsoring Organizations of the Treadway Commission

- **ITIL:** IT Infrastructure Library

- **GLBA:** Gramm-Leach-Bliley Financial Modernization Act

- **HIPAA:** Health Insurance Portability and Accountability Act

- **PCI Data Security Standard:** Payment Card Industry (PCI) Data Security Standard

Integrated diagramming features enable NCM to generate network diagrams automatically based on the configurations database. This diagram is always up to date with the latest information. Documentation is one area that auditors typically find lacking during assessments. Figure 6-7 shows an example of the automated diagramming feature in NCM.

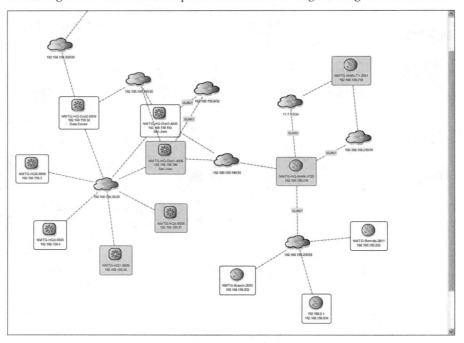

Figure 6-7 *NCM Automated Network Diagram Functionality*

NCM is more than just an assessment and best practice enforcement tool. It also provides software image management and vulnerability matching, so that an organization knows whether its network devices need to be upgraded because of a newly found security weakness. NCM can deploy new software images to devices and recommended workaround configurations. Figure 6-8 shows an example of the software vulnerability report in NCM.

NCM key assessment features include the capability to:

- Maintaining comprehensive configuration change history archive for security audits

- Monitoring and enforcing compliance with security standards such as Visa CISP / PCI for credit card transactions

- Creating security compliance policies (regex pattern match on firewall configurations) and checking if firewall configurations are in compliance with applied security policies

- Providing RBAC and lockdown to devices and their configurations

- Provisioning configuration changes on firewall devices

- Maintaining an up-to-the-keystroke level audit trail of changes made on firewall devices

- Maintaining a history of changes made to ACLs

- Easily deploying ACL changes

- Viewing and searching current ACLs, historical ACLs, and audit trails

- Setting policies to track compliance

- Enforcing policies in real-time

- Providing centralized patch management

- Telnet/SSH Proxy

Assessing networks with NCM is a great way to automate the auditing process and move it from a quarterly or yearly event to an almost real-time snapshot of a company's compliance posture.

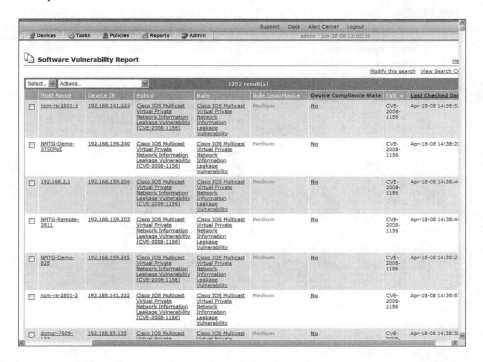

Figure 6-8 *NCM Software Vulnerability Report*

Checklist

Table 6-4 details areas of assessment for policy and compliance and includes recommendations for gathering the audit evidence. It can be used as a starting point for building your assessment process.

Table 6-4   *Policy Compliance Checklist*

Assessment Area	Assessment Technique
Does the organization have a documented security policy that is endorsed by management, HR, and legal?	Review the security policy to determine the level of commitment from management. Interview HR and legal regarding the policy.
Is the security policy actively enforced?	Interview HR and supervisors to determine whether policy is enforced.
Are there clear disciplinary measures associated with noncompliance to the policy?	Review each policy for disciplinary measures. Interview HR to determine whether any employees have been disciplined (not names, just evidence that policy violations have consequences).
Is the policy up to date and does it have a periodic review cycle?	Review policy for change and review dates.
Are there documented procedures and standards that accompany security policies?	Review security standards and procedures for each policy.
Do personnel follow security standards and procedures?	Interview IT staff and observe whether they adhere to standards and procedures.
Are essential security policies present?	Review the following policies: • Acceptable use • Desktop minimum access • Network access • Remote access • Internet access • User account management • Data classification • Change management • Server security • Mobile devices • Guest access • Physical security • Password security • Malware protection • Incident handling • Audit policy • Software licensing • Electronic monitoring

continues

Table 6-4 *Policy Compliance Checklist (continued)*

Assessment Area	Assessment Technique
Is there a formal risk management program?	Review risk management policy documents and results.
Is a risk assessment conducted periodically?	Review risk assessment policy and last risk assessment finding documents.
Are periodic security audits or assessments conducted?	Review audit policy and last audit assessment finding documents.
Are periodic vulnerability assessments conducted?	Review vulnerability assessment policy and vulnerability scan results.
Has the organization identified regulatory or industry requirements with which it must comply?	Review risk management and compliance documents that the company has created. Determine if they have identified all laws with which they must comply.
Are compliance requirements integrated into corporate security policies?	Map regulatory compliance requirements to policies and security controls.
Does the organization review and monitor security events?	Review policy and procedures documents and pull reports from MARS. Review case management tools in MARS.
Does the organization have an incident response plan?	Review incident response policy and procedures. Interview personnel to determine if they know what to do during a live incident.
Does the organization conduct periodic security-awareness training?	Review security awareness documentation. Review training logs and employee-signed attendance documents.
Is there a mechanism for review and update of security-awareness training?	Review policy and interview staff to determine update cycle and retraining schedules.
Are roles and responsibilities clearly defined for each IT staff member?	Review employee-manning documents and interview employees to determine their day-to-day workflows.
Is there a separation of duties principle followed for IT staff?	Review management application configurations to determine who has access to make changes and approve changes.

Summary

Assessing policy and compliance requires understanding business goals and risks. This chapter covered many areas of policy and compliance that define the security culture of an organization. Having policies that are well written and effectively communicated is essential to protecting an organization from external and internal threats. In summary:

- Policies are not just nice to have but required by a number of laws and industry regulations.

- Policies are best measured against a maturity model to identify how well they are integrated into the business processes of the organization.

- You must balance access with security to make a policy effective and not cause users to either ignore the policy or look for ways to circumvent it.

- Assessing policies for compliance requires a strong understanding of an organization's business to map compliance requirements to policies and security controls.

- Cisco technologies can help to automate the auditing process by providing access to audit evidence and even automatically enforce compliance at the user level.

References in This Chapter

Guel, Michele. *A Short Primer for Developing Security Policies*. SANS, http://www.sans.org/security-resources/policies/Policy_Primer.pdf.

SANS Policy Project, http://www.sans.org/security-resources/policies/.

RFC for developing security policies

RFC2196 Site Security Handbook

NIST 800-100 Information Security Handbook: A Guide for Managers

Chapter 7

Infrastructure Security

The network infrastructure acts as the plumbing that provides the transport mechanism for data communication to occur. Without this critical facility, applications don't work, products don't get shipped, and your Facebook status doesn't get updated. The network's contribution is significant to the business process, making it a natural target for attackers. Cisco IOS is a mature platform that provides the intelligence and protective mechanisms that must be enabled by businesses to maximize a security posture. This chapter focuses on the auditing of routers, switches, and wireless devices for good security practices. It also covers the necessary security controls that keep these devices running while under attack.

Infrastructure Threats

The threats faced by infrastructure devices are focused at the device itself, its capability to pass data, or the manipulation of data in transit. The primary threats to the network infrastructure are:

- Unauthorized access

- Denial of service

- Traffic capture

- Layer 2 attacks

- Network service attacks

Unauthorized Access

Gaining unauthorized access to network infrastructure devices gives the attacker full control of the device and how and where the device forwards network traffic. This can result in the attacker having the capability to disable security features, logging, and management access to the device. Use of insecure management protocols, weak passwords, misconfiguration, and insecure in-band management can lead to unauthorized access to network devices.

Wireless networks take unauthorized access threats to a much higher level than wired connections. Radio frequencies are difficult to control and limit effectively, so unless the company creates a Faraday Cage around its building, the wireless signal will be visible outside the physical walls of the company. Without the proper security mechanisms in place for wireless, you might as well have an Ethernet jack in your company's parking lot that anyone can use and abuse.

Denial of Service

Denial of service can occur when WAN or Internet connections are saturated with traffic, services are attacked and left in an inoperative state, or a network device's packet-processing capabilities are saturated. A denial of service is more than a nuisance and can cost A company money lost productivity and the inability to operate the business.

Routers face denial of service through attacks targeting the bandwidth companies use to access the internet, VPN connections to branch offices, and WAN links. A distributive denial of service is the most common form of attack, and this kind of attack leverages a vast army of compromised devices on the Internet to disable access through bandwidth saturation or by exhausting TCP connection capabilities. Routers can also be vulnerable to denial of service attacks targeting routing protocols such as BGP that prevent the router from advertising or receiving routing information from other devices, isolating it from the network. Other router denial of service attacks are targeted at resource exhaustion on the router, maxing out CPU or memory utilization, which can cause the router to drop legitimate traffic.

A switch is designed to handle massive amounts of bandwidth, so denial of service from a switch is typically targeted at the switch protocols such as spanning tree. Creating switching loops or manipulating forwarding topologies can bring even the mightiest switch to its knees. A switch can also be susceptible to memory exhaustion and MAC address table flooding, which can impact traffic forwarding.

Wireless denial of service can take the forming of jamming, traffic flooding, or wireless protocol attacks. Each of these techniques results in the disruption of wireless service.

Traffic Capture

Loss of confidentiality can occur at the network infrastructure level through packet capture or sniffing. There are numerous techniques used to monitor network communications. An attacker can manipulate routing tables on a network, forcing traffic to flow through a controlled device that also secretly stores all packets that go by. On switches, an attacker can flood the switch with bogus MAC addresses in an attempt to fill its address tables and force the switch to broadcast packets received on a particular VLAN to all ports in that VLAN. Spanning tree can be manipulated to force a switch to think that the attacker has the root bridge in the network, forcing switched traffic to flow to the attacker instead of the core of the network. ARP poisoning is another mechanism that is also used to allow sniffing in a switched network and can be targeted at specific network devices. If the attacker can gain administrative control of the switch, he can also enable switchport monitoring functions called *span ports*, which can be used to monitor traffic entering or exiting the switch uplink ports.

The risk that people most often associate with wireless networking is eavesdropping. With communication between legitimate clients and the access point floating around in the ether, it is not difficult for an attacker with the right hardware to attempt to intercept this traffic. The attacker's success or failure greatly depends on the strength of the security controls used to protect the network.

Layer 2 Threats

Some of the most common network attacks are at layer 2 of the OSI model. These attacks are typically focused on trying to hijack a user's network connections, intercept traffic, or spoof a device's identity. These types of threats are relevant to both wired and wireless network infrastructure access methods.

- **Spoofing:** Spoofing occurs when an attacker masquerades as a legitimate device on the network using the IP and/or MAC address of another computer. This can be for forging network traffic or bypassing access control mechanisms based on simple IP address schemes. Attackers often use this mechanism to launch attacks on other systems to hide their real identities.

- **ARP spoofing:** Typically, when two devices communicate, they use ARP to resolve the MAC address of the device they want to communicate with and place that information in their ARP tables. ARP spoofing takes advantage of the ARP process by announcing to the network the IP and MAC address of another computer or the next hop router through a gratuitous or unsolicited ARP. When other devices receive this announcement, they update their tables and start sending traffic intended for the real destination to the fake one that the attacker controls. ARP spoofing works on wired or wireless connections and is a common method used to steal network credentials and sensitive information.

- **Session hijacking:** Session hijacking, also known as a man-in-the-middle attack, attempts to take control of an active or authenticated session, so that the attacker can bypass username and password access controls or steal credentials. TCP connections (such as web sessions) are most commonly attacked, and if the attacker is successful, he gets full visibility of the data being sent back and forth and he has the ability to modify it on the fly. The end system usually cannot tell that a connection has been compromised, making this a dangerous attack.

Network Service Threats

Two of the most important network services are DNS and DHCP, without which devices would not be able to resolve names to IP addresses or receive automatic configuration of network addressing. These services are not typically authenticated, and based on their importance, this makes them targets for attackers to compromise network devices.

DNS attacks on the network can occur when an attacker is able to sniff network requests for DNS lookups and respond to the requestor faster than the real DNS server can. Because the real DNS server is usually not on the same VLAN segment when the attacker replies with bogus information, the reply is accepted by the client because the attacker's DNS reply is the quickest to respond. Attackers do this so that they can control the victim's web browsing or network connections for session hijacking or eavesdropping. The attacker can run a proxy server that connects to the real servers or websites that the user wants to visit and record their sessions and passwords.

With DHCP attacks, attackers can configure rogue DHCP servers on a VLAN to respond to DHCP requests from network clients. Just like with DNS attacks, the attacker's DHCP server can respond to the client request quicker than the legitimate DHCP server, enabling the attacker to set the victim's IP, DNS, and next hop router configurations to point to the attacker for eavesdropping and session hijacking purposes.

Policy Review

Network infrastructure policy should create a strong foundation for the delivery of networking services to end users and business applications in a secure manner. Policy should help to address network threats by requiring security controls that take into account the organization's level of risk.

- **Administrator accounts:** All administrators should have their own accounts for the configuration of network devices. The purpose of this policy is to ensure that logging and accounting can be used to identify connection times, dates, and any changes made. Accounts should ideally reside in a centralized authentication, authorization, and accounting (AAA) system such as Cisco ACS. Local accounts should be used only for fall back logins in the event that the AAA server is not reachable, and not for general administrator login through a single account.

- **Passwords:** Password strength should be enforced in accordance with good security practices. Passwords should be stored in a protected format. All network devices should utilize password encryption so that they are not shown in an easily recoverable fashion in configuration files. Passwords should also be changed on a regular basis. One-time passwords through hardware tokens are preferred for preventing password compromise of sensitive administrator authentication credentials.

- **Secure management protocols:** All network management protocols should use the highest level of security as possible. SSHV2 and HTTPS should be used for interactive network device management. Access control lists (ACL) should be used to prevent access to management interfaces from unauthorized IP addresses or subnets.

SNMPV3 with encryption and authentication should be used for management systems whenever possible.

■ **Device hardening:** Devices should have all unneeded services disabled to present a smaller attack surface. Policy should enforce a baseline security configuration that follows recommended security practices.

■ **Login banners:** Login banners should be configured on all network devices. They should clearly state that unauthorized access is prohibited and that all connections are logged and monitored in accordance with appropriate laws.

■ **Change control:** Changes should be made in conjunction with a defined change control process. Policy enforcement of the change control mechanism makes it clear that changes outside of this process are strictly prohibited. Changes should be approved and logged with rollback capabilities.

■ **Least privilege access:** Access to network devices should follow the principle of least privilege, limiting configuration and modification to specific job roles. Help desk and first level administrators should be limited to monitoring and basic test functionality, and higher level access should be approved and reviewed on a regular basis.

■ **Wireless security:** It is important that an organization have a complete wireless policy that includes how and when access points should be configured. This policy should also outline how users are allowed to access the wireless network. Only approved wireless devices are to be used and connected to the company network. Wireless access points should have a baseline security configuration before being deployed. When the wired network adapter is active, the wireless is disabled. Some organizations also dictate that clients use a VPN when connecting with wireless or that wireless networks be firewalled from the production network.

Infrastructure Operational Review

During an infrastructure operations review, an auditor assesses the processes and procedures a business follows to manage the security of infrastructure network devices. To do this, an auditor typically starts with a review of network documentation to better understand the network services offered and to ensure that the organization has a clear picture of how the network is deployed. Networks have the tendency to grow at an exponential pace, and as businesses embrace the power of connecting on a global scale, the logical and physical data connections used must be clearly identified. In a perfect world, network documentation would always be up to date and accurately reflect every connection to every device. Unfortunately, as IT budgets are compressed and people are asked to do more with less, these are some of the important areas that often get overlooked.

Network documentation is not the only area that auditors should examine in an infrastructure operational review. The other aspects that should be reviewed are:

■ Administrative access

■ Configuration management

- Vulnerability management
- Disaster recovery

The Network Map and Documentation

When an auditor examines the network map, he looks for interconnections where assets of value could be at risk to identify areas that need to be inspected more closely. In addition to looking for risk, he also checks to see whether or not there is a process for updating IT configuration and documentation. How seriously a company takes standardization and documentation can be an indication of how well the operational aspects of security are conducted overall. The daily execution of security processes directly impacts the protection of key systems, and one ignored policy or procedure can result in a significant breach. Not many engineers like the documentation process, but few would argue about how important it is when there is a security incident.

Logical Diagrams

Logical diagrams detail the types of devices and protocols in use on the network. These diagrams don't show every port, but they indicate the flow of information through devices. A logical diagram helps the auditor identify potential high-risk areas to explore in-depth during the assessment process. A logical diagram is like an outline of the network and can be used as a basis for understanding how security features should be deployed, such as firewalls, IPS, or other technology.

Network service, VLANs, and logical network separations would be included in this type of document. An auditor should be able to look at this diagram and ascertain major network connectivity points and paths used to reach end systems. The point of a logical diagram is to be able to see quickly how the network is designed at a high level.

Physical Diagrams

A physical diagram tends to be the most detailed and is useful for troubleshooting a network problem or a security incident. Knowing what ports plug into what devices is essential for planning security defensive strategies and protecting network connections. Because of the level of detail and the rapidly changing environment, physical diagrams can be the most out of date. When assessing this type of documentation, you should also identify if the organization has a formal process for keeping physical diagrams current and recommend such a process if none exists. Management applications such as Cisco Works can automate the collection of physical connectivity information down to the switch port level.

Asset Location and Access Requirements

Knowing where key assets are located logically and physically on the network helps an auditor identify risk against the assets. Asset documentation should be kept up to date on all critical assets and include as much detail as possible regarding the services and connectivity requirements for each system. Knowing where an asset is located is a good start, but in addition, a review of access requirements detailing who should have access to the system is also relevant at this stage. Firewalls are covered more fully in Chapter 8, "Intrusion Prevention," VLAN separation by work group and baseline access control filtering in the infrastructure can go a long way toward protecting these systems. Knowing who should and should not be able to access the system makes creating and inspecting ACLs much easier later. Filtering network connections at multiple levels reduces risk by limiting exposure. Baseline access control features are available in all Cisco infrastructure devices and are an important part of defense in depth.

Data Flow and Traffic Analysis

How can you identify abnormal traffic if you don't know what normal traffic looks like? Most attacks are initially identified by rapid increases in traffic on either nonstandard ports or commonly used ports that are used to tunnel through firewalls and access devices. Having a network traffic baseline can help identify these anomalies and allow for quicker response. Auditors can also use this information to identify unneeded protocols and ineffective access lists. If a current baseline is not available, then the auditor can perform packet captures or configure netflow accounting to get an idea of what traffic actually goes across the wire. Many organizations are surprised when they compare what is supposed to be on the network versus what is actually on it. Network management platforms that understand netflow and Cisco MARS provide this information automatically in a nicely formatted report.

Administrative Accounts

Administrator accounts should be handled with the utmost care to prevent them from falling into the wrong hands. This might seem obvious, but auditors are often surprised to find that some organizations share the same username and password for administering network infrastructure devices. Each person who requires network device administrative access should have his own unique credentials that follow good password complexity practices. Utilizing usernames such as admi or administrator is discouraged because these are often targeted by attackers. Usernames should be constructed in a manner that makes them unique but does not give an indication about the access level of the account.

The creation of administrative accounts should have a documented process with management approval required for any accounts that allow modification of configuration and settings. Quarterly access reviews should be conducted to ensure that the principle of least privilege is followed. Locally configured fallback accounts are often configured to enable network device access in the event that the AAA server is unreachable. These accounts should not be used by employees, and the usernames and passwords should be stored securely in a safe, only to be used in case of emergencies. Employee termination should initiate immediate account suspension or deletion and password changes for fallback network device accounts.

Configuration Management

Configuration management processes and procedures should be in place to document and approve any and all changes to infrastructure devices. Organizations that have not developed and implemented change management systems are encouraged to do so to prevent uncontrolled device configuration that can become a troubleshooting nightmare and the source of security vulnerabilities.

All commands entered into network infrastructure devices should be logged through AAA and/or syslog. This record of activity is useful for identifying inappropriate behavior and to provide a history of network device interaction to assist with troubleshooting and security incident handling.

Network device configurations should have electronic and/or hard copy backups to archive current operating settings. Electronic backups should be stored in a secure manner with password protection and access control mechanisms to prevent unauthorized access.

Vulnerability Management

Organizations should stay up to date on vulnerabilities that might exist in the software on which network devices run. Vulnerability management is the process used to identify and remediate software or configuration weaknesses. Not following good vulnerability management practices can result in prolonged exposure to risk. Cisco offers email and SMS alerts from the Product Security Incident Response Team (PSIRT) that can give administrators warning if a vulnerability is found in Cisco devices. The alerts include details about the issue found, software versions where the bugs were fixed, and workarounds necessary to protect the system until it can be updated with new software.

Vulnerability scans should be conducted on a regular basis to identify weaknesses that might have been overlooked. The key to successful vulnerability management is an updated software and hardware inventory for the organization. That way, when a vulnerability is discovered, it's easy to look at the inventory to see what needs to be addressed. Automation of this process is recommended through management applications such as Cisco NCM because there is nothing more useless than outdated software or hardware inventory documentation.

Disaster Recovery

When disaster strikes, a good disaster recovery plan is critical to restoring service as quickly as possible. Networks should be designed with resiliency in mind, and that includes network device redundancy and failover capabilities. Disaster recovery planning uses a risk management process that is similar to risk identification in security. This subject is broad and not the main focus of this book; however, auditors must consider disaster recovery and planning documents as a part of network infrastructure operations reviews and should be on the lookout for single points of failure and weak recovery processes that could cause difficulties when dealing with a security incident.

Wireless Operations

All operational aspects discussed so far also apply to wireless security. Network maps, configuration management, and disaster recovery need to be considered when auditing a wireless installation. There are, however, some unique challenges that wireless presents that can be better managed by a specialized management application. The Wireless Control System (WCS) is software that helps wireless administrators effectively manage wireless security on their networks. It centralizes administration of the APs, the Wireless LAN Controllers (WLC), users, policies, logging, and reporting all on one console. With security-related information streaming from all connected controllers, the WCS can simplify the daily operations associated with managing wireless security.

Infrastructure Architecture Review

Without a secure networking environment, protecting applications and data becomes significantly more difficult. An auditor must inspect routers, switches, and wireless network devices to ensure that they are properly configured to afford the maximum amount of resiliency and protection of the routing and switching processes to keep packets flowing to their intended destinations. To that end, an auditor can group security functions together in a way that logically separates their configuration to make assessments easier. Cisco describes this separation of function as *logical planes* and provides a wealth of capabilities in IOS to protect network devices from attack and exploitation.

Logical planes group the various functions a network device must perform to pass traffic and interact with the network. Each of these logical planes operates at different levels in hardware and software. For example, the primary purpose of an IOS device is to move data from one interface to another as quickly as possible; to do this, the network device must understand the topology and which interface to send data through. Routing updates used to build topology awareness are sent to the network device and are handled by the CPU at the control plane, whereas data sent through the device destined for another computer on the network flow through the data plane, which uses dedicated forwarding hardware and barely impacts the CPU. Each plane has unique attack and defense characteristics that can be addressed through IOS security features. The three IOS security planes are:

- **Management plane:** Protocols and services necessary for authorized personnel or applications to configure and interact with the network device. The management plane can be thought of as the interactive plane in that this plane deals with all mechanisms used to send configuration tasks to the device.

- **Control plane:** The routing protocols and services that control traffic flow through the device. This type of traffic is directly processed by the network device itself.

- **Data plane:** The transmission of packets or frames going through the device. In this plane, the network device performs its primary functions of moving data from one part of the network to another. Policy enforcement also occurs here, and it directly controls what network traffic is allowed through or discarded.

The next sections cover general network device protection mechanisms that can apply to any IOS device. Subsequent sections cover router and switch-specific features. It's important to note that with the proliferation of switching modules in routers and route processors in switches, the concepts of router and switch are more about functions. Auditors need to truly understand how the network device is used and the protective capabilities available. Not all security features are available on all Cisco platforms, so glancing through the device documentation is recommended to make sure that the appropriate security controls are implemented.

Management Plane Auditing

Maintaining and protecting management control of network devices is the first area that should be assessed when auditing IOS devices. Many attacks today that target network devices look for common mistakes in configurations, such as leaving default passwords or using insecure protocols such as telnet to manage network devices. If an attacker can gain administrative control of a networking device, he has absolute control over how that device transmits data and where it sends it. Limiting access to these services enables the administrator to take advantages of GUI configuration tools such as Cisco Configuration Professional without opening up a web interface to the Internet and potential attack.

Disabling unneeded services and features is fundamental to device hardening. If you don't use a feature, turn it off because a disabled service—even one with a vulnerability—cannot be exploited directly if it's not enabled. Network devices with default configurations should never be allowed on a production network because they simply beg to be hacked. Cisco has done a good job of making its devices easy to configure and install, but as with any "easy" install, there is usually a tradeoff in security. Default passwords and services need to be changed and disabled. It falls on you as an auditor to ensure device configurations reflect these best practices.

Currently, Cisco-recommended best practices regarding the protection of the Management plane require adherence to the following:

- **Restrict device accessibility:** Limit who can gain access to configuration ports and protocols, and the networks address ranges that can interact with the device.

- **Present Legal Notification:** Ensure that all interactive login prompts have the appropriate legal banners in place so that those connecting understand that the device should be connected to by authorized personnel only and that all connections and activities are monitored and logged.

- **Authenticate all access:** All users and groups should be authenticating with unique credentials.

- **Authorize all actions:** Limit administrative access to the least privileges necessary.

- **Ensure confidentiality of device configurations and sessions:** Protect all configuration files and data with encryption and limit the ability to view and copy protected data. Always encrypt configuration sessions that travel over insecure mediums such as the Internet or user-facing subnets.

■ **Log and account for all device access:** Log all access and configuration changes to network devices.

Cisco Device Management Access

Cisco devices can be managed in numerous ways. These management interfaces are designed to give command-line access directly to the IOS, connectivity to built-in, web-based device management software, or SNMP access for centralized management systems. To protect these connections, it is important to disable any management options not used and to restrict access to those that are. Cisco provides four classes of management capabilities for IOS network devices:

■ **Physical ports:** Console port for direct serial connection into the device cli, Aux (auxiliary) port for dial backup, or out-of-band management in case the device is not reachable.

■ **VTY (virtual) ports:** Software terminal ports that can be reached via IP and run configurable services such as telnet and SSH.

■ **Web ports:** An internal HTTP and HTTPS server are available for providing access to internal web device management software.

■ **SNMP:** Cisco supports SNMP v1-3 as management access to a network device with read and write capabilities.

Physical Ports

The aux port is useful only if you have a modem attached to it for dial backup or some other out-of-band management purpose. This port happily accepts a connection just like a console port, and network engineers sometimes forget to protect it. The following example shows what to look for in the configuration to ensure that the aux port is disabled.

```
line aux 0
  no exec
  transport input none
```

Virtual Ports

Virtual terminal sessions are useful for gaining access to a network device across an IP network for management purposes. By default, there are five virtual terminal ports enabled on IOS devices (numbered 0–4), but more can be added if needed. These ports are generally used by a protocol such as telnet or SSH. Consider these connections just as you would physical ports; if they are not used, they should be disabled. This is easily accomplished with the following commands:

```
line vty 0 4
 login
 no exec
```

For many organizations, the benefit of virtual terminal connections for remote management means that disabling them is not an option. Because telnet sends all traffic in clear text, it is highly recommended that SSH be used for communicating to Cisco IOS

Table 7-1 *IOS Management Access Restriction Examples*

IOS Device Management Access Restrictions	Commands Applied to Physical or Virtual Ports
No incoming connections	transport input none
No outgoing management connections from the device	transport output none
Only SSH permitted for incoming connections	transport input ssh
Only telnet permitted for incoming connections	transport input telnet
SSH or telnet permitted for incoming connections	transport input telnet ssh
Only SSH permitted for outgoing connections	transport output ssh

devices. If telnet must be used, limit the networks that can access telnet to only management subnets by using the **access-class** command to specify the IP address range. There are various methods for restricting access to specific protocols for virtual terminal connections. Table 7-1 shows a few examples of access restrictions and the commands that auditors look for in the configuration.

The following example shows what the configuration would look like for a network with a management subnet of 192.168.1.0 and a policy that specifies only ssh is allowed to manage network devices and that ssh sessions must originate from the management subnet. The session is also configured to time out after being idle for 3 minutes.

```
access list 15 permit 192.168.1.0 0.0.0.255
line vty 0 4
 access class 15 in
 transport input ssh
exec-timeout 3
```

Note The configurations used in this chapter are examples and do not indicate every possible way a device can be configured. It is up to the auditor to test the device to ensure that the necessary security functions are achieved.

SSH

SSH is a much more secure management protocol for interaction with IOS devices over the network. It is not enabled by default, but luckily, it is easy to configure. Before SSH can be configured, the IOS device needs a hostname and domain name. These are used to help generate the SSH key that authenticates the device. The following commands are entered to configure hostname and domain:

```
hostname Myroutername
ip domain-name mydomain.com
```

After you have the host name and domain configured, you can now generate an RSA key. You will be asked how large of a key you want to generate (between 360–2048 bits), with larger being more difficult to break. The following example shows the command to generate an RSA key with a 1024-bit modulus:

```
crypto key generate rsa modulus 1024
```

You should also configure a few other parameters to better protect SSH from brute force password-guessing attacks and management sessions being left unattended, namely time-out and authentication retries. These parameters are configured with the following commands:

```
ip ssh time-out 60
ip ssh authentication-retries 2
```

Web Ports

Web-based configuration and device management tools for Cisco network devices can dramatically improve the productivity of network administrators by providing a graphical alternative to command-line configuration. The Cisco Configuration Professional provides configuration capability for many of the advanced security and connectivity features available in routers. Likewise, on switch and wireless devices, there is a built-in graphical device manager. The integrated device managers require that web-based access be enabled to connect to these applications. Most Cisco devices come from the factory with basic configurations applied and these tools enabled, so if they are not to be used because of the presence of enterprise management applications such as Cisco Security Manager, then it is a simple process to turn them off. To disable access to http and https configuration capabilities, you simply type the following commands:

```
no ip http server
no ip http secure-server
```

Organizations that use the functionality of the built-in device manager can secure those connections by enforcing the use of SSL encryption. This is accomplished by enabling https instead of http and ensures that configuration management sessions are not sent in clear text. It's also recommended that ACLs be implemented to restrict access to the device management service from approved network address ranges and set timeout values for idle connections. The following configuration example shows what an auditor would look for to determine whether web access is properly secured:

```
no ip http server

ip http secure-server

ip http timeout-policy idle 180 life 7200 requests 100
```

```
access-list 10 permit 192.168.1.0 0.0.0.255
access-list 10 deny any log

ip http access-class 10
```

Local Authentication and Password Protection

Local authentication can be used for IOS devices and simply involves configuring a username and password into the device. Whenever there is a password stored in an IOS devices configuration, it's important to make sure that the command **service password-encryption** is present to prevent someone who gains access to the configuration files from viewing the passwords. You then tell the device to require authentication credentials for management connections by applying the login command to the configuration to each virtual terminal port and the console port. The following configuration example shows how this is accomplished:

```
username admin secret password
line vty 0 4
login local
```

Cisco IOS provides 16 levels of access control at the router level to define individual user roles and the commands that they can use. Most organizations don't use anywhere close to this level of granularity, but these features are useful in defining limited support monitoring roles for a helpdesk by controlling access down to the command level. By default, when a user first logs into an IOS device, they are at privilege level 1 (denoted by a > at the command prompt). To access configuration and diagnostic options, they enter enable and input an enable password that grants them level 15 (denoted by a # at the command prompt). When defining a username and password, there is an option to supply a default privilege level, which immediately places the user at the appropriate access level after successful authentication. The following command is an example of what an auditor would see for a user named "support" with full configuration privileges and an encrypted password.

```
username support privilege 15 secret $1$ACdo$bP9ojwtxHv.2GsCdURTOy/
```

Of course this manual method leaves a lot to be desired from a security standpoint because it does not allow differentiated user access or logging of activities. Although AAA is the preferred method for addressing management control of IOS devices, local authentication should be configured in conjunction with AAA as an authentication option of last resort, in case the authentication server that AAA uses becomes unavailable. The account created for this purpose should be protected and only used in an emergency.

AAA

Authentication, authorization, and accounting can be used to centrally manage and log all login and configuration activity on IOS devices. Best practices recommend using AAA for access control of network devices, as it provides robust logging and centralized user authentication. AAA is a framework used to logically separate three security functions that control IOS device administration.

- **Authentication:** User identity and credential verification
- **Authorization:** User privileges and access rights
- **Accounting:** Records session activity details and connection information

AAA is enabled with the aaa new-model command that follows:

```
aaa new-model
```

After enabling AAA, you must identify the authentication servers used. AAA supports a wide range of servers, including the Radius and Cisco TACACS+. Radius and TACACS+ provide similar capabilities, except TACACS+ offers the ability to define command-level authorization requirements for IOS devices. The commands that follow show how to configure a Radius and TACACS+ server and a shared secret key used for authentication.

```
radius-server host 192.168.1.1
radius-server key Wx2rfsd2QQ
tacacs-server host 192.168.1.1
tacacs-server key Wx2rfsd2QQ
```

After the server or servers are configured, enable their use for AAA by specifying the authentication method to be used and in what order. You can specify multiple authentication methods, as shown in the following configuration, but the second or third methods are used only if the IOS device cannot reach the first authentication sever. A credential check failure results in denied access and no other login mechanisms are used. As a backup in the event of an authentication server failure, it is recommended to use a local username and password for these situations. This can be accomplished by using an authentication method local at the end.

```
aaa authentication login default group tacacs+ radius local
aaa authorization exec default group tacacs+ radius local
```

After the authentication and authorization methods are defined, the accounting function should be configured to log all configuration and authentication activities on the IOS device. Auditors should ensure that accounting is configured to record the following at a minimum:

- Authentication failures:

    ```
    aaa accounting send stop-record authentication failure
    ```
- Sessions to the IOS device, including username, date, start and stop times, the device IP address, and the user source IP address:

    ```
    aaa accounting exec default start-stop group tacacs+
    ```

- Commands entered, username, and time on the IOS device:

```
aaa accounting commands 15 default start-stop group tacacs+
```

- System-level events such as the system reboots or when accounting is turned on or off:

```
aaa accounting system default start-stop group tacacs+
```

Legal Notices

All network devices must have an appropriate legal notice presented to the user whenever they connect to the IOS device, to remind the user that the system they are connecting to is only for authorized personnel, and that their actions will be monitored. Legal notices can be defined for any type of interactive session. It's important to make sure that all legal banners are approved by the company's legal counsel to ensure that all appropriate laws and regulations are adhered to. The following is an example of a standard banner and the commands used to configure it:

```
login banner %
UNAUTHORIZED ACCESS TO THIS DEVICE IS PROHIBITED
You must have explicit, authorized permission to access or configure this device.
Unauthorized attempts and actions to access or use this system may result in civil
and/or criminal penalties.
All activities performed on this device are logged and monitored.
%
```

This banner should be applied to all connections and can be applied to virtual terminal and console connections. The key to writing a good banner is to make sure that it is written in a way that leaves no question that the network device is for authorized personnel only and that connections are logged and monitored.

SNMP

SNMP is the mostly widely deployed management protocol for network devices. Many network management platforms use SNMP for configuration and reporting on interface state, traffic load, and other statistics. Cisco NAC also uses SNMP to configure user network ports to the appropriate VLAN after authentication. Securing this facility is critical to protecting network devices.

There are three versions of SNMP:

- **Version 1:** The original and least secure
- **Version 2c:** The most widely supported
- **Version 3:** Supports authentication and encryption

The biggest problem with SNMP from a security perspective is that version 1 and 2c have no authentication mechanism, and all data is sent in clear text. Community strings are used as a form of "password," but sniffers pick this off of the wire quickly. Access to any management interface with no authentication is a risky proposition. If SNMP is not used, then it is a good idea to disable it. By default, Cisco IOS devices do not have SNMP enabled. To disable SNMP, the following command is entered from the global configuration prompt:

```
no snmp-server
```

There are a number of SNMP security practices that auditors should be on the lookout for when inspecting IOS devices:

- Be selective in SNMP use.

- Restrict SNMP to read-only queries.

- Deny SNMP requests to download IP routing and ARP tables with SNMP view configuration.

- Community strings are like passwords; treat them accordingly.

- Never use default community strings.

- Use strong password practices to create community strings.

- Restrict incoming SNMP access attempts to authorized SNMP management stations with ACLs.

- Use SNMP v3 when possible for authentication and encryption.

- Ensure SNMP traps are regularly monitored.

Syslog

Syslog is a standard-based logging facility that IOS devices can use to record security events, operational data, system status, traffic information, and connection information. This information is critical for security because it acts as a day-to-day record of network device activity. Good security practices require centrally logging syslog data from all network devices. Enabling syslog is a simple process that requires selecting a source interface for sending a syslog server address and the level of detail you want to send. There are eight levels of logging available, as shown in Table 7-2.

The default level of logging is informational and includes all of the messages that would be generated at any of the numerically lower levels. Debugging is the highest and can generate a significant amount of logging information on a heavily used device.

The configuration that follows shows an example of what the configuration would look like for an IOS device configured to send debugging level logging information to a syslog server:

```
logging source-interface ethernet 0
logging host 192.168.1.5
logging trap debugging
```

Table 7-2 *Syslog Logging Levels*

Log Level	Alert Level	Types of Messages
0	Emergencies	System is unusable.
1	Alerts	Immediate action needed. Failover events.
2	Critical	Critical conditions. Denied packets and connections because of failure condition.
3	Errors	Error identified. AAA server connection failure, CPU, memory, and routing issues.
4	Warnings	ACL denial, fragmentation, and routing protocol errors.
5	Notification	Device configuration changes, user connections, invalid logins, and user session information.
6	Informational	AAA events, ACL logging, DHCP activity, TCP/UDP connection, and teardown.
7	Debugging	Detailed debugging information, TCP/UDP packet handling, IPsec, and VPN tunnel creation.

NTP

Configuring Network Time Protocol (NTP) on a router is important for making sure that log messages accurately reflect time. Time is used to correlate log messages between multiple devices and can be essential in piecing together a chain of events during a security incident. It is recommended that all IOS devices be set up to receive NTP from a trusted source and use authentication whenever possible.

When configuring NTP for the purposes of logging, there are two commands that need to be entered to make the router time stamp each log and debug message:

```
service timestamps debug datetime localtime show-timezone msec
service timestamps log datetime localtime show-timezone msec
```

A router can perform multiple roles in an NTP solution. It can receive time as a client or provide time to other devices as an NTP server. Following are examples showing two of these roles: one as NTP client and another one acting as an NTP server.

■   Set the time zone for the router:

```
clock timezone PST -8
```

■   Set daylight savings time if appropriate:

```
clock summer-time PDT recurring
```

- Allow NTP to update the hardware clock on the device:

```
ntp update-calendar
```

- Define the NTP server IP address client uses for NTP:

```
ntp server 192.168.1.10
```

- Set up NTP authentication with matching passwords and key numbers:

```
ntp authentication-key 10 md5 00071A1507545A545C 7
ntp trusted-key 10
```

- Indicate that NTP is using authentication:

```
ntp authenticate
```

- If the router is to provide time to other devices, set as master:

```
ntp master
```

Netflow

Originally developed as a mechanism to count packets used in billing service provider customers, Netflow has become a useful source of security event data by allowing routers and switches to gather traffic information that can be used to create a baseline of network usage. This baseline can then be used to detect anomalies that might represent an attack or worm outbreak. Practically all Cisco routers and many Cisco switches support Netflow, and it can drastically improve visibility into what is traversing the network at any given moment. Combine Netflow accounting with a product like MARS that uses Netflow to automate traffic baselining and anomaly detection, and you can start to see the extensive network visibility afforded by this technology.

Netflow is enabled on an interface-by-interface basis for any interface or VLAN that traffic monitoring is required. The example that follows shows the two different ways to enable Netflow on an interface and then the optional export to a Netflow collector like MARS:

```
ip cef
!
interface FastEthernet0/0
ip route-cache flow
```

Or:

```
ip cef
!
interface FastEthernet0/0
ip flow ingress
```

Configuration for Netflow export to a Netflow collector is as follows:

```
ip flow-export version 9
ip flow-export destination 192.168.1.7 9997
```

Control Plane Auditing

An IOS device's control plane is responsible for topology awareness and building routing tables used in directing traffic. Control plane traffic is sent to the IOS device and consists of services such as routing updates, spanning tree, ARP, and Cisco discovery protocol. While the control plane of a network device is robust, direct attacks targeting these services can bring the device's processor to its silicon knees if the proper protection mechanisms and defensive strategies are not in place. IOS hardening and control plane policy are two of the most important areas that auditors inspect to defend router processing resources.

IOS Hardening

For the most part, many services that are unnecessary in modern networks and used to be turned on by default in IOS versions prior to 12.X are disabled in current versions of software. This doesn't mean that they can't be turned on by accident, though, and as such, it's up to the auditor to make sure that they are not enabled in configurations. Because these commands are disabled by default, you will not see them in an IOS device configuration unless they have been explicitly added. These services can be used by attackers to gather information on remote networks. Placing no in front of each command disables these unnecessary services if they are accidentally enabled.

Global services disabled by default are:

```
no ip finger
no ip identd
no service tcp-small-servers
no service udp-small-servers
```

IP-directed broadcast has been disabled by default on all interfaces since the 11.2 version of IOS. It used to make certain DoS attacks possible by allowing the IOS device to pass data sent to the broadcast address of a subnet across the network, forcing every device on that subnet to respond. Most host systems have updated TCP/IP stacks that do not allow these types of attacks to work. When auditing configuration, look for the command **ip directed-broadcast** on any interface. The following command disables the feature if it is inadvertently enabled:

```
interface Ethernet 0
no ip directed-broadcast
```

There are a number of services enabled on IOS devices for legacy compatibility that are not disabled by default. Some of these services provide some value in initial device setup, but they are not useful in production.

Source routing can allow an attacker to manipulate the way an IOS device forwards received packets by influencing what devices are considered the next hop for routing. Source routing ignores the routing table all together and looks inside the IP packet to figure out where to go next. This should be disabled on all interfaces.

```
no ip source-route
```

The bootp service is used when an IOS device is first turned on and has no configuration information. The device attempts to get an IP address from bootp and then download a configuration via tftp. This behavior can be exploited, so the recommendation is to disable the bootp feature:

```
no ip bootp server
```

PAD is a legacy protocol from the X.25 days that enables character-mode terminals to connect to the network. There is little security in this protocol and it has practically no use in today's networks. The following command is used to disable this feature:

```
no service pad
```

Cisco Discovery Protocol (CDP) is a Layer 2 protocol used to automatically discover other Cisco devices that are directly connected on a network segment. CDP provides information about IP addresses, IOS versions, devices types, and other useful troubleshooting data. From a security standpoint, CDP has no authentication mechanism, and it blindly sends information out regardless of who or what sees it. It is recommended you turn off CDP completely on devices where it is not used; however, in situations where it is actively part of a network management application or where IP Telephony is used, it should be disabled on all public or user-facing interfaces where it is unnecessary. The following commands are used to disable CDP globally or on a specific interface.

To globally disable CDP, use the following command:

```
no cdp run
```

To disable CDP on public or user-facing interfaces, use the following commands:

```
interface Ethernet 0
no cdp enable
```

It is also recommended you disable MOP (Maintenance Operations protocol), which is another legacy protocol used to support Digital Equipment Corp terminals. Unless these terminals make an unforeseen comeback, this protocol is safe to turn off. It is enabled by default on Ethernet interface and can be disabled using the following commands:

```
interface eth 0
no mop enabled
```

IP redirects and IP proxy ARP are two other IP protocol options that are enabled by default and should be disabled. IP redirects are used when a router sends an ICMP packet to a host redirecting its output to a different router on the same subnet. It is used to help hosts find the best default gateway, so it can be used for reconnaissance or other attacks on a network. Proxy ARP is a mechanism where a router can respond to an ARP request for a MAC address on a remote subnet that it knows about from its routing tables. This lets the router respond for the remote host if the local host does not have a default gateway set. This function can be used to perform ARP poisoning attacks on remote devices that would normally not be possible because ARP should not pass through the router. To disable this feature, the following commands must be entered under each interface:

```
interface eth 0
no ip redirects
no ip proxy-arp
```

Routing Protocols

When verifying secure configuration of routing protocols on routers and switches, the main area to look at is peer authentication. Peer authentication is used to restrict unauthorized peers from exchanging routing information and influencing the routing process. Not only should routing peers be authenticated, but the authentication should be protected with MD5 rather than exchanging passwords in clear text. The use of MD5 reduces the risk of someone sniffing the shared secret password. Peer authentication is accomplished in different ways depending on the routing protocols in use. The following examples show how each routing protocol is configured for peer authentication and what to look for when inspecting a router's configuration:

- BGP

```
router bgp 65001
neighbor 192.168.19.21 remote-as 65002
neighbor 192.168.19.21 password 7 05080F1C22431F5B4A
```

- OSPF

```
interface FastEthernet0/0
  ip address 192.168.192.1 255.255.255.0
  ip ospf message-digest-key 1 md5 cisco123
!
router ospf 20
  network 192.168.192.0 0.0.0.255 area 0
  area 0 authentication message-digest
```

- EIGRP

```
key chain authchain
  key 1
```

```
   key-string cisco123
 !
interface FastEthernet0/0
 ip address 192.168.192.1 255.255.255.0
 ip authentication mode eigrp 100 md5
 ip authentication key-chain eigrp 100 authchain
 !
router eigrp 100
 network 192.168.192.0
```

■ RIP

```
key chain authchain
 key 1
 key-string cisco123
 !
interface FastEthernet0/0
 ip address 192.168.192.1 255.255.255.0
 ip rip authentication key-chain authchain
 ip rip authentication mode md5
 !
router rip
 network 192.168.192.0
 version 2
```

Protecting the Control Plane

Control plane policing (CoPP) is a technique used on routers and switches to protect the control plane of the network device. CoPP utilizes QoS and ACL features in the IOS to permit, deny, or rate limit traffic to the device's route processor. The IOS uses these capabilities to protect against DoS attacks, reconnaissance, and other situations that can overwhelm a network device's capability to process network traffic. To accomplish this protection, the IOS uses the modular QOS command line to configure policies based on traffic classification schemes that can be used to segment, prioritize, and rate limit routing control and management processes to maintain device functionality under attack.

The key to a successful implementation of CoPP requires a strong understanding of the types of traffic that exists on the network and classifying the protocols and services that are essential to router function and management. Grouping services makes it easier to create the ACLs and policy maps used to differentiate traffic and apply enforcement policy. The following list is a sample classification structure that can be used for an organization:

■ **Routing:** BGP, OSPF, EIGRP, and ECT

■ **Management:** Interactive configuration, reporting, and monitoring

- **Undesirable:** Known unwanted or malicious packets

- **Default:** Other traffic that might be destined for the device

After the classification scheme is constructed, ACLs are used to identify matching traffic being sent to the device. The following code example shows the ACLs that would match the previous sample classification scheme:

```
ip access-list extended coppacl-routing
permit tcp any gt 1024 192.168.19.0 0.0.0.255 eq bgp
permit tcp any eq bgp 192.168.19.0 0.0.0.255 gt 1024 established
permit tcp any gt 1024 192.168.19.0 0.0.0.255 eq 639
permit tcp any eq 639 192.168.19.0 0.0.0.255 gt 1024 established
permit tcp any 192.168.19.0 0.0.0.255 eq 646
permit udp any 192.168.19.0 0.0.0.255 eq 646
permit ospf any 192.168.19.0 0.0.0.255
permit ospf any host 224.0.0.5
permit ospf any host 224.0.0.6
permit eigrp any 192.168.19.0 0.0.0.255
permit eigrp any host 224.0.0.10
!
ip access-list extended coppacl-management
permit tcp 192.168.0.0 0.0.255.255 host 192.168.19.2 eq ssh

ip access-list extended coppacl-undesirable
permit icmp any any fragments
permit udp any any fragments
permit tcp any any fragments
permit ip any any fragments
permit udp any any eq 1434
permit tcp any any eq 639 rst
permit tcp any any eq bgp rst
ip access-list extended coppacl-default
permit tcp any any
permit udp any any
permit icmp any any
permit ip any any
```

The classification access lists are then applied to class maps:

```
!
class-map match-all coppclass-routing
    match access-group name coppacl-routing
class-map match-all coppclass-management
    match access-group name coppacl-management
class-map match-all coppclass-undesirable
```

```
    match access-group name coppacl-undesirable
class-map match-all coppclass-default
    match access-group name coppacl-default
```

After the class maps are configured, they are used to create the protective policy maps, which control how much data from each class of traffic is allowed to the processor of the network device:

```
!
policy-map copp-policy
     class coppclass-undesirable
           police 8000 1500 1500 conform-action drop exceed-action drop
     class coppclass-management
           police 100000 20000 20000 conform-action transmit exceed-action drop
class coppclass-routing
     police 1000000 50000 50000 conform-action transmit exceed-action transmit
class coppclass-default
     police 10000000 100000 100000 conform-action transmit exceed-action drop
```

The final step is to apply the policy map to the control plane. This is accomplished with the following commands:

```
!
control-plane
    service-policy input copp-policy
```

CoPP is available in multilayer switches and routers and can be complicated to configure depending on the network environment. Auditors need to understand this feature from a control perspective to realize where it fits in protecting infrastructure devices.

Not all switching platforms support CoPP, so auditors are encouraged to review the Cisco feature navigator for more information about whether or not a specific device has this feature. For the most part, it is available in routers running IOS 12.3t and above and Catalyst 4500k and 6500k switches. For more information, go to http://tools.cisco.com/ITDIT/CFN/.

Data Plane Auditing

The data plane consists of the traffic generated by the various end systems connected to the network. The primary purpose of this aspect of network devices is to make sure that only authorized traffic is allowed to pass through the network device. There are many attacks that use abnormal data or manipulated packets to exploit other systems and gain information about firewall rules and services. Filtering data so that only expected traffic is allowed through and the logging of abnormal ports and protocols can go a long way in identifying malicious behavior. For the auditor, data plane auditing involves inspecting ACLs and essential data plane protection features such as spoof prevention.

Access Control Lists

ACLs are the building blocks of network policy control. ACLs are used extensively to identify host addresses and protocols for not only traffic control, but many other security features, many of which have been described in this chapter.

ACLs come in three forms:

- **Standard access lists:** These are designed to permit or deny based on source address.

- **Extended access lists:** These permit or deny based on source, destination, and protocol or ports used.

- **Named access lists:** These provide a much more descriptive way of identifying access lists and allow for the editing of individual lines in a multi-line list.

ACLs can be used for many purposes on a router. Having an ACL that is not applied to an interface or service serves no function, so it is important to track down where the ACL is being used to verify its intended purpose. Some examples of ACL commands include:

- Standard access list:

  ```
  access-list 1 permit 10.1.1.0 0.0.0.255
  ```
- Extended access list:

  ```
  access-list 101 permit ip any 10.1.1.0 0.0.0.255
  ```
- Named access list:

  ```
  ip access-list extended inside_to_outside
  permit tcp host 10.1.1.1 host 10.10.1.10 eq telnet
  ```

iACLs

Infrastructure ACLs (iACL) are commonly used by service providers and by companies to help prevent direct attacks against their internal networking devices from the Internet. The goal is to create a basic ACL that blocks traffic that you know does not belong on the network, such as private addresses detailed in RFC1918, and special use addresses detailed in RFC3330. These ACLs can help prevent spoofing of an organization's assigned IP ranges by denying any external source trying to use the organization's own assigned addresses. This type of ingress filtering can be a basic first line of defense deployed before a firewall on the edge network devices. The following example configuration shows how the access list can be applied for an iACL that would be deployed on an edge router.

■   RFC 3330 addresses:

```
access-list 110 deny ip host 0.0.0.0 any
access-list 110 deny ip 127.0.0.0 0.255.255.255 any
access-list 110 deny ip 192.0.2.0 0.0.0.255 any
access-list 110 deny ip 224.0.0.0 31.255.255.255 any
```

■   RFC1918 addresses:

```
access-list 110 deny ip 10.0.0.0 0.255.255.255 any
access-list 110 deny ip 172.16.0.0 0.15.255.255 any
access-list 110 deny ip 192.168.0.0 0.0.255.255 any
access-list 110 deny ip 169.223.0.0 0.0.255.255 any
```

■   Block spoofing of an assigned IP address range:

```
access-list 110 deny ip any your.ip.range.0 0.0.0.255 any
```

Unicast Reverse Path Forwarding

Unicast Reverse Path Forwarding (uRFP) automates the process of providing antispoof protection for networks by adding the capability for an IOS device to look into its forwarding tables and determine whether or not the traffic sent to it is supposed to be reachable from the interface in which it was received. If there is not a route to the source address of the packet through the interface, the packet is dropped. This feature requires Cisco express forwarding to be enabled to work.

There are two modes available for configuring uRFP: strict mode and loose mode. Strict mode is designed for networks that typically have one path available to a particular destination and the destination is reachable only from that interface.

Configuration of uRFP strict mode:

```
interface ethernet 0
          ip verify unicast source reachable-via rx
```

Loose mode is useful for networks that have multiple interfaces that can receive a source address because of load balancing or redundant connections. This mode allows the packet's source destination to be reachable from any interface on the device, not just the one it was received on.

Configuration of uRFP loose mode:

```
Interface serial 1
          Ip verify unicast source reachable-via any
```

Layer 2 Security

Switches, if properly configured, can act as a first line of defense for the network. Unlike a router, switches can be taken out of the box, plugged into the wall, and will happily start passing traffic with no configuration. Of course, these default configurations leave the switch vulnerable to many types of attacks, which is one of the reasons Cisco has added so many security features and capabilities to switching software. Properly configured switches can make a powerful security device, which means that auditors need to inspect the switch to make sure that the organization is making the best use of the features available. This section covers a number of best practices that should be followed to minimize risk present at the entry point to the network.

VTP

VLAN Trunking Protocol (VTP) is a layer 2 protocol used for automatically configuring and sharing VLAN database information in a Cisco switched network. This protocol eases the administrative burden on VLAN management across switches and can prevent misconfiguration or inconsistencies in VLAN naming and numbering. By default, a switch shares this information with other directly connected switches without requiring authentication, making it vulnerable to manipulation through this protocol.

VTP has three modes of operation:

- Server mode enables a switch to create and share VLANs with other switches.

- Client mode lets a switch receive VLAN configurations and pass VTP information, but it cannot create or modify VLANs locally.

- Transparent mode prevents a switch from accepting VTP configuration information from a VTP server, but it passes VTP packets to other switches.

VTP requires the creation of a VTP domain that is used to determine what VLANs are configured for a given set of switches. To participate in VTP, the domain must be the same. Secure authentication is enabled through a password that prevents unauthorized devices from joining the VTP domain and is a required practice for secure use of VTP. The following commands show how to configure a VTP with a password:

```
vtp domain ciscolab
vtp password cisco123
vtp mode server
```

VTP is not a required service for a switched network to operate and can be disabled with the following command:

```
vtp mode off
```

Port Security

MAC flooding is a common attack used to force packet capture on a switch. The attacker floods the switch with bogus MAC addresses, filling up its address table databases. After the tables are exhausted, the switch forwards all packets to every port (instead of the ones that the traffic is destined for). In a switched network, this can be used to allow the capture and reconstruction of any traffic on a particular VLAN segment. Cisco helps address this problem through a switch feature called *dynamic port security*. Dynamic port security configures the switch to learn a specified number of MAC addresses, limiting how many devices can communicate on the port and prevent MAC address table exhaustion. Setting the switch to only accept two MAC addresses provides access for a phone and a PC and prevents any more from being learned. Following is an example of how port security is configured:

```
interface GigabitEthernet0/1
 switchport mode access
 switchport port-security maximum 2
 switchport port-security
 switchport port-security violation restrict
```

DHCP Snooping

DHCP is an essential infrastructure service that provides network configuration information for end-user network devices. Protecting this service can prevent an attacker from setting up his own DHCP server on a user VLAN to control endpoint configuration parameters such as default gateways and DNS server addresses. Cisco offers DHCP snooping that monitors DHCP requests and replies to create a binding table to map IP addresses to switch ports and to prevent unauthorized devices from responding to DHCP requests. In addition, DHCP snooping can also verify the MAC address if the request is the same as the MAC address on the switch port to prevent attackers from imitating a denial of service through DHCP starvation attacks. This feature is enabled per VLAN and is used in a number of other layer 2 protection mechanisms. The following is an example configuration of DHCP snooping:

```
ip dhcp snooping
ip dhcp snooping vlan 1-100
ip dhcp snooping verify mac-address
```

After DHCP snooping is enabled, interfaces that are connected to DHCP servers (or are supposed to respond to requests) must be identified individually. The following command appears on these interfaces:

```
interface GigabitEthernet 0/1
ip dhcp snooping trust
```

Dynamic ARP Inspection

ARP is used for devices to query the network for IP-to-MAC address resolution. In typical network communications, devices reply to ARPs, but devices also have the capability to announce their MAC address through an unsolicited ARP, aptly named gratuitous ARP. An attacker can send a gratuitous ARP packet claiming to have the IP address of another endpoint (such as a phone) on the voice VLAN. The default behavior in TCP/IP is for all devices that receive the gratuitous ARP to change their ARP tables with the newly learned IP-to-MAC address. Any traffic destined for the spoofed system flows to the attacker, allowing for sniffing or other mischief. This technique is often used for man-in-the-middle attacks. To combat this, Dynamic ARP Inspection can be configured on a Cisco switch to work in conjunction with DHCP snooping to record the IP and MAC addresses of devices that receive IPs from a DHCP server. If an attacker attempts to send a gratuitous ARP pretending to be another device, it will be blocked by the switch because it does not match what the switch has recorded. The configuration of Dynamic ARP Inspection is configured for selected VLANs globally on a switch with the following command:

```
ip arp inspection vlan 1-100
```

To allow multiple ARP requests on switch trunk ports, you must tell the switch to trust the trunk port to prevent blocking on these links. The following commands are an example of what you see on switch trunk links:

```
interface GigabitEthernet 0/48
ip arp inspection trust
```

IP Source Guard

Spoofing an IP address is as easy as typing the address in the configuration settings on a network interface card. To prevent this, IP Source Guard can be configured to filter IP traffic based on addresses and MACs learned through DHCP snooping or manually configured addresses. Any attempt to communicate on the network with an address not learned from DHCP will be blocked, preventing an attacker from spoofing a legitimate endpoint. If IP and MAC source guard is enabled, the following command is present on switch ports:

```
interface GigabitEthernet 0/1
ip verify source port-security
```

Disable Dynamic Trunking

Cisco IOS has many features designed to make installation easy, and the plug and play nature of modern switches definitely makes use of them. Dynamic trunking is a feature that allows any port that connects to another Cisco switch setup and automatic trunk port to pass VLANs between the switches. Although this sounds like a nice feature during installation, leaving this enabled is not recommended in a production environment for security reasons. Best practices dictate that trunking should be explicitly configured and not left up to an automatic feature that could be potentially exploited. It is also recommended to predefine the VLANs that are allowed to pass. A properly configured trunk port will look like the following example on both switches:

Trunk port:

```
Switch(config-if)# switchport mode trunk
Switch(config-if)# switchport trunk encapsulation dot1q
Switch(config-if)# trunk allowed vlan 2-10,243
```

For access ports that user are connected to that are not involved in trunking, the following configurations are used to specify access mode and what VLAN the port is to be placed in. You also should ensure that the no negotiate command is present for verification that the dynamic trunking protocol is completely disabled.

Access port:

```
Switch(config-if)# switchport mode access
Switch(config-if)# switchport access vlan 10
Switch(config-if)# switchport nonegotiate
```

Protecting Spanning Tree

Spanning tree is a protocol used to create loop-free environments for bridge networks. It was designed with little thought for security, and it is easy to manipulate for someone with evil intentions. Bridge Protocol Data Units (BPDU) are sent out by switches to determine whether redundant links are available to the root switch, which is determined by a simple priority mechanism. This allows anyone that can manipulate BPDUs to be in a situation where they can force a device under their control to then become the root switch, making man-in-the middle attacks easy to accomplish. Cisco provides two powerful features, BPDU Guard and Root Guard, for protecting spanning tree and should be enabled to defend against these attacks.

BPDU Guard prevents the switch from accepting BPDUs from user ports by automatically shutting down the port or silently discarding BPDUs. BPDUs are used to calculate the root bridge in a spanning tree and can be manipulated to reconfigure the forwarding topology of a VLAN.

```
interface fastethernet 0/1
spanning-tree portfast
spanning-tree bpduguard enable
```

Root Guard prevents the root bridge from changing to an unapproved root bridge port. This feature allows the use of BPDUs to prevent loops at the port level while protecting the spanning tree root bridge path. Root Guard, when enabled, will disable any port that detects another switch trying to claim root. It is configured on a port-by-port basis and should be configured on all ports that should not become root as shown in the following example:

```
interface fastethernet 0/2
spanning-tree guard root
```

Spanning tree is the mechanism that switches use to learn where to forward traffic to and create a loop-free layer 2 network. Protecting spanning tree can prevents an attacker from manipulating that topology and prevent topology changes that could cause an attacker to become the spanning tree root and have all voice traffic forwarded for capture.

Switch Access Controls Lists

There are three types of switch ACLs that can be configured to enforce infrastructure access policies. PACLS, VACLS, and RACLS might sound like alphabet soup, but they represent the first level of policy enforcement for controlling access. Each type has a different enforcement focus and can be used together with PACLS taking priority. Auditors might see these configured in networks and should understand their functionality.

PACL are port-level ACLs that can filter at layer 2 through MAC addresses and ether types or at layer 3 at the IP address level. The following commands show the configuration of both a MAC and IP PACL on a switch port:

```
mac access-list extended example-mac
permit host 1111.1111.1111 any

ip access-list extended example-ip
permit ip host 192.168.1.1 any

interface GigabitEthernet0/1
ip access-group example-ip in
mac access-group example-mac in
```

RACL ACLs on switches are configured the same as on traditional routers and are used to control packets received on layer 3 interfaces configured on the switch. The following is an example RACL configured on a VLAN to block packets destined to network 172.16.1.0 from VLAN 1 but allow any other destination:

```
Access-list 102 deny ip any 172.16.1.0
Access-list 102 permit ip any any

interface Vlan1
ip address 192.168.1.253 255.255.255.0
ip access-group 102 in
```

VLAN access lists can be configured to control both switched and routed traffic into and out of an entire VLAN and are not limited to a single interface like the other switch

ACLs. The following example shows a VACL that is configured to allow any IP traffic into and out of VLANs 12-16 and deny all other source addresses:

```
Access-list 101 permit ip any 192.168.1.0 0.0.0.255
Access-list 101 deny ip any any log

vlan access-map example_vacl 10
match ip address 101
action forward
exit

vlan filter example_vacl vlan-list 12-16
```

Protect Unused Ports

Unused switch ports can be a liability if left enabled, where anyone can connect and gain access to the network. This fact makes it important to protect switch ports as you would any other type of access into your network. The recommendation is to disable switch ports that are not being used by turning them completely off. This can be accomplished with the following command:

```
interface GigabitEthernet0/1
 shutdown
```

If the port is not disabled, then at a bare minimum it should be placed into a VLAN that is nonroutable. A nonroutable VLAN is one that is not configured for IP access. Simply placing the unused port into a VLAN without an IP addressing structure and no routing function will prevent that port from being used to gain IP access to the network. The following shows a switchport configured for a nonroutable VLAN and other layer 2 security features that should also be applied to prevent attacks:

```
interface GigabitEthernet0/52
switchport access vlan 999
switchport trunk encapsulation dot1q
switchport trunk native vlan 999
switchport trunk allowed vlan none
switchport mode access
switchport nonegotiate
switchport port-security
spanning-tree portfast
spanning-tree bpdufilter enable
spanning-tree bpduguard enable
spanning-tree guard root
```

Wireless Security

More and more companies today use wireless to reduce infrastructure costs, improve workforce productivity, and provide access to guest users. Companies often choose to use wireless networks because they are easy to deploy and because of their capability to provide network access to a large area with relatively few wired network drops. As an auditor, you should take a critical look at the design and configuration of a wireless network to ensure that all precautions have been taken to protect this facility with the appropriate controls.

Wireless Network Architecture

Cisco wireless networks can be deployed in either an autonomous or a controller-based fashion. When configured autonomously, every access point acts independently and all administrative functions such as link encryption, user authentication, and access control are done locally at each access point. These types of installations are common with smaller organizations where a smaller number of access points have been deployed.

The other deployment method is through a Wireless LAN Controller-based system. A *Wireless LAN Controller (WLC)* is a standalone appliance or a module installed in a router or switch that centrally manages the configuration and operation of the access points. This is accomplished through a protocol called *Lightweight Access Point Protocol (LWAPP)*. When the AP is initialized in a lightweight model, it first identifies a local WLC, builds a LWAPP tunnel with the WLC, registers itself, and then downloads its configuration information from the WLC. The main benefit of this model is that it simplifies administration and control of a wireless network, allowing for consistent policy and configuration parameters across all of the organizations access points. Figure 7-1 shows an example of an LWAPP network deployment.

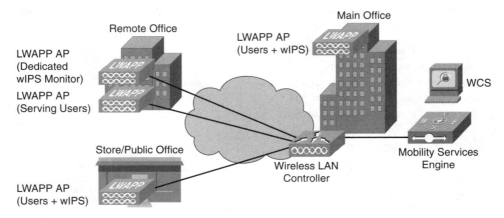

Figure 7-1 *LWAPP Network Deployment*

Cisco Adaptive Wireless Intrusion Prevention System

Wireless IPS (wIPS) is an important part of managing the security and availability of your wireless network. A traditional IDS or IPS detects attacks at layer 3 through 7 of the OSI model, but it does not have the capability to identify layer 1 and 2 wireless activity where most wireless attacks occur. If a company has deployed wireless using lightweight access points and a Wireless LAN Controller, then IPS can be enabled in two ways. First, the WLC itself has a collection of signatures that should be enabled to detect and prevent some reconnaissance and attacks against the wireless devices on your network. These can be verified from the Security tab of the wireless controller. Figure 7-2 shows the protection policies enabled on a WLC.

These protection policies can provide visibility into and protection from common wireless attacks such as reconnaissance and layer 2 denial of service attacks such as deauthentication floods. For more complete protection, the Mobility Services Engine can be deployed.

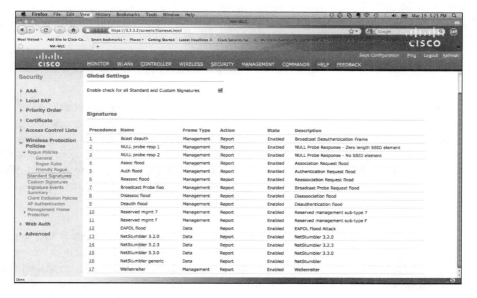

Figure 7-2   *WLC Protection Policies*

The second method of providing IPS in a wireless network is through the Adaptive Wireless Intrusion Prevention System built on the Cisco Mobility Services Engine (MSE). The MSE is an appliance-based platform for wireless services enablement and control. The MSE provides a much more robust collection of protection policies for your wireless network. It is designed to holistically look at the wireless environment to identify and defend against threats and provide a full packet capture of traffic for forensic analysis. The MSE's wIPS functionality is enabled through a license and is managed by and reported on through the Cisco Wireless Control System (WCS). The MSE has many more signatures and detective capabilities over the small number of integrated signatures in the WLC and the capability to define custom polices.

Protecting Wireless Access

Security controls for wireless networks have continued to evolve over the years to adapt to hacker attack techniques. Early encryption techniques used RC4 and Wired Equivalency Privacy (WEP) to protect the integrity of communications. This technique was found to be inadequate, and tools were developed that were able to break the static shared key encryption method by analyzing the hash collisions. This led researchers to develop numerous tools that have made the process of breaking a WEP key trivial and fast, under 5 minutes in most cases.

In 2004, the IEEE ratified the 802.11i architecture, which was designed from the ground up to address the security shortcomings of WEP. This time, they chose not to limit themselves as they had with WPA to be backwards compatible with existing devices. 802.11i, or WPA2, as it is more commonly known, did this by implementing AES encryption using a co-processor and Counter Mode Cipher Block Chaining Message Authentication Code Protocol (CCMP) for key management. Today, a wireless network configured using WPA2 with AES is considered to be the most secure. The one thing consistent with the risks discussed so far is the presence of a static shared key to encrypt the communications. This practice has been shown time and time again to be ineffective for protecting wireless networks, because either weak, preshared keys are chosen allowing brute force key compromise or technology is developed that exploits a flaw in how or when the shared key is used.

Another common issue with shared key authentication is the management of the key itself. If the key is compromised or a device that has been configured to access the network is lost, administrators need to change the key on all of the devices. This becomes almost impossible as the number of devices grows. The most effective way to deal with this issue is to implement 802.1x or EAP to mutually authenticate users to APs and APs to users. There are various EAP types today that have varying levels of effectiveness in providing a more secure means of authenticating users:

- **LEAP (Lightweight Extensible Authentication Protocol):** A proprietary EAP type developed by Cisco that allows single sign-on to Windows NT domains or Active Directory. This protocol does not require user- or server-side certificates and relies on the complexity of the username/password combination for security. Based on demonstrated dictionary attacks against this protocol and the fact that users are notorious for not selecting strong passwords, this EAP type is not preferred.

- **EAP-FAST (Flexible Authentication via Secure Tunneling):** An EAP type developed by Cisco in 2004. It is still username- and password-based without the need for a PKI infrastructure; however, it is not susceptible to the dictionary attacks that plague LEAP, due to a mutually authenticating tunnel. This EAP type can also provide single sign-on with Windows NT domains and Active Directory.

- **EAP-TLS (Transport Layer Security):** EAP-TLS is the most flexible EAP type with support for the most client devices and backend authentication databases, but is arguably the most difficult to install and maintain. EAP-TLS is based entirely on PKI, where both the server and the client that participate in the 802.1x authentication must have their own certificates.

■ **PEAP (Protected Extensible Authentication Protocol):** PEAP is an open standard developed jointly by Cisco, RSA, and Microsoft. It is flexible and supported by many operating systems. PEAP requires only a server-side certificate for deployment, making it easier to operate than EAP-TLS. PEAP comes in several flavors, from PEAP-GTC (Generic Token Card) to PEAP-MSCHAPv2 (Microsoft Challenge Authentication Protocol), and it supports authentication into Active Directory, Novell, or even one-time password databases.

Including EAP (802.1x) as part of the authentication process reduces the risks of shared key encryption. 802.1x and identity are discussed in greater detail in Chapter 8. Table 7-3 shows the capabilities of the various EAP types.

There are situations in which extended authentication or strong encryption using WPA2 might not be possible. Hand scanners, point-of-sale systems, wireless scales, and other devices might be too old or might not have the hardware to support the advanced encryption or EAP required to properly secure a wireless network. In these cases, segmentation of the wireless devices from the rest of the network and encryption of the transmitted data where possible are recommended.

Wireless Service Availability

Wireless is quickly becoming as fast as wired networks. With the IEEE ratification of 802.11n, wireless transmission speeds have increased into the 400–600 Mbps range. This makes it attractive for companies to start using additional services on top of wireless that were not normally seen when APs were limited to a shared 54 Mbps. It is not uncommon to see voice, video, and application data traversing the wireless network. In new construction applications, businesses are giving significant thought to installing less wired connections and using wireless as the primary means of communication. This places a greater emphasis on protecting the availability of the wireless network by reducing interference or a targeted denial of service attack.

Table 7-3 *EAP Type Capabilities*

	LEAP	EAP-FAST	EAP-TLS	PEAP
Requires server-side certificate			x	x
Requires client-side certificate			x	
Supports Windows single sign-on	x	x	x	x
Supports WPA and WPA2	x	x	x	x
Password expiry and change		x	N/A uses Certificate for Auth	x

Interference to a wireless network can come from many sources. Other access points that share the same wireless channel or an overlapping channel, cordless phones, and microwave ovens can cause interference. WLANs are based on Carrier Sense Multiple Access with Collision Avoidance (CSMA/CA) or "listen-before-talk." If another wireless device is already transmitting on the frequency you intend to use, the device is instructed to wait until the first device is finished transmitting. This protocol is what helps multiple access points and other wireless devices coexist in the same frequency ranges and share time across the spectrum.

While preventing a layer 1 interference or an attack is nearly impossible, the capability to identify and remediate the source is important to companies who run their businesses on wireless. Cisco offers an application to help organizations deal with this risk called *Cisco Spectrum Expert*.

Cisco Spectrum Expert is a software application that is normally installed on a laptop that can be carried around an organization to analyze, locate, and mitigate the source of the wireless interference. Figure 7-3 shows a screen shot of Spectrum Expert.

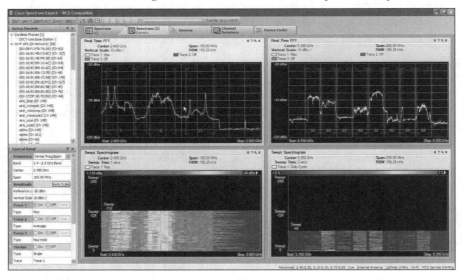

Figure 7-3   *Spectrum Expert*

Rogue Access Point Detection

Knowing which access points are authorized to be on a network and finding the ones that are not can be a challenge for most organizations. Access points can purchase at any electronics store for as little as $30 and require little technical knowledge to bridge the company's production network to RF. In most cases where this occurs, the offending employee puts little or no encryption on this wireless network, making it an easy target for an attacker. Because the rogue access point allows access to the internal network over RF, security appliances such as firewalls or IPS devices are completely blind to this traffic and cannot stop an attacker from attaching to the network. Businesses need to quickly identify and eliminate any unauthorized access points from the network.

Identifying rogue access points manually is a time-consuming and unreliable process. A laptop is loaded with software that monitors all wireless channels for AP beacons, and then someone has to physically walk through the building with the laptop in front of them like an RF-sniffing Frankenstein monster (that step is not strictly required but makes a dull job fun). The software then enumerates all of the active access points that were found during the walkthrough. After the list of APs is compiled, an administrator then needs to determine whether any of the discovered APs are new and that the APs are actually connected to the corporate network and not some other company's wireless device. If the organization is large, has multiple remote offices, or is in a densely populated are with a large number of identified rogue access points, this process can be ineffective and the results can be inconclusive.

The Cisco Unified Wireless System simplifies the process of identifying and removing the access points that are not supposed to be connected to your network. The APs can handle client communication while also monitoring the air around them for other access points. This information is then fed back into the WLC, which analyzes the data and correlates it with the information that other APs report back. If an AP is detected and is not managed by the WLC, it automatically reports as a rogue access point.

The WLC attempts to determine whether a discovered rogue AP is connected to the local network in one of two ways.

- **RLDP (Rogue Location Discover Protocol):** If the discovered AP does not utilize encryption on the link, one of the APs that identifies it can disassociate its connected clients and attempt to connect to the AP as a client. If it can get an IP address and is able to send the local controller a packet on UDP port 6352, it can definitively determine that the identified rogue is also connected to the local network.

- **Passive operation:** If the rogue AP uses some form of encryption and the lightweight AP is not capable of associating to the rogue AP, the local controller passes the list of rogue client MAC addresses that it doesn't know about to the detecting AP. The AP then scans all of the configured subnets for ARP requests. If it sees a match, it can identify the rogue AP as being connected to the wired network.

After a rogue AP is identified, the WLC can notify administrators about the presence of the rogue and take additional actions such as preventing clients from associating with the AP and sending deauthentication messages to existing clients. This isolation protects the organization until the rogue can be located and removed from the network.

The WCS can graphically depict the approximate location in the building where the rogue AP was detected to make it easier to remove. Figure 7-4 shows the location identification capabilities of WCS.

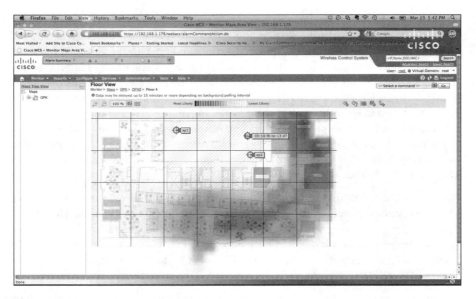

Figure 7-4   *Rogue AP Location*

General Network Device Security Best Practices

General network device best practices are the foundations for which all security configurations should be measured against. To minimize exposure, the following general rules
regarding network device configuration are recommended:

- **Stay current on any Cisco security advisories for your devices:** Cisco provides a
  wealth of information at the Cisco Security Center to keep you informed about any
  new vulnerabilities or threats against your IOS devices. The Cisco Security Center is a
  great place to go to stay current on new threats. Cisco also offers a fee service called
  IntelliShield, which can provide security vulnerabilities and recommendations for all
  products, not just Cisco.

- **Always use the most secure protocols available when interacting with IOS
  devices:** Telnet sends all information in clear text, as does FTP and TFTP. Make sure
  that you recommend at least SSH and Secure Copy. Sniffers can be anywhere.

- **Use AAA whenever possible:** Storing administrative credentials directly on a network device might work in very small networks, but if you have more than one person who can configure or control network devices, there is a need to authorize and
  log all actions individuals perform on network devices, and AAA does that well.

- **Use secure passwords for all devices:** Weak passwords are the single most pervasive vulnerability of Internet-connected devices. If you can figure out the password, a potential hacker won't have to go through any custom coding or find a zero
  day exploit.

■   **If you log it, review it:** Logging security information is useless unless you have a mechanism in place to review the data gathered. This can be labor-intensive, and using products such as Cisco MARS can help pinpoint security problems that would be the equivalent of finding a needle in a haystack by parsing logs manually.

Technical Testing

Verification of security controls used to protect the network infrastructure is accomplished through testing the network's response to the attacks that hackers are likely to deploy. Not all attack methods are tested like a penetration test, but performing these basic assessments can provide evidence of policy compliance and adherence to good infrastructure security practices.

Scanning network infrastructure devices shows the auditors what services are enabled on a device. This simple test speaks volumes about whether or not the organization configures its devices in a security-conscious manner.

NMap is the easiest tool to run for doing a quick scan of network devices. The auditor looks to find any insecure services that an attacker could potentially compromise. Services such as telnet, SSHv1, and web management interfaces that are easily accessible from user network segments, or even worse, public network segments, can be used as attack vectors against the device. Auditors should also be on the lookout for any other unnecessary service that is open. The following shows a basic NMAP TCP connect scan with OS and service detection against a Cisco router:

```
nmap -A 192.168.1.1


Starting Nmap 5.21 ( http://nmap.org ) at 2010-03-06 13:55 EST
Nmap scan report for 192.168.1.2
Host is up (0.0041s latency).
Not shown: 996 closed ports
PORT     STATE SERVICE   VERSION
22/tcp   open  ssh        Cisco SSH 1.25 (protocol 1.99)
|_sshv1: Server supports SSHv1
| ssh-hostkey: 1024 75:4b:5f:2d:d7:4a:f1:f1:00:b3:be:e1:05:7b:4a:40 (RSA1)
|_1024 d4:3d:6d:0f:b9:ab:dc:24:99:ae:9b:93:5e:07:d9:e9 (RSA)
23/tcp   open  telnet    Cisco router
80/tcp   open  http      Cisco IOS administrative httpd
|_html-title: Site doesn't have a title.
| http-auth: HTTP Service requires authentication
|_ Auth type: Basic, realm = level_15_access
443/tcp open  ssl/http Cisco IOS administrative httpd
|_html-title: Site doesn't have a title.
| http-auth: HTTP Service requires authentication
|_ Auth type: Basic, realm = level_15_access
MAC Address: 00:13:C3:44:4D:78 (Cisco Systems)
```

```
Device type: router¦WAP
Running: Cisco IOS 12.X
OS details: Cisco 836, 1751, 1841, or 2800 router (IOS 12.4 - 15.0), Cisco Aironet
AIR-AP1141N WAP (IOS 12.4)
Network Distance: 1 hop
Service Info: OS: IOS; Device: router
```

This scan highlights a number of security problems an auditor might find. First off, the administrator configured management access for both Telnet/SSH and HTTP/HTTPS access for the router. Unencrypted network device interaction is a big security no-no, and it should be disabled to prevent password capture and other common attacks. SSH v1 is used, which is known to be susceptible to man-in-the-middle attacks and should be replaced with SSH v2. Another issue is the fact that the management interfaces are configured on user-facing VLANs. Dedicated management VLANs are preferred, with ACLs configured on network devices to prevent access from IP ranges outside of the management network. At a minimum, SSHv2 and HTTPS should be the only mechanisms used to manage Cisco devices.

Testing for SNMP is another scan that can be performed with NMAP. SNMP can operate on TCP or UDP and uses ports 161 and 162. The latest version of NMAP includes built-in scripting capabilities that attempt to read SNMP information from the device. The following scan shows that SNMP is in operation using SNMPv1 and using a community string of public.

```
nmap -sU -sC -p 161,162 192.168.1.2
Starting Nmap 5.21 ( http://nmap.org ) at 2010-03-06 15:40 Eastern Standard Time
Initiating UDP Scan at 15:40
Scanning 192.168.1.2 [2 ports]
Discovered open port 161/udp on 192.168.1.2
Completed UDP Scan at 15:40, 1.21s elapsed (2 total ports)
NSE: Script scanning 192.168.1.2.
NSE: Starting runlevel 1 (of 1) scan.
Initiating NSE at 15:40
Completed NSE at 15:40, 0.01s elapsed
NSE: Script Scanning completed.
Nmap scan report for 192.168.1.2
Host is up (0.0022s latency).
Scanned at 2010-03-06 15:40:29 Eastern Standard Time for 2s
PORT     STATE          SERVICE
161/udp open           snmp
¦ snmp-sysdescr: Cisco IOS Software, 2800 Software (C2800NM-ADVENTERPRISEK9-M),
Version 15.1(1)XB, RELEASE SOFTWARE (fc1)
¦ Technical Support: http://www.cisco.com/techsupport
¦ Copyright 1986-2009 by Cisco Systems, Inc.
¦ Compiled Mon 21-Dec-09 01:14 by prod_rel_team
¦_ System uptime: 0 days, 2:46:48.58 (1000858 timeticks)
```

```
162/udp open¦filtered snmptrap
MAC Address: 00:13:C3:44:4D:78 (Cisco Systems)
```

After SNMP is identified, it often helps to show the gravity of the situation by showing an example of the types of things an attacker can do through this protocol. Figure 7-5 shows how a tool like Cain can pull a configuration file off of a router through SNMP.

While these general network device tests have been conducted against a router as an example, they work against any Cisco IOS powered device and are a good starting point for testing.

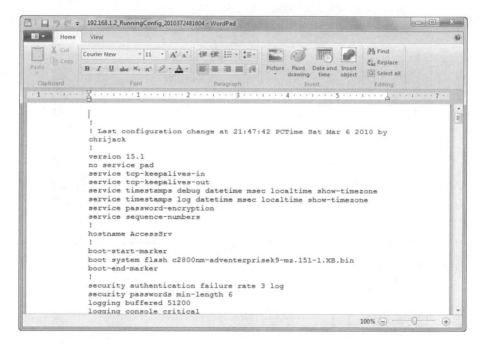

Figure 7-5   *SNMP Configuration File Download Through Cain*

Router Testing

Routers should be tested against best practices for secure configuration. As mentioned in Chapter 4, Cisco has integrated a quick and free security audit function in Cisco Configuration Professional (CCP). This compares the routers configuration against 35 Cisco recommended security parameters. CCP is designed for smaller networks and does not scale to assessing large numbers of routers.

RedSeal is a good commercial security best practices assessment tool, which can handle large networks. The best practices analyzer identifies configuration and software vulnerabilities in Cisco routers and firewalls. After the device's configuration has been imported into SRM, it is compared with NIST security best practices and any custom configuration requirements dictated by policy. Figure 7-6 shows best practices assessment on an individual router.

Dynamic routing protocols should be protected from attack by utilizing MD5 authentication on routing updates. To test if these features are enabled, auditors can use a sniffer such as Wireshark to see whether routing updates are authenticated, or they can use a tool called *Cain and Abel* to make it easier. Cain and Abel sniffs the network for routing the update packet and lists all routes being advertised and whether routing authentication is being used. Figure 7-7 shows Cain and Abel discovering poor routing protocol security.

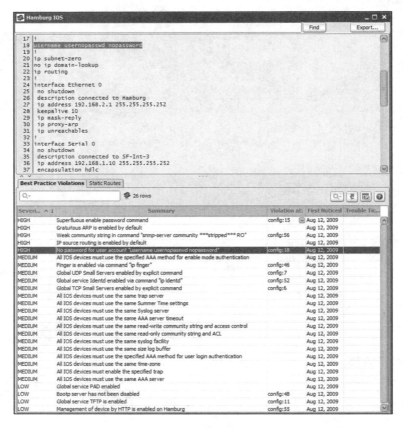

Figure 7-6 *Router Best Practices Assessment with RedSeal*

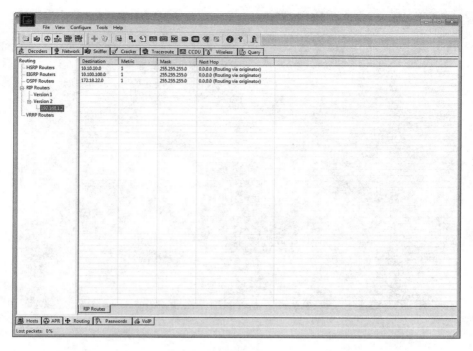

Figure 7-7   *Cain Detecting Routing Protocols with No Authentication*

Switch Testing

Probably the best tool in existence for testing layer 2 security features on switches is Yersinia. Named after a type of bacteria that spawned the bubonic plague (I don't get why they named it after the plague either), this tool has it all. As a layer 2 security testing suite, Yersinia includes protocol support for CDP, VTP, HSRP, DTP, STP, 802.1Q, and 802.1X. It runs as a command-line tool, interactive terminal application, and it has an experimental GUI that is still a work in progress. Using the tool is easy and is included in Backtrack4. Figure 7-8 shows the protocol support list for Yersinia.

Auditors can use Yersinia to test a switch's response to spanning tree attacks, trunking attacks, and other malicious activity that Cisco switches should be configured to prevent. Allowing BPDUs to be sent to the switch from user-facing VLANs should be prevented by enabling BPDU Guard on all user switch ports. To test this feature, simply launch Yersinia, select STP protocols, and send a BPDU to the switch. If properly configured, the switch port is disabled automatically. Figure 7-9 shows a Yersinia BPDU attack selection.

Figure 7-8 *Yersinia Layer 2 Protocol Support*

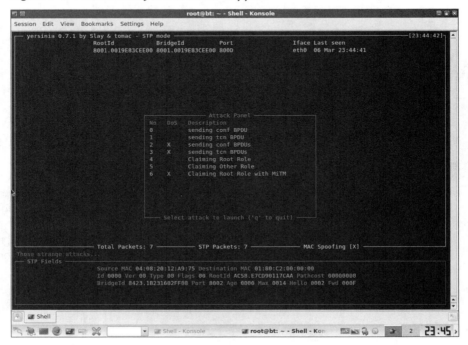

Figure 7-9 *Yersinia BPDU Attack Detection Test*

If the switch is properly configured, you would see the following displayed on the console port of the switch, and your Ethernet port would be disabled:

```
3w4d: %SPANTREE-2-BLOCK_BPDUGUARD: Received BPDU on port Gi0/13 with BPDU Guard en-
abled. Disabling port.
3w4d: %PM-4-ERR_DISABLE: bpduguard error detected on Gi0/13, putting Gi0/13 in
err-
disable state
3w4d: %LINEPROTO-5-UPDOWN: Line protocol on Interface GigabitEthernet0/13, changed
state to down
3w4d: %LINK-3-UPDOWN: Interface GigabitEthernet0/13, changed state to down
```

MAC flooding can be tested with MACof from the DSniff suite of tools. This little application can generate thousands of MAC addresses per second, which is useful for testing MAC flooding protection on Cisco switches. MACof is easy to use and has command-line help available for setting options if you need to conduct a more specific test of MAC address handing. Be careful running this tool with no parameters set to limit the number of MACs generated because it impacts switch performance and can cause a denial of service if port security is not configured. Setting it to send five MAC addresses is usually enough for testing, and can be accomplished with the following command:

```
macof -i eth0 -n 5
```

Figure 7-10 shows MACof in operation against a switch performing a MAC flooding attack. If properly configured, the switch drops excessive MAC addresses or disables the port depending on how port security is configured.

Testing for defense against ARP spoofing can be accomplished with a number of tools. These attacks are designed to force user traffic to flow through the attacker's machine to hijack sessions and grab login credentials. Ettercap, Arpspoof, Cain and Abel, and many other hacking tools can perform ARP spoofing attacks, which is why it is so important to prevent this type of activity from occurring. These types of tools highlight how easy it is to perform sniffing on switched networks without the appropriate safeguards like Dynamic ARP Inspection. With Dynamic ARP Inspection enabled, the switch prevents the ARP table poisoning performed by these tools by comparing the ARP sent to the switches' DHCP snooping tables, which include IP-to-MAC address information for all of the devices in the VLAN. If an ARP is sent that doesn't match the table, then the switch discards it. Figure 7-11 shows Ettercap being used to sniff network connections through ARP poisoning.

A rogue DHCP server can be configured to manipulate automatic network configuration for malicious purposes. One of the best tools for auditors to test DHCP handling on a network is Gobbler. This tool is available on Unix-based operating systems and includes a whole suite of attacks against DHCP that determine whether a switch is configured properly to defend against them. If the switch is configured for DHCP snooping, then it is able

Figure 7-10   *MACof MAC Flooding Attack*

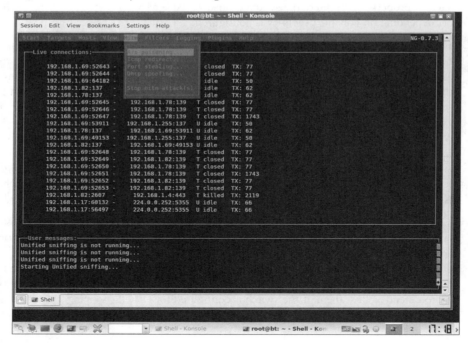

Figure 7-11   *Ettercap ARP Poisoning Test*

to prevent DHCP address assignments from coming from any other ports other than the ones that are trusted. Yersinia can also be used to test these security features. Figure 7-12 shows Yersinia being used to create a rogue DHCP server that will provide IP addresses, router, and DNS pointing to an attacker.

Auditors should also test how the switch responds to IP spoofing attacks. IP Source Guard can be used to prevent spoofing on local addresses by comparing the DHCP snoop table to the MAC address of a particular port. If the address matches, the switch allows the packet through; if it doesn't match, the switch drops it.

Figure 7-12   *Yersinia Creating a Rogue DHCP Server*

Wireless Testing

Testing wireless security features requires finding the wireless access points and the encryption mechanisms that are in place. The best tool to catalog access points in range is Kismet. Kismet is available on Windows, Mac OSX, BSD, and Linux and is an essential wireless auditing suite (www.kismetwireless.net). It is a passive scanner that can detect nonbroadcast SSIDs by listening to the wireless traffic beacons. Beacons are sent across the RF network in clear text, and Kismet can identify this traffic that would not be visible to a scanner that relied on the AP responding to active probes. Figure 7-13 shows the main Kismet interface.

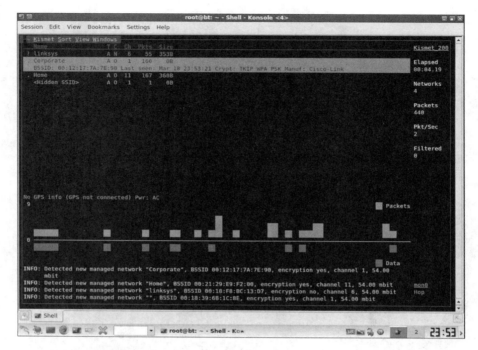

Figure 7-13 *Kismet Interface*

From the Kismet interface, you can also identify the encryption techniques that are used and clients that are communicating with the selected access point. You can also add a GPS for pinpointing exactly where networks are located. These features are useful for ensuring that the access points in range operate with standard encryption mechanisms such as WPA2 and not running weak protective suites such as WEP.

While WEP and WPA pre-shared key encryption has been easily broken for many years now, as an auditor, you might be asked to demonstrate the weakness in these technologies to prove the risk associated with using them.

Auditing WEP-encrypted networks requires the use of a WEP-cracking tool such as Aircrack-NG. Aircrack-NG is a powerful suite of applications designed to identify, capture, analyze, and inject packets onto a WEP-protected wireless network. These tools make the job of finding a WEP-encrypted network's shared key trivial. Aircrack-NG was initially written for Linux platforms, but has since been ported to Windows and other platforms. One popular option for auditors has been to use Backtrack4 with the Aircrack-NG applications and the required wireless drivers already loaded. To crack WEP, you have to capture enough packets to exhaust the 24-bit initialization vector (IV). This requires that you put your wireless adapter into monitor mode and configure a capture file to save the raw capture. The following commands are entered to perform the capture:

```
airmon-ng start <interface>
airodump-ng -c <channel> -w <capture file> <interface>
```

This can take a long time on a wireless network that does not have a lot of traffic on it. To speed up the process, you can associate to the AP and then start replaying captured traffic back to the AP to quickly generate packets. This generates errors on the AP, causing a flood of responses back to the client. The first command performs a fake authentication with the target access point, which prevents the AP from just ignoring the replay traffic you send at it because your wireless card's MAC address is not in its tables.

```
aireplay-ng -1 0 -e <target's SSID> -a <target APs MAC address > -h <your wireless
MAC address> <interface>
```

This command listens for ARP requests sent to the access point and will replay them back to the network. ARP is used here because it causes the AP to generate a new IV with every packet, enabling the auditor to gather a large number of IVs in a short period of time.

```
aireplay-ng -3 -b <target's BSSID> -h <your wireless MAC address> <interface>
```

You then open another terminal window and run Aircrack-NG on the capture file that is created. After it has found enough IVs, the WEP key is displayed. The following command can be used to launch Aircrack-NG:

```
aircrack-ng -a 1 -0 -n 128 <capture file>
```

Figure 7-14 shows Aircrack-NG decoding the WEP encryption key.

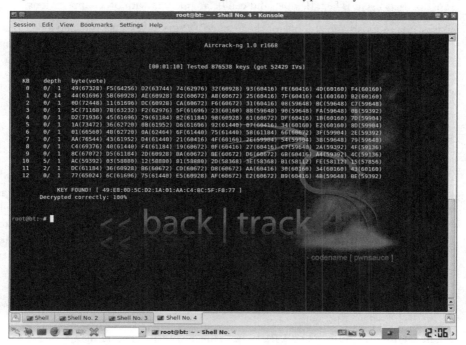

Figure 7-14 *Aircrack-NG WEP Encryption Key Crack*

With WPA-PSK, you don't need to collect a large number of packets to recover the key used to encrypt wireless traffic. When a client begins a session with an access point, he can exchange a series of four packets called the *handshake*. By capturing these four packets, you can perform an offline brute force dictionary attack and hopefully recover the key quickly.

The BackTrack4 Linux live distribution that is commonly used for cracking WEP is also particularly useful for cracking WPA-PSK. The Aircrack-NG suite can be used to put your wireless adapter in monitor mode and capture the required handshakes.

Begin by putting your interface into monitor mode and setting up a capture file:

```
airmon-ng start <interface> <channel>
airodump-ng -c <channel> -w <capture file> <interface>
```

At this point, you have two options: Either wait until a legitimate connection completes a handshake with the AP or send a client a deauthentication frame that should force them attempt a reconnect:

```
aireplay-ng -0 5 -a <BSSID of AP> -c <MAC address of client> <interface>
```

If you see that you have captured at least one handshake for the target network you are auditing, you have enough information to conduct the rest of the work offline. Now you need an application to perform the brute force; coWPAtty is a useful application for this function because it is fast, flexible, and can be augmented with other applications.

One of the originals and still one of the best, coWPAtty takes a capture and a dictionary file and then runs through each entry in the dictionary to try to find a match to the captured key. Obviously, the larger the dictionary, the better chance you have of finding a match to the pre-shared key. There are a number of sites that produce dictionary files optimized for this purpose.

```
cowpatty - f <capture file> -d <dictionary file> -s <SSID>
```

Figure 7-15 shows coWPAtty decoding all of the WPA preshared keys it finds.

This process uses an enormous amount of processing power on a computer because coWPAtty computes the hash for the SSID using every word in the dictionary file until it comes up with a match. This can also take a long time, so to speed it up, you can use an application called pyrit. Pyrit can make use of the advanced number-crunching capabilities of your video card's processor to more quickly compute and compare the hashes to the captured traffic. Pyrit does the computation and then sends it to coWPAtty to make the comparison. It has been shown to cut the time to audit a WPA-PSK by up to 90 percent. The following command is used to launch pyrit and coWPAtty:

```
pyrit -e <SSID> -i <dictionary file> -o - passthrough ¦ cowpatty -d - -s <SSID> -r
<capture file>
```

Figure 7-16 shows pyrit and coWPAtty decoding a wireless capture file.

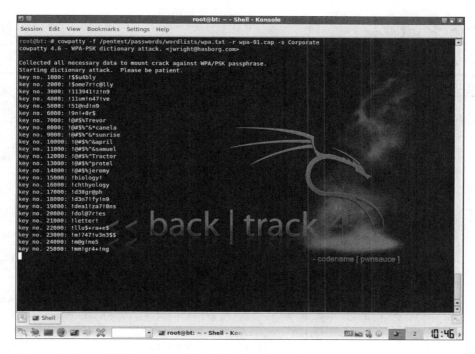

Figure 7-15 *coWPAtty Decoding WPA Pre-Shared Keys*

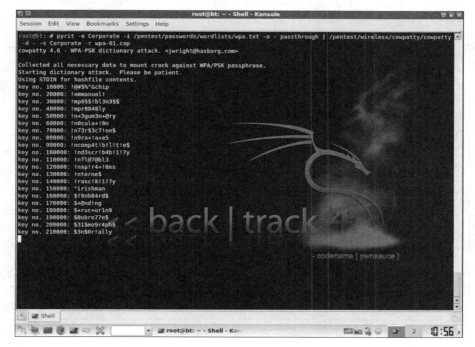

Figure 7-16 *Pyrit and coWPAtty Working Together*

Checklist

Assessment Area	Assessment Technique
People	
Does the password policy require strong passwords and periodic changes?	Review the password policy for password complexity requirements, password history, and password change frequency.
Are secure management protocols required by policy?	Infrastructure device policies should prohibit management access without using encrypted protocols such as SSH and HTTPS.
Is least privilege access required for access to infrastructure devices?	The policy should require least privilege access be granted for all network users and administrators.
Is a change management policy in place?	Review the change management policy.
Is a wireless access policy in place to forbid unapproved and/or user installed wireless devices?	Wireless access should have a dedicated policy prohibiting unauthorized installation of wireless devices by employees as this represents a significant risk.
Are polices and standards used when configuring network devices?	Inspect policies and standards for configuration of network devices to determine whether they are followed.
Process	
Are all key computing assets identified and documented?	Review documentation to determine location of servers, databases, and other critical systems.
Is there sufficient network documentation to identify physical and logical configurations of devices?	Review physical and logical documentation for completeness. Determine how often it is updated and review update procedures.
Has a traffic flow analysis been conducted?	Look for evidence that administrators have conducted a traffic flow analysis to determine what protocols are used on the network.
Are administrator accounts unique and assigned to a single individual?	All administrator accounts used to connect to network infrastructure devices should be unique for the purposes of auditing and non-repudiation.

continues

Assessment Area	Assessment Technique *(continued)*
Is configuration management and change control conducted?	Configuration backups should be made of all network devices and kept electronically in a secure manner, and a hardcopy stored in a safe if possible. All configuration changes should be reviewed with a formal approval process and rollback mechanism.
Is there a process in place to review product security advisories?	Interview staff and determine procedures used to identify new vulnerabilities in network devices. Staff should subscribe to PSIRT reports.
Are vulnerability scans conducted on network devices?	The organization should conduct periodic vulnerability scans of network devices and have a software version inventory to quickly determine whether vulnerable software is installed on infrastructure devices.
Is a network disaster recovery plan in place?	Review the disaster recovery plan for good practices.
Are logs stored in a central repository and reviewed on a regular basis for security issues?	All infrastructure device logs should be stored in a central database that enables easy searching and review of security and operational events.
Is wireless device management and monitoring conducted?	Wireless management should be in place to address wireless-specific security issues, such as denial of service, hacking, rogue APs, and RF spectrum problems. Wireless should be monitored on a regular basis to quickly resolve security problems.
Technology	
General Network Device Security	
Management Plane	
Are unused management ports (aux, console, and vty) disabled?	Unused management ports should be disabled to prevent physical access to the configuration if it is not used for management. At a minimum, all ports should require authentication.

continues

Assessment Area	Assessment Technique *(continued)*
Are management login best practices followed?	Ensure that failed login attempts are limited, the maximum number of concurrent sessions are limited, idle timeouts are enforced, and all commands entered are logged.
Are there access control mechanisms in place to prevent connectivity to management ports from unauthorized subnets?	Review documentation and configuration to determine whether access lists are properly applied to management interfaces.
Are network device terminal and management ports not in use disabled?	Review all terminal and management ports for use.
Are secure access protocols such as SSH or HTTPS being used prior to device access?	Review configuration for management access methods.
Are secure passwords required for all network devices?	Review the password policy and inspect against actual configuration.
Are local login accounts on network devices used for fallback access only?	Network devices should be configured only to use local authentication in the event of a failure to reach a AAA server. If the network is small (less than five devices), then local authentication can be used, but each user must have his own credentials.
Are network device passwords in configurations secured with encryption?	Review configurations for service password encryption.
Is AAA utilized with unique logins and least privilege principles applied to all network device access?	Review configurations to determine authentication methods for network devices.
Are logging and accounting enabled for network devices to track users and system state?	Ensure that logging is enabled and there is reporting to a central logging system. Identify how often logs are reviewed.
Are legal banners in place and presented before login attempts?	Inspect configurations for appropriate legal notification.
Is SNMP configured in a secure manner?	Review configurations to determine whether default settings are removed and secure practices are followed for using SNMP.
Is syslog configured for network- device reporting and is it archived?	Syslog should be configured to report to a central syslog server and record device status, logins, management activities, and other pertinent security information.

continues

Assessment Area	Assessment Technique *(continued)*
Is NTP configured for all network devices in the organization?	Review configurations to determine whether NTP is enabled along with appropriate authentication.
Control Plane	
Are unused IOS services disabled as outlined in hardening best practices?	Inspect configurations to ensure that services disabled by default have not been re-enabled.
Is routing protocol peering configured for authentication and encryption?	Review configuration for routing protocol passwords and that MD5 hashing is used to encrypt updates.
Is control Plane Policing enabled to protect the IOS device from DoS attacks?	Review configurations to identify control plane protection mechanisms in place.
Are iACLs deployed to reduce the risk of spoofing and prevent unapproved control plane traffic from being received by the IOS device	Review configuration for iACLs and check the access lists to ensure effectiveness.
Is Netflow configured to improve network visibility?	Netflow should be configured where appropriate to give insight into traffic patters and protocol usage.
Data Plane	
Are access lists configured to prevent unnecessary or prohibited network protocols and access?	Access Lists should be configured in accordance with approved traffic flow requirements. Prohibited network protocols and services should be blocked.
Is uRPF enabled to reduce spoofing of internal addresses?	Review configurations for the presence of anti-spoofing access lists or technologies like uRPF.
Is the Committed Access Rate and QOS flooding protection enabled to prevent DoS attacks?	Committed Access Rate and QOS should be configured to prevent flooding attacks on the network.
Layer 2 Security	
Is VTP protected with a password or disabled?	VTP should be disabled if it is not used to manage switch VLANs. If configured, a VTP domain and password should be configured to prevent unauthorized modification or access to VLANs.

continues

Assessment Area	Assessment Technique	*(continued)*
Is port security configured to prevent MAC flooding attacks?	Review configuration for port security features, minimizing the number of MAC addresses a switch port can learn. No more than three should be configured for a normal user port.	
Is DHCP snooping enabled to protect DHCP servers?	Review configuration for DHCP server protection through DHCP snooping.	
Is dynamic ARP inspection enabled to prevent ARP poisoning attacks?	Dynamic ARP inspection should be enabled to prevent ARP attacks that can be used to hijack user sessions.	
Is IP Source Guard enabled to prevent IP address spoofing?	IP Source Guard should be configured to prevent IP address spoofing on local VLANs.	
Is dynamic trunking disabled on non-trunk ports?	Inspect switch configurations to determine whether access ports are configured for no trunking.	
Are spanning tree security best practices utilized?	Inspect configuration for appropriate spanning tree protection features. BPDU Guard and Root Guard should be present.	
Are VLAN ACLs used to enforce VLAN traffic policies?	VACLS are present in switch configurations to provide policy control at the switch port or VLAN level. Review configurations for appropriate access control.	
Are unused switch ports disabled and/or placed in a nonroutable VLAN?	Review configuration to ensure unused ports are protected from unauthorized access.	
Wireless		
Are WEP or WPA configured on any APs?	Review the configuration to ensure that WEP and WPA pre-shared keys are not used for wireless networks.	
Are wireless protection policies or wIPS enabled?	If using a control-based architecture, wireless protection policies should be enabled to prevent common wireless attacks. For higher security requirements and better visibility into wireless attacks, wIPS is recommended.	

continues

Assessment Area	Assessment Technique *(continued)*
Are rogue AP detection features enabled?	Rogue AP detection features should be enabled if available to automate detection and containment of unauthorized APs.
Are pres-hared keys used for encryption?	Pre-shared keys for wireless are not recommended, but if used, should follow good complexity requirements to increase the time for brute-force cracking. Just like passwords, these keys should also be changed on a regular basis.
Are weak encryption keys used?	Audit the network for weak encryption keys.
Is 802.1x used for authentication?	802.1x provides strong authentication and key management for wireless networks and is recommended for secure wireless connectivity.

Summary

This chapter covered security practices and auditing for the devices that make up the network infrastructure. Routers, switches, and wireless provide the plumbing that enables businesses to harness the power of technology. The network provides the foundation for connectivity of business systems; considering the importance of its role, it should be configured in a manner that will ensure the availability and visibility necessary to protect customer and business data. In summary:

- Proper documentation is essential in troubleshooting and incident handling, and it should be reviewed by the auditor for completeness and accuracy.

- Network operations must adhere to good security practices and leverage change control processes that implement standard configurations for all network devices.

- When auditing infrastructure security, it helps to view IOS protective mechanisms as they apply to the different functional planes of security.

- Layer 2 protection is critical to ensuring the proper defense of network resources and the clients that use those resources.

- Wireless networks increase productivity, but they also increase risk if they are not adequately protected.

- Auditors should test network security controls to make sure that they are working as expected and enforce policy.

References in This Chapter

Schudel, Gregg and Smith, David. *Router Security Strategies: Securing IP Network Traffic Planes*. Indianapolis, IN: Cisco Press, 2008.

Vyncke, Eric and Paggen, Christopher. *Lan Switch Security: What Hackers Know About Your Switches*. Indianapolis, IN: Cisco Press, 2008.

Cisco Safe Reference Guide, http://www.cisco.com/en/US/docs/solutions/Enterprise/Security/SAFE_RG/SAFE_rg.html

DISA Network Infrastructure Security Technical Implementation Guide, Version 7, Release 1 http://iase.disa.mil/stigs/stig/network_stig_v7r1_20071025.pdf

NIST 800-97, "Establishing Wireless Robust Security Networks: A Guide to IEEE 802.11i," http://csrc.nist.gov/publications/nistpubs/800-97/SP800-97.pdf

Chapter 8

Perimeter Intrusion Prevention

Protecting a network perimeter used to be a simple thing: Stick a firewall on your Internet connection, lock down all of the unused ports, and monitor on a regular basis. Today the concept of the perimeter has expanded to encompass more than just the Internet edge. The perimeter now represents logical zones of trust that are created to protect against internal and external threats. Network borders have become fluid, while the need for secure access to data has increased dramatically. Defending the applications and services that provide this data is accomplished through perimeter defense controls such as firewalls and intrusion prevention systems (IPS).

Firewalls and intrusion prevention systems are a crucial layer of protection for business assets. Firewalls are equivalent to locks on doors, and an IPS is like an alarm system and security guard all rolled into one. Security architects use these devices to limit access to only the ports and protocols necessary to provide network services, monitor access, and stop malicious activity. Not having adequate perimeter controls leaves a business completely exposed to the many attack vectors commonly used to gain unauthorized access to networks today. Auditors must understand how these perimeter protection controls work and how businesses can properly leverage them to reduce risk. This chapter discusses techniques used in assessing network perimeter protection controls and good defensive practices.

Perimeter Threats and Risk

Potential threats are never in short supply, which is where countermeasures such as firewalls and IPS come into play. If you have vulnerability in Secure Shell (SSH), but access to SSH is blocked by a firewall rule, then the potential vulnerability has no direct way of being exploited. The vulnerability is not gone, but the countermeasure reduced the risk of attack by preventing access. Some threats do not pose significant risk to a company based on the types of services that the company offers to its customers via the Internet. This does not mean that a low risk today might not be of concern in the future, as the business grows or new services are added.

Threats can come from the inside of the network through compromised hosts, or from other sources on the Internet. The SAFE design guide from Cisco identifies the following threats to the network perimeter. Although this is not a comprehensive list of all possible threats that an organization faces, it is a good starting point for auditors to use in the identification of threats.

- **Service disruption:** Service disruption is a threat that targets the availability of network resources from applications to bandwidth. Denial of service attacks are common occurrences that can have significant impact on a company's capability to conduct business.

- **Network abuse:** Network and application services are enticing targets for attackers who want to break in to the network. These are usually the areas where the most exploitable vulnerabilities can be found through custom code and insecure deployments of applications. Other threats included in this category center around network acceptable use policy violations from insiders using prohibited network services such as P2P file sharing, unapproved instant messaging, and web services.

- **Data theft:** There is value in data, which includes customer credit card numbers, personal information, or a secret formula used in making a product. This makes data theft a serious threat with a wide range of attack strategies to steal sensitive information for resale to the highest bidder.

- **Intrusions and takeover:** Attackers can cause significant harm by vandalizing websites or loading malware on a compromised web server and infecting customers. Defending against intrusions is one of the most important goals of perimeter defense.

Policy Review

A perimeter protection policy provides guidance on how network traffic is to be controlled when entering and exiting the organization or traversing between security zones. Perimeter protection policies list the requirements for proper network segmentation and defining services that are allowed or explicitly denied within the network. A firewall rule set, for example, is the implementation of the perimeter protection policy and might not achieve the goals of the policy, which is discovered during an audit. These failures to implement policy appropriately are often because of poorly written, contradictory, or vague requirements. A good policy that is the result of a proper risk analysis lists detailed handling instructions for services and applications to overcome protocol weaknesses and reduce the attack surface. This information should be used as the source for creating the system of controls to protect the perimeter and enable proper monitoring and response. A good perimeter policy includes standards for the following:

- Ports and protocols allowed into the organization

- Network address translation (NAT)

- P2P and instant messaging policy

- Whether or not the business allows open access to the Internet or restricted to specific protocols for users

- Monitoring and IPS requirements

- Change control process and procedures

- Physical protection of perimeter devices

- Auditing of perimeter controls

Managing perimeter controls is not an easy task. Nothing can cause you to be in the unemployment line quicker than making a rule configuration mistake or disabling a critical signature that as a result enables an attacker to access credit card info or other sensitive customer information. It is like leaving the doors unlocked to your warehouse. You might come in the next day and have all of your inventory missing. For this reason, it is essential for all businesses to have a policy that addresses how to manage and control perimeter defenses. The policy should include the following:

- Individuals authorized to configure and manage perimeter controls

- A statement that specifically requires adherence to all standards outlined in the policy

- Device configuration requirements and references to standards documents

- Required process for testing and review before new perimeter controls are allowed into production

- Requirements for change control and monitoring of perimeter security events

Perimeter Operations Review

When an auditor performs a perimeter operations review, he or she is typically looking at much more than just the technology. The auditor must always look for areas that can be improved in design, support, maintenance, and operation of the security system. This section covers four of the most important aspects of perimeter defense management, change control, monitoring, and incident handling.

IPS devices and firewalls can determine whether there is an incident that needs to be investigated, but only if the events are reviewed and acted on. Logging security information and never looking at it is not only a waste of time and resources, but it will ultimately limit the business's ability to recognize attacks and fine-tune the effectiveness of policy.

Management and Change Control

Configuration control processes and procedures need special attention during an audit. Poor adherence to policy and mismanagement in this area can leave an organization vulnerable and wide open to attack. Any user who has access and authorization to make changes to perimeter access rules must be monitored, and all changes should be reviewed to help minimize mistakes.

At a bare minimum, there needs to be a change control process that details the date of the change, who made the change, why the change was necessary, what the change was, and who approved the change. This can be a physical form or an automated change control application, depending on how sophisticated the organization's change controls processes are.

Cisco Security Manager (CSM) provides a sophisticated workflow and approval tool that can automate this process. The auditing capabilities in CSM also enable a record of changes that can be rolled back if necessary. It is also a good practice to have a syslog server available and configure all perimeter devices to send configuration and change messages to it for a secondary audit trail.

Figure 8-1 shows a change report for a firewall configuration in CSM.

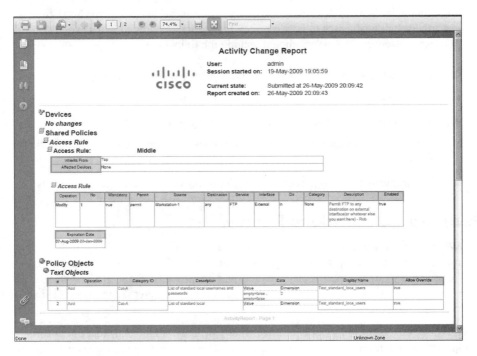

Figure 8-1   *Change Activity Change Report in CSM*

Monitoring and Incident Handling

The final aspect of perimeter architecture review is to assess how the organization conducts monitoring and responds to security events. There is a wealth of security data generated by your typical firewall or IPS, but without regular and automated review this information might as well not even exist. It's not uncommon to get thousands of syslog messages a day from just a handful of devices, so automating this process is very beneficial for businesses.

Products such as Cisco MARS take all of the data generated and sort through it to correlate and identify the most relevant and important events that should be followed up on. The capability to have a single dashboard for security events makes the detection of malicious activity not only faster, but also something that is significantly less labor intensive. Figure 8-2 shows the MARS dashboard, which is a single application for monitoring the security status of all devices.

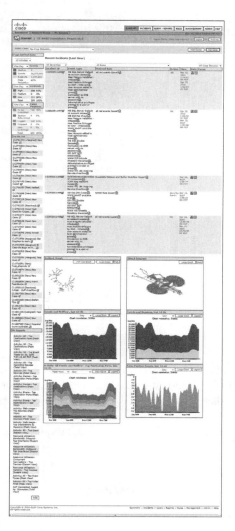

Figure 8-2 *MARS Dashboard*

Incident handling is another area that businesses should assess because it's not a matter of if there will be an incident but when. Having a plan in place to quickly respond can mean the difference between a painful monetary loss or a company's name splashed all over the news. Don't wait until after a security incident occurs to figure out who to call and what to do next. Auditors need to review these procedures for effectiveness and a clear process. Cisco MARS has built-in incident-handling capabilities and can assign incidents to individuals for follow-up. Figure 8-3 shows the MARS case creation function.

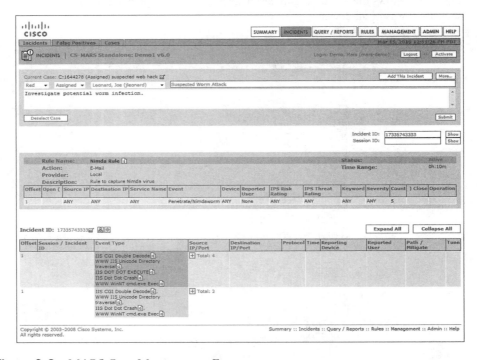

Figure 8-3   *MARS Case Management Features*

Log archives and storage of perimeter devices are required by a number of regulations such as PCI and SOX. This information can be used for forensics in the event of a breach, as a way to piece together what happened. Log data also provides a valuable source of trending information that can help with capacity planning and other functions. At a minimum, an organization needs to archive all changes, inbound connections, and alerts generated by perimeter security devices.

Perimeter Architecture Review

Assessing perimeter protection devices should always begin with an architectural review of perimeter security. Networks have a tendency to grow organically over time, and what was once a solid protective posture can end up becoming difficult to manage and ultimately a vulnerable collection of old firewall rules and exposed services. It is not uncommon to see firewall rule sets that number in the thousands on larger networks, with little coherence and significant overlap. IT engineers are good at "just making it work," and sometimes it is at the expense of security.

Access rules are not the only areas that need attention in an architectural review. Intrusion preventions systems act as the eyes, ears, and active defense for the network. An improperly deployed IPS provides little value, and many organizations do not tune their IPS to defend against their own unique risk profile. A perimeter architecture review gives the auditor a top-level view of perimeter defenses and enables the auditor to better tailor the audit for identifying security weaknesses that could be exploited.

What Are You Protecting?

Effective security architectures entail a solid understanding of the assets that need to be protected first and foremost. The requirements for protecting a database server that houses an ecommerce gateway, for example, is much more involved than protecting a nonessential FTP server. Gathering this information into a chart can be a great way to make sure that nothing is missed, and the assets with the most business value are highlighted and given priority. The following information is useful in assessing protection mechanisms:

■ **Asset details:** The type of device including operating system version

■ **Applications and services:** A complete list of applications and services for each piece of hardware or asset

■ **Connectivity requirements:** Communication flow requirements for the asset, to the IP port and service level

■ **Business value:** The criticality identification to business operations the device or asset represents

Table 8-1 provides an example of an asset classification chart.

Table 8-1 *Asset Classification*

Asset Details	Apps and Services	Connectivity Requirements	Business Value
Windows 2008 Server E-mail Server	Exchange 2007	SMTP, IMAP, HTTPS, DNS, MS AD	High
Windows 2003 Database Server	MS SQL Server	SQL, MS AD	Mission critical
Ubuntu Linux 8.04 Web Server	Apache, Mysql	HTTP, HTTPS, SFTP, SSH	High

Perimeter Design Review

Reviewing the current design involves assessing the logical and physical placement of security controls. During this part of the review, the auditor takes all of the collected information thus far and begins to piece together how each control works towards the goal of keeping the network secured. Looking at the perimeter from a logical perspective first prevents the natural engineering tendency of getting caught up in the nuances and details of the design and missing the big picture. At this stage, the auditor spots the security issues and determines security requirements based on good practices and policy. After a logical map of security requirements is constructed, it is compared to the physical implementation to determine what is missing or can be improved upon.

Logical Architecture

Devices that are accessible from the Internet are by definition at more risk than those buried behind layers of firewalls and hidden behind NAT. A good technique for spotting and evaluating risk at the perimeter is to create security zones in which you can group like applications and services. These zones can then be used to separate services and security control requirements into their own parts of the network. This technique also makes it much easier to create firewall rules and helps to reduce complexity.

The primary objective of grouping assets into security zones is to create natural policy enforcement points among different security levels. An ecommerce zone, for example, has a higher risk level because of its proximity to the Internet and its criticality, where as an internal network print server farm has a lower risk level, because it is on a trusted internal network and not a significant target for attack. Risk helps determine the countermeasures needed, and grouping services into zones shows an auditor the level of risk each zone faces. Table 8-2 groups assets into security zones.

Table 8-2   *Asset to Security Zone Mapping*

Asset	Security Zone
Ecommerce Server	Web Service
E-mail Server	Web Service
AD Domain Server	Internal Server

The flow of data into and out of the organization should be identified to determine whether policy and good security practices are followed. For an easy way to do this, create a logical flow diagram and an application and service chart that highlights how data moves through different zones of the network. Figure 8-4 shows what a logical data flow diagram looks like.

Each zone should have its communications requirements mapped, including the direction of communication (either incoming or outgoing), which enables the auditor to determine what controls should be present at various points in the network. The logical diagram should be tested through traffic analysis and scanning to verify assumptions, but provides a good start in evaluating perimeter defenses. Table 8-3 represents data flow requirements between security zones.

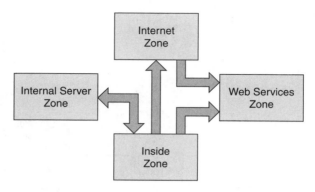

Figure 8-4 *Logical Security Zone Data Flow*

Table 8-3 *Intra Security Zone Communication Requirements*

Source Zone	Destination Zone	Protocols
Internet	Web Services	HTTP, HTTPS, DNS, FTP, SMTP, POP3
Web Services	Internet	DNS, FTP, SMTP
Internal	Web Services	HTTP, HTTPS, DNS, SMTP, POP3, SSH
Internal	Internet	HTTP, HTTPS, DNS, FTP

Physical Architecture

A physical architecture review is used to assess the deployment of security countermeasures for optimum protection. A physical diagram shows the routers, switches, and security appliances that are used as security controls and how they are physically connected. The logical diagram can then be compared against the physical diagram to make sure that nothing was missed during the security design phase and that defense in depth is utilized. Figure 8-5 represents a simple physical perimeter diagram.

In network perimeter design, the concepts of inside, outside, services networks, and the DMZ (demilitarized zone, a term borrowed from military security) are central to building strong perimeter defenses. Networks that are under a business's administrative control and not freely accessible from the Internet are usually considered inside networks with a higher degree of trust, and those that are accessible from the Internet or outside of a business's administrative control are considered to be untrusted outside networks. The concept of the DMZ stems from the simple fact that services designed to be accessible from the Internet or available to third parties are naturally greater targets of attack and warrant special handling and segmentation from the rest of the network. Another zone that is often used in security design is the services network. The services network is a logical classification for internal services that can be grouped together by function to simplify policy enforcement. A business typically has a number of services networks that are not open to the Internet but warrant special handling and protection because of their importance to operations and productivity. These four security zones are basic examples

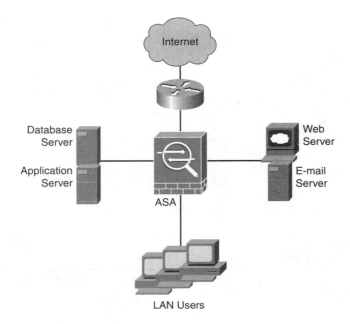

Figure 8-5 *Physical Perimeter Diagram*

that can be used to define a perimeter defensive strategy. Each network boundary provides an opportunity to deploy security countermeasures, which affords another layer of
protection. Regardless of the size of the business and network, segmenting services is an
effective way to control access and reduce risk.

What Is the Risk?

Now that you know some of the threats and vulnerabilities of perimeter systems, the next
logical step is to determine the level of risk to these systems. Chapter 1, "The Principles
of Auditing," discusses the risk assessment process in detail, and following these techniques enables an auditor to create a ranked list of risks that need to be addressed
through countermeasures. Most auditors know that placing an unpatched Windows server on the Internet is a pretty risky move, because it is well known that there are many
attacks that could exploit the vulnerabilities of an unpatched system. But what if there is
a legitimate reason for not patching to the latest software release? Maybe a patch breaks
other critical functionality, or the organization has not had time to test the patch to
ensure that the same level of service will be maintained. Scenarios like this happen all the
time, and risk, just like any other aspect of the business, must be managed to minimize
impact. It's the auditor's job to recognize these risks and ensure that the proper countermeasures and compensating controls are in place to limit exposure.

Creating a table that represents each security zone, zone risk rating, and threats identified
for each zone is useful for identifying which zones are deficient based on the available
countermeasures and controls for each threat. Table 8-4 shows an example chart for mapping security zone to threats.

Table 8-4 *Security Threats by Zone*

Security Zone	Risk Rating	Threats
Internet	5	DDoS, spoofing, reconnaissance, malware, and spam
Internal Server	3	Data theft, malware, data manipulation, and theft of trade secrets
DMZ Network	3	SQL injection and credit card theft
Inside Network	3	Malware, insider threat, spam, phishing, and data leakage

Good Design Practices

The Internet is a great source for examples of good practices and perimeter security design, and auditors should review the organization's designs against good practices. For example, it is a good practice to place a screening router on the outside connection in front of a firewall, as a way to add another layer of filtering capabilities. This can be extremely useful to help reduce filtering load on the firewall itself, because it's always better to drop traffic as close to the source as possible.

The Cisco website provides numerous examples of perimeter protection schemes for businesses both large and small, including Cisco validated designs that encompass complete solutions. Cisco has also released some significant updates to the safe design guides for use as architectural references. You can go to www.cisco.com/go/safe for the current design guides.

Auditing Firewalls

Firewalls are top on the list of critical security devices that businesses use to protect their assets. Cisco firewalls are available as dedicated appliances through the ASA product line, and integrated into Cisco routers. Even though Cisco firewalls come in all shapes and sizes, they operate on the same basic principle that you should limit the exposure of computer systems to only those protocols and ports necessary to provide services, thus reducing the size of the attack surface of the system. The auditing of a firewall primarily revolves around inspecting the firewall rules to make sure that they are accurately enforcing security policy, and providing as high a degree of protection as feasible.

Firewalls block unauthorized traffic, but if an organization wants to follow good practices, then it needs to layer on other security countermeasures to defend against attacks that firewalls are not designed to prevent. If you have an attack against an authorized port and service, and your server is compromised, it isn't the firewall that failed but the lack of defense in depth. Of course the concept of what a firewall is just isn't as clear as it used to be in the days of single purpose firewalls. We live in a unified threat management world, and today's firewalls perform a great many security tasks. IPS and VPN has been integrated into the Cisco ASA firewall line and IOS firewalls, and as such Cisco offers one of the most complete and advanced firewall platforms available. Unified Threat

Management (UTM) devices operate as a combined threat management device, but the foundational elements of the firewall are central to how the device operates. This section discusses how to conduct an assessment of Cisco firewalls and the firewall rule base.

Review Firewall Design

Assessing firewall design requires that the auditor understand the various ways in which a Cisco firewall can be deployed. There are many factors that cause an organization to choose one design over another, and technical requirements sometimes are shaped by politics and budget as well. The firewall is a policy enforcement tool that should be placed at key network zone boundaries. It is ultimately up to the business to determine its tolerance for risk and deploy the countermeasures that make sense. The following examples illustrate common firewall designs that an auditor might find.

Simple Firewall

The simple firewall design is common for small or branch networks and involves a firewall or router (configured as a firewall) between the Internet and the internal network. NAT is typically used, and providing Internet access is the primary function of the firewall. There might be port forwarding configured to internal servers for e-mail delivery or limited web hosting. These designs typically suffer from minimal layered security, but are by far the least expensive deployment method to connect a very small remote office or mobile worker situation. Figure 8-6 shows a diagram of a simple firewall deployment.

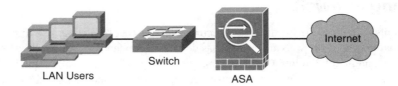

Figure 8-6   *Simple Firewall*

Screening Router and Firewall

A screening router provides frontline defense at the network edge. Not only does this router act as a basic firewall, but can also perform services such as routing, Netflow collection, quality of service, and anti-spoofing. The point of a screening router is to provide defense in depth and another place where access rules can be applied. Figure 8-7 shows a screening router and firewall design.

Figure 8-7   *Screening Router and Firewall*

Firewall with DMZ

A better design for an organization that hosts its own websites, e-mail, or other Internet-facing services is the firewall with DMZ design. This design provides segmentation of Internet-facing services to their own dedicated subnet where policies and access control can be better enforced. Typically the firewall provides NAT services to the web applications, and also conducts application layer inspection to enforce RFC compliance and application use policies. Layering in an IPS via an SSM module inside the ASA or through a dedicated appliance can give full IPS protection for all traffic passing through the device. Figure 8-8 shows a firewall with DMZ design.

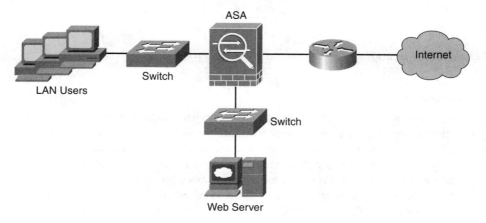

Figure 8-8   *Firewall with DMZ*

Firewall with DMZ and Services Network

As the criticality of web services increases, a single DMZ can sometimes become crowded with applications and services. The more applications, the more complicated the access rules can become, and before long policies become difficult to implement on a single DMZ. Creating service networks on separate firewall interfaces addresses this, by grouping like services together to simplify policy enforcement. Web servers can go into the DMZ, and internal servers can go into the services network. The amount of configuration starts to increase as the number of interfaces increases, but the capability to be able to create more effective policies is vastly improved. Figure 8-9 shows a firewall with a DMZ and services network.

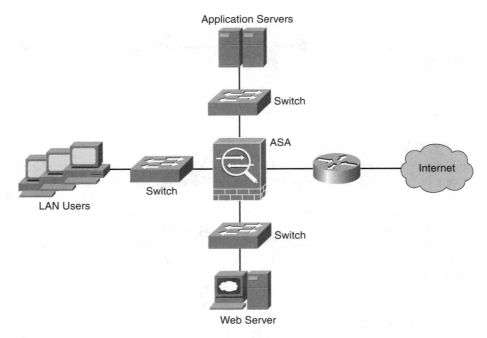

Figure 8-9   *Firewall with DMZ and Services Network*

High Availability Firewall

High availability firewall designs are common in organizations that rely on the Internet as both a source of revenue and an important mechanism for reaching customers. For these types of organizations, downtime can create significant monetary loss, so the expense of a redundant architecture is well worth it. Cisco firewalls can support active/standby, where one firewall forwards traffic and the other takes over in the event of a failure. Another high availability option is active/active where both firewalls enforce policy and pass traffic at the same time, and in the event of a failure of one device all traffic flows through the single remaining firewall. The benefits of active/active over active/standby are that both firewalls are being utilized and can support higher data rates than a single firewall. The downside to active/active is that both firewalls must be able to support their own traffic loads in addition to the other firewall if one fails or the organization must be able to accept reduced throughput during the failure condition. Figure 8-10 shows a high availability firewall design with two ASAs.

IOS Firewall Deployment

Cisco IOS firewalls are typically deployed in small or branch offices, retail, or teleworker environments where integrated security into a single device is preferred to having a dedicated security appliance. An IOS firewall can provide the same foundational policy enforcement capabilities as a firewall appliance. These platforms are deployed as an edge

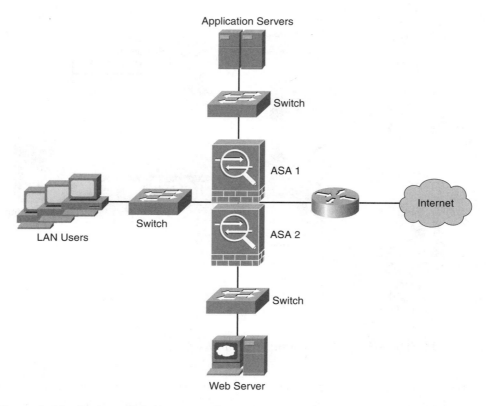

Figure 8-10 *High Availability Firewall Design*

router terminating wide-area network (WAN) and Internet connections, and in the case of a branch office or teleworker application, will terminate Virtual Private Networks (VPNs) back to corporate headquarters. From a design perspective IOS firewalls can be used interchangeably with firewall appliances, but usually with performance and feature trade-offs associated with the extra processing load on the router.

Figure 8-11 shows an IOS firewall deployment at a branch office.

Review Firewall Configuration

Cisco ASA firewalls are built from a hardened operating system designed specifically for duty as a security appliance. This means that for the most part, they do not require the extensive tweaking or service removal of a general-purpose operating system. However, it is possible to enable features and services that could degrade the security of the firewall, and for this reason an auditor should review the firewall configuration for mistakes and unnecessary services.

A Cisco router configured as a firewall should follow router hardening and security configuration best practices to ensure that it is set up appropriately for duty as a

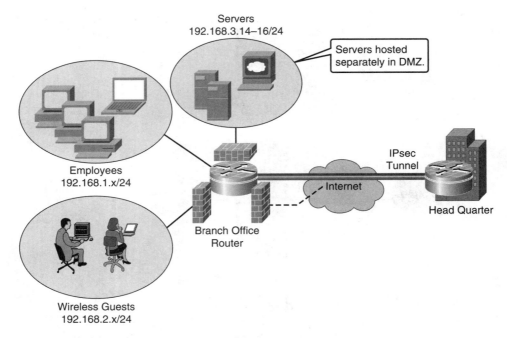

Figure 8-11 *IOS Firewall Deployment at a Branch Office*

security device. Chapter 7, "Infrastructure Security," discusses many of the baseline configurations that should be present, such as AAA services, login banners, and other protective features for IOS devices.

Auditing a firewall's configuration can be conducted from Adaptive Security Device Manager (ASDM) on the ASA or Cisco Configuration Professional (CCP) for IOS devices, a configuration file, the command line, or by using CSM.

Firewall Modes of Operation

Cisco Firewalls can be configured to operate in either routed or transparent mode. Routed mode is the most common way a firewall is configured and is also the factory default. In this mode, the firewall is set as a next hop gateway and provided an IP address on the network segment it is connected to. NAT can be used in this mode, and the firewall can also be configured to participate in routing protocol updates through Open Shortest Path First (OSPF), Routing Information Protocol (RIP), or Enhanced Interior Gateway Routing Protocol (EIGRP).

Transparent mode is introduced as a way to enable firewalls to operate without requiring that they be given IP addresses on the network. For all practical purposes, the firewall is configured to bridge segments together and control security in a stealth manner. The two segments are configured on switches as two separate VLANs that share a common IP address scheme. The transparent firewall bridges these connections together and then can

enforce security policy by being directly in-line with the traffic stream. The primary benefit of a design like this is that it does not require any re-addressing of the network IP
space, and a firewall can literally be dropped into any segment where extra security and
access control needs to be implemented. The firewall is not only able to control traffic at
a layer 2 level but also can enforce application layer security and perform NAT if
required. Figure 8-12 shows how the two modes are deployed in the network.

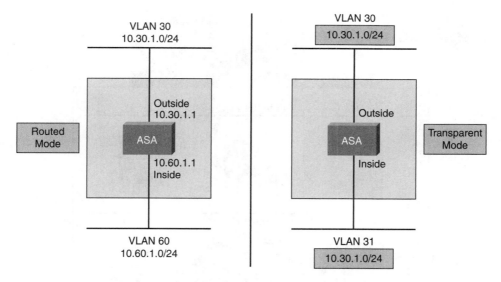

Figure 8-12 *Routed and Transparent Firewall Deployments*

Firewall Virtualization

Firewall management can sometimes be the source of contention within an organization,
where different groups need control over specific applications in a single firewall rule
base. Cisco introduced firewall virtualization capabilities into the ASA, in the form of
multiple security contexts, as a way to take a single firewall and have it appear, from a
management, configuration, and policy standpoint, as multiple firewalls. Each context is
configured independently and can have a number of interfaces, both physical and VLAN
trunked, applied to that context. Multiple context mode can support both routed and
transparent mode enabling maximum flexibility. Figure 8-13 shows a firewall deployed in
multi-context mode.

Filtering Methods

Cisco networks use the following three categories of filtering to enforce network traffic
policies.

- **Packet filter:** The packet filter is the simplest filtering method, and usually resides on
  routers and switches in the form of an access control list. Access control lists filter
  based on source, destination, protocol, and ports. This type of filtering is generally

fast from a processor standpoint, but there are no advanced features or inspection capabilities. From a defense-in-depth standpoint, this is typically the type of filtering performed on an edge router and can be used to offload some of the filtering requirements of the internal firewall. Of course, the downside of this filtering technique is that it is relatively easy to bypass, and there are limited logging capabilities for drop packets.

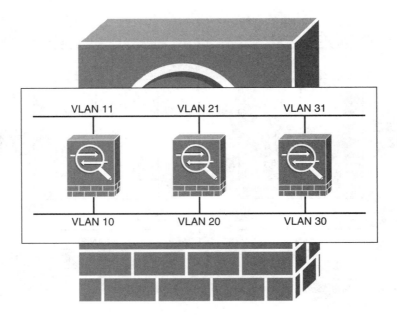

Figure 8-13 *Firewall Multiple-Context Mode*

- **Stateful inspections:** Every packet that is processed by a Cisco firewall is run through a stateful inspection algorithm, known as the adaptive security algorithm, to determine whether the packet should be allowed to pass or not. When a computer on the inside of the firewall wants to communicate to a host on the outside of the firewall, it forwards those packets to the firewall. As long as the connection is allowed by policy, the firewall will send the packet and store the connection information in its state table. The response from the host on the outside is received causing the firewall to look into its state table to ensure that it is a valid reply to an existing connection. If there is a match in the state table, the firewall will then pass it on to the inside host. This way the firewall can dynamically enable authorized communication to take place and deny unauthorized communication.

- **Application inspection:** Application inspection, also known as an application layer gateway, is a process that is layered onto stateful inspection to enable the firewall to further analyze a packet for malicious activity, and conformance to RFC standards. It's common for applications to try to circumvent firewall policy by tunneling their communications through well-known ports such as HTTP, because most firewalls are configured to allow outbound web traffic. With application inspection, the firewall identifies the fact that an application was operating on the ports used by web traffic but did not follow standard HTTP communication methods. Application inspection is accomplished through the modular policy framework, which is discussed next.

Network Address Translation

NAT was originally conceived as a method to alleviate some of the issues around the fact that the IPv4 address space was quickly becoming consumed by the explosive growth of the Internet in the 1990s. RFC 1918 addresses, or private address ranges, were allocated to enable business and home users to hide entire networks behind a single Internet address. Although this is not typically thought of as a security feature, it does help to hide a network's topology from being easily scanned and connected to from the Internet. This lack of direct Internet connectivity to hosts behind a NAT gateway limits exposure from connection initiated from the Internet and is considered a good security practice for organizations to adopt for users and devices that do not provide services on the Internet.

There are two basic types of NAT:

- **Full network address translation:** One address is translated to another address in a one-to-one fashion on a firewall or router.

- **Port address translation:** A single network address is shared for multiple hosts simultaneously.

Cisco firewalls support the following methods for implementing NAT:

- **Dynamic NAT:** Dynamic NAT provides a pool of globally reachable Internet addresses that are assigned to devices that initiate outbound communications. The address stays with the devices until the session times out or communication is ended. This type of NAT is intended only for communication initiated from the inside of a network going outbound and not for hosting services.

- **Dynamic PAT:** Dynamic Port Address Translation (PAT) takes one real Internet address and shares it with multiple internal hosts. A table is created that maps ports to hosts, and those ports are forwarded to the host that initiated the outgoing connection to receive return traffic. PAT maps ports above 1024 to communicating hosts for each connection they initiate, and clears the translation after 30 seconds of inactivity. Dynamic NAT and Dynamic PAT can be configured to work together to enable practically limitless scalability.

- **Static NAT:** Static NAT is typically used for devices that need fully bi-directional Internet connectivity. There is a one-to-one translation configured between a globally reachable Internet address and an Internet private address.

- **Static PAT:** Static PAT is used to map specific ports from a globally reachable Internet address to internal hosts. You can take a single address and map port 80 and 443 (web and SSL) to one host and port 21 (FTP) to another host, for example, and only have to use one real IP address.

Good security practices dictate that you should always limit connectivity and exposure to the least amount of services possible. Using NAT and PAT can help to achieve these goals by limiting the capability for Internet devices to initiate connections to ports and services that are not essential to service delivery. Auditors should be on the lookout for firewall configurations that provide static NAT to end users for direct access from the Internet because these users could be inadvertently compromised.

Secure Management

The configuration review should begin with an inspection of management interfaces to ensure adherence to good security practices:

- SSHv2 should be configured for command-line configuration.

- If the ASDM web management interface is used, HTTPS should be configured.

- Use AAA for user authentication and authorization.

- Create a local fallback account in the event that the AAA server is unreachable.

- Encrypt all local account passwords.

- Make sure that user sessions time out after inactivity.

- If using SNMP for monitoring, use SNMPv3 with encryption.

Logging

Use the Network Time Protocol (NTP) to synchronize device time for correlation of log records to a common time:

- Use syslog to log all systems messages and connections through the firewall.

- Make sure that timestamps are used in syslog messages.

Other Configuration Checks

Perform the following configurations:

- Check that the built-in DHCP server is disabled.

- Ensure that antispoof configurations are present.

- Make sure that all access control lists end with an explicit deny all and log.

- Check the Cisco website for any Product Security Incident Response Team (PSIRT) or vulnerability notice for the version of software that the firewall is running.

Review Rule Base

Firewall rules appear to magically grow by themselves. The first day a firewall goes into production is like the first day you take a new car home from the dealership. It's shiny and new, it has that smell everyone loves, and you are careful to make sure that it stays neat and clean. Of course, that usually lasts about a week before the inevitable fast-food bag is thrown into the floorboard next to you. Before long, it takes a crime scene investigator to determine what those stains are on the seat, and a chisel to get the dried bird poop off the hood. Luckily, most organizations ban birds from perching on top of the firewall, so at least you won't have that to worry about during an audit. You are, however, required to look at many years' worth of rules and determine which rules implement policy and reduce risk and which ones don't.

As discussed earlier in the chapter, policy dictates the types of rules that need to be in place and the firewall is simply the enforcement of policy. By this point, the auditor has gathered all of the information necessary to review the firewall rules. When it comes time to sit down and actually review the rule base, it definitely helps to interview the firewall administrator during the review to get more context as to why questionable rules were added, and for the auditor to validate his or her knowledge of the business requirements that required the rules in the first place. The goal is to make sure that the rule base follows good security practices, enforces policy, and is manageable and optimized. Keeping the rule base simple is the key to achieving that goal.

Cisco Firewall Rule Basics

Cisco firewall rules are built from the physical or logical interface perspective. Each interface is given a security level from 0 to 100, with 0 being untrusted (outside network) and 100 reserved for trusted networks (inside network). By default, interface 0 on the firewall is considered the outside interface, and interface 1 is considered the inside interface. These security zones become important in rule development because a Cisco firewall automatically enables communication initiated from a trusted network to an untrusted network, and deny traffic initiated from an untrusted network to a trusted network. These implicit permits and denies create the basis for an organization's firewall rule base. Security levels are classified by the following:

- **Security level 0:** Untrusted outside interface. Cannot receive inbound traffic unless explicitly configured.

- **Security level 100:** Trusted inside interface. Any traffic received on the inside interface is allowed to pass to any lower-level interface by default.

- **Security level 1-99:** If you want to add other networks to the firewall, such as a DMZ network, create the interface, provide it a name, and give it a security level. For a single DMZ network, 50 is commonly used. This enables communication to be initiated from the inside network to the DMZ, and from the DMZ to the outside network. All other traffic is blocked unless permitted by making additional firewall rules to enable bi-directional communications.

After you get the hang of this interface-centric model, understanding how the firewall rules affect policy becomes much easier. Like the security level, the access control rules are applied to the interface in an incoming or outgoing direction. Cisco firewall rules consist of the following components:

- **Interface:** Specifies the interface the access control entry is applied to

- **Action:** Permit or deny packet

- **Source:** Source network or group

- **Destination:** Destination network or group

- **Service:** Protocol and ports to match

- **Logging level:** Option to log and how detailed the log entry will be

Optional components of a firewall rule include:

- **Time range:** Time range in which the firewall rule is enforced

- **Description:** Optional, but good practices recommend documenting the reason for a rule in the configuration if possible

The firewall rule itself is applied on the interface and can be configured as an incoming rule or outgoing rule. These directions are in reference to the interface itself, and do not effect rules on any other interface. If you want to allow web traffic into the firewall from the outside network, configure the permit rule on the outside interface in an incoming direction. If you want to block all web traffic except from a single host (for a proxy server, for example), you can deny it on the outside interface in an outgoing direction and not have to create individual incoming rules on every interface on the firewall to block web traffic, which can greatly simplify configuration. Good practices in firewall rule creation recommends that if you are going to block something, block it on the interface it was received (incoming interface), because if you are going to have the firewall process the packet just to drop it on another interface, then you are wasting processing resources.

Another important tool for firewall rule creation is the use of object groups to link common devices and services into a logical object that can then be configured into access control lists. Object groups can include the following entries:

- **Network objects/groups:** Contains one or more host IP addresses of network devices

- **Service object:** Contains IP protocols, Internet Control Message Protocol (ICMP) ports, TCP ports, and UDP ports

- **TCP service group:** TCP port lists

- **UDP service group:** List of UDP ports

- **TCP/UDP service group:** Combined TCP/UDP port lists

- **ICMP group:** Groups for ICMP types

- **Protocol group:** IP protocol groups

Creating service objects can dramatically simplify configuration requirements and provide all of the ports protocols and IP address communications needed for a specific network segment, such as an e-mail or web server farm. The service group details required ports, and a network object group can reference the IP addresses. Instead of having an access control list (ACL) for every IP address and port used, with object groups one ACL can cover all similar servers and ports in that need to be accessible. If there is ever a change, such as the addition of a new server, that new IP address can be added to the network group object and inherit the configuration of the service group. It is also possible to nest groups within each other so that an ICMP group of approved ICMP types can be used within a service group. There is a significant amount of configuration flexibility here and even the most complicated network rules can be represented.

Rule Review

The firewall rule base for a small network can be as simple as 15 rules. If there are no services being hosted that need access from the Internet, then there might only need to be a handful of rules. Some organizations can have thousands of rules and hundreds of applications that need various levels of access. The key to strong firewall rule base security is to keep the rules as simple as possible. Firewall rule misconfiguration is a serious issue that is not easy to detect, which is why it is so important to have a well-documented standard configuration method for implementing firewall rule changes and additions.

There are a number of ways to get access to the firewall rule base. Auditors can simply review the configuration file itself if they have a good knowledge of Cisco firewall configuration techniques; they can access the built-in device manager for a much easier-to-read graphical representation of the rule base; or they can access Cisco Security Manager. All three ways get the information required, but for complex rule bases it's almost always easier to use the graphical tools. Figure 8-14 shows firewall rules from the built-in device manager within the ASA.

There are a number of good practices for firewall rules that every auditor should note. Following these practices well help to achieve defense in depth, and can act as a baseline for checklists:

- Allow only approved services and ports, and deny everything else inbound.

- Always use an explicit deny all at the end of the interface rules with logging. This provides a wealth of information on potential attacks and helps with troubleshooting if the firewall configuration is a bit too strict.

- Block all RFC 1918 addresses. Use spoof protection.

- Be as specific as possible on source and destination addresses during rule creation. It is easy to use ANY as a source, but it enables spoofed or addresses outside the approved range to be sent through the firewall.

- DMZ traffic going outbound should be controlled.

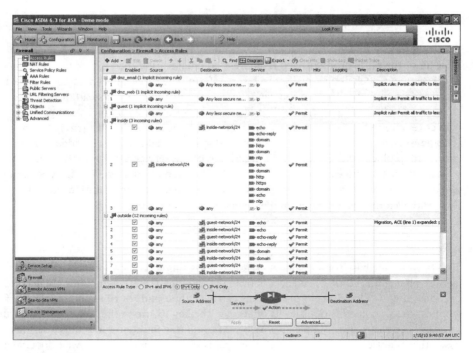

Figure 8-14 *ASDM Rule Base Display*

- DMZ segments should not have the capability to initiate connections to internal networks.

- Provide a description of every rule.

- Allow only approved Internet protocols to be sent to the Internet from user segments. Botnet masters and spammers love overly permissive outbound firewall policies.

Rule Optimization

Rule optimization is the process of reordering rules to make them more efficient, consolidating redundant rules, and pruning obsolete or unnecessary rules. Rule optimization is like firewall rule spring cleaning. Cisco firewalls process rules in order, and in many cases, the most commonly used rules are not at the top of the list, which makes the firewall have to keep checking until it gets a match. This matching process can also run into problems if a less specific rule comes before a more specific rule. The less specific rule always matches first, and the more specific rule is never processed, which means that the policy that rule is intended to enforce is ignored.

The number of rules a firewall has to check can also have an impact on performance. Many rules can be combined into a single rule, which, given enough rules, can drastically decrease the amount of processing the firewall needs to perform. Using network objects and service groups enables the configuration of entire classes of devices with a single rule, instead of each device having to be configured separately. The improvement in consistency using these techniques can also help reduce the chances of misconfiguration.

Rule optimization can be done manually by examining the firewall rules and inspecting the logs to find the ones that are most heavily used. These should go first, based on the number of hits that they have received. Typically, HTTP traffic and DNS will be at the top of the lists, but if there are many firewall segments and they are protecting internal network connections to servers, the wide range of ports that can be in use can seem overwhelming. For that reason, the auditor can save an enormous amount of time by using a commercial tool such as Algosec Firewall Analyzer to automate the optimization process. Figure 8-15 shows the Algosec Firewall Analyzer optimization report with a 62 percent increase in efficiency achieved by reordering and consolidating the rules of this particular firewall.

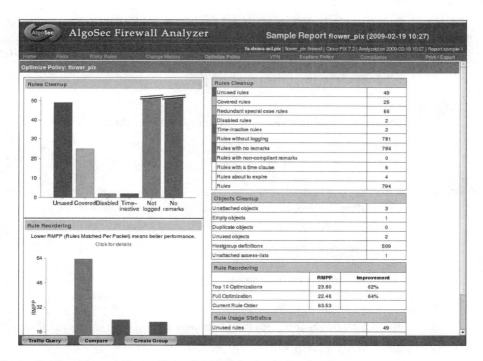

Figure 8-15 *Algosec Firewall Analyzer Rule Optimization Report*

The ASA Modular Policy Framework and Application Inspection

One of the most powerful features in Cisco firewalls is the Modular Policy Framework (MPF). The MPF is the mechanism that the firewall uses to identify specific traffic flows for the application inspection process. After a traffic flow is identified, the following features can be leveraged:

- **Traffic policing:** Uses QoS features to rate limit types of traffic such as ICMP or P2P file sharing to prevent abuse

- **Application inspection:** Uses deep packet inspection to look for malicious activity or tunneling

- **Quality of service:** Sets priority for mission critical apps or delay sensitive communications such as VoIP

- **TCP normalization, connection limits, and timeouts:** Enables the firewall to enforce TCP RFC standards conformance, limit the number of connections allowed over a period of time, and set the timeouts of session establishment

To better understand the modular policy framework, look at an example of how this technology can be used to enforce policy. The following example shows how a company can block instant messaging and P2P connections from employees through the use of the MPF and application inspection.

Step 1.   Be certain class maps are in place. The class maps identify the type of traffic you want to process; they use an access control list to accomplish this. The first class map looks at all traffic to search for tunneled instant message traffic:

```
class-map IMBlock
    match any
```

The second class map looks for P2P traffic tunneled through http ports:

```
class-map P2P
    match port tcp eq www
```

Step 2.   After the class maps are in place, a policy map is created to determine what will be done with the identified traffic. The following commands drop MSN or Yahoo instant message traffic:

```
policy-map type inspect im impolicy
 parameters
 match protocol msn-im yahoo-im
  drop-connection
```

The second policy map uses pre-programmed regular expressions that can detect gator and kazaa P2P traffic, plus drop and log any traffic that matches:

```
policy-map type inspect http P2P_HTTP
 parameters
 match request uri regex _default_gator
  drop-connection log
 match request uri regex _default_x-kazaa-network
  drop-connection log
```

The following policy map is used to combine the previous two policy maps into a single policy map statement:

```
policy-map IM_P2P
 class imblock
  inspect im impolicy
 class P2P
  inspect http P2P_HTTP
```

Step 3.   Apply the policy to an interface and in this case the combined policy is
applied to traffic originating from the inside interface:

```
service-policy IM_P2P interface inside
```

Although this is a single example to show what these commands might look like in the
configuration of an ASA, the actual implementation could cover any number of applications or policies. The extreme flexibility of application inspections requires that the auditor understand the basics of how it is applied. Consult the firewall documentation for further examples and options.

IOS Zone-Based Firewall

The IOS firewall has evolved significantly over the years. As of 12.4(6)T, it has moved
from an interface-centric firewall deployment model known as Classic Firewall (or
Context Based Access Control for you veteran Router Jockeys) to a zone-based approach
that enables firewall rules to be defined globally. Multiple interfaces can be assigned to
the same zone, making configuration and policy implementation much easier.
Organizations that are still running context-based access control (CBAC) are encouraged
to migrate to Zone-Based Firewalling (ZFW) because of the many improvements in policy enforcement, and because no new features will be added to the old firewall method. If
CBAC is in use by a company being audited, refer to Cisco documentation for more
information.

A ZFW policy provides stateful inspection and policy enforcement based on traffic moving into and out of defined security zones. Policy is no longer limited to physical interfaces and can be applied to logical regions of the network that might encompass multiple
interfaces. Each zone boundary is denied communication with other zones and must be
explicitly configured to the ports and protocols allowed to communicate between the
zones. Figure 8-16 shows three security zones defined within an IOS firewall.

Auditors need to understand the configuration process for ZFW in order to audit these
types of firewall rules. The configuration is not difficult and is similar to the ASA

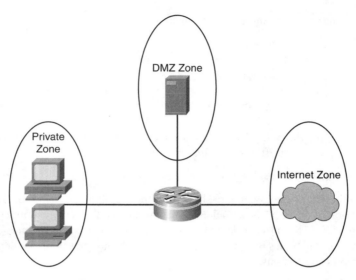

Figure 8-16   *IOS Zone-Based Firewall*

modular policy framework. IOS ZFW policies are applied by using Cisco Policy Language through a five-step process:

Step 1.   Use class-maps to select the protocols that are to be permitted:

```
class-map type inspect match-any allowed
match protocol http
match protocol https
match protocol dns
match protocol smtp
match protocol ftp
```

Step 2.   Use policy-maps to apply the protocols that are to be inspected:

```
policy-map type inspect allowed-policy
class type inspect allowed
inspect
```

Step 3.   Define the zones.

```
zone security private
zone security internet
```

Step 4.   Configure the interfaces for the zones they will be in:

```
Interface GigabyteEthernet 0/0
zone-member security private

interface GigabyteEthernet 0/1
zone-member security internet
```

Step 5.   Configure the zone pair in the direction of traffic flow and apply the policy:

```
zone-pair security private-internet source private destination internet
service policy type inspect allowed-policy
```

This simple policy highlights how the configuration might look from the command line. If the policy is complex, with many zones defined and very specific rule enforcement, auditing from the command line can be difficult to follow. Unless you truly want to wade through hundreds of lines of code, using CCP or CSM is a much easier way to analyze the rules. Figure 8-17 shows the IOS Firewall rules configured on a router in CCP.

Figure 8-17   *IOS Firewall Rules in CCP*

Auditing IPS

An IPS works in conjunction with a firewall to provide much deeper inspection of network traffic. While a firewall locks down ports and minimizes potential attack vectors of a network device, an IPS will inspect authorized traffic to make sure that it is legitimate and also look for malicious behavior. An IPS is an essential component of defense in depth and should be placed throughout the network at key junctions between security zones. Auditing an IPS is similar to auditing a firewall in that much of the testing is conducted at the packet level, but more emphasis is placed on effective detection and proper tuning of the IPS.

How IPS Works

The intrusion prevention system is an evolution of the intrusion detection system (IDS), which takes what was essentially an alarm system and turns it into an active policy enforcement device. Early IDS products were notorious for creating an incredible amount of logging information and alarms. This led many businesses to avoid using them because the people that had to monitor and manage them simply could not keep up with the amount of alarms generated. The other problem with a typical IDS deployment was the fact that even if a packet was detected as being malicious, the IDS could do very little to prevent damage because it was not in a position to drop the bad packet. This all changed with the invention of the IPS, because the IPS essentially acts as a network bridge and has full view and enforcement capabilities on all traffic that goes through it. This means that the IPS can detect and stop malicious activity in midstream, instead of just creating alarms.

Because an IPS has the capability to be able to drop traffic on the fly, it is responsible for differentiating good packets from bad packets. Packet analysis is not only a science but also an art, and many factors come into play to determine the intent of a communication flow. The easiest way to understand how the IPS handles these tasks is to quickly review how packets are processed within the IPS. Figure 8-18 shows the IPS process flow.

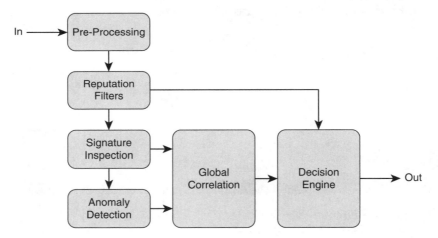

Figure 8-18   *IPS Packet Flow*

As a packet enters a Cisco IPS through its network interface, the first thing to occur is the packet is sent to the appropriate virtual sensor. Virtual sensors are independent policy configurations that can be applied to different networks or segments the IPS protects. Each virtual sensor can be set up for a specific purpose, such as to protect a web server farm with all of the appropriate signatures and settings. This enables an organization to deploy a single sensor and have it protect multiple segments without having to develop a single all-inclusive configuration.

After the appropriate virtual sensor is identified through IP address range or VLAN assignment, the packet goes through the IPS detection modules:

- **Pre-processing:** The normalizer engine is designed to pre-process packets to prevent attackers from using evasion techniques to trick the IPS into letting bad traffic pass. All IP and TCP packets are checked for RFC compliance, and anything that falls outside of this is either fixed (normalized) or dropped. The normalization function that occurs during pre-processing can stop many attacks that rely on manipulation of the IP and TCP parameters without needing a signature.

- **Reputation filters:** Reputation filters leverage Cisco sensor base to dramatically increase the effectiveness of detecting malicious activity. Based on the reputation of the network address that the packet came from, the IPS can respond to packets from networks that are known to be owned by the bad guys without having to run through the detection engine. For packets that come from questionable networks but not bad enough to drop immediately, the actual reputation score is sent to the Global correlation engine to be used by the decision engine. Chapter 11, "Endpoint Protection," discusses Reputation and Sensorbase in more detail.

- **Signature inspection engines:** Signatures are used to identify malicious packets through a scanning process preformed on the IPS. The signature engines are unique in that they are written for the vulnerability and not just the exploit code. The exploit can change or mutate over time, but because the Cisco IPS is looking for the vulnerability (such as a buffer overflow condition), a single signature can apply to multiple variants of the same attack that result in much more accurate signatures. Cisco accomplishes this through its use of universal protocol decoding engines as well as specific protocol engines for technologies such as VoIP.

- **Anomaly detection:** Anomaly detection provides the IPS sensor a way to learn normal behavior of the network through statistical analysis of traffic parameters. If there is a sudden increase of traffic on a port outside of normal thresholds, it might be an indication of a brand-new threat. The IPS creates a knowledge base of how traffic flows on the network by default every 24 hours.

- **Global correlation engine:** The global correlation engine influences the risk rating of a packet based on information from sensorbase and the results from signature inspection and anomaly detection. The IPS has the capability to participate in sensorbase by sending new attack data back to Cisco. The correlation engine also enables the IPS to identify malicious behavior by employing a meta-event generator to detect attack patterns. It's common for attacks today to be a multistep process that acts like normal network communications, which taken packet by packet would be no reason to raise an alarm. If, however, you look at the sequence of events over time, a pattern appears indicating that you might have an attack on your hands. The on-box correlation engine identifies patterns from suspicious, but not obviously malicious, activity.

After the detection process has been completed, it's up to the IPS to determine what to do with the packet in question. The decision engine follows a risk-based process to determine the impact of letting the packet through. The risk rating is computed from the following variables:

- **Attack severity:** Attack severity measures the potential impact of the packet. If this is an actual buffer overflow packet, the severity is high because it represents a potential compromise.

- **Signature fidelity:** Signature fidelity measures the accuracy of the signature at being able to detect an attack, or if it is prone to false positives.

- **Attack relevancy:** If the attack packet is crafted for a Windows machine and it is being sent to a UNIX server, the attack is not relevant so this value is lower. This relevancy information is learned by the sensor through passive fingerprinting, or manually configured.

- **Asset value of target:** This is a user-supplied value and enables the administrator to specify a target value. A financial server has a high asset value of mission critical, and a print server has a normal value.

- **Watch list:** Watch list information can be applied from other security products such as CSA. CSA can be configured to interoperate with the IPS and share information regarding any hosts that it has put into a watch list because of suspicious behavior.

All of these values are added together to come up with a risk rating based on a 0–100 scale. By default, a risk rating less than 34 produces an alarm, at 35–84 the IPS will alarm and log the packet, and at 85–100 the IPS will drop the packet inline.

Review IPS Deployment

Risk drives the deployment strategy and in many cases, firewalls and IPS are deployed together for in-depth defense. The most important factors for effectively utilizing an IPS are a solid understanding of what the IPS is protecting and what type of traffic should be inspected. Although the default configurations of an IPS are relatively effective out of the box, there is no "one-size-fits-all" configuration for IPS. Tuning is part of IPS administration and should not be overlooked.

An IPS can only inspect as much traffic as it is rated for, and an overworked IPS drops packets. Under sizing the IPS can lead to network communication problems and a degraded level of security. The IPS can be configured to fail closed, and drop packets that it cannot inspect, which is a way to handle unusually high traffic loads and end enforce policy, but it is always best to perform traffic analysis first to determine how much bandwidth the hardware needs to handle.

Cisco IPSec come in multiple forms, from standalone sensors to integrated modules in routers and firewalls. All of the hardware-based IPS sensors use the same software, which makes configuration consistent across all of the platforms. A common deployment technique for an IPS is to put it between the firewall interface and the network segment that it protects. This type of deployment inspects all traffic entering and exiting the firewall interface, and enables the IPS to focus on the ports and protocols that the firewall allows through. IPS deployments are also effective in front of critical servers or assets where any attack could be costly in terms of downtime or loss.

Physically deploying the IPS can occur in a number of ways, depending on the current network architecture. Figure 8-19 and the list below illustrate common deployment examples.

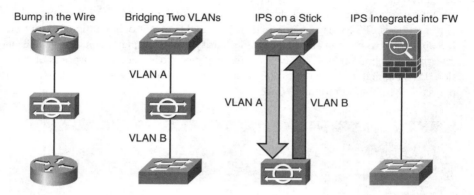

Figure 8-19   *Common Deployment Examples for IPS*

- **Bump in the wire:** The IPS is physically cabled between two network devices.

- **Bridging two VLANs:** The IPS connects two separate VLANs that use the same IP subnet. The IPS acts as a bridge in this case connecting the two VLANs at layer 2.

- **IPS on a stick:** The IPS is connected to a single switch and configured to support VLAN trunks, and inspected traffic makes a u-turn through the IPS and back into the switch.

- **Integrated into a firewall:** The IPS resides on a module in the firewall, and the sensing interface resides on the backplane of the device. Traffic to be inspected is funneled to the sensor.

Review IPS Configuration

Just like the ASA firewall, the Cisco IPS is built on a hardened operating system that does not require any tweaking of services to secure. Many of the same good security practices that are used for firewalls also apply to an IPS, and this section covers a number of areas that auditors need to be aware of when reviewing the IPS configuration.

Configuration review on the Cisco IPS platform can be accomplished five different ways:

- From the command-line interface

- By direct review of the configuration file

- Using an integrated IPS device manager

- Through IPS Manager Express

- Through CSM (for large deployments)

The command-line interface is a quick way to do a spot check on the configuration. The integrated device manager gives you the same information with a graphical interface and is a lot easier to get around in if the auditor is not familiar with Cisco IPS command-line configurations. IPS Manager Express (IME) is capable of not only configuring up to ten IPS appliances, but it can also receive IPS security events, display them in real-time, and save them to a built-in SQL database for reporting purposes. For the purposes of this section, IME highlights where the various configuration options are located. Figure 8-20 displays the IME configuration interface.

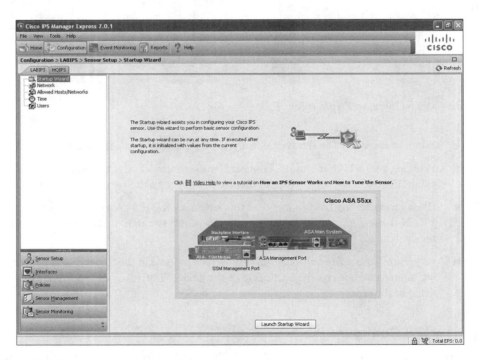

Figure 8-20 *IME Configuration Interface*

Protect the Management Interface

The IPS platform by nature is invisible on the wire, so outside of an unpatched vulnerability, there are minimal ways in which an IPS can be directly compromised. The management interface, however, should be segmented to a protected, management-only VLAN if possible. The management interface is not only responsible for configuration of the IPS, but also generates alarm traffic, rate limiting, and shunning commands for edge routers.

The IPS also has the capability to control which IP addresses are allowed to initiate communications with the management interfaces. Limiting access to a VPN-accessible, protected management subnet is a practical way to allow access from anywhere in a secure manner that does not expose the management interface to unauthorized traffic. Consult the security policy to determine what is permissible. Allowed hosts/networks for management are shown in Figure 8-21.

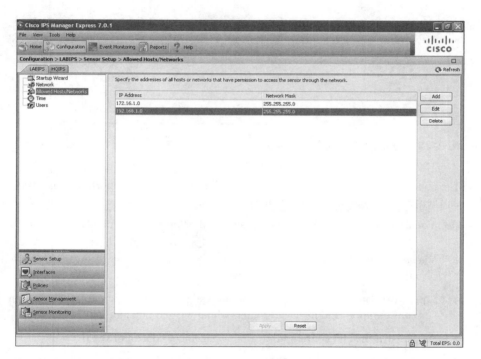

Figure 8-21   *Allowed Hosts/Networks for Management*

Administrative Access and Authentication

A Cisco IPS can be managed via the built-in web interface encrypted with SSL, SSH, and telnet. Although the IPS supports telnet, it is not recommended to enable it for interactive management of the device because the entire session is sent in clear text. The preferred method of command-line management is SSH v2. Telnet should be disabled for management. Figure 8-22 shows telnet disabled and SSL used for web management.

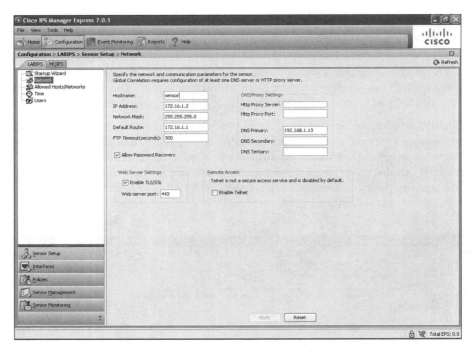

Figure 8-22 *Telnet Disabled for Management and SSL Web Access Enabled*

The built-in device manager has multiple levels of management support, for businesses that separate configuration and monitoring duties.

User management roles in IME and IDM are listed below and illustrated in Figure 8-23:

- **Viewer:** Allowed to view configuration and events, but can't make any configuration changes except to his or her own password

- **Operator:** Can view all configurations and make changes to signatures, virtual sensor configuration, and managed routers (shunning and rate limiting)

- **Administrator:** Full configuration and management control of the IPS

- **Service:** A special account built for low-level troubleshooting of the IPS subsystem. Allows this user to bypass the standard configuration shell, and primarily used for Cisco technical support personnel to assist with troubleshooting.

The IPS can also enforce strong password requirements, login attempts before lockout, and the number of historical passwords remembered for user accounts. Figure 8-24 shows these settings in the configuration.

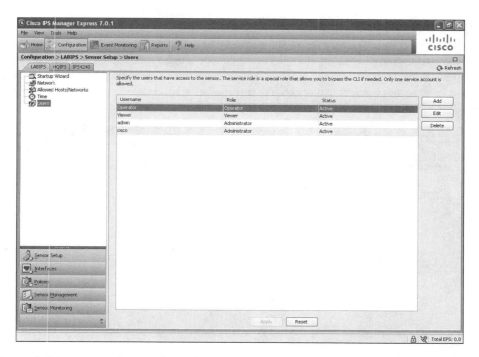

Figure 8-23 *User Roles Configured*

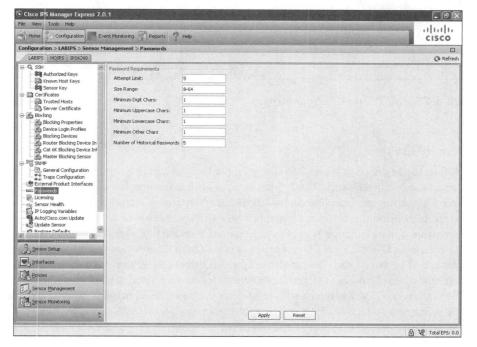

Figure 8-24 *Password Requirements for IPS Management*

NTP Configuration

NTP should be configured for all IPS devices. Time is an important element in logging and enables the correlation of events between multiple devices. All logs generated by the IPS include a timestamp, and NTP can synchronize the timestamps. NTP can be spoofed, so good security practices dictate using authentication to a trusted time source. Figure 8-25 shows NTP configuration parameters in IME.

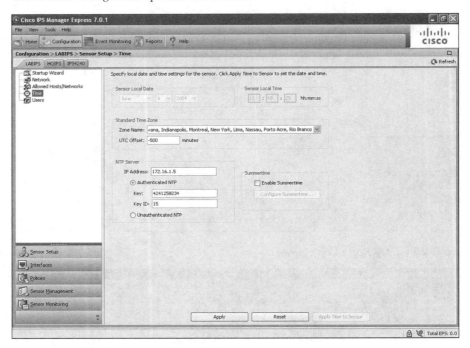

Figure 8-25   *NTP Time Configuration*

Signature Updates

IPS signatures need to be updated on a regular basis to add protection from the latest attacks and vulnerabilities. The IPS has an auto update feature that enables the IPS to pull latest signature and scanning engine updates directly from Cisco or a network share, if the organization wants stricter control of how IPS updates are distributed. The built-in signature update function is configured separately on each IPS sensor, and in order to update from Cisco directly, you simply supply a Cisco Connection Online (CCO) username and password with IPS signature download rights. Select an update interval, based on how often the organization wants to check for new signatures. For larger sensor deployments, CSM has the capability of deploying updates in mass to many sensors at the same time, which can be a considerable timesaver. Figure 8-26 shows the IPS Signature update configuration options in IME.

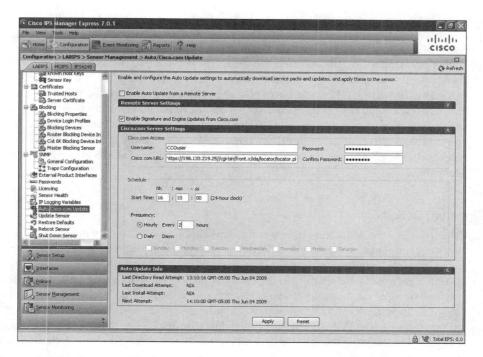

Figure 8-26 *Signature Update Configuration*

Event Logging

Cisco IPS uses SDEE and SSL encryption as a secure IPS log transportation method. SDEE uses a subscription model where a logging device makes a connection to the IPS and pulls down the logs. There is little configuration needed within the IPS to make this work: If IME is used, the logging function is enabled as soon as the IPS device is added. For MARS, the IPS sensor needs to have the MARS appliances certificate added to the list of trusted hosts.

Logging is turned on by default for many signatures, but some signatures, such as the ones that operate within the normalizer engine, are not set to log because the enormous amount of events the engine would create makes it not worth logging. This also means that a few packets in an attack might be dropped, but no log is generated because they were stopped by the normalizer. This typically occurs with packet manipulation attacks (overlapping fragments or invalid TCP options), where the normalizer discards the packet because of failure to comply with TCP/IP RFCs.

All IPS logs should be collected, reviewed, and stored for archival purposes. Auditors should review the logging function to make sure that it is operating as expected.

Review IPS Signatures

An IPS is only as good as its detection capabilities, and Cisco has spent thousands of hours tweaking the default signatures in the IPS to provide the maximum protection possible for the widest range of deployments. Although the default signatures are good for general-purpose use, it's impossible to plan ahead for every network application or service. For that reason IPS tuning is an essential part of IPS deployment and is unfortunately one of the primary areas where organizations fail when configuring their IPS. The auditor's role is not to configure it for them, but to make sure that the IPS is providing the appropriate level of protection based on the value of the assets the IPS is responsible for defending.

Signature Definitions

The IPS signature definitions represent the core of IPS policies, and by default all of the most critical signatures are enabled. Reviewing the signatures allows the auditor to see what is enabled and help to determine whether the IPS is appropriately configured. The IME is a great place for auditors to review signatures, because it provides not only categorized views of the signatures themselves, but also a handy filter function that displays only specific signatures by name, scanning engine, severity, whether or not it is enabled, or signature ID. The IME also includes a window that displays detailed description information and history for selected signature. Figure 8-27 shows the signature definitions for virtual sensor 0 (VS0).

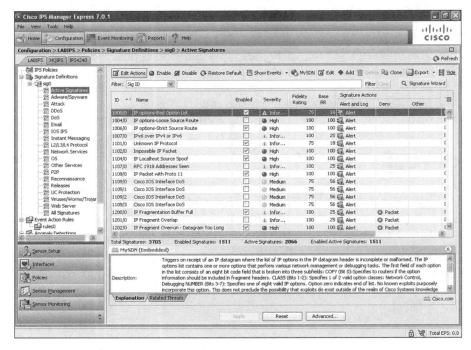

Figure 8-27 *IME Signature Definitions*

There are three different states for a signature in the IPS:

- **Enabled:** An enabled signature is loaded into the inspection engine and is used for inspection.

- **Disabled:** A disabled signature is still loaded into the inspection engine, but is not currently active or enforcing policy.

- **Retired:** A retired signature is unloaded from the inspection engine and is not taking up any CPU cycles or memory.

Each security zone can have its own virtual sensor and will be assigned signature polices that reflect the type of services and hosts that reside on it. If the security zone is full of Linux servers acting as a web farm, then the signatures should be tuned for identifying and stopping relevant attacks. Retiring Windows-specific signatures in this case helps increase sensor performance and keeps the logs clean of irrelevant information. Retiring unused signatures is considered good practice for tuning.

Event Action Rules

Signatures are responsible for identifying bad traffic on the network, but it's the event action rules that enforce policy and make the decision on what to do with the offending packet. By default, a Cisco IPS drops any packet that produces a risk rating of 85 or above. This is set so that the IPS will react to any critical attack while minimizing chances of a false positive stopping legitimate traffic. Event actions can be configured to support different actions based on risk rating. There are three built-in risk categories that can be used: high risk, medium risk, and low risk. The risk threshold can be modified to create a multitude of custom policies.

Target Value Rating

Asset target values influence the IPS actions by increasing the risk value associated with assets that are more important to the business. It is recommended to input target value ratings for assets that could benefit from a stronger enforcement response based on their criticality to the business. The following values can be assigned to devices:

- **Mission critical:** Strictest IPS malicious behavior actions for extremely high-value assets

- **High:** Assets that are high value but not mission critical

- **Medium:** Assets that represent an average level of importance

- **Low:** Assets that are little importance but represent inconvenience

- **None:** No change in risk rating of packets for this level

Figure 8-28 shows target value configuration.

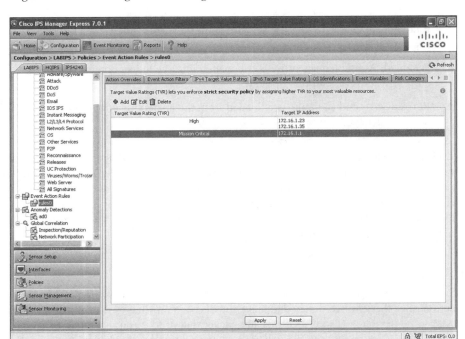

Figure 8-28   *Target Value Rating Configuration*

IOS IPS

IOS routers have the capability to run a subset of the IPS scanning engines available in Cisco IPS appliances in software. This enables organizations to load a smaller set of signatures to detect and stop major threats at the router level. There are over 2,900 signatures available that can be implemented. Cisco has two categories of signatures: IOS Basic and IOS Advanced. These two signature categories enable a select number of signatures based on current threat levels, active exploits, and the latest viruses and worms.

IOS IPS does not provide all of the scanning engines or advanced features of the appliance, but it can be useful for implementing application-specific protection, such as voice services. The ability to deploy attack detection capabilities to branch offices with no dedicated IPS appliance or IPS module installed in the router increases network visibility and provides defense in depth. Figure 8-29 shows IOS IPS signatures in CCP.

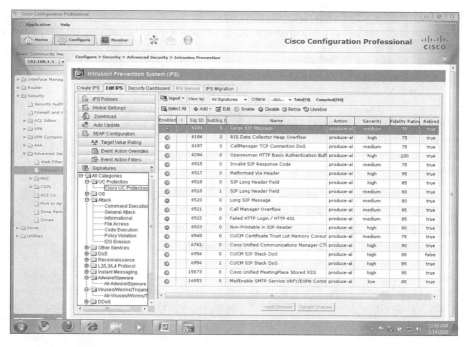

Figure 8-29 *IOS IPS Signature Review in CCP*

Technical Control Testing

Testing perimeter defense controls consists of firewall rule testing for firewall policy performance and IPS testing for attack prevention and detection. The following tests can be conducted by auditors to validate control capabilities and the organization's capability to be able to detect and respond to real attacks.

Firewall Rule Testing

Firewall rule testing is the process of validating rule configuration by sending test packets and analyzing the firewall's response. The goal of the auditor in this case is not to conduct a penetration test, but to ensure that the firewall rules are enforced, and that only approved ports and services are visible. In firewall rule testing, the auditor typically sends traffic through the firewall to other segments to analyze how the firewall reacts.

The first test is to scan the firewall itself for open ports. One of the best tools for the job is Nmap. Knowing what ports the firewall has open might uncover misconfiguration of management access control rules or insecure services. The only ports you see open on a Cisco firewall are management protocols that are available on the interface you scan, or ports that are forwarded through PAT.

The following is an example scan with Nmap on an inside network with access to the management interfaces. You would not expect to see any ports showing on a scan from the outside interface. This is a default syn connect scan with the service identification function turned on. Auditors should be on the lookout for any insecure management ports such as telnet.

```
nmap -sV 172.16.1.1
Starting Nmap 5.21 ( http://nmap.org ) at 2010-03-14 19:58 Eastern Daylight Time
Nmap scan report for 172.16.1.1
Host is up (0.0012s latency).
Not shown: 997 filtered ports
PORT     STATE SERVICE  VERSION
22/tcp  open  ssh       Cisco SSH 1.25 (protocol 2.0)
443/tcp open  ssl/http Cisco Adaptive Security Appliance http config
MAC Address: 00:12:D9:49:09:3D (Cisco Systems)
Service Info: OS: IOS; Devices: firewall, security-misc
```

After scanning the firewall, start scanning hosts on each firewall segment to see what ports and services are available. This information should be checked against policy to make sure that only approved services are visible. These scans should be conducted from every network and security zone protected by the firewall. These scans can take quite a while, especially if UDP scanning is preformed, too. The scans can be run against the entire subnet or just the known hosts. Scanning the known hosts not only speeds up the scan, but also enables the auditor to spend more time assessing the most important services. The following types of scans can be used to identify services available through the firewall.

- Perform a ping scan to see whether systems respond to echo requests.

  ```
  nmap -sP 172.16.1.0/24
  ```

- Standard TCP connect scan with host pinging disabled for all TCP ports. This scan can take 5 minutes per host, but will scan all 65,535 possible ports. Adding –F causes Nmap to scan only the top TCP ports, making it faster.

  ```
  nmap -PN -sT -p1-65535 172.16.1.0/24
  ```

- Ack packet scanning.

  ```
  nmap -PN -sA 172.16.1.0/24
  ```

- Fin packet scanning.

  ```
  nmap -PN -sF 172.16.1.0/24
  ```

- Fragment TCP packets with –F to test how the firewall handles fragments.

  ```
  nmap -PN -sT -f 172.16.1.0/24
  ```

- Scan all UDP ports. Optionally use the –F option for fast mode, which scans well-known ports only.

  ```
  nmap -PN -sU -F 172.16.1.0/24
  ```

After each network, which has a firewall, is scanned, test each rule to make sure that only approved traffic is allowed through. This involves crafting packets on one side of the firewall and sniffing the results on the protected side to determine whether any traffic makes it through. Various TCP options should be tested in addition to fragmentation and evasion techniques.

The last part of the test is to review the findings and inspect any logs generated. Scanning is typically a noisy process, so the firewall logs should be full of this information. Testing logging and detection capabilities are an added benefit of the scanning process, and can often uncover weak log management and review procedures.

Testing the IPS

IPS testing conducted during an audit is typically not to the level of a penetration test. For the most part, the auditor is trying to determine whether the IPS is operating in accordance with policy, and that suspicious activity is detected and reported. It is also not a good idea to launch malicious packets against important business resources just to test whether the IPS will stop the attack or not. An auditor is assessing for compliance, not to see whether he or she can break in. Leave those tasks to the penetration testers, and focus instead on detection, mitigation, and reporting capabilities of the IPS.

Effectively testing an IPS requires strong knowledge of applications, vulnerabilities, and potential exploits. The scope of this book doesn't allow for getting into all of the nuances of IPS testing, but a basic knowledge of testing techniques can be useful in assessing network security. There are three primary types of IPS tests that auditors can conduct:

- **Baseline/well-known attacks:** These are useful in verifying IPS detection and reporting capabilities. This type of test just looks at basic detection, prevention, and reporting.

- **Attack mutations:** This tests the capability for the IPS to detect attack variations and the quality of signatures by changing attack shellcode and encoding methods. The Cisco IPS signatures are written against the vulnerabilities and fairs well against these types of attacks.

- **Evasion testing:** IPS evasion and obfuscation is as much an art as it is a science. These techniques test how well the IPS performs protocol normalization, packet reassembly, and signature fidelity.

Testing IPS is not just about throwing packets at it to see what happens. As an auditor, you must be methodical and have a purpose as to what you are looking to confirm. Having a test plan document is essential to a well-run objective IPS test. The test plan document should include:

- Policies to test

- Applications to test

- Specific threats (SQL injection, buffer overflow, and so on)

- Operating systems

- Tools that will be used

- Testing strategy/checklist

Your test plan document is a guide through the assessment process and ensures that you are targeting the right areas.

Conducting an IPS Test

When conducting an IPS assessment in a production environment, care must be taken to not adversely impact normal business transactions. Because the purpose of this test is to determine whether the IPS can detect real attacks, real attacks must be launched on the network, which presents a very good chance that services could fail. Most auditors want to create a "sacrificial" server that they can use to direct this traffic to. The server should have similar services and operating systems to the devices that the IPS is protecting. It is relatively easy to load a server on a laptop and connect it to the network for testing purposes; plus, the added mobility of the laptop enables it to be reused on other service networks as well. It is also a good idea to load a packet capture program such as wireshark or tcpdump and record all of the packets sent and received during the test for later analysis. The goal is to make the test as real and replicable as possible.

There are many tools that can be employed for generating traffic for the test itself. The following are a mixture of free and commercial tools useful in IPS testing:

- **Nmap (Free):** Scanner used for testing IPS reconnaissance detection

- **Metasploit (Free):** Penetration test framework great for creating live attacks and testing IPS evasion detection

- **Core Impact (Commercial):** Commercial-grade, penetration-testing tool

- **Karalon Traffic IQ (Commercial):** Purpose-built IPS and firewall packet replay assessment tool

After the environment is set up, determine what tools to use in order to generate attack traffic to see whether the IPS will detect it. There are two primary methods used to generate traffic:

- **Live attack testing:** The easiest and most common method for testing IPS detection is to utilize a penetration-testing tool such as Core Impact or Metasploit and conduct live attack testing against a target server. The benefit of this type of testing is that it simulates real-life as closely as possible; the downside is if you have a lot of IPSes to assess, it can take a long time because of the manual nature.

■ **Packet capture replay:** Another method for IPS testing is to replay packet captures of real attacks. Tools such as TCPrelay and Karalon IQ Traffic Pro are designed for this purpose. These tools can simulate the attacked host without having to create a "sacrificial" host to point traffic to. You simply configure a laptop with two network interfaces and connect them on the input side and output side of the IPS. These tools separate the send and receive functions of the packet capture to make it communicate like a real attacker and victim, which is essential for proper IPS testing. The quality of the packet captures and the capability for the tool to modify the captures to work on any topology determine how well these types of tools work for testing. For the most part, a quality-testing tool such as Karalon Traffic IQ can save an enormous amount of time in creating capture files, there are hundreds already included, and it is updated regularly as new attacks are discovered. Karalon Traffic IQ Pro is shown in Figure 8-30 sending the slammer worm through an IPS.

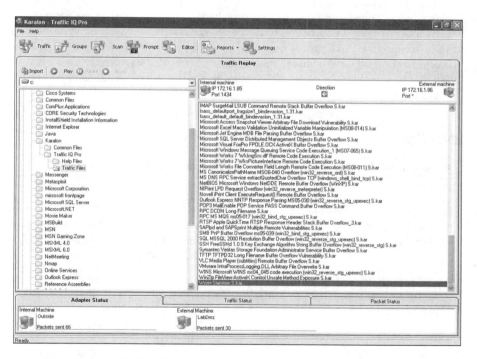

Figure 8-30   *Karalon Traffic IQ Pro*

One of the easiest baseline type tests to perform is an Nmap scan to determine whether the IPS can detect the reconnaissance attempt. The default settings on Nmap generate a lot of easily identifiable traffic that follows a specific pattern that IPS signatures can pick up.

Sending attack packets to the test host to simulate attacks against applications and services that the service segment would normally see, checks that the IPS detects real attacks and stops them in line. It's also helpful to use obfuscation and evasions techniques to test signature effectiveness.

Reviewing the Logs

All of the traffic generated during IPS testing should have created a significant number of logs. These logs can be stored locally, in IME, or forwarded to Cisco MARS. There are also a number of third-party products that can read SDEE-formatted logs, so regardless of the storage facility they should be reviewed and reported on. Having the IPS test plan and checklist makes the log review much easier to perform, and the auditor can determine what the IPS did with the traffic. It's not uncommon to also find, especially in the case of the normalizer engine, that certain packets were indeed dropped, but a log message was not generated. This behavior is designed to help reduce the storage and processing load on the IPS and is not necessarily a bad thing. Having a packet capture of the test also enables the validation of the test to ensure that nothing actually got through. Logs might not show everything, which is why it is important to have the packet captures.

With all of the noise being generated during the test, there should have been alarms ringing and e-mails flying. If no one noticed that the IPS was under test, there are probably much bigger issues than signatures to deal with, namely that there is not an adequate incident review process. This part of the test is by far the most important, because it tests the organization's ability to absorb the information provided by security controls and make informed and timely decisions that can reduce the risk of significant loss during a real event.

Checklist

Assessment Area	Assessment Technique
People	
Are perimeter and intrusion protection policies adequate for the organization's level of risk?	Review applicable security polices (firewall, IPS, and WAN) and configuration standards and compare them with good practices (CIS, NIST, and ECT).
Are all service networks and DMZs identified by zone with appropriate controls in place?	Review security architecture for application and service grouping of similar devices. Network services and protocols allowed should be documented as part of policy and standards.
Are all applications and communication protocol requirements documented between security zones?	Review logical traffic flow between zones to ensure principles of least privileges and minimum device exposure.
Does firewall policy follow good security practices?	Review the policy and ensure that it addresses risk and adheres to good security practices.

continues

Assessment Area	Assessment Technique *(continued)*
Is there an active IPS monitoring policy that all employees have been informed of?	Review monitoring policies to ensure they are present, and check with legal counsel to determine legality requirements.
Process	
Are all key assets grouped into zones based on risk?	Review logical design and zones to assess identification of risk.
Does the physical design adhere to policy and standards?	Review physical design and assess against good security practices.
Are threats and vulnerabilities accounted for in the perimeter architecture?	Review risk assessment documentation. Identify all risk areas that are not being addressed.
Are security zones assigned risk ratings?	Review risk assessment documentation.
Does the security architecture follow good security practices?	Ensure that logging is enabled and reported to a central logging system. Identify how often logs are reviewed.
Are change management processes in place and followed?	Review change management procedures. Interview security administrators, and review and change control documentation.
Are all changes logged to syslog and reviewed?	Review logs and device configuration for change logging.
Is there a vulnerability and patch management process for perimeter-protection devices?	Security appliance software should be monitored for vulnerabilities and necessary patches.
Are configuration backups and disaster-recovery processes in place?	Configuration backups and rules should be stored electronically in a protected manner, and hard copies of the configuration stored in a safe.
Is there a process in place for rule-base modifications?	A formal process should exist to request firewall rule modifications. This process should include a risk analysis and review of the proposed change. All changes should also be tested before implementation.
Are all device alerts logged to syslog and monitored for potential intrusion?	Review log management configurations and logs.

continues

Assessment Area	Assessment Technique	*(continued)*
Is there a defined procedure for incident handling?	Assess incident-handling capabilities.	
Technology		
Firewall Review		
Does current firewall design provide for segmentation of security services and policies through security zones?	Review topology and design.	
Does the firewall design address single point of failure and availability?	Assess firewall design for single points of failure.	
Does the firewall configuration follow baseline security measures and practices from Chapter 7?	Assess firewall configuration for good security practices.	
Is advanced application inspection configured to reduce the risk of tunneled traffic and application attacks?	Review modular policy framework and inspection classes.	
Is NAT used effectively to hide internal network addressing and topology?	Review configurations.	
Are secure management practices utilized for device configuration and logging?	Review configuration for utilization of SSHv2, SNMPv3, and web management access control lists.	
Do firewall rules reflect policy requirements?	Review firewall rules for policy compliance.	
Do firewall rules follow good security practices?	Compare firewall rules against good security practices.	
Is denied traffic logged and reviewed?	Inspect configuration and firewall log review procedures.	
Are firewall rules optimized and consolidated for faster operation?	Review firewall rule usages and recommend optimization where needed.	
Are firewall rules verified through technical testing?	Verify firewall rules, and expose the least access necessary for services and applications to function. Utilize tools such as NMAP and Firewall Analyzer to check for compliance.	
IPS Review		
Is the IPS management interface protected from unauthorized access and utilize secure protocols?	Review configuration.	

continues

Assessment Area	Assessment Technique *(continued)*
Is NTP configured for time stamping IPS logging events?	Inspect configuration for NTP configuration and appropriate time settings.
Are all corporate assets assigned asset target values within the IPS?	Review documentation and IPS configuration.
Are signature updates configured to automatically update to the latest signatures?	Review configuration for device level signature updates or through CSM auto update function. Review update procedures and policy and check for compliance.
Is event logging configured and sent to a security logging platform for archival and storage?	Check configuration to ensure that all logs are transmitted to a platform such as MARS or IME for log storage and review.
Is the IPS configured to leverage security zones to target IPS protection?	IPS should be configured to protect essential services for each security zone they are deployed in. Review configuration and IPS design for proper segmentation and signature deployment.
Does the IPS provide the appropriate level of protection against security zone threats?	Review signature configuration and test with NMAP and packet generation tools.
Do security logs reflect the IPS tests?	Review IPS logs to see whether all IPS test packets were detected and the appropriate mitigation was preformed.
Did the organization under test detect the simulated attacks?	Review detection procedures and tools.

Summary

Securing the network perimeter is top priority for most organizations, and this chapter is focused specifically on assessing firewall and IPS technologies for network defense. This network edge is the frontline of defense, and auditors must ensure that the network under audit complies with both policy and good security practices. This chapter discussed the following:

- Security zones and service networks are essential to architecting manageable security solutions for the perimeter.

- Understanding the risks faced by each service network and security zone better equips an auditor to evaluate whether deployed controls are sufficient in protecting assets.

- A firewall and IPS work together to protect against a wide range of threats and should be deployed together as a system complementing each other's strengths.

- It's not enough to simply review firewall and IPS configurations for compliance; manual testing is required to validate expected results and find areas that can be improved.

References in This Chapter

ISACA Firewall Auditing Procedures, http://www.isaca.org/Template.cfm?
Section=Home&Template=/ContentManagement/ContentDisplay.cfm&ContentID=18782

NIST 800-41 Rev1: Guidelines on Firewalls and Firewall Policy, http://csrc.nist.gov/
publications/nistpubs/800-41-Rev1/sp800-41-rev1.pdf

NIST 800-94: Guide to Intrusion Detection and Prevention Systems, http://csrc.nist.gov/
publications/nistpubs/800-94/SP800-94.pdf

Cisco SAFE, www.cisco.com/go/safe

Chapter 9

Access Control

Throughout history, people have struggled with protecting their valuables by limiting who is allowed to access them in a multitude of ways. From a pirate's buried treasure that can be accessed only with detailed maps, sophisticated locks, and skeleton keys, to the digital certificates and biometric identification devices of our digital age, one thing is common: Restricting access and authorization is a proven method for reducing risk, because you can't steal or damage what you can't interact with. This chapter covers techniques for auditing Cisco network access control technologies and best practices for securing access.

Fundamentals of Access Control

Access control is the process of establishing an individual's identity and determining what resources with which he is allowed to interact. This process represents one of the most basic and fundamental aspects of protecting digital assets. It is subsequently the most targeted by attackers attempting to gain unauthorized access. It is usually much easier to try to steal a username and password than attempt to compromise an operating system vulnerability or break in through layers of firewalls or other security technologies. If you can get the key, you can simply unlock the front door and walk in.

From a Cisco perspective, the main objectives of access control are to protect the network from unauthorized access and to reduce the risk of exposure to devices that do not comply with security policy. The key areas addressed by access control are:

- Preventing unauthorized access
- Authenticating users
- Authorizing all user access based on the user's role
- Enforcing acceptable use policies
- Enforcing mobile and desktop security standards

- Identifying and monitoring guest user access

- Controlling access to non-PC devices

- Monitoring and reporting on all network access

Identity and Authentication

In its most basic form, an *identity* consists of a username that references an individual's electronic login and a password that is used to authenticate that the users are who they claim to be. A login ID should be unique for each user and not shared between multiple people for the simple reason that access control is also about user accountability and enforcing that responsibility. To detect malicious activity, you have to be able to connect activities performed with individual users to make the users accountable for how they interact with the system. If a group of people shares a login, it is difficult to determine who is actually logged in during a security incident. This makes taking corrective actions and enforcing policy a significant challenge.

Usernames address who the users are, and authentication attempts to prove that the users are who they claim to be. Authentication is usually accomplished with one or more of the following methods:

- **Something you know:** Passwords or PIN numbers

- **Something you have:** Physical tokens and certificates

- **Personal characteristics:** Biometrics (fingerprints, retina scan, and so on)

- **Location:** Where (physically) you are attempting to log in

Each of these methods represents an authentication factor. If a password alone is used for authentication, it is called single-factor authentication, because a single factor is used for validation. Two-factor authentication makes use of multiple authentication components, such as when you use something you know (pin number) and something you have (hardware token) to verify identity. The more factors you use, the more assurance you have that the individual is who she says she is and should be authorized access to system resources.

Biometrics has become increasingly popular as a form of authentication because it leverages a physical characteristic of an individual such as a fingerprint, an eyes iris pattern, or retina scan as validation. Users are much less likely to forget their fingerprints at home or share them with a coworker, which can make biometrics an attractive solution. The downside to biometrics is that they can be prone to false readings.

Using location as a factor is useful for adding the context of the login as a component of authentication. Users might be authorized to connect to their network within their assigned work area but not able to connect while in the finance department. Using location as a factor can also be useful in addressing physical access policies.

Protecting user identities can be a challenging prospect because it requires reliance on the end user to comply with policies and ensure the confidentiality of the username and passwords. Everyone who has ever worked in IT has probably seen a sticky note with a username and password stuck to a monitor or hidden under a mouse pad. Issues like these are typically user education and compliance problems but can stem from a poorly implemented password policy (where the requirements might be far too complex) or the lack of policy enforcement.

Access Control Threats and Risks

The threats to access control revolve primarily around attacks against authentication and authorization of network resources. Access controls work to minimize the risk of inadvertently exposing sensitive information or services and encompass all aspects of provisioning user accounts, authentication processes, authorization process, and safeguarding access credentials. The risks to access controls include the following:

- **Unauthorized/accidental disclosure:** Unauthorized disclosure of sensitive data is the top risk of weak access control methods. Businesses want to protect their secrets from falling into the wrong hands, which is why authentication and authorization is used in the first place. It's not just the risk of third parties gaining access to sensitive data that is a concern, but also the threat of inadvertently disclosing information to employees who do not have a role that requires access to the data. Although it might be interesting to see how much money all the directors in a company make, unless you are in finance, that information should not be accessible. This type of risk is common and one of the reasons why auditors are often asked to conduct access reviews.

- **Unauthorized changes:** Access controls are also meant to prevent modification or destruction of data assets. Management of this risk is one of the primary tenets of the Sarbanes-Oxley act, which federally mandates that publically traded companies have controls in place to prevent modification of accounting data.

- **Unauthorized Access:** The risk of allowing unauthorized access to the network can result in many of the risks mentioned previously, but also can represent a risk of its own. Network access is a resource that has value, which can be used for malicious purposes. If an attacker gains access to network devices, he can steal network services, host malware, and provide access to stolen software to others. Abuse of the network usually happens because of a poor access control enforcement mechanism.

Some of the most common threats facing access control technologies are:

- **Password sniffing:** Password sniffing exposes clear text passwords on the wire and is an easy way to gain unauthorized access to the network.

- **Password cracking:** Weak passwords that do not follow complexity rules or utilize easy-to-guess, dictionary-based words are trivial for an attacker to compromise.

- **Vulnerable hosts:** Letting vulnerable hosts on the network can result in those devices being used to gain unauthorized access to the network.

■ **Social engineering:** Poor user awareness training regarding proper access credential handling can lead to social engineering attacks directed at employees to trick them into divulging their passwords.

■ **Third-party access:** Uncontrolled guest access is a threat to the network because without access control technologies, there is no way to differentiate legitimate guests from potential attackers or reduce the risk of providing access.

Access Control Policy

Access control policies provide the framework for building access rules and enforcement. An access policy review should be conducted to determine if the organization has defined its goals, standards, and requirements for users to make use of the network. Auditors should ensure that the following policies exist and effectively utilize good security practices:

■ **Access-granting policy:** For a new user to be granted access, there needs to be a formal process for requesting and granting the appropriate level. This process is enacted through an access-granting policy. The principles of least privilege and need to know should be followed to provide the minimum access required to do the job. The access-granting process should have a physical or an electronic audit trail that shows who requested access and who approved access. Auditors should review the documents of the process to determine whether the organization is following the appropriate practices.

■ **Access-revocation policy:** The review of access-revocation policies and procedures is useful to ensure that the business does not accidentally leave access to corporate systems after an employee is terminated and to review entitlement of employees who change jobs inside the company or simply no longer need access to a particular system. This process should be documented with an auditing trail showing the chain of events necessary for termination.

■ **Password policy:** The password policy outlines password strength, password age, and any other password-related requirements that are usually detailed in standards documents. This type of policy addresses prohibiting password sharing.

■ **Access auditing and logging:** Access auditing and logging policies define the requirements for reviewing and auditing access logs. This policy usually includes how long logs should be retained and how often they should be reviewed. In addition, standards should be in place for a centralized and searchable logging format.

■ **Asset classification:** There should be a policy that requires an asset classification scheme be put in place to differentiate authentication and authorization for sensitive systems and data. Auditors should look for evidence that asset and data classification reviews are conducted periodically. Each asset classification should also have an approved authentication mechanism (pin, password, certificate, or hardware token) and a list of which job roles are allowed access if following role-based access control (RBAC) principles.

- **Guest/third-party access policies and procedures:** Contractors and guests need access to the network to collaborate on projects and keep up with e-mail and other requirements. Although it is a welcome courtesy to provide access, access should not be offered at the expense of security. Guest and third-party access should be offered only with specific terms and conditions that dictate acceptable use during their time connected to the network. Individuals must also be made aware that their activities can and will be monitored. Utilizing technologies that also provide a unique identifier for the sessions can be used to create a guest access audit log.

- **Posture-assessment policy:** Posture-assessment policies detail minimum host requirements that are assessed as a condition of granting network access. The host system should have all major operating system and high-risk vulnerabilities patched. All security software should be enabled, and signatures and policy definitions should be updated. The remediation process should also be documented, and the user should be educated about what to do to fix any deficiencies found. These requirements are often part of the acceptable use policy.

All policies should be reviewed and updated on a regular basis as new technologies are added to the business. The review process needs to be documented and changes disseminated to the organization in an efficient manner. The best method is to provide an internal repository or website that is easy to update. Management and personnel should be required to review the site on a regular basis and document their acceptance.

Access Control Operational Review

Access control operational reviews enable the auditor to assess the processes and procedures used in monitoring and managing access control technologies. This type of assessment analyzes common access control practices such as identity, password enforcement, designing authorization strategies, and asset classification schemes.

Identity Operational Good Practices

Login IDs represent 50 percent of the user access equation, but are not usually treated with the same level of importance as the password itself. Using logins such as Admin or Root invites attackers to launch their password-guessing programs against these accounts because they can assume that if they compromise them, they have high-level privileges that can be used to exploit the system. It's also not a good idea to provide departmental or job-related designations as part of the login ID because this type of information can help hackers better target their attacks. In general, the following good practices should be followed whenever possible:

- Revaluate user access requirements on a regular basis to determine whether the user still needs access to the resource and to determine whether any account not used after a given amount of time should be disabled.

- Configure all user logins with an idle timeout to prevent a session remaining open if the user forgets to logout.

- Create all user accounts that are globally unique to the organization.

- Disable user accounts immediately upon employee resignation or termination.

- Never reassign a login ID as this can interfere with investigations and review of old audit logs.

- Use single sign-on whenever possible to maintain a single login ID for all accessed systems.

Password complexity requirements can sometimes make you feel like you are competing in the finger dexterity Olympics. The reason for putting users through this form of digit torture is to reduce the risk of someone using a password-guessing program to gain unauthorized access. Following is a list of good password practices:

- Passwords should be a minimum of eight characters.

- Passwords should be constructed with a combination of three of the following alpha, numeric, upper and lower case, and special characters: !"#$%&'()*+,-./:;<=>?@[\]^_`{|}~.

- Passwords should not be based on dictionary words or user information such as the user's name, pet's name, mother's maiden name, favorite singer, and so on.

- Passwords should be changed every 60 days.

- Password histories should be used to prevent the reuse of old passwords from the last 12 months.

- Passwords should be disabled for an hour after the fifth incorrect attempt or the account is locked out completely, which requires an administrator to reset the account.

Authorization and Accounting Practices

The principle of least privilege states that you give users the rights and access to only the resources and data they need to accomplish their jobs and nothing more. No one needs root access to the operating system to run a spreadsheet, and excess privilege is one of the primary ways for malware to infect a computer's operating system. All organizations should review who has privileged accounts or access on a regular basis.

Another fundamental aspect of authorization is found in the concept of separation of duties. Separation of duties has its origins in the financial world and is used to create checks and balances for detecting fraud and malicious activity. The goals of this concept are to prevent malicious or fraudulent acts and to detect mistake and security failures. For example, if a bill needs to be paid, someone in accounting might prepare the check, but only a supervisor is authorized to sign the check. This separates the job (or duty) into a multistep process that requires two individuals to agree on the appropriate action to take. This way an individual cannot just write a check, sign it, and then cash it. From an IT perspective, separation of duties can be used to catch malicious activity, but also to prevent downtime from misconfigurations or other activities where having another set of eyes and perspective can prevent costly mistakes. This aspect is used in change management as part of the change control workflow by including an approval process for all changes.

Many other aspects of network security can benefit from this process. Figure 9-1 shows the ISACA segregation of duties matrix for IT that highlights potential weaknesses when job functions are combined.

	Control Group	Systems Analyst	Application Programmer	Help Desk and Support Manager	End User	Data Entry	Computer Operator	Database Administrator	Network Administrator	Systems Administrator	Security Administrator	Systems Programmer	Quality Assurance
Control Group		X	X	X		X	X	X	X	X		X	
Systems Analyst	X			X	X		X				X		X
Application Programmer	X			X	X	X	X	X	X	X	X	X	X
Help Desk and Support Manager	X	X	X		X	X		X	X	X		X	
End User		X	X	X			X	X	X			X	X
Data Entry	X		X	X			X	X	X	X	X	X	
Computer Operator	X	X	X		X	X		X	X	X	X	X	
Database Administrator	X		X	X	X	X			X	X		X	
Network Administrator	X		X	X	X	X	X						
System Administrator	X		X	X		X	X	X				X	
Security Administrator		X	X			X	X					X	
Systems Programmer	X		X	X	X	X	X	X		X	X		X
Quality Assurance		X	X		X							X	

X—Combination of these functions may create a potential control weakness.

Figure 9-1 *ISACA Segregation of Duties Matrix for IT*

After a user's identity is authenticated, the user is then authorized with specific privileges and rights to the network or application. There are three primary models used to determine access:

- **Mandatory access control (MAC):** MAC represents controls that are defined at the administrative level and cannot be changed by data owners or users. In a MAC environment, a tag is applied to each asset that is compared against a user's privilege level.

If the tags match, the user gains access; if not, no access is granted. Security classifications or tags are defined by policy and are applied directly to the asset. The military often uses MAC for sensitive information and uses confidential, secret, and top secret as its tagging mechanism.

- **Discretionary access control (DAC):** DAC is a method of access control that allows the asset owner the right to determine who gets access to the asset. Discretionary access control is a flexible system of access control that works well in a decentralized management structure. Policies must be well written and adhered to for this type of access control to work, because inconsistency in the way asset managers provide access can lead to mistakenly granting excessive privileges. DAC and MAC can work together and are not mutually exclusive; the key to either of these and any access control method is to ensure proper security classification of data and resources.

- **RBAC:** RBAC takes a different approach than MAC and DAC. Instead of assigning access rights to individuals, rights and privileges are assigned to the individual's role in the company. Roles are analogous to groups from an implementation perspective, and a single individual can have multiple roles in an organization. One of the biggest problems organizations face when provisioning access for users is in consistently applying appropriate privileges. RBAC makes provisioning much simpler by assigning specific roles to the user instead of a multitude of individual privileges and rights. As users change jobs at the company, this becomes even more advantageous, because the user can then be assigned the new role and removed from the old role without making any other configuration changes.

Of these three models, RBAC is the most popular due in no small part to its scalability and ease of administration after roles and rights are defined. In organizations where users can change roles and responsibilities often, RBAC makes the most sense. Cisco has embraced RBAC concepts in both Network Admission Control (NAC) and Identity-Based Networking Services (IBNS).

Administrative Users

"Who watches the watchers?" This quote from the Roman poet Juvenal has been used throughout history to represent the problem of monitoring those individuals who are put into authoritative positions over others. It is an appropriate concept for auditors to employ when assessing identity and access controls for network administrative users. All admin accounts must be subject to auditing and all activities monitored and stored for later retrieval. Cisco provides facilities in IOS via AAA to write log messages for every command entered. This audit trail functionality should be enabled on all devices.

Administrative users must be given rights to the network commensurate with their job responsibilities. Role-based access control works well in these scenarios and enables the organization to differentiate access to networking devices. To do this, each administrator must have her own unique username and password. Sharing an admin account between multiple administrators in not a good practice because the business cannot know for sure which admin made a change or if the username and password is compromised. Audit trails become possible with unique accounts, and as mentioned previously, they can be used for not only detecting malicious behavior, but also for troubleshooting. It's also a good practice to change the default administrator account names because identity is determined by both the username and password, which leaves a default username that enables attackers the ability to target these well known accounts and focus their efforts.

Cisco IOS role-based access controls can provide an authorization requirement for specific commands that can be viewed as a security threat. A user might be allowed to use certain show commands that provide troubleshooting information but not be allowed to enter interactive configuration modes with the device.

Classification of Assets

Asset classification is the process of compiling all physical and logical assets and applying a tag or classification that represents how the asset needs to be managed from a security prospective. This classification takes into account the sensitivity of the asset, the value, and importance to the businesses mission. An example classification scheme might use Public, Internal, Confidential, and Restricted. Table 9-1 shows an example asset classification matrix.

Table 9-1 *Asset Classification Matrix*

Asset	Public	Internal	Confidential	Restricted
Web Server	✓			
E-mail Server		✓		
Database Server			✓	
HR Applications				✓
Networking equipment			✓	
Printers		✓		
Keys and Access Cards		✓		

After the business's assets are classified, it can then create an access control matrix to determine what job roles or individuals should have access to what resources using the principles of least privilege as a guide.

Access Control Architecture Review

Assessing access control security should always include an architectural review of access control devices.

Identity and Access Control Technologies

Cisco offers a wide range of products and technologies to enforce access control policies. The core function of the Cisco access control technologies is to address policy in three primary ways:

- User and device authentication

- User role and privilege authorization

- User and device policy enforcement

One of the first steps that many organizations take to combat the risks of uncontrolled access is to enable user and device authentication. User and device identity addresses authentication for all classes of users, from corporate users with corporate-owned devices to guest users, contractors, and consultants. Laptops and computers that have a user driving their activities are not the only types of devices. In many cases there can be hundreds to thousands of non-interactive devices such as printers, phones, and uninterrupted power supplies (UPS). These devices can be given access through a white listing process by either manually entering the MAC address into an approved list or by utilizing Cisco Profiler to automatically catalog and identify devices.

There are many classes of users on a typical network, ranging from the most trusted positions, such as a CEO, to a part-time mailroom clerk. All these users have specific network access requirements for accomplishing their jobs. The goal of user role and privilege authorization is to ensure that each user has the necessary access to perform his duties, without exposing sensitive systems that he has no need to access. Segmenting the users by role in the network makes it easier to create policy enforcement boundaries. Groups of users can then be monitored based on normal traffic patterns, allowing administrators the ability to better spot unusual activity on the network.

Cisco has two approaches to network access control: NAC and IBNS, which both fall under the Cisco TrustSec umbrella. The primary differences between NAC and IBNS are the support of posture assessment and 802.1x. NAC is a technology that is layered over the top of the network and does not rely on any other protocols on the client side. NAC is best known for its assessment capabilities for end-user devices to ensure compliance to policy. IBNS is the Cisco 802.1x solution that integrates support on Cisco catalyst switches with an 802.1x client to perform authentication and VLAN assignment for network devices. This section covers these two network access control technologies.

Network Admission Control

Cisco NAC operates as an overlay on to the existing network and works with any switch or wireless device. The Cisco NAC solution performs four primary security functions:

- **Authentication and RBAC:** NAC can authenticate the user, assign role-based privileges, quarantine noncompliant devices, and assist the user in remediation steps to become compliant.

- **Endpoint posture assessment:** The capability for a NAC solution to enforce endpoint compliance to policy is one of the key benefits of NAC, and it enables the business to determine the minimum acceptable posture of a client machine before gaining entry.

- **Quarantine of devices out of compliance:** If policy dictates that client machines must have antivirus software enabled and up-to-date plus any critical service packs to the operating system, then the NAC appliance can be configured to perform checks on the machine to validate compliance and minimize the risk to the rest of the network through quarantine of the host until detected problems are fixed.

- **Remediation of noncompliant systems:** Remediation occurs dynamically, and the user is quarantined to a segmented VLAN that enables updates and patches to be applied before the user is allowed access to the rest of the corporate network. NAC supports more than 350 antivirus and security applications from a multitude of third-party vendors and Microsoft WSUS and other patch remediation solutions.

NAC also enforces role-based access policies by mapping a user's identity and role to specific VLANs on the network if used in conjunction with Cisco switches. Each user role has a different level of risk based on the required access to the network, and depending on how it is deployed, NAC can enforce access rules such as a firewall or change the user's VLAN and apply unique role-based policies. NAC allows for more stringent checks to be performed on clients that are in high-risk roles (from an information leakage and sensitivity perspective) such as finance, HR, and corporate executives. This allows user roles to be in the same VLAN with the same access control policies applied no matter where they are physically located in the building or how they connect to the network (wired, wireless, or even remote VPN).

NAC Components

The Cisco NAC solution consists of a number of individual components that work together to deliver access control and policy enforcement. See Figure 9-2 for the components that make up the NAC solutions.

The core components of the NAC solution consist of the following:

- **Cisco NAC Manager:** NAC Manager is the configuration repository for all policies, user roles, compliance checks, and remediation methods for the NAC solution. The NAC manager leverages a Web-based interface for configuring and managing the NAC deployment, and all configuration tasks and reporting are performed here.

- **Cisco NAC Server:** NAC Server is the enforcement point for policy, conducts compliance checks on clients, and authenticates users.

NAC Components

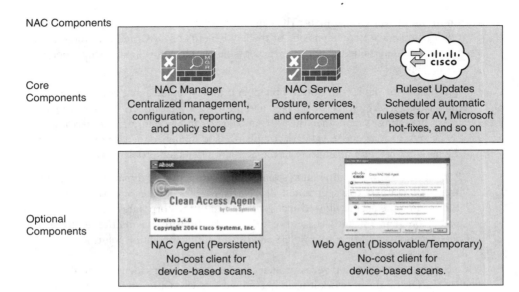

Core Components

Optional Components

Figure 9-2   *NAC Solution Components*

Optional components address specific needs:

■ **Cisco NAC Agent:** NAC Agent can be deployed on client machines to utilize single sign on with Microsoft active directory and NAC for Windows devices, plus perform a deep operating system level inspection of the client device. The agent can be installed permanently on a client.

■ **Cisco NAC Web Agent:** The Cisco NAC Web Agent enables the NAC solution to perform posture assessment and authentication on a device that has not already been preloaded with the NAC Agent. This component is referred to as a temporal agent because the software deletes itself after the agent completes the assessment.

How NAC Works

Cisco NAC works by blocking initial access to the network (either wired or wireless) until the user has logged in via Microsoft Active Directory, through the NAC Agent, or by launching a web browser and logging in via the Web Agent. Logging in via Active Directory initiates a single sign-on process on Windows platforms that utilizes the supplied username and password for both the domain login and NAC. Having the NAC Agent loaded is required for the single sign-on function to operate properly. If the user is not part of the domain, then the NAC Server redirects the user's browser to point to the NAC Web Agent and prompts for a username and password. Lightweight Directory Access Protocol (LDAP) is also supported for credential authentication for nonMicrosoft networks. Figure 9-3 shows a Cisco NAC Agent login screen.

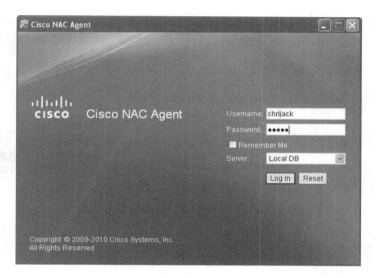

Figure 9-3   *NAC Agent Login*

After the user is authenticated, NAC assesses the user's system to determine patch levels and device configuration and looks for vulnerabilities. These assessments are configured by user role, which is why the assessment process happens after authentication and allows for differentiated policy enforcement by role. If the device is determined to be noncompliant, access is denied and the system is quarantined. During this quarantine process, the user is presented with options for fixing the identified vulnerabilities or non-compliant configuration. These options can point to locations for downloading patches, can kick off antivirus update programs, or even initiate Microsoft patch downloads. After the user addresses any vulnerabilities and is determined to be within policy, NAC then provides access to the network based on the user's role-based privileges. This whole process is typically fast, and unless the user has been away for an extended period of time and not kept up with the patches, the process does not add significant time to the login. The user's access is then allowed unimpeded until she logs off the network, or the administrator configurable session timer has counted down to zero. When the session timer expires, the user has to go through the authentication and assessment process again to ensure compliance with policy.

Figure 9-4 shows a graphical presentation of how NAC works.

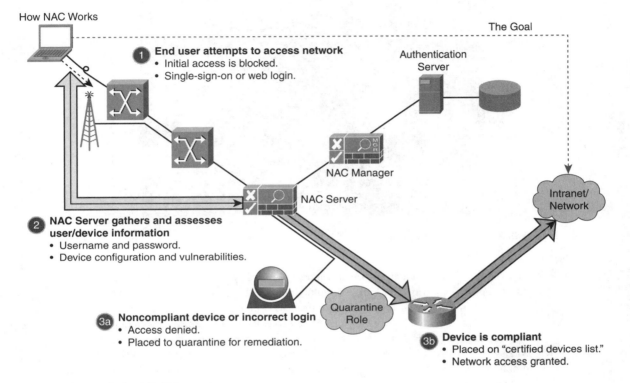

Figure 9-4 *NAC Operation*

NAC Deployment Considerations

Understanding how the deployment of NAC can affect access control enforcement gives the auditor a better grasp of how to properly assess a NAC solution. Many factors come into play when determining how NAC is deployed, and Cisco provides an enormous amount of flexibility with NAC.

There are two major deployment methods for Cisco NAC: in-band and out-of-band. The difference between the two methods is in the policy enforcement mechanism used. An in-band deployment places the NAC Server directly in line with the user, allowing the NAC Server to enforce compliance and implement policy like a firewall. All user traffic flows through the NAC appliance, and it is responsible for access control and bandwidth limiting. In-band can be used for VPN, wireless, campus, and remote LANs. The NAC Server can be configured with an IP address like a gateway router, or configured like a transparent bridge between the user and a gateway router. The NAC Server also supports VLAN trunking, which enables it to enforce policy on multiple logical network segments. The only limitation in these designs is that the a single NAC Server supports about 1 Gb of aggregate throughput, but even this can be overcome through load balancing devices.

An out-of-band deployment is designed for Cisco campus LANs and wireless LAN controller deployments and uses SNMP to change the user's physical port VLAN by role or to move it from a quarantined VLAN to a network access VLAN on the controller in the case of wireless. In this deployment method, the NAC Server directly interacts with the user during authentication and assessment. After authentication and assessment, the user's switch port is placed into the appropriate VLAN. Existing VLAN access control lists on the switch are used to enforce access policies, and the NAC Server's job is complete. Because the NAC Server is no longer in the flow of traffic sent by the user, access control with the NAC Server is not possible in an out-of-band deployment. Likewise, bandwidth controls, which rely on the NAC Server being in line with the user, are not possible either.

NAC Posture Assessment

Cisco NAC automatically downloads the latest service pack and hotfix updates for Windows machines and supports more than 350 security and management applications. These updates are used to assess the client's machine to determine whether required patches are installed through the client-scanning process. This process inspects registry entries, file dates, and the presence of running services. Figure 9-5 shows the NAC Agent having quarantined a noncompliant user's machine due to not having the appropriate patches or updated antivirus software.

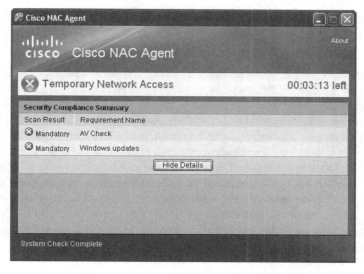

Figure 9-5 *NAC Agent Temporary Access*

Identity-Based Networking Services

IBNS provides the capabilities of delivering secure access to corporate networks utilizing features present in software on Cisco switches and wireless LANs. IBNS leverages 802.1x technologies as the control mechanism for wired and wireless devices enabling authentication and authorization, based on the user's role and privilege level.

The standards-based port authentication protocol 802.1x requires a client (or supplicant) to be present on the endpoint device, an authenticator (network access device), and AAA server running radius. Cisco IBNS is used today for Authentication, Authorization, and Accounting and does not perform policy compliance checks on endpoints like NAC, but this is likely to change in subsequent releases because Cisco has committed to combining the two technologies under TrustSec. See Figure 9-6 for 802.1x terminology.

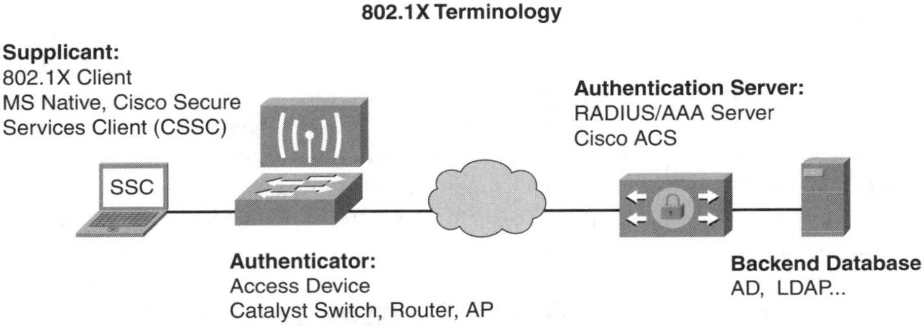

802.1X Terminology

Supplicant:
802.1X Client
MS Native, Cisco Secure
Services Client (CSSC)

SSC

Authenticator:
Access Device
Catalyst Switch, Router, AP

Authentication Server:
RADIUS/AAA Server
Cisco ACS

Backend Database
AD, LDAP...

Figure 9-6   *802.1x Terminology*

802.1x is an IEEE standard for port-based (wired and wireless) access control and authentication and is based on Extensible Authentication Protocol (EAP). EAP was leveraged as the authentication method and modified to operate over LANs and WLANs, which ultimately became EAPoL (EAP over LAN). This alphabet soup-sounding protocol enables the supplicant (host wanting to connect to the network) to authenticate to the network device (authenticator) by sending a username and password or a digital certificate that is then checked against the credentials stored on the authentication server. The default state of a port configured for high security 802.1x is to deny all access except for EAPoL, which restricts interaction with the network without authentication. After the network device has successfully authenticated, the server can then reconfigure the port to allow access granted by the user's role and the radius server applies any access control list configured for the user.

Refer to Figure 9-7 to see a visual representation of the IBNS components.

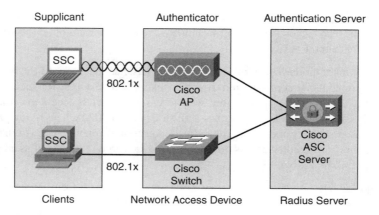

Figure 9-7 *IBNS Components*

The core components of the Cisco IBNS solutions are:

- **Cisco Secure Access Control Server (ACS):** The Cisco ACS is an enterprise class Radius and Tacacs+ server first and foremost, but it has been extensively enhanced to provide RBSC and to integrate with Cisco IOS to provide a suite of security services that make up the IBNS solution. ACS is the policy management server for IBNS and is used to integrate user authentication with other directory services, such as Microsoft's active directory and LDAP.

- **Cisco Secure Service Client (SSC):** Cisco SSC is an 802.1x suppliant that can be loaded on any Microsoft Windows operating system to provide a single authentication mechanism for wired and wireless networks. Cisco SSC manages user and device certificates and eases the administrative burden of deploying 802.1x to client computers; it allows the import of a single xml file that configures the SSC for applicable corporate settings and prevents the modification of those setting to reduce support calls.

- **Network Authentication Devices:** Any Cisco Catalyst switch or wireless access point that supports 802.1x can be used as a network authentication device. These devices are responsible for authenticating the users through 802.1x back the Cisco ACS.

Deployment Methods

802.1x has typically been a challenge to deploy because in the past it was an all-or-nothing proposition. A gradual migration was difficult and a manual process. Cisco has added a number of capabilities to ease the deployment of 802.1x and handling clients without supplicants. Cisco recommends three functional methods for the deployment of 802.1x based on the security requirements of the business and how far down the path of 802.1x security the organization wants to proceed:

- **Monitor mode:** Allows unobstructed access to the network, but allows authentication if an 802.1x client is available. This provides little security, but can assist with the 802.1x migration by allowing users to get used to 802.1x and allowing administrators time to deploy supplicants and work through any issues before going fully into production. The biggest benefit of this mode is the identification of all the 802.1x-capable clients in the network.

- **Low impact mode:** This mode gives all users basic connectivity to the network utilizing open mode configuration, which enables selective access for specific protocols such as DNS, DHCP, and possibly Web access, but restricts access to critical network resources, unless the user has authenticated via 802.1x. This mode provides increased security and allows the radius server to implement dACLS (dynamic ACLS) on the port to enforce access policies. This mode can be thought of as a hybrid mode and is flexible.

- **High security mode:** High security mode prevents the port from sending or receiving any traffic except for EAPoL. After the user has authenticated via the 802.1x port, he is then moved into the appropriate VLAN and any access control lists are applied. This is the most strict security mode.

NAC Guest Server

Guest user access features found in the NAC solution can enable organizations to provide network access for guests without compromising security policy. The Cisco NAC Guest Server has a simple web interface that allows you to provide a guest with access codes that can be sent via SMS or e-mail that is valid for the duration of the guest's visit. All the activities that the user performs are logged, and all applicable policies are enforced during the user's stay.

The NAC Guest Server is configured to allow sponsors in the company to provision guest access on a temporary basis for both NAC deployments and IBNS 802.1x. NAC Guest Server is a standalone solution that also integrates with Cisco WLAN controllers to provision access via wireless. Figure 9-8 shows the provisioning page company employees see.

NAC Guest Server creates records of who provisioned guest access and any activities conducted on the network through detailed logs. These logs track not only when and where the users connected, but also what websites they visited and protocols and services they attempted to use. Figure 9-9 shows an example of one of the activity reports available in NAC Guest Server for an individual user.

NAC Profiler

Cisco NAC Profiler keeps track of noninteractive devices such as phones, printers, and PDAs by dynamically cataloging and identifying any device that tries to communicate on the network. It allows for a rapid deployment of 802.1x by automatically profiling the type of device and applying the necessary security policies to the port to which it is connected. If an inventoried device moves or changes, then NAC Profiler updates its database and changes access requirements accordingly. This catalog of devices can then be used as the source list for white listing in NAC Appliance and MAC Auth-Bypass in IBNS, greatly reducing the amount of manual work that an administrator has to do to keep these lists up to date.

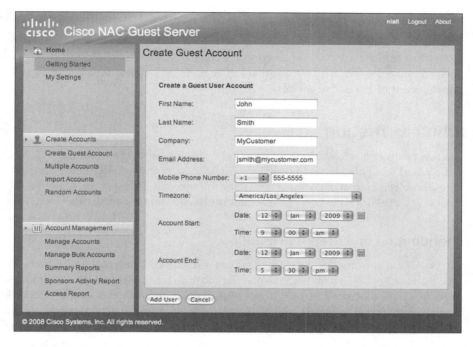

Figure 9-8 *NAC Provisioning Page*

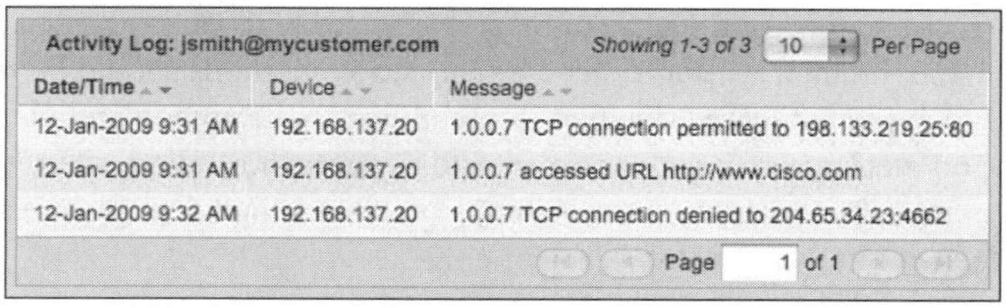

Figure 9-9 *NAC Guest Server User Activity Report*

These noninteractive devices can be placed into specific VLANs and monitored for any type of behavioral change. If a phone stops acting like a phone (by unplugging the phone and plugging in a laptop), an alert is sent and the device might be taken offline.

The NAC Profiler solution consists of a Profiler server and collector. The server is responsible for cataloging devices and holds the database of MAC addresses. The server also leverages Netflow to analyze the behavior of each device. The collector is responsible for monitoring the network by looking at the protocols and services a device uses to communicate. Cisco NAC Server includes an integrated collector, which can be incorporated into the Profiler deployment. If a full NAC solution is not deployed, a dedicated collector server must be used. Integration with Cisco switches via SNMP also delivers Mac address information and 802.1X data to the profiler solution.

Reporting features in NAC Profiler provide a complete picture of all devices that are connected to the network. This information can be useful in handling the monitoring and management of interactive devices.

Technical Testing

Access control assessments test the technical controls used to determine the who, what, where, and when of network access. The area of security that administrators have the most problems enforcing policy in is identity management. This section details the aspects of network access control that auditors should test for compliance.

Authentication and Identity Handling

To assess authentication and identity handling in a network, the auditor must first review the password policy, network access polices, and any technical standards. This gives the auditor a basis to determine the types of tests to run based on how access control technology is supposed to enforce policy. After the organizational standards are determined, the auditor can then move to the actual testing. Many methods can be used to ask a user for authentication credentials. The strength of these methods should be equal to the value of the data or asset they are used to protect. At this stage, it is useful to review asset and data classifications schemes to further streamline the assessment process and highlight weak controls. Multifactor authentication for high-value assets is a must. Hardware token, biometrics, and other authentication methods should be reviewed for weakness and exploitability. Ultimately though, the most common and most vulnerable authentication mechanism is the password, and as such, the auditor needs to pay special attention to how passwords are provisioned, stored, and used. Password testing are covered in detail later in this section.

Account lockout procedures should also be in place to prevent brute force guessing attempts. This can give the organization early warning if there is an attempt to compromise an account based on a defined number of invalid password attempts. There is always a balancing act required for this type of control though, because one of the most common and time-consuming calls help desks receive is for resetting passwords. Setting the number of invalid passwords too low floods the help desk with calls.

Sniffing for passwords sent in clear text is another common practice attackers use to gain access. Use of telnet and unencrypted passwords on the network does not follow good security practices, but is unfortunately still in use today. Auditors should use sniffers and password-scanning tools to identify if any unencrypted passwords are used.

Auditors should also be on the lookout for poor password handling by taking a stroll through the work place and looking for any unsecured passwords, badges, or access cards. Passwords taped to monitors or under mouse pads are a huge security risk.

Utilizing single sign-on capabilities not only makes it easier for the user to work with access control, but also helps with the administration of the user's accounts and access rights. Cisco provides single sign on with Windows through native Active Directory integration with both NAC and IBNS solutions.

Posture Assessment Testing

NAC provides posture assessment capabilities to help reduce the risk of exposing the network to computers that do not meet policy requirements for antimalware and patch levels. NAC can be configured to inspect machines with the NAC client or through a Web Agent. The inspection process is assigned to the role of the user, and if the client is found deficient, then NAC offers methods for patching or updating to become compliant.

When auditing posture assessments, the auditor needs to compare policy requirements with what is configured on NAC. Antivirus software version checks and patch levels are automatically downloaded from Cisco at regular intervals, and they can be used to automatically look for noncompliance to policy. NAC can look for the presence of specific services and whether or not they are enabled, such as antimalware software. These checks ensure that the user is compliant with a policy that requires these services be turned on.

When assessing posture assessment, the auditor should test how the network reacts to policy violations, such as turning off AV, or uninstalling required services. The auditor can test patch and hotfix detection through connecting a freshly installed laptop or removing a required service pack to ensure that NAC catches the security vulnerability.

Remediation is configured by pointing the user to either the Internet, in the case of using Microsoft update service, or launching the WSUS service to download the latest patches. NAC Agent can also start the update process for the user's antimalware software to get the definition files and policies up to current levels. Remediation should be tested to ensure that if a missed patch is discovered, NAC provides a link to download the appropriate updates.

Testing for Weak Authentication

There are two primary methods used to test password strength: interception and brute force. Interception obtains the password in clear text, encrypted, or hashed off the network or from the air in a wireless environment.

Password interception is relatively easy to do and can require little to no skill. The only requirement is that you have the ability to sniff or intercept the traffic between the user entering the login credentials and the host where the user is trying to access resources. This is normally accomplished through a general-purpose packet sniffer or a specially designed password-auditing tool that can intercept and decode raw packet information. The goal of testing is to identify poor password-handling processes in applications and weaknesses in network device deployment that attackers can exploit.

There are numerous tools and applications to assist an auditor in capturing, decoding, decrypting, and displaying user passwords. Two packet-capture applications covered in Chapter 4, "Auditing Tools and Techniques," are tcpdump and Wireshark. The best thing about tcpdump is that it is easy to use and can create portable capture files that can be analyzed by other tools for password recovery. Wireshark's graphical interface makes it easier to filter the packets it collects and display only the relevant information, thus making the job of an auditor looking for items such as clear-text passwords trivial. The built-in session tracking functions can be used to follow a single user session without having to create complex filtering rules, which makes it perfect for monitoring specific applications a user might interact with that could have weak password handling. Figure 9-10 shows Wireshark decoding a telnet session username and password.

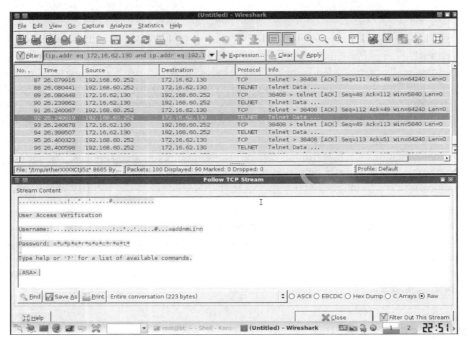

Figure 9-10   *Wireshark Password Auditing*

Although both tcpdump and Wireshark do a fantastic job finding sensitive information on networks, they were designed for network troubleshooting and diagnostics as their primary purposes. For a more focused approach to password auditing, there is nothing better than Cain & Abel. Developed by Oxid.it, it is a purpose-built cracking application with numerous add-ons for intercepting and decrypting passwords sent over the network. This application does not require that the attacker have an in-depth understanding of packet construction or even network architecture because it takes care of grabbing information off the network and automatically displaying any clear-text passwords or hashes that it finds. If the password is encrypted or hashed when it is intercepted, Cain has tools that can handle both simple and complex decryption and hash decode capabilities including dictionary and brute force. Figure 9-11 shows Cain displaying a weak password used for the web administration of a network device.

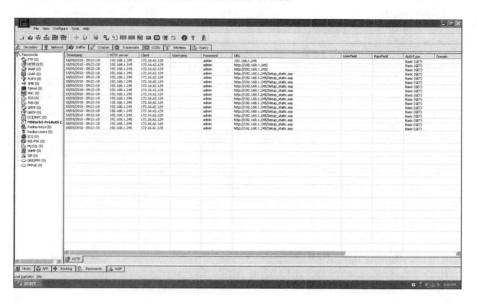

Figure 9-11   *Cain Displaying a Captured Password*

One of the challenges of password auditing is positioning your network password assessment tools at a place in the network where it can see the network traffic from other clients on your network segment. In the early days of networking, when hubs roamed the Earth, this process was easy. Hubs work on a shared media architecture, where all traffic is copied to every port on the device. You did not need to do anything except listen for this traffic, and it would be sent to you. With the introduction of switches, this process became a little more difficult. A switch sends traffic to and from the port that initiated it based on the MAC address of the source and destination devices. If you want to intercept a conversation that you did not initiate, you have to either have access to a span port or trick the switch into sending traffic to you by using an ARP attack. As discussed in Chapter 7, "Infrastructure Security," Cain and Ettercap have built-in ARP poison capabilities to force network clients to send their network traffic to the auditor's machine allowing for easy password auditing.

Another method that auditors can use to attempt to gain access to systems and applications is brute force. This method requires little skill or expertise regarding a target system. An attacker simply finds a valid username (such as administrator) and then attempts to guess the password for that account. Most brute force attacks are conducted through an application whose primary job is to send different passwords repeatedly to a target system as fast as it can.

Several tools are available to assist with the tedious task of brute forcing. THC Hydra is one of the original and still the most popular brute force tools. It can attempt to guess a password over HTTP, POP3, FTP, SMB, mySQL, VNC, Telnet, and a number of other protocols. Hydra is available as part of the Backtrack Linux distribution discussed in Chapter 7. As mentioned earlier in this chapter, the best method to counter a brute force attack is to implement user account lockout after a certain number of incorrect passwords. In addition, administrators can limit the number of attempts that can be made within a certain time range. However, neither of these controls prevents an offline attack.

An auditor can also conduct and offline brute force decoding of passwords if he is able to capture encrypted or hashed password information off the network. This enables the auditor the ability to conduct the password analysis after hours, which is typically how an attacker operates to avoid detection. An offline password analysis tool compares the password information captured against password values for which it generated a hash. After it finds two hashes that match, the password is discovered. This type of attack is most often used with NTLM, NT LAN MAN hashes, and with WiFi Protected Access (WPA) handshakes in a wireless environment.

In addition to Cain, two applications that are great at systematically running through hashes are John the Ripper and L0pht Crack. These applications use the captured hashes as an input and with some patience determine the user's password. Another technique to speed this process up is to use a rainbow table to compare hashes. Offline password attacks can be conducted at lightning speed with the use of rainbow tables and dictionary files. A rainbow table is basically a database of passwords and hashes that has already been computed from a dictionary file. The only limit to this is memory and drive space, which are inexpensive today. John and L0pht use a significant amount of processing power and memory to hash each possibility every time the application is run, whereas rainbow tables use a database of precomputed hash values and compare the captured hash to every entry in the database. This database of hashes can be as little as 100 MB for a simple password scheme or might consume hundreds of gigabytes for more complex passwords.

Checklist

Assessment Area	Assessment Technique
People	
Are Identity and Access control policies adequate for the organizations level of risk?	Review applicable identity policies: Asset classification, Access Granting policy and procedures, Access Revocation policy, Guest and third-party access policy, and Posture assessment policy.
Are the acceptable use, monitoring, and access control policies signed by all users?	Review documentation of signed agreements or electronic click to accept.
Process	
Has an asset classification and inventory been conducted on all network resources?	Review documentation of assets in security classification.
Are appropriate authentication methods selected based on risk and asset value?	Review access control matrix for appropriate single or multifactor authentication.
Are strong passwords requirements outlined in policies and procedures?	Review password policies to ensure adherence to good security practices.
Are the principles of least privilege used in granting access?	Review user access rights to ensure unnecessary privileges have not been granted.
Are appropriate separations of duties principles followed?	Review user roles to ensure separation of duties are followed.
Are access-granting procedures well documented and include sign off from management?	Review access-granting procedures to determine adherence to good security practices.
Do access revocation procedures effectively remove terminated employees?	Review access revocation procedures and user accounts for any terminated employees left active.
Is a periodic entitlement review conducted for all employees and job roles?	Review documentation of entitlement review, and inspect user access for unnecessary privileges.
Is there a well documented approval process for access changes?	Review access change procedure procedures.
Are administrative users actively monitored and their activities logged?	Assess administrative user monitoring and logging capabilities, and review reports.

continues

Assessment Area	Assessment Technique	*(continued)*
Are guest users required to sign acceptable use policies before gaining access to the network?	Review guest user provisioning process and ensure appropriate documentation and acceptance of acceptable use policies.	
Are physical password protection procedures followed?	Conduct a site walk-through looking for passwords on sticky notes or written down in work areas. Also, be on the lookout for any type of credentials such as badges or other physical access devices.	
Technology		
Are all vendor supplied default passwords changed?	Run vulnerability assessment tool to check passwords.	
Are all network devices configured with inactivity session timeout and accounting lockout after a specific number of invalid logins?	Review network device configuration, and test user account lockout and inactive session timeout.	
Do all users have unique assigned usernames and passwords?	Review user access to ensure that account and password sharing is not allowed. Inspect network device configuration to prevent multiple logins from the same user.	
Are user VLANs segmented by role, and have appropriate access control restrictions?	Ensure network is configured for role-based access control.	
Are non-interactive devices (UPS, printer, IP phone, and so on) cataloged, and are Mac addresses used for white listing?	Inspect network device configuration for compliance.	
Are users authenticated before access is granted to the network?	Review configuration for appropriate port level access control.	
Are unused switch ports administratively disabled or placed in not routed VLANs?	Review device configuration for compliance.	
Does the organization actively monitor failed login attempts?	Review documentation and reports of failed logins.	
Does the organization have appropriate security incident detection capabilities in place?	Review detective controls to monitor for password attacks, repeated invalid logins, and other security risks.	
Are passwords sent in clear text on the network, or are any insecure services present?	Conduct password sniffing assessments on user VLANs.	

continues

Assessment Area	Assessment Technique	*(continued)*
Are strong passwords used throughout the organization?	Conducted password analysis reviews utilizing brute force and off-line password assessment techniques.	

Summary

The technologies and procedures used to validate a user's identity are essential to reducing the risk of exposure to data loss and unauthorized access. This chapter highlighted many security good practices for protecting identity and controlling how a user authenticates to the network and interact with it. NAC and IBNS play a big role in the Cisco portfolio for identity management. These technologies, in conjunction with effective security policy and user administration procedures, can help protect critical business information and assets. In summary:

- The strength of identity control methods should be appropriate for the value of the asset they protect.

- Passwords are still the weak link in protecting access to the network; solid user education and password-handling procedures are essential to keeping passwords secret.

- The principle of least privilege should be utilized when granting access to the network, and RBAC can help to better implement these types of policies.

- Both NAC and IBNS provide the capability to authenticate to the network before access is granted, which creates not only an audit trail of access, but also reduces the risk of uncontrolled ports to the network. In addition, NAC can also provide posture assessment capabilities to ensure the client machines have the appropriate security countermeasures in place and are patched to the latest service packs and hotfixes.

- Auditing identity and access control require policy assessment, configuration, architecture review, and hands-on testing to make sure policy is properly enforced.

- Many tools are available for conducting password-assessment exercises. The simplest of these is the sniffer. However, more specialized tools are available and currently being developed, which highlight the clear need for strong passwords and using encryption whenever feasible when users interact with network applications and services.

References in This Chapter

ISACA Access Control Auditing Procedures, http://www.isaca.org/AMTemplate.cfm?Section=Standards,_Guidelines,_Procedures_for_IS_Auditing&Template=/ContentManagement/ContentDisplay.cfm&ContentID=37906

Cisco SAFE, www.cisco.com/go/safe

Chapter 10

Secure Remote Access

Not long ago, high-speed network connectivity was something that only large companies could afford, and it usually required dedicated circuits that connected remote sites in a point-to-point fashion. Bandwidth was expensive, and most network connections were measured in kilobytes per second. Today, broadband is the norm, and cell phones have faster Internet access than businesses did five years ago. As a result of all of the bandwidth and connectivity options, the Internet now provides a cost-effective way to connect remote sites and users to corporate networks, which increases productivity and collaboration across the globe. As Virtual Private Networks (VPN) continue to replace dedicated circuits as a means to connect decentralized groups of users, the security implications of this virtual network should be a priority because sensitive company data can be transported anywhere at the blink of an eye. VPNs are called upon to help maintain the confidentiality, integrity, and availability of communications sent over the public, and in many cases, actively hostile Internet. This chapter covers the technologies Cisco offers for VPN access, good VPN security practices, and the process for auditing site-to-site and remote access VPN solutions.

Defining the Network Edge

The physical location is where a company's employees' work has become more flexible for many businesses. Information workers are consistently armed with laptops and smart phones that provide real-time access to e-mail and nonpublic corporate information across the Internet, which increases employee effectiveness and productivity and enables them to better interact with customers. Over the years, as businesses have come to realize that people are able to work independently and effectively without having to sit in an office building eight hours a day, the use of remote technologies has exploded. Many organizations provide some level of remote access for various classes of their workforce, from after-hours e-mail and work-related tasks to full-time telecommuting, which enables an employee to work from home. Although remote access has been shown to provide an enormous amount of benefit to the employee and employer, all this productivity-enhancing access does increase the risk of exposing confidential information if it is not properly protected.

As if protecting sensitive data wasn't hard enough, the boundaries that used to represent the network edge are not as easily identified as they once were. Traditional network security design classifies the inside of the network as trusted and the outside of the network as untrusted. With VPN technologies, however, your network edge can be anywhere there is an Ethernet or wireless connection. This, in effect, makes the endpoint device the new network edge, which means that the focus must shift away from network borders and move to protecting the flow of information as it moves outside of the organization's corporate boundaries. Ultimately, when assessing VPN solutions, the auditor must focus on the movement of sensitive information and determine if the controls in place to protect the confidentiality, integrity, and availability of that data are effective.

VPN Fundamentals

The term VPN is commonly used to describe a technology that enables the creation of a private network over a public medium, such as the Internet. The word "private," when referring to a VPN, does not always mean encryption technologies are used. A common misconception about VPNs is that they automatically include some type of confidentiality protection or encryption. Most mobile user access VPNs include encryption by default, but in the case of tunneling technologies, such as PPTP, L2TP, GRE, and MPLS, encryption must be configured separately to protect the confidentiality of these connections. It is never a good idea to send any data across the Internet unencrypted, unless you are absolutely sure that you would not care if it was read by anyone.

For the purposes of this chapter, the focus is on commonly used VPN technologies that use encryption for confidentiality. This chapter does not delve into the mathematical formulas or intricate workings of the encryption algorithms, but does provide guidance about some of the most common configurations used in Cisco VPNs.

The effectiveness of a VPN is usually measured by its capability to adequately protect the following three areas:

■   Confidentiality

■   Integrity

■   Authentication

Confidentiality

Keeping private information private is the goal of confidentiality, and Cisco supports standards-based encryption methods and technologies. Crypto analysis is a branch of science that delves into the nuances of mathematical formulas that are used in encryption. Auditors do not need to know encryption to this level of detail when assessing network security, but a good working knowledge of the basics is important in understanding whether the organization being audited has selected the appropriate mechanisms to safeguard its VPNs. At its most basic, the function of encryption is to take a plaintext message, run it through an algorithm, and mathematically produce cipher (encrypted) text. The cipher text can then be decrypted by authorized systems by reversing the mathematical formula to recover the original message. The mathematical process uses unique data strings called keys to do the encryption, and without those keys, the cipher text cannot be decrypted. Figure 10-1 shows a graphical representation of this process.

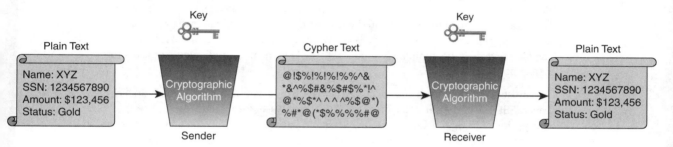

Figure 10-1 *Basic Encryption*

The history of encryption is quite old; in Roman times, generals used simple substitution ciphers in which each letter in a message was substituted with another letter in an agreed upon manner. In World War II, the electro-mechanical encryption machine Enigma helped the Allies win in the European theater. Luckily, encryption today does not require paper and pencil or complicated wiring and gears. Computers have already completed the hard stuff. The challenge is in understanding the pros and cons of the various cryptographic mechanisms that can be used to ensure that the business has selected the appropriate technologies based on the level of risk they are willing to accept.

There are two main types of encryption algorithms in use today: symmetric and asymmetric. The biggest differences between the two are in how they handle the encryption keys used to encode data and the level of data transmission performance that can be obtained.

Symmetric Encryption

Symmetric encryption uses the concept of a "shared secret" key to encode and decode data. The key is the same for both systems and must be shared prior to data transmission. One of the benefits of symmetric encryption is that it is computationally fast to process. This fast processing capability provides a significant speed boost, which makes symmetric encryption ideal for use in encrypting high-speed data transmissions on networks. The downside to this method of encryption is in managing and distributing the encryption keys. Symmetric encryption by itself has no mechanism for sharing keys across a public network in a protected manner and must rely on other protocols or preinstalled keys to set up the session.

There are two classes of symmetric encryption algorithms: stream ciphers and block ciphers. Stream ciphers encode unencrypted plain text data in various lengths directly with the encryption keystream. The keystream is generated by the use of a pseudorandom number generator mathematically computed against a fixed length key, allowing one bit of plain text data to be encrypted with one bit of the keystream, which produces the encrypted cyphertext. For this process to work securely, the keystream used to encrypt the plaintext must be completely random. If the keystream is predictable, it makes for weak encryption.

The most commonly used stream cipher is RC4, which can be used in Secure Sockets Layer (SSL), Wired Equivalent Privacy (WEP), and Wi-Fi Protected Access (WPA) encryption. Although RC4 is extremely fast and can be easily implemented in software, it has been shown to be a poor encryption mechanism. In the case of WEP and WPA, the RC4 algorithm has failed to provide secure connections based on a poor implementation of the initialization vector used to "randomize" the cryptographic process. The use of a 24-bit initialization vector and the sheer computational power of modern computers have enabled the quick cracking of this form of encryption, and as such, these types of stream ciphers are not recommended for use. It's not uncommon to find RC4 in use today in SSL VPNs for backward compatibility with older systems that might not have the processing performance necessary to run Advanced Encryption Algorithm (AES) encryption, and as such, auditors should look out for any SSL VPNs making use of RC4 and recommend switching to a more secure cipher.

Block ciphers operate by breaking data into 64- or 128-bits chunks or blocks. These blocks are then run through a process that mathematically combines the keysteam, an initialization vector to generate randomness and the data block to produce the first block of cipher text. This process is then repeated by chaining further iterations together to scramble the data further. Key size is the single most important factor to determine how crackable a block cipher is. Current security practices recommend that an 80-bit key be the minimum key size given the computational power of the average computer. The larger the key, the harder it is to brute force (sequentially guess at the key). Figure 10-2 shows how a block cipher produces its output.

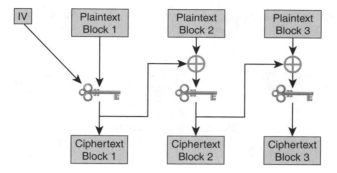

Figure 10-2 *Block Cipher*

The following block ciphers are the most commonly used in Cisco networks:

- **Data Encryption Standard (DES):** A 56-bit symmetric encryption algorithm that is considered weak protection considering current computing performance standards and should not be used for protecting sensitive data.

- **Triple DES (3DES):** Uses DES 56-bit algorithm preformed three times to provide the equivalent of 112-bits of encryption. This is a much slower algorithm than DES, but it is more secure.

- **Advanced Encryption Algorithm (AES):** A 128-bit symmetric block cipher that can use 128-, 192-, and 256-bit keys. AES is considered more efficient and secure than DES and 3DES and should be the standard for corporate encryption.

Asymmetric Encryption

In asymmetric encryption, the keys to encrypt a piece of data are not the same as the ones used to decrypt. This form of encryption is often referred to as public-key cryptography and uses two keys, one public and one private for each device. Two network devices that want to communicate securely simply need to share their public keys. The public key can then be used by the sending system to encrypt data that can be decrypted only by the receiving system that holds the private key. Figure 10-3 shows how the public and private keys are used to communicate.

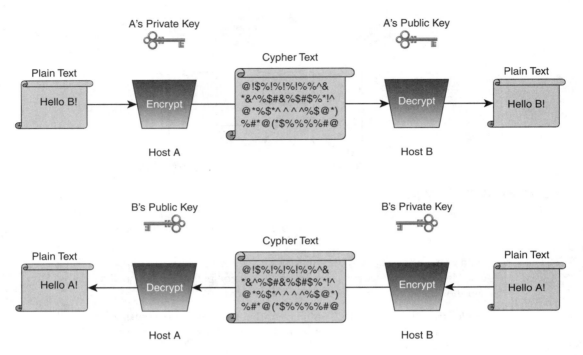

Figure 10-3   *Asymmetric Encryption*

There is no known method for mathematically deriving the private key from the public key, making this an effective cryptography mechanism for establishing secure and confidential connections over a public network. Asymmetric encryption does require more involved mathematical computations that use significantly higher computer resources, and thus are slower. For this reason, asymmetric encryption is often used for key exchange and setting up the encryption session only. After the keys are securely set up, the job of encrypting the data stream is then passed on to symmetric encryption algorithms for better throughput on the network. The asymmetric key exchange is typically implemented as a component of other cryptographic suites. The following are a few widely used examples:

■   **SSL/TLS:** Provides end-to-end encryption across the Internet for many different applications. The most common is for encrypting web browser sessions and for remote access VPNs. Supports 1024- and 2048-bit encryption strength.

■   **Internet Key Exchange (IKE):** IKE is used by IPsec to securely exchange encryption keys prior to establishing an IPsec session association.

■   **Secure Shell (SSH):** SSH is used as a replacement for telnet to protect interactive session to network devices. There are two versions of SSH, with SSH v2 addressing many of the security flaws present in version 1. It is recommended you use SSHv2 whenever possible. SSH can also be used for secure FTP, file copy, and network traffic tunneling between host systems. Although Cisco network devices fully support SSH as a replacement for telnet, they do not terminate SSH tunnels for remote access to networks.

- **RSA:** Encryption method capable of encryption and used to verify authenticity of digital signatures; it supports 1024- and 2048-bit keys.

Integrity

To protect a VPN from external tampering and to ensure that the VPN session occurs between two authenticated systems, Hashed Message Authentication Code (HMAC) is often used. Without this technology, it would be possible for someone to change a value of the data being sent without either party knowing. A $100 banking transfer could become $10,000.

A hash function creates a fixed length numeric value that is computed based on the whole block of data being sent. A hash function works in one direction and acts like a digital fingerprint of the original data. If a single bit is changed, the hash does not match the data, and the two communicating systems drop the offending bits of data. As shown in Figure 10-4, an HMAC uses a hash algorithm. It also adds the encrypted key as a seed value, which makes it even harder to impersonate the remote system without the appropriate key. This can help even MD5 (which is known to have cryptographic weaknesses) be significantly more difficult to impersonate.

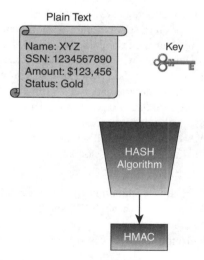

Figure 10-4 *Creation of a Hashed Message Authentication Code*

After the receiving system receives the message and decodes it, the receiving system generates its own HMAC value based on the message it receives and the encryption key and then compares that value to the HMAC value in the original message. If the two HMAC values match, the receiving system can assume that the message is authentic and has not been tampered with. SHA-1 is the currently preferred choice for hash algorithms and should be configured on VPN connections. An HMAC code is often computed for use in SSL/TLS and IPsec to ensure the integrity of the connection.

The two hash methods supported by Cisco are:

- **Message Digest 5 (MD5):** A 128-bit fixed length hash computed by breaking data into 512-bit blocks, it is widely used to sign digital certificates as means for file integrity checking and VPN security protocols. MD5 is computationally fast, but security weaknesses in the hashing algorithm have made MD5 vulnerable to collisions, allowing attackers to fake the authenticity of data that uses MD5 hashes. The risk of using MD5 in VPNs is reduced by the use of HMAC, which leverages cryptographic keys, but for all other uses, MD5 is discouraged. It is recommended you use SHA1 in its place.

- **Secure Hash Algorithm 1 (SHA1):** A 160-bit fixed length hash computed based on 512-bit data blocks, SHA1, although more secure than MD5, has also been found to have some weaknesses. SHA2 (256-bit and a 512-bit version) has been slow to be added as options, but are starting to appear in Cisco and other vendors VPN products. When SHA2 is available, migration to it is advised.

Authentication and Key Management

The method used to securely exchange keys when a VPN is first initiated is accomplished utilizing asymmetric encryption to set up secure sessions across a connection that is not secure. The initiating system can sign the data with its private key, and the receiving system is able to compare the message with the public key it has in its key chain to ensure that the system sending the data has the private key. This provides proof (outside of a compromise of the private key) that the data was legitimately from the appropriate system. This process occurs in both directions for mutual authentication of the session. After both systems have set up this bi-directional authentication, they can then digitally sign (and encrypt) the VPN session key and send it to each other with confidence that the only system that can view the VPN session key is the one that holds the private key used in the public key encryption exchange.

Diffie Helman is one of the most common key exchange mechanisms in use today. It is used to set up session keys in IPsec through IKE and can be used with SSL. Diffie Helman groups determine the strength on key protection employed. The following shows the Diffie Helman (DH) groups in use on Cisco VPN devices.

- **DH Group 1:** 768-bit; considered low key protection

- **DH Group 2:** 1024-bit; minimum recommended key protection level

- **DH Group 5:** 1536-bit; more secure but also requires more processing power

Public key cryptography facilitates the secure transfer of keys, but it doesn't address the problem of distributing the public keys to all the devices to which you might want to create a VPN connection. This is where public key infrastructure (PKI) comes in to play; it utilizes asymmetric encryption as a digital authentication architecture. X.509 V3 is the current standard for PKI and was designed as a mechanism for distribution, formatting, and revocation of digital certificates.

Regardless of the strength of encryption used, if the encryption keys are compromised then confidentiality goes out the window. The two most common methods for provisioning Cisco VPN device authentication for the exchange of keys are pre-shared keys and PKI.

Pre-shared keys are applicable for a small number of VPN endpoints and are used to identify remote devices or users to the VPN concentrator. This method is common because it is easy to set up. As the number of devices in a VPN grows, pre-shared keys become impractical to manually administer. Many pre-shared key deployments also make the mistake of using the same key for all VPN connections, increasing the chance of the key becoming compromised.

PKI, on the other hand, can use digital certificates and X.509 to validate the identity of a remote device and set up a secure connection. Management of digital certificates also enables the revocation of a certificate in the event device is being compromised. The Certificate Authorities (CA) can grant or revoke devices on an as-needed basis, giving the administrator the capability of revoking a single device or user and not having to reconfigure every device with a new key. The Certificate Revocation List (CRL) handles this process.

PKI is a multistep process that verifies an end system's identity. These steps are:

Step 1.   Request the certificate from the CA.

Step 2.   The CA verifies the requester's identity.

Step 3.   The CA issues the certificate to the requestor.

Step 4.   The certificate is presented to users.

Step 5.   The user asks the CA to verify the certificate.

Step 6.   The CA checks that the certificate is valid and hasn't been tampered with.

Step 7.   The CA confirms that the certificate is valid.

Step 8.   The user can now create a trusted connection to the device.

A digital certificate is typically held with a third-party CA and is digitally signed by the CA vouching for its authenticity. Larger organizations might even have their own CA and have the capability to grant and revoke their own certificates. Cisco includes a local CA in the ASA that can be used for issuing certificates to VPN clients. A digital certificate includes the following information:

- **Serial number:** A number used to identify the certificate

- **Subject:** The individual or system identified

- **Signature algorithm:** Algorithm used in creation of the certificate

- **Issuer:** The name of the CA verifying the certificate

- **Valid From:** The date and time the certificate can be used

- **Valid To:** Expiration date of the certificate

- **Key usage:** Encryption, signature verification, or both

- **Public key:** The public key to use to encrypt a message to the certificate's owner

- **Thumbprint algorithm:** Hash algorithm used to identify certificate tampering

- **Thumbprint:** Hashed value

IPsec, SSL, and dTLS

The two most common VPN protocol suites that tie together all of the components previously mentioned into a useable framework are IPsec and SSL. In addition to IPsec and SSL, dTLS is a common encryption method that is based on SSL but designed to better handle delay-sensitive traffic such as voice. These technologies are essential for encrypted communications even though they are not perfect. A basic understanding of how IPsec, SSL, and dTLS work is important when assessing VPNs. VPN security relies on the proper configuration and implementation of these two technologies.

IPsec

IPsec is the de-facto standard protocol suite used to secure point-to-point connections across the Internet today. It provides confidentiality, integrity, and authentication of data packets that match user-defined selection criteria such as source and destination. IPsec is flexible and extendable, and by its modular nature, it can use any cryptographic or authentication mechanisms in use today.

IPsec has two modes of operation:

- **Transport mode:** Transport mode is used for host-to-host communication, such as from a client to a server. Transport mode encrypts only the IP payload (data portion), leaving the IP header intact.

- **Tunnel mode:** Tunnel mode, on the other hand, encrypts the entire IP datagram and then wraps another IP header on top of that to leave the original packet untouched. Tunnel mode is the method used for remote access and site-to-site VPNs.

IPsec is composed of three protocols that are responsible for securely exchanging encryption keys, providing authenticity, maintaining integrity, and creating encrypted sessions:

- **Internet Security Association and Key Management Protocol (ISAKMP):** Used to negotiate encryption methods, keys, and authentication used to set up security associations between network devices. This service is provided on UDP port 500 and utilizes IKE to securely exchange encryption keys when bringing up a security association. IKE can use pre-shared keys, digital signatures, XAUTH (username and password), and digital certificates for authentication.

- **Authentication Header (AH):** A protocol that can be used for protecting the integrity and authenticity of the IP payload and datagram by ensuring that nothing has changed from the originally transmitted packet along the way before it is received at its intended destination. AH cannot be used if network address translating occurs anywhere along the data path because AH provides integrity protection for the IP header itself. It is important to note that AH does not provide encryption.

- **Encapsulating Security Payload (ESP):** More than just a geeky-sounding name, ESP provides encryption, integrity, and authentication of IP packets. It does this by protecting the header and data of the packet, but ignoring the IP header fields that could be changed due to network translations or routing. Because ESP does not protect the IP header, it does not have the same limitations of AH, namely with Network Address Translation (NAT).

When an IPsec VPN is first initiated, ISAKMP uses IKE to initiate the VPN. ISAKMP has two phases of operation when establishing a VPN. The first phase, appropriately named Phase 1, is responsible for negotiating a secure communication channel by using a Diffie Helman key exchange to create a shared secret key and appropriate encryption methods. This creates a security association that can then be used to exchange encryption keys for creating IPsec security associations. IKE can operate in main mode or aggressive mode. With main mode, the identity of the two devices is protected, whereas with aggressive mode, it is not. Aggressive mode was initially intended for mobile users and can reduce the initial key exchange time in half. The problem with aggressive mode is that it passes the user or device name in clear text, which makes it possible to sniff VPN user names. When aggressive mode is used in conjunction with pre-shared keys, the pre-shared key hash is also sent in clear text, which can then be cracked offline given enough time.

After Phase 1 is complete and encryption keys are exchanged, Phase 2, or quick mode, then selects the IPsec encryption methods and protocols and brings up a one-way security association in each direction between the two IPsec peers. These two SAs are then used to transfer encrypted data for the duration of the session. Quick mode can also make use of Perfect Forward Secrecy (PFS) to generate completely new encryption keys throughout the session, which can prevent the compromise of an earlier negotiated session key from being used to decrypt traffic. Because PFS requires frequent rekeying, the number of computations that the VPN devices must perform increases, but the security benefit is substantial.

IPsec's use of ESP allows for a number of encryption methods and integrity hashing algorithms that offer different levels of protection. This is where IPsec implementation can get complicated. IPsec has a long history and as such, a number of legacy protocols can be implemented that today are considered cryptographically weak. The other challenge in selecting the appropriate level of cryptography comes from the fact that each algorithm has a cost in computational resource utilization. Both the VPN network device and the IPsec client must pay this cost. For the most part, modern clients have more than enough raw computational power to support the most cryptographically secure protocols, but care must be taken to properly scale VPN access because each network device has a limit of how many connections they can support. The following is a list detailing the different encryption algorithms supported by Cisco IPsec VPNs:

- **Esp-aes:** ESP with AES 128-bit encryption

- **Esp-aes192:** ESP with AES 192-bit encryption

- **Esp-aes256:** ESP with AES 256-bit encryption

- **Esp-des:** ESP with DES 56-bit encryption

- **Esp-3des:** ESP with 3DES (168-bit/112-bit effective) encryption

- **Esp-null:** ESP with no encryption

HMAC is often used in addition to encryption with ESP to ensure integrity and authenticity of the security association created. Although it is possible to create security associating without using HMAC, this is not recommended. The HMAC hashing algorithms used for Cisco VPNs are MD5 and SHA1.

Secure Socket Layer

Originally created by Netscape in 1994 as a means to protect e-commerce websites, SSL has become the standard for web-based security. SSL has since been ratified as an IETF standard and been reborn as Transport Layer Security (TLS). The name SSL has become synonymous with web-based security, and as such, it is used interchangeably with TLS.

SSL and TLS consist of two layers: the handshake protocol and the record protocol. The handshake protocol layer includes a number of subprotocols that perform the work of setting up the secure session, whereas the record protocol is responsible for the encrypted transmission of data. The handshake layer subprotocols and their functions are:

- **Handshake protocol:** The purpose of the handshake protocol is to facilitate authentication, the exchange of cryptographic keys, and the negotiation of encryption technologies.

- **Change CipherSpec:** This protocol is responsible for informing the peer in the TLS/SSL session that the sender wants to start using a new set of cryptographic keys.

- **Alert:** This protocol provides information on session status and any errors that might have been detected.

The encryption algorithms supported are as follows:

- **DES:** DES encryption is considered weak and should not be used for protecting SSL sessions.

- **RC4:** RC4 is available in 40-bit and 128-bit encryption strength. RC4 is a fast stream cipher that is not recommended for SSL VPN use.

- **3DES:** Provides 168 bits (112 bits effective) of encryption and is sufficient for encrypting VPN traffic.

- **AES:** Available in 128-bit and 256-bit encryption strength and is the best choice for creating a VPN if all clients support it.

With SSL, authentication typically occurs on the server side, with the server authenticating to the client. TLS, on the other hand, operates identically to SSL for server authentication but also provides the capabilities of mutual authentication between both client and server, making it useful as a VPN technology. TLS also leverages HMAC for data integrity and supports MD5 and SHA1 hashes.

Datagram Transport Layer Security (dTLS)

Datagram Transport Layer Security (dTLS) was designed to make TLS more efficient for real-time traffic, such as voice. TLS by itself is not capable of directly supporting UDP traffic and must tunnel it in TCP to work with TLS/SSL. TCP requires more overhead than UDP, which doubles when TLS tunnels UDP over TCP. If any data is lost in transmission, both the application and TLS have to retransmit, which results in significant slowdown. For voice and video traffic, this can make TLS a challenge to control quality of service (QoS) for real-time applications. dTLS enables TLS to operate over port 443 UDP to solve this problem, which enables low latency and faster transmission of voice and video traffic.

Remote Access Threats and Risks

Remote access devices and technologies by their nature are directly attached to the Internet, and as such, they are subject to a significant number of threats that can put an organization at risk of a security breach. Without the appropriate controls and countermeasures, such as access control and granular policy enforcement per user, the VPN can be used as a way to bypass outside security mechanisms. The risks to a remote access VPN include the following:

- **Lack of physical controls:** One of the most obvious threats to remote access systems is the lack of physical control over the devices being used to access the network. Laptops and smart phones are often lost or stolen, which means they could end up in the hands of individuals looking to profit from the information contained in the device.

- **Mobile network boundaries:** Not knowing where the users are when they connect to the network can make it difficult to determine what types of threats are present. Most organizations assume a hostile environment, and rightly so.

- **Use of public networks:** The use of a public network such as the Internet is what makes VPNs so attractive from a connectivity standpoint. However, a public network that is available to anyone means that any data traveling across it is at risk of disclosure to anyone with the technology and the desire to capture it.

- **Remote devices infecting internal systems:** Mobile devices connecting to unsecured networks are at a much greater risk of being infected by malware then those sitting safely behind a corporate firewall with advanced endpoint protective controls. If infected, the device poses a threat to the internal network by allowing malware the ability to use the VPN connection as a means to compromise other devices behind the firewall.

■ **Theft of confidential data:** Theft of confidential data is one of the greatest risks of using remote access technology. All data should be classified and protected according to sensitivity, especially when access is granted via VPN.

■ **Theft of access credentials:** Theft of access credentials can happen in a number of ways, from shoulder surfing, where an attacker watches the user input his username and password, to man-in-the-middle attacks, where access credentials are captured as they are entered when logging into the network. When uncontrolled, Internet kiosks are used to access the corporate network and there is a possibility that a keystroke logger (in the form of software or hardware) could be utilized to steal the user's access credentials.

■ **Backdoor network access:** After a mobile device is compromised, it can be used as a jump point for an attacker to be able to traverse the mobile access VPN and gain access to the internal network. Split tunnel access can allow an attacker to ride a client's VPN connection back into the corporate network if they can compromise the user's computer.

■ **Weak cryptography:** Choosing the wrong cryptographic technologies can result in poor security. VPNs have an enormous number of optional configuration parameters that can greatly impact how well confidentiality is maintained. 56-bit DES encryption was considered strong when it was first released, but the amount of processing that a typical CPU can perform has far surpassed its ability to provide adequate protection.

Remote Access Policies

VPN policies and standards should be reviewed to determine whether remote access risks are properly identified and good security practices are followed before network access is granted. The following security elements should be addressed in the organization remote access policies and standards:

■ **Access requirements:** Not everyone in the organization needs access to a VPN. Policies must be developed to determine which individuals or groups are authorized access to the VPN. Account provisioning must be requested in writing and approved by an employee's direct supervisor. Employee access should be limited to the applications and services they need to perform their jobs remotely.

■ **Account review:** A user account review process that includes access rights review should be conducted on a regular basis. The purpose of this policy component is to remove unnecessary accounts or access privileges.

■ **Authentication:** Authentication standards should be defined with two-factor authentication being preferred. Digital certificates provide a much higher level of security versus pre-shared keys and make for more manageable device credentials for site-to-site VPNs. User authentication can also be tied to active directory, radius, or LDAP for centralized management. The best option for mobile access users is one-time passwords, derived from hardware or software tokens.

- **Role-based user classification:** Each job function can have different security requirements based on the types of data with which the role interacts. Classification of all user types should be completed and access control standards in place for each role.

- **Minimum access standards:** Minimum standards set forth the requirements for host access to the VPN. These include operating system patch-level requirements for antivirus, antispyware, and personal firewalls. Antimalware and personal firewalls should be required of any endpoint connecting to the VPN.

- **Posture assessment:** The requirement for posture assessment of remote endpoints before access is granted should be detailed in the VPN policy. This element is often a component of the minimum access standards.

- **Noncorporate assets:** Use of noncorporate assets such as personal computers or even Internet kiosks can represent an increased level of risk to the business of data loss and should be addressed in policy.

- **Split tunneling:** Split tunneling should be explicitly prohibited, as should any user configuration or modification of VPN software.

- **Prohibited network activities:** Specific activities like peer-to-peer file sharing or other bandwidth-intensive or policy-prohibited activities should be listed.

- **Encryption standards:** Encryption standards should be documented and include specific protocols and authentication mechanisms allowed.

- **Monitoring and logging:** Monitoring and logging of all remote connections should be required by policy, and logs should be reviewed on a regular basis.

Remote Access Operational Review

Site-to-site VPN operations are often conducted in a similar manner to managing wide-area network (WAN) connections. VPNs have become the virtual pipes used to connect branch offices, making bandwidth utilization, latency, and packet loss key metrics for meeting acceptable service levels. Mobile user VPNs, on the other hand, require more security focus because of the volume of connections and the authentication and authorization of user sessions. This section discusses some of the operational components that should be in place to securely deliver these services.

VPN Device Provisioning

VPN device provisioning should follow good security practices that protect the integrity of device configuration during the installation of new VPN endpoints. There are a number of ways to securely provision site-to-site VPNs that can make it easier on the network

administrator. The following are methods that organizations can use to securely deploy a
site-to-site or home office VPN:

- **Configure and ship:** The configure-and-ship method requires that network engineers
  perform VPN device configurations before they are sent to the new VPN site. This
  enables the network engineers to implement all the security configuration requirements and test functionality without requiring IT personnel at the remote site. The
  downside to this method is the cost of shipping and the scalability of network engineers. Large VPN deployments can be a challenge logistically.

- **Secure token:** A secure token is a USB key that is encrypted and stores the configuration and authentication credentials necessary for a network device to connect back
  to the corporate VPN. A network device can be shipped unconfigured to a remote
  site, and by inserting the etoken into the USB port of the device, the full configuration is installed.

- **Zero touch deployments:** Zero touch deployments are a form of automated self-provisioning that utilizes Cisco Security Manager, Cisco Configuration Engine, and
  Cisco Secure Device Provisioning. These components make up the core of the Cisco
  Virtual Office solution and can scale extremely large VPN deployments. Using templates enables engineers to provision a new device by having a user at the remote site
  log in via a web browser to the VPN device through a username and password. This
  kicks off automatic configuration and the assignment of certificates to provide secure connectivity to the corporate network.

Mobile Access Provisioning

The process for provisioning mobile access VPNs should follow the same rules as all user
accounts. Chapter 9, "Access Control," discusses many of the role-based access requirements that are also applicable to VPN access. The key is to ensure that users are given
access to the application and devices they need to accomplish their jobs. VPN access
controls should be configured based on user roles to provide a consistent and enforceable
policy that all users must follow.

User credentials can consist of a user name and password, certificate, or electronic token.
Pre-shared keys can be used for mobile VPNs but represent a significant security risk and
are discouraged because it's too easy for them to be compromised. Hardware tokens that
provide a one-time password are more secure and reduce the administration associated
with resetting forgotten passwords.

Client deployment software for IPsec requires that the organization install a compatible
client on the user's device, which has to be done manually or through a third-party software deployment mechanism. With IPsec, there is no automatic deployment function.
SSL VPN software can be deployed automatically by authenticating to the SSL VPN concentrator (ASA or IOS router) and downloading the AnyConnect client. If a new version
of the AnyConnect client is required, the next time the user connects to the VPN, it is
automatically installed.

Mobile User Role-Based Access Control

Each user role has different requirements for access to applications and services, making role-based access control (RBAC) useful for mobile user VPNS. The integrated access control functions available for an IPsec mobile user VPN are limited to access control lists that restrict a user's network access, whereas SSL VPNs open a wide range of access controls and features that take into account posture assessment and host scanning. Cisco utilizes a technology called dynamic access policies (DAP) to implement access control for SSL VPN users. Cisco NAC can also be integrated with a mobile user VPN to provide posture assessment and remediation of vulnerabilities (see Chapter 9 for more information on NAC). Regardless of the approach an organization takes for implementing policy controls for mobile user VPNs, having well-defined user roles is critical to their proper implementation.

VPN access methods should also be determined by user role. Some users are allowed a full tunneling client, whereas others, such as business partners, might be allowed connectivity only to a web portal for sharing files or placing orders. The organization should have a mapping from user role to access requirements for each mobile user class. Table 10-1 shows an example access mapping:

Table 10-1 *Mobile User Access Requirements*

Role	Access	Applications	Access Control
Executive	Web Portal, AnyConnect Client	E-mail, Financial Dashboard, Telephony	Corporate laptop with security features enabled: access to financial dashboard Other access method or outside policy: deny protected services
Sales	Web Portal	E-mail, Sales Dashboard, Customer Relationship Management, Telephony, Web	Corporate laptop with security features enabled: access to financial dashboard Other access method or outside policy: deny protected services
Engineering	Web Portal, AnyConnect client	E-mail, Remote Desktop, Development application, Telephony, Web	Corporate laptop with security features enabled: access to development application and Remote Desktop Other access method or non compliant to policy: e-mail and web only
Network Admins	AnyConnect Client	Email, Remote Desktop, SSH, Web, Telephony	Corporate laptop with security features enabled: full access Other access method or noncompliant to policy: e-mail and web only
Business Partners	Web Portal	Partner Data Exchange application, Sharepoint	Access denied from IP address ranges not used by business partner

Monitoring and Incident Handling

The monitoring of a VPN solution can be accomplished with Cisco Security Manager and the built-in graphical configuration monitoring tools available on the router and ASA. Cisco Security Manager enables the integration of Cisco Performance Monitor, which tracks VPN usage statistics and other useful data for determining how well the VPN performs. Keeping track of this type of data can identify anomalies that might represent a security incident. Using Radius accounting and syslog can help track invalid login attempts that might represent someone trying to brute force a user's credentials.

The use of IPS technologies is a great complement for VPNs because they allow for the monitoring and inline preventions of malicious traffic entering and exiting the VPN tunnel. This functionality can detect attacks that attempt to use the VPN to exploit corporate resources. IPS sensors can be integrated as hardware modules in the ASA and IOS router products. Without this visibility into the VPN tunnel, organizations are blind to security issues that can threaten the organization from remote networks or compromised end-user devices. A security incident management application such as Cisco MARS can provide intelligent analysis of the logs and events generated from the VPN network reducing the burden on support staff from having to sift through log files.

Remote Access Architecture Review

How a VPN is deployed has a major impact on the security posture of the organization. Assessing the VPN architecture enables the auditor to identify any weaknesses in the current design and determine whether or not technical controls are implemented to reduce the risk of attack or disclosure of confidential information. An architecture review starts by examining any documentation pertaining to the VPN deployment, which includes identifying how and where the VPN connects to the external network and the method in which it is integrated into the internal network authentication process and access controls.

A VPN can be deployed on routers, firewalls, or as a dedicated VPN appliance, and there are many factors that determine how a business chooses to implement the VPN. Cost plays an important role, too, which is why many organizations choose an integrated solution that leverages existing hardware purchases. An auditor's role in the architecture review is to look for weaknesses in these deployments. Some of the key factors that determine whether a VPN design is adequate for protecting business assets are:

- Ease of management
- Sufficient controls to enforce policy
- Monitoring and analysis capabilities
- Protection of the VPM from direct attack
- VPN failover and redundancy addressed

- Meets the requirements for remote access and policy

- Follows principles of least privilege

- Strong authentication

This section describes the architectural elements of how Cisco VPNs are deployed for site-to-site and mobile user access and the various controls available to enforce policy.

Site-to-Site VPN Technologies

In general, a VPN can be deployed in one of two ways: site-to-site or by remote access. A site-to-site VPN typically uses IPsec to connect remote offices to a headquarters' site or each other. The primary purpose of a site-to-site VPN is to provide a confidential and protected transport for network traffic from one location to another and as a more cost-effective replacement for dedicated point-to-point circuits.

In its most basic form, the site-to-site VPN simply requires that two network devices (a headquarters and branch router or firewall) be configured to encrypt traffic using IPsec to and from the networks configured behind them. The users and devices behind the VPN network device are typically unaware that they are traversing the VPN. Figure 10-5 shows a simple site-to-site IPsec connection.

Figure 10-5 *IPsec Site-to-Site Tunnel*

Many configuration options enable the site-to-site connection to more closely operate like a physical dedicated circuit, improve scalability, and improve fault tolerance. The following are some methods used for site-to-site VPNS.

Easy VPN

Cisco Easy VPN dramatically reduces the amount of configuration required to bring up a VPN connection for a small office or home office. The small office's router or firewall is configured with the VPN head-end IP address, and after it connects, it is authenticated and all VPN policies and connectivity requirements are pushed to the device from the head-end that establishes the VPN. Configuration settings and policies are centrally controlled in an Easy VPN configuration. Routing is handled through reverse route injection, without the need for static IP address configuration. Easy VPN supports only one IP subnet behind the easy VPN client, which makes it most suitable for small offices without complex VLAN configurations.

IPsec and Generic Router Encapsulation (GRE)

Generic router encapsulation (GRE) is an overlay technology that can be used to create a logical network connection between two devices on the Internet that operates like a hardwired point-to-point link. GRE enables dynamic routing and multicast to traverse an IPsec VPN. All the traffic that is to be secured is sent through a GRE tunnel interface, which is then encrypted by IPsec. The GRE tunnel is configured between routers through manually configuring the IP address of the remote hosts allowing for the creation of a single security association for all networks passing through the GRE tunnel, instead of one for each network making for simpler configuration. Figure 10-6 shows a GRE tunnel protected by IPsec.

Figure 10-6 *GRE Tunnel Protected by IPsec*

IPsec GRE tunnels start to become administratively difficult to manage as the number of connections rise. GRE tunnels are typically configured in a hub-and-spoke pattern, with each remote device having a GRE/IPsec tunnel to the headquarters' router. This design causes all traffic to flow through the headquarters' device to reach other parts of the VPN network. When a branch office wants to communicate to another branch office, the traffic must be sent to the head-end and then back down another VPN tunnel to the appropriate branch office router. This effectively doubles the bandwidth requirement at the head-end and increases latency for the connection. The alternative is to create a fully meshed environment where each VPN device has a tunnel configured for every other VPN device. The issue here is in the amount of configuration that must be performed as networks get larger. The number of tunnels rises exponentially. Figure 10-7 shows hub-and-spoke and fully meshed topologies.

Dynamic Multipoint VPN (DMVPN)

IPsec tunnels and GRE are a good overlay technology to make secure point-to-point links, but as mentioned in the previous section, they must be set up in advance and can lead to significant administrative difficulties as networks grow. The need for branch office-to-branch office secure connectivity is essential for enabling new services like

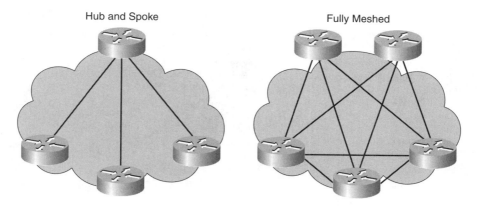

Figure 10-7   *Hub-and-Spoke Topology and Fully Meshed Topology*

voice. Voice communication using the VPN is a fantastic way to save money on toll calls, but with GRE tunnels, it becomes difficult to manage all of the possible calling destinations for each branch. Dynamic Multipoint VPN (DMVPM) can provide a scalable and administratively easier way to provide branch-to-branch connectivity.

DMVPN is configured in a hub-and-spoke manner with the hub typically being a headquarters' site. Each spoke router has one permanent IPsec/GRE tunnel configured to connect to the hub router. The spoke then registers the addresses of the networks it supports to the HUB through Next Hop Resolution Protocol (NHRP). NHRP then builds a database of the spoke routers, so when a spoke wants to communicate to a network at another spoke, it can query NHRP and find the address of the destination spoke router and then dynamically build an IPsec/GRE tunnel to communicate. After the session is idle after a preconfigured amount of time, the tunnel is torn down automatically. Figure 10-8 shows an example of DMVPN in action.

Multi Protocol Label Switching (MPLS) and Virtual Routing and Forwarding (VRF) VPNs

Traffic segmentation is key to limiting exposure, as it separates logical paths that data follows as it travels across the network to its ultimate destination. Segmenting a network used to require dedicated network interfaces and complex rules, but through the creation of Virtual Routing and Forwarding (VRF) and Multi Protocol Label Switching (MPLS), Cisco IOS routers and switches have the capability of operating with multiple routing tables on a single device. This technology, for all practical purposes, operates as if you had multiple routers handling specific network connectivity requirements without having the expense and complexity of dedicated devices. Because VRFs keep data paths separate, they operate in much the same manner as a typical VPN without all of the configurations and peer setups. The biggest benefit of VRFs is that overlapping IP addresses can be used in a network, because each VRF has its own view of the network and the VRF tag is really what differentiates the traffic, from the network device's perspective. VRFs

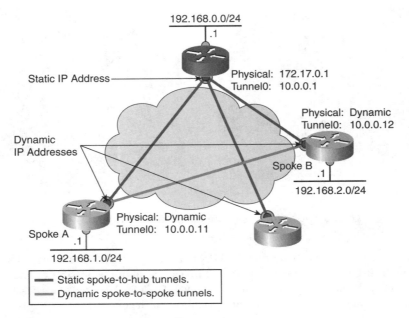

Figure 10-8   *DMVPN Dynamic Tunnel Creation*

have become common as a means for reducing the scope of PCI audits by setting up dedicated VRFs for the network path used to process credit card transaction, segmenting that traffic from the rest of the network.

MPLS is a technology that uses VRFs to create VPNs and leverages tags or labels to identify traffic destinations instead of routing tables when transporting data across a WAN. MPLS has become popular for service providers to deploy for connecting customers' branch offices, as it rides entirely over an IP network and can be used to logically separate customer traffic while providing QOS and other services as well. This gives the customer a logically separated network that operates in the same manner as a dedicated point-to-point circuit but at a reduced cost. MPLS adds extensions to BGP to include label routing information for dynamically updating network paths through the Internet.

RFC2547 is the guiding RFC for layer 3 MPLS VPNs and is a good read for any auditor looking to understand more about MPLS VPNs. The layer 3 MPLS VPN consists of three functional devices:

- **Customer Edge (CE) router:** This is the router that connects the customer network to the service provider network.

- **Provider Edge (PE) router:** This is how the customer router connects to the service provider network and is the first hop for MPLS. This device is typically an aggregation point for multiple customers.

- **Provider (P) router:** The router inside the core of the service provider network and is responsible for switching MPLS tagged traffic to its ultimate destination.

MPLS functions by placing a MPLS header on packets that include a label that uniquely identifies a customer network to the service provider's network. In addition, there are QoS fields to differentiate high priority packets from lower priority packets. After a packet is forwarded by the CE router, it is passed on to the PE router to enter the service provider's network. The PE router looks up the network information of the packet and adds an MPLS header that identifies the customer network and VRF. The PE router then looks up the destination PE router, adds another MPLS header identifying the destination PE router, and forwards it to the appropriate provider router within the service provider's network. The P routers send it hop by hop, swapping the outer label based on the P router label table, until it reaches the destination PE. The outer label is popped off. The PE then looks at the remaining label and determines the proper customer VRF to send the packet. The final label is popped off, and the packet is sent to its intended destination on the customer network. Figure 10-9 shows MPLS VPN traffic passing through a service provider's network.

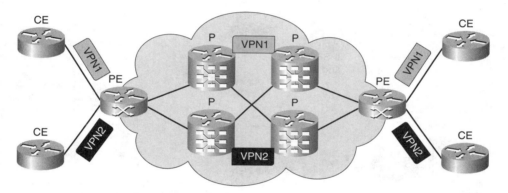

Figure 10-9 *MPLS VPN Traffic Flow*

MPLS VPNs usually stay within a single service provider, and although they use IP as a transport, they do not traverse the Internet like other VPN technologies. This doesn't mean that there are not threats to an MPLS network. There is no inherent security within MPLS and without encryption, and there is no guarantee that a misconfiguration within the service provider's network would not expose sensitive data.

MPLS design and deployment is a complicated subject. Auditors are not expected to know every nuance of getting MPLS working, but it is important for auditors to understand the basics from a security perspective.

GETVPN

Cisco GETVPN is a technology that allows for encryption of traffic that can be deployed within an MPLS network. GETVPN preserves all of the original IP address and header information, while encrypting the data portion. This is considered a "tunnel-less" encryption technology because it does not require any setup in advance to communicate between devices in the GETVPN domain. Each device is already authenticated and holds an agreed-upon shared key that allows instantly encrypted communication. GETVPN uses group domain of interpretation (GDOI) to distribute keys and leverages IPsec for encryption.

There are three components to GETVPN: the key server, group member, and GDOI protocol. A group member is responsible for encrypting and decrypting traffic between other groups. The key server handles distributing the key used for all communications, which enables all group members to communicate without having to setup direct connections to each other and exchange keys. Group members register with the key server, using GDOI to authenticate and authorize the device for communication. GDOI informs the group member of the IPsec policy and the keys being used. After the group member is registered and has received the traffic encryption key (TEK) and key encryption key (KEK), it can then communicate to any other group member without having to go through the key server. Figure 10-10 shows the components used in GETVPN.

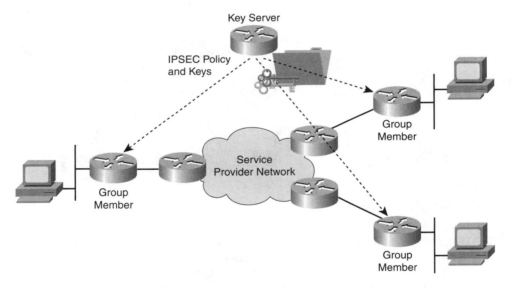

Figure 10-10 *Get VPN Example*

Mobile User Access VPN

A remote access VPN improves productivity by allowing employees to spend less time in the office and more time in front of customers. The technology Cisco uses provides the flexibility to tailor access to the type of user. SSL and IPsec can be used together on the same network device at the same time. IPsec has been used for many years as a mobile user technology, whereas SSL VPNs are starting to takeoff in no small part due to their ease of configuration and easier deployment.

IPsec Client

IPsec remote access requires a pre-installed software client and is typically deployed on company-managed laptops or smart phones. Many modern operating systems also have IPsec clients that can be used to connect directly to Cisco VPN devices. Cisco provides a free IPsec client with integrated firewall, autoupdate, and centralized policy push from the VPN head-end.

The IPsec client supports both pre-shared keys and PKI for authentication. When pre-shared keys are used, aggressive mode is enabled for authentication, which causes the VPN device to send the username and pre-shared key hashes in clear text. Cisco VPN devices can be configured to not use aggressive mode to prevent this from happening.

Split tunneling can be enabled to allow a VPN client the ability to access local LAN print servers and other devices, but it can also used by an attacker as a method to gain access to the VPN tunnel. Split tunneling does allow for more efficient utilization of bandwidth by not having to force all traffic to the VPN head and then be routed back onto the Internet. DNS is another configuration option that can be pushed from the VPN head-end to the client to enforce known good DNS servers. DNS poisoning and hijacking is often used as an attack vector for getting users to go to malicious websites or man-in-the-middle attacks, which is why having a trusted DNS source is an essential security precaution.

The Cisco VPN client also has integrated firewall capabilities that enable VPN personal firewall policies to be enforced at the end point when connected to the corporate network through the VPN. The client can be configured to check for the presence of Cisco Security Agent before initiating the VPN tunnel. These rudimentary posture and enforcement functions offer some policy control, but nowhere near the level of assessment capabilities of Cisco's SSL solution, which are discussed next.

Clientless SSL VPN

Cisco clientless SSL VPN leverages a user's web browser to access everything from file shares, web applications, and a number of TCP-based applications. Many users do not need a full tunneling client because they only use a few applications like email, connect to file shares, or use remote desktop applications. For these types of users, the clientless SSL solution meets their functional requirements and decreases the risk to the organization of having to provision a full tunneling client for every user. Access can be limited to a very small subset of applications and internal sites by implementing a web portal that operates as proxy between the user and the internal network. There are a number of client/server plugins that can be implemented as well that can give browser based access to the following applications:

- Citrix Metaframe

- RDP

- RDP2

- SSH/Telnet

- SSH2

- VNC

Cisco ASA VPNs also support port forwarding and smart tunnels that allow client side applications that use TCP to use the SSL Tunnel to access internal resources. This enables the user to continue to utilize supported application while not requiring an SLL VPN client.

The main web portal page appears after logging in and displays a list of bookmarks for internal websites and applications approved by the organization for the user to interact with. The page can be configured per user role. Figure 10-11 shows the clientless SSL VPN portal page.

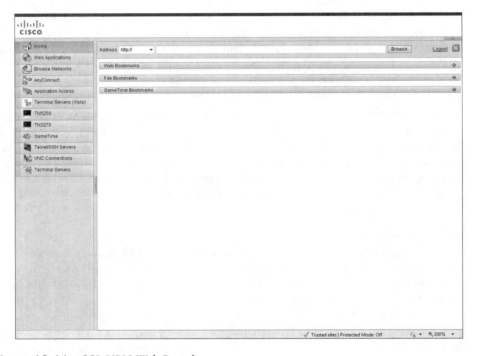

Figure 10-11   *SSL VPN Web Portal*

Cisco Secure Desktop

Cisco Secure Desktop (CSD) is designed to reduce the risk of data leakage by providing a secure workstation environment and handling the cleanup of information that might be left behind after the session is complete. CSD can be configured to check security parameters and enforce policies while the user is connected. CSD creates a secure vault that stores all cache files, browser history, and any downloaded data in an encrypted file that is erased by overwriting it seven times in a U.S. Department of Defense approved manner after the session disconnects. No files or history can be retrieved outside of the VPN session. Cache cleaner is another feature that can be used with Windows and non-Windows systems to erase the browser cache on termination of the VPN for instances when the vault cannot be used or is not supported.

DAPs are features used in conjunction with Cisco Secure Desktop that allows the results of a posture assessment and policy checks to influence how much access a user is granted. CSD scans for registry entries, certificates, file settings, or the presence of keystroke loggers and malware to determine if the system meets minimum access standards or is corporately owned. This allows for differentiated policies based on potential risk. If users connect to the VPN on a shared computer or kiosk, they might have only basic access, as opposed to full access when connecting with their corporate laptops with security features enabled.

The CSD host scan can be used to perform three levels of endpoint assessment on a laptop:

- **Basic scan:** System service pack levels, processes running, filenames, and registry keys.

- **Endpoint assessment:** Scans for FW, AV, antispyware, and signature and definition levels.

- **Advanced endpoint assessment:** Allows for limited remediation of noncompliant systems. Enabled antimalware software, updates signature definitions, and applies approved rules to personal firewalls.

Cisco Secure Desktop enables a number of security controls to protect an SSL VPN connection. The events and actions are as follows:

- CSD prelogin process:

    1. The user connects to the VPN appliance.

    2. The VPN appliance pushes CSD to the clients system.

    3. CSD performs checks to identify the location of the user. It views certificates on the machine and looks at IP ranges, registry entries, and other identifying files or processes running.

    4. Based on the results obtained, CSD applies location and assessment policies.

- CSD login process:

    5. CSD checks for keystroke loggers and host emulation and based on the policies configured permit or deny access to the VPN.

    6. If access is allowed, CSD then creates the encrypted secure vault and switches to Secure Desktop mode on the client.

    7. A login is presented to the user for authentication.

    8. The host scan information gathered previously is checked against DAPs to determine the network access level to be granted.

- CSD post-login process:

    9. DAP is applied to control what the user can access based on compliance to security policy and location.

    10. The VPN connection is now active and the user is able to access resources.

    11. After the session is complete or an idle timeout occurs, CSD post-session cleanup is preformed. CSD clears all cookies, browser history, and files downloaded, and it erases the secure vault with a DoD-grade erase (writing over the secure vault data location seven times).

Figure 10-12 shows a windows device protected by the CSD vault.

Figure 10-12   *Cisco Secure Desktop Vault*

SSL Full Tunneling Client

The Cisco AnyConnect client is a thick VPN client that is loaded on a remote client system to enable full tunneling access through an SSL VPN. The AnyConnect client can either be preloaded on a workstation or can be automatically provisioned when the user connects to the web portal. The AnyConnect client supports a wide range of operating systems from Microsoft Windows (32- and 64-bit), Mac OSX, Red Hat Linux, and Windows Mobile devices.

Split tunneling is also supported on the AnyConnect client (with the same risks as the IPsec client) and can be pushed down through policy configurations from the SSL appliance. The AnyConnect client can make use of TLS and DTLS for better support of voice and video traffic across the SSL VPN. The AnyConnect client also has an auto update feature that checks for newer version whenever it connects to the SSL VPN appliance.

VPN Network Placement

The placement of a VPN device is an important factor to consider when auditing a VPN network. When assessing VPN deployments, the auditor must take into consideration protecting the VPN device itself and what could happen if the VPN connection is compromised. The following are common VPN designs that help to highlight the pros and cons of VPN placement. The VPN appliance can be either a router or an ASA.

- **Integrated with the firewall:** Many organizations choose to leverage an existing firewall, either a router or ASA, as a VPN device. The most obvious benefit of this type of deployment is in cost savings. The VPN is able to use existing firewall rules and policies, which can save on administration efforts as well. If, however, there is a misconfiguration, security can be impacted on the VPN side and the firewall. Care must be taken to follow strong change control processes to help prevent these types of errors when using a single device. Figure 10-13 shows this design option.

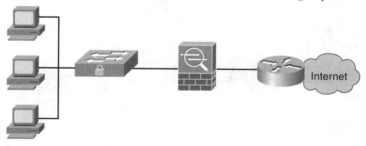

Figure 10-13 *Integrated VPN with Firewall*

- **Parallel to the firewall:** In a parallel deployment, the VPN device sits alongside the firewall, with one interface directly connected to the Internet and the other interface terminating to the internal network. The biggest benefit of this type of design is typically seen in the performance of both the VPN and firewall, because the firewall does not have to process the VPN traffic. The VPN device in this instance should be configured with firewall rules and strong access control mechanisms because of its direct proximity to the internal network. If a VPN is compromised in this case, direct access to the internal network is granted to an attacker. Figure 10-14 shows this design option.

- **DMZ network:** The VPN device decrypts traffic from the Internet and sends it to a DMZ interface for access control and inspection of unencrypted traffic by the firewall. This design does require that the VPN have firewall capabilities to protect itself because of it is directly attached to the Internet, but all unencrypted traffic is subjected to firewall rules and inspection on the DMZ. This design can also be modified by using two DMZ interfaces and allows the firewall to completely control traffic going into and out of the VPN device, which protects the VPN device and the internal network from malicious activity. Figure 10-15 shows this design option.

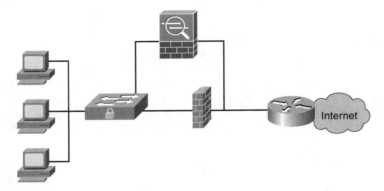

Figure 10-14   *VPN in Parallel with Firewall*

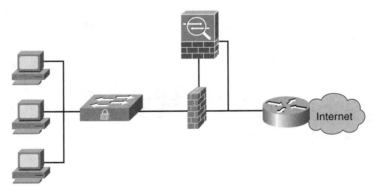

Figure 10-15   *VPN Inside Interface on DMZ of Firewall*

VPN Access Controls

VPN access controls represent the first line of defense to protect the internal network against malicious activity and ensure that only applications and services that are approved by policy are allowed through the VPN. Access control implementation is based on the type of VPN deployed: site-to-site or mobile user access.

Site-to-Site Access Controls

Site-to-site VPNs rely on IPsec as a mechanism for encrypting the connection between sites. If IPsec is not used with a tunneling technology like GRE, then each subnet must be selected with an access control list to identify the traffic that is to be encrypted. Any IP subnet that is not specifically defined passes unencrypted or is dropped by access control policies. With GRE, a tunnel interface is created that operates like a physical interface and can have access control lists applied to prevent the transmission of unapproved protocols and services through the VPN connection. GRE is available only for router-based VPNS and is not supported on the ASA.

All VPN devices should implement access control lists or (preferably) firewall rules to limit the ports and services to better comply with policy. It's tempting to just give full access across the VPN tunnel for a site-to-site VPN, because it's easier from a configuration standpoint, but this wide-open access can be misused if a host on the other end of the VPN is compromised. Chapter 8, "Perimeter Intrusion Prevention," examined how to create these rules and should be reviewed for VPN deployments. Having a complete list of the applications and services available to the remote site enables easier creation of those rules.

Handling remote access web traffic is another policy decision that must be addressed for site-to-site VPNs. The decision to allow remote sites to have Internet access can help to reduce the amount of bandwidth used to connect to a headquarters' site, which can be advantageous, specifically for increasing application responsiveness and voice over IP, which fights for bandwidth through the VPN tunnel. Of course, by doing this, policy enforcement of Internet usage must be performed at the remote site.

Quality of service (QoS) should also be implemented for the VPN tunnel to prioritize essential traffic from nonessential traffic. QoS can also be used to ensure management access from the headquarters' site to the remote site for troubleshooting and maintenance of remote devices. QoS can be an integral part of enforcing access control policy.

Mobile User Access Controls

A mobile user access VPN has many potential pitfalls that should be addressed from an access control standpoint. The first issue to address is whether or not the organization provides full tunneling access or simply utilizes a webportal or application proxy. If users only need access to Outlook Web Access or maybe a content management server, it makes little sense to give them a complete tunneling client that can allow any application to communicate back into the internal network. Webportal deployments can significantly reduce the access control requirements and attack vectors of malware, because they operate by proxying communications between the client and the backend servers that create a buffer to protect applications from direct interaction. Some organizations allow only terminal services to secured and controlled virtual desktops, giving users a remote desktop that allows them to work without the risk of dataloss through saving or transferring sensitive documents to their mobile machines.

Outside of the webportal, there is also the ability to use a clientless SSL VPN for TCP-based applications. This prevents the need to deploy a full tunneling client and still provide full encryption capabilities for traffic from supported applications. This can be useful for remote administrators who need to leverage SSH to communicate back to internal devices within the network. Access control is limited with this method to just these key applications, which reduces administration.

Deploying a full tunneling client, which uses either IPsec or SSL, gives a remote user full access to the internal network for any application via TCP or UDP. This type of deployment is typically used for supporting virtual office environments, where multiple applications and services on the client machine need to communicate back to corporate resources on the internal network. If this type of deployment is leveraged, then it is recommended to have intrusion prevention inspection capabilities either within the VPN or between the user and the internal network to monitor for malicious applications or behavior. From a risk standpoint, the full tunneling client requires that more stringent access controls are implemented than a webportal.

Remote Access Good Practices

Reducing the risk presented by enabling remote access can be achieved by following good VPN security practices.

- **What level of access do users need?** Many VPN technologies can help to enable remote access. Understanding what users need to accomplish their jobs and the level of access required is essential before deploying the VPN solution. Each user role should also have a list of what applications and resources are approved for use. Not every user needs a full tunnel into the organization; web portals or even protected access to e-ail alone may be sufficient. A thorough review of all applications, protocols, and services should be conducted.

- **Use of strong encryption:** Strong encryption helps to maintain the confidentiality of remote VPN connections. A good rule of thumb for VPNs is to use the strongest level of encryption possible. Although this sounds easy in theory, in practice, it's much more difficult because of the many compatibility and user laptop and device hardware differences. As the required number of VPN users increases, the processing time required to support the strongest authentication and encryption can greatly reduce the number of users who can be connected to a single VPN appliance. The current recommended levels of encryption for IPsec and SSL VPNs are 3DES or AES encryption. Hashing should also be enabled to prevent any manipulation of packets in transit, and the current hashing algorithm recommended is SHA1. The lifetime of a security association should never be more than a day and not less than eight hours before rekey of the encryption keys is performed, to prevent heavy load on the VPN appliance. For remote access IPsec VPNs, IKE Main mode should be used whenever possible over-aggressive mode to prevent the exposure of the VPN users name. Perfect forward secrecy is also recommended as a method for generating new session keys with each rekey of the VPN. PFS prevents the compromise of a single session key from being used in the future to gain access to the data protected by the VPN, because each rekey uses a different value not derived from the original key. Diffie Hellman should always be used for IKE with group 2 or greater and 3DES or AES encryption for protecting the key exchange of an IPsec security association.

- **Strong authentication mechanism:** Authentication of VPN connections is the single weakest link of the entire process of providing remote access. Although it is easy to configure pre-shared keys for a small number of devices, the challenges faced as

VPNs get larger require more scalable solutions, such as the use of PKI. Certificate authorities can then be leveraged to provide verification of digital certificates and the revocation of certificates when a client no longer needs access to the VPN. Remote access VPN authentication can utilize a wide range of authentication mechanisms. Single sign-on with integration to LDAP, Radius, or active directory is a common mechanism for allowing VPN access. User passwords ideally should be two-factor to prevent the compromise of a single password.

- **Granular access control:** For full tunneling clients, it is recommended to provide RBAC that defines where a particular user can go within the network after connected via the VPN. Cisco provides the ability to finely tune access controls based on the user's group and how they connect to the VPN. Port protocols and applications should be defined only with those services enabled.

- **Client posture assessment:** Cisco provides posture assessment scanning features, either through network admission control for IPsec clients or with the integrated Cisco Secure Desktop host scan feature for SSL VPN. Host scanning provides another layer of control to ensure that the remote system meets minimum standards before allowing access. After it is enabled, the host scan feature can look for keystroke loggers, ensure antimalware applications are up to date and activated, and determine whether or not the user is connecting on a corporately on machine. Client posture assessment can also provide differentiated access based on the results of these scans. Posture assessment can reduce the exposure to certain types of malware and to ensure policy compliance before access is granted.

- **Data and system classification:** Providing remote access is the easy part; preventing data leakage and theft of trade secrets is much harder. This is where a strong data and system classification scheme can help to provide the appropriate level of security for sensitive systems and information. Access to the finance servers might not be worth the risk of losing sensitive information, so access to that server across the VPN is denied. Policy works best when access control and information control are practiced together.

- **User access review:** User access should always be reviewed on a regular basis to ensure that users are given least privilege access and that the access is still necessary. Any VPN connection not used can be a potential vector of attack.

Although this list of good practices is not exhaustive, it does provide some key areas in which auditors should focus their attention when assessing VPNs. Much of the attention of the auditor is focused on remote access VPNs, because those are the ones that are typically not as easy to control. Site-to-site VPNs, when properly designed, do not require a significant amount of change. The more access VPNs introduce the user into the equation, the more complicated policy enforcement and compliance.

Technical Testing

Technical testing is conducted to verify that policy and standards have been implemented and that all technical controls are working as expected. VPN testing should be conducted on site-to-site VPN and remote access, which encompasses IPsec and SSL VPN technologies. An exploitable VPN is a significant security risk, and through testing, the auditor can identify control weaknesses that can be used to gain entry.

The first technical review should always start with a vulnerability assessment on each VPN device to identify any out-of-date software. Cisco's Product Security Incident Response Team (PSIRT) posts vulnerability information on the Cisco website, detailing any identified security issue; it includes workarounds or bug-fixed versions of software. If the organization does not have a good vulnerability management program, it's not uncommon to have vulnerable code sitting on a device.

After ensuring that no vulnerable software is running on VPN devices, the following tests should be conducted:

- Authentication
- IPsec
- SSL
- Site-to-site access control
- Mobile user access control
- Monitoring and log review

Authentication

Auditors need to pay particular attention to authentication and credential handling. As discussed earlier in this chapter, authentication can make or break a VPN. Poor authentication mechanisms can leave the VPN vulnerable to a multitude of attack techniques, from brute force to man-in-the-middle attacks. The use of pre-shared keys can represent a big security risk when it comes to VPNs. The handling and provisioning of pre-shared keys is in many ways similar to passing out sticky notes with passwords written on them. Pre-shared keys are a weak security mechanism that is typically easier to implement than certificates, but the overall risk they pose dramatically outweighs the benefit.

Two-factor authentication should be the standard for remote access VPNs. They prevent password reuse, sniffing, and brute force. Auditors should observe how users are authenticated and look for any weakness in the process that can be exploited. If passwords are used, complexity requirements should be checked to verify policy conformance.

Auditors should also look at user lockout mechanisms for multiple invalid password attempts to help prevent brute force password cracking. Lost passwords can also represent a procedural vulnerability in how the organization handles delivering new passwords to users that have forgotten them. Account lockout can be configured in Radius, active directory, and even for the internal user database within the VPN appliance itself.

IPsec

IPsec testing involves scanning VPN appliances to determine which cryptographic features are enabled and ensuring that IKE is configured in accordance with good security practices.

Ike-scan is an open source IPsec VPN assessment tool that allows for detailed testing of VPNs. IKE is responsible for setting up security associations and key exchange, and is the most critical aspect of creating a secure tunnel. Ike-scan can be used to look for aggressive mode IKE and the use of any weak cryptographic transforms. Aggressive mode bypasses the protective features of main mode during the initial security set up and exposes tunnel groups and VPN IDs. Aggressive mode, used in conjunction with pre-shared keys, is especially dangerous because the pre-shared key hashes are sent to the client and can then be saved and cracked off-line. Ike-scan supports storing the pre-shared key hashes in a format that can be used by IKEcrack. IKECrack attempts to brute force the hash files until it finds a match. Figure 10-16 shows ike-scan being used to test for aggressive mode and IKECrack uncovering the VPN pre-shared key.

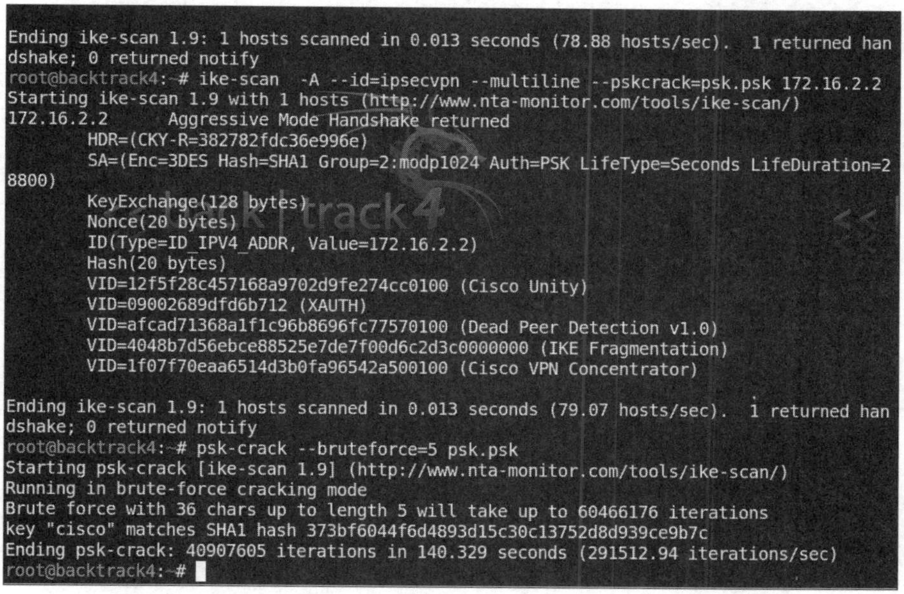

```
Ending ike-scan 1.9: 1 hosts scanned in 0.013 seconds (78.88 hosts/sec).  1 returned han
dshake; 0 returned notify
root@backtrack4:~# ike-scan  -A --id=ipsecvpn --multiline --pskcrack=psk.psk 172.16.2.2
Starting ike-scan 1.9 with 1 hosts (http://www.nta-monitor.com/tools/ike-scan/)
172.16.2.2      Aggressive Mode Handshake returned
        HDR=(CKY-R=382782fdc36e996e)
        SA=(Enc=3DES Hash=SHA1 Group=2:modp1024 Auth=PSK LifeType=Seconds LifeDuration=2
8800)
        KeyExchange(128 bytes)
        Nonce(20 bytes)
        ID(Type=ID_IPV4_ADDR, Value=172.16.2.2)
        Hash(20 bytes)
        VID=12f5f28c457168a9702d9fe274cc0100 (Cisco Unity)
        VID=09002689dfd6b712 (XAUTH)
        VID=afcad71368a1f1c96b8696fc77570100 (Dead Peer Detection v1.0)
        VID=4048b7d56ebce88525e7de7f00d6c2d3c0000000 (IKE Fragmentation)
        VID=1f07f70eaa6514d3b0fa96542a500100 (Cisco VPN Concentrator)

Ending ike-scan 1.9: 1 hosts scanned in 0.013 seconds (79.07 hosts/sec).  1 returned han
dshake; 0 returned notify
root@backtrack4:~# psk-crack --bruteforce=5 psk.psk
Starting psk-crack [ike-scan 1.9] (http://www.nta-monitor.com/tools/ike-scan/)
Running in brute-force cracking mode
Brute force with 36 chars up to length 5 will take up to 60466176 iterations
key "cisco" matches SHA1 hash 373bf6044f6d4893d15c30c13752d8d939ce9b7c
Ending psk-crack: 40907605 iterations in 140.329 seconds (291512.94 iterations/sec)
root@backtrack4:~#
```

Figure 10-16 *Ike-Scan and IKECrack in Action*

SSL

SSL VPNs should be tested in a similar manner to IPsec remote access VPNs. These VPNs are tested like any web service.

SSL VPNs rely on certificates to create the initial trust a connection to the VPN concentrator. The certificate should not be self-signed; it should be issued from a trusted third-party CA.

SSL scan is a tool that can be used for assessing SSL VPNs. It identifies which SSL and TLS encryption ciphers are being used for the VPN concentrator. This is useful for identifying weak cryptographic technologies and shows information regarding the certificate of the server itself. The following command launches sslscan and shows only the encryption ciphers that are enabled on the SSL VPN appliance through the no-failed option.

```
sslscan —no-failed 172.16.2.2


Testing SSL server 172.16.2.2 on port 443

  Supported Server Cipher(s):
    Accepted  SSLv3  256 bits  AES256-SHA
    Accepted  SSLv3  128 bits  AES128-SHA
    Accepted  SSLv3  168 bits  DES-CBC3-SHA
    Accepted  SSLv3  128 bits  RC4-SHA
    Accepted  TLSv1  256 bits  AES256-SHA
    Accepted  TLSv1  128 bits  AES128-SHA
    Accepted  TLSv1  168 bits  DES-CBC3-SHA
    Accepted  TLSv1  128 bits  RC4-SHA


  Preferred Server Cipher(s):
   SSLv3  256 bits  AES256-SHA
   TLSv1  256 bits  AES256-SHA
 SSL Certificate:
   Version: 2
   Serial Number: -3680765514
   Signature Algorithm: md5WithRSAEncryption
   Issuer: /CN=asalab/unstructuredName=asalab.ciscolab.com
   Not valid before: May 10 05:23:39 2009 GMT
   Not valid after: May  8 05:23:39 2019 GMT
   Subject: /CN=asalab/unstructuredName=asalab.ciscolab.com
   Public Key Algorithm: rsaEncryption
   RSA Public Key: (1024 bit)
```

```
    Modulus (1024 bit):
        00:9b:a7:04:89:9e:bc:f1:ec:49:37:e1:85:dd:d4:
        3b:80:f3:85:78:09:cc:5e:5e:12:fa:6f:ab:a2:84:
        f1:e8:a2:85:c0:0f:76:bc:95:b4:12:28:3a:fe:b8:
        9f:b9:93:5b:64:fe:40:5f:6d:c0:fe:67:17:dd:96:
        b2:2f:a4:34:d1:30:0b:3e:3a:ee:1e:a1:f8:5b:68:
        fa:ab:9e:41:d1:4b:98:f0:77:d2:e9:8e:f8:5b:32:
        a3:98:ec:1c:05:3f:93:d6:b0:a0:52:fc:85:64:2a:
        ff:c6:2b:44:92:e3:9c:29:2e:72:f1:7a:f8:9c:50:
        99:43:eb:e2:26:4a:d5:c1:d5
    Exponent: 65537 (0x10001)
 Verify Certificate:
   self signed certificate
```

The preceding example shows rc4 and DES enabled, which means that a client could request those ciphers and make a connection that is cryptographically weak. An auditor should recommend the removal of these weak ciphers. In addition, the VPN device's SSL certificate is also shown identifying that this device is using a self-signed certificate instead of one issued by a third-party CA.

Site-to-Site Access Control Testing

Access control testing for site-to-site networks can be conducted with Nmap to determine what services and protocols are allowed to traverse the VPN. Chapter 4, "Auditing Tools and Techniques," covers NMAP in detail and should be referred to for more information on how NMAP can be used here. Auditors should also test intrusion prevention features as well, if deployed, to protect and monitor VPN connections.

Mobile User Access Control Testing

Testing mobile user VPNs requires that the auditor connect to the VPN as different roles and verify the access control requirements are aligned with policy. Standard tools, such as ping and NMAP, can be used to test network access rules for full tunneling clients. Dynamic access policies are configured to enable host scanning and version checking of antimalware applications for SSL VPNs, and they should be tested. An easy way to do this is to disable security applications and use old antivirus definition files, which denies access if host scanning were properly configured.

Split tunneling should be disabled for user access, and only local LAN access should be enabled if access to print servers and other devices is required. If there is a legitimate reason for using split tunneling, then it is wise to reduce access for that user type to non-critical systems so that the client machine cannot be used as a backdoor into the corporate network.

Webportal access should be tested to ensure that applications and file shares do not provide more access than necessary.

Monitoring and Log Review

All VPN connections should be monitored and reviewed for failed logins. Having IPS integrated into the VPN concentrator or inline between the concentrator and the network can provide a much higher level of visibility into the activity that occurs on the VPN. Policy violations and malicious behavior can be identified and logged. Without this capability, the organization has limited detection capabilities. During the course of these tests, logs should have been generated for failed login attempts and account lockout. Any scanning or testing of the IPS also creates security alerts that the organization should be able to spot.

Checklist

Assessment Area	Assessment Technique
People	
Are remote access policies adequate for the organization's level of risk?	Review applicable remote access policies: asset classification, access granting policies and procedures, access revocation policies, and posture assessment policies.
Have users signed remote access acceptable use and monitoring policies?	Review documentation of signed agreements or electronic click to accept.
Are strong passwords or two-factor authentication required for VPN use?	Review VPN authentication standards. Passwords should meet complexity and minimum length with two-factor authentication preferred.
Is access granted to the VPN for business partners or contractors?	Review acceptable use policies and contracts for third parties.
Process	
Has a user role-based access matrix been developed?	Review documentation showing user roles with systems and applications that each role is able to access from the VPN. Ensure that the principle of least privilege is followed.
Have endpoint client security controls and standards been created?	Review documentation of required security controls for end-point access, standards security applications, and personal firewall rules.
Have encryption standards been identified and do they follow good security practices?	Review encryption standards documents for use of 3DES, AES, and SHA1 hashing for VPN access.
Are access-granting procedures well documented, and do they include signoff from management?	Review access-granting procedures to determine adherence to good security practices.

continues

Assessment Area	Assessment Technique *(continued)*
Do access revocation procedures effectively remove terminated employees?	Review access revocation procedures and user accounts for any terminated employees left active.
Is a periodic entitlement review conducted for all employees and job roles?	Review documentation of entitlement review and inspect user access for unnecessary privileges.
Is there a well documented approval process for access changes?	Review access change procedures.
Are change control procedures and configuration backup implemented?	Review change control and the configuration backup process.
Technology	
VPN Architecture	
Is the VPN device protected from direct attack?	Firewall features should be enabled on VPN device with DoS protection.
Does VPN use appropriate encryption and hash algorithms?	VPN device should be assessed to ensure that DES and RC4 are not in use. SHA1 or MD5 should be used for HMAC hashing with SHA1 preferred.
Is PKI implemented and used where appropriate?	PKI can provide a much stronger and manageable mechanism for VPN device authentication and is preferred over pre-shared keys.
Are self-signed certificates used on VPN devices?	Self-signed certificates are useful only in a lab environment and should never be used in production on the Internet.
IPsec-Specific Architecture Review	
Do IPsec encryption and key exchange use good security practices?	IPsec encryption should be AES or 3DES and use DH group 2 or 5 for IKE.
Do security associations use good security practices?	SA lifetimes should not last longer that 24 hours and not rekey before 8 hours to prevent excessive load on the VPN device.
Is perfect forward secrecy used?	PFS should be enabled to prevent the compromise of an old encryption key from being used in the future.

continues

Assessment Area	Assessment Technique	*(continued)*
Is IKE aggressive mode disabled for pre-shared keys?	IKE aggressive mode should be disabled to pre-shared keys due to the lack of protection during the exchange of pre-shared key hashes.	
Do security associations use HMAC for integrity and authenticity of received data?	HMAC should be configured for all security associations.	
Site-to-Site VPN Review		
Is the provisioning of VPN devices accomplished in a secure fashion?	Provisioning VPN should be a control process, which ensures the protection of keys certificates and any other credentials. Automating this process can greatly improve its security.	
If pre-shared keys are used, are they unique for each device?	Pre-shared keys should be unique for each VPN device so that in the event of a compromise, only one device and key need to be reconfigured.	
Is QoS implemented to protect the VPN tunnel?	Review the network design to ensure QoS is configured for the VPN tunnel to prioritize control and administrative access traffic.	
Remote Access VPN Review		
Do all VPN users have unique assigned usernames and passwords?	Review user access to ensure that account and password sharing is not allowed. Inspect network device configuration to prevent multiple logins from the same user.	
Are client assessment checks performed before access is granted to ensure policy compliance?	Ensure the post posture assessments are conducted for key-stroke loggers, personal firewall is active, and antimalware enabled.	
Are dynamic access policies used to control user access based on posture results?	Check the configuration for the dynamic access policy.	
Has session clearing technology been configured for SSL remote access?	Cisco provides session cache cleaning via its cache cleaner or the complete Cisco secure desktop to create an encrypted vault that stores all session data transfers to the remote client and is erased after disconnect.	
Are clients required to authenticate with complex passwords or two-factor authentication?	Review device configuration to determine whether password complexity meets security standards or two-factor authentication is used.	

continues

Assessment Area	Assessment Technique *(continued)*
Are VPN devices configured to disconnect idle sessions and are user accounts locked out after a specific number of invalid logins?	Review network device configuration and test user account lockout and inactive session timeout.
Is split-tunneling disabled when connected to the VPN?	Check the VPN device configuration to determine whether split tunneling has been disabled and that this configuration is being actively pushed to all VPN clients.
Technical VPN testing	
Conduct vulnerability assessments on VPN devices.	Review the software level of each device for vulnerabilities.
Review the authentication mechanism.	Check the authentication mechanism to ensure compliance to policy.
Run Ikescan on IPsec VPN to test for aggressive mode.	Ikescan should be used to identify encryption methods used and whether or not aggressive mode is enabled.
Review the certificate revocation process.	Review the certificate revocation process and make sure that individual certificates can be revoked and test that function.
Run an SSL scan for SSL VPNs and review encryption methods.	SSL scan can quickly identify what encryption mechanisms are configured on the SSL VPN and show the certificate used by the VPN device.
Test each configured role for access to the internal network.	Test each role for least privilege access and access control features should be conducted. Ping and NMAP are used.
Test session cache cleanup and Cisco secure desktop secure vault utilization.	Test the functionality of cache cleanup features and Cisco secure desktop to ensure that session information is not left on clients after disconnect.
Test incident handling and intrusion prevention system protection of malicious activity.	While connected to the VPN, test intrusion prevention and detection capabilities by running Metasploit or Core Impact against a testing host.
Review VPN logs and alerts.	Session logs should be reviewed for login and logout time-stamps, invalid login attempts, and any alarms generated during testing.

Summary

This chapter provided an overview of VPN technologies and architectural design decisions that organizations might make when deploying VPN technologies for remote access and site-to-site connections. VPNs have become an important connectivity option for businesses today, and the security of these connections is critical to maintaining the confidentiality of data being sent between locations. Assessing the VPN requires a strong understanding of VPN configuration, encryption, and authentication as each aspect can directly impact the overall security of the VPN solution. In summary:

- The security of a VPN is measured by its capability to adequately address confidentiality, integrity, and authentication.

- An organization should choose encryption algorithms that are appropriate for the sensitivity and value of the data they are being used to protect.

- Authentication is one of the most important areas of good VPN deployments. Digital certificates and two-factor authentication provide stronger and more scalable authentication capabilities than pre-shared keys.

- Site-to-site VPNs can be deployed in many different ways depending on the goals and connectivity requirements of the organization. Regardless of how the VPN is deployed, following good security practices for IPsec is critical for maintaining secure connectivity.

- User-access VPNs must be well planned with granular RBAC configured to ensure users have access only to the resources they need.

- VPN standards and remote access policies provide guidance for configuration of VPN devices and should be based on a solid risk assessment and current cryptographic standards.

- All remote clients should have enforceable security controls deployed and access based on those controls being enabled and up to date.

- Intrusion prevention systems should be used with VPNs to allow for monitoring and detection of malicious behavior on the VPN connection.

References in This Chapter

NIST SP800-77: Guide to IPsec VPNs, http://csrc.nist.gov/publications/nistpubs/800-77/sp800-77.pdf

NIST SP800-113: Guide to SSL VPNs, http://csrc.nist.gov/publications/nistpubs/800-113/SP800-113.pdf

Chapter 11

Endpoint Protection

Wouldn't networks be so much easier to protect if you could just keep people from getting on them? Every network security professional has dreamed of a world without constant security awareness training and the need to figure out new controls to combat the latest attacks aimed at taking advantage of employees and their computing devices. Endpoint security is by far the hardest aspect of securing a network, because users never cease to amaze us with their abilities to disappoint by opening suspicious file attachments and applications.

In many cases, it's not the user's fault when a security incident occurs, but more a problem with how fast the evolution of collaborative technologies has outpaced previous security paradigms. Attacks are coming through the web and e-mail in unique ways that require a new set of skills, because the attacks are no longer just targeted at technology but are aimed at the people who use technology. This chapter is focused on auditing various protective mechanisms that Cisco offers to defend a business from threats that come from the web and e-mail and that target the endpoint.

Endpoint Risks

Organizations face significantly higher levels of risk from endpoint security breaches than ever before, due to our highly mobile and connected workforce. The whole security paradigm of inside versus outside assumes that company employees are trusted insiders, and everyone else is an outsider. Security, when applied in terms of this paradigm, has shown to be incomplete at best, unworkable at worst. The insider threat is not about a few disgruntled employees with malicious intents because of grudges against the company, but the fact that every employee has the potential to represent a threat to the organization by introducing malware into the internal network where most security technologies are weakest. The threats companies must deal with today are generally targeted with the intention to make money or steal valuable data. They are quieter and harder to detect than the mass infection network worms popular in years past. More often than not, the attackers go after vulnerabilities in the user's web browser to gain access to internal systems and services to commit fraud or steal valuable data. Some of the key endpoint risks organizations face today are:

- **Loss of private information:** Privacy is becoming a major concern for businesses of all sizes. Social networking sites such as Facebook allow for unprecedented access into individuals' lives and habits, making it much easier for attackers to target specific people and groups.

- **Loss of reputation:** Reputation is one of the most important intangible assets corporations have. Severe damage to reputation can even result in the death of viable businesses as customers move to competitors. Loss of data usually results in loss of customer trust.

- **Intellectual property:** Loss of intellectual property and trade secrets can directly impact a company's bottom line. Products, processes, and formulas are how companies differentiate and achieve a competitive advantage, which can be sold to the highest bidder.

- **Financial loss:** Direct financial loss through scams or bank fraud happen to businesses. A targeted attack against the accounting department of a company might result in unauthorized funds transfers and other attempts at theft.

- **Service outages:** Service outages and downtime from restoring infected systems cost time, money, and lost productivity. It's common for organizations to spend hundreds of hours a year dealing with these types of issues.

This list of risks is just a sampling of some of the most prevalent threats organizations face. Every organization should conduct a risk assessment to identify specific areas that need controls to help minimize the impact of an endpoint security incident.

Endpoint Threats

Attacking endpoints is big business for criminals, and the methods they use to exploit systems and steal information are unfortunately effective. This section classifies common threats that use the web and e-mail as a means to compromise computers and spread malware. Knowing these threats enables an auditor the ability to better assess network security countermeasures.

Malware

It would be difficult to find someone who has worked with computers for any length of time who did not have a story or two to tell about being infected by malware. The term malware is used to describe the constantly evolving and expanding class of malicious software that is being used to irritate, steal, extort, and generally make life difficult for users and IT organizations trying to defend against such a constantly changing threat. The types and uses of malware have exploded over the years as criminals have discovered that the endpoint is a target rich environment for illegally making money. What was once an area of computer science that attracted antisocial people looking for their 15 seconds of fame by coding evil software in their basements has morphed into a serious business model with development processes and teams that would rival many legitimate software firms. There is now a virtual marketplace to buy and sell unknown vulnerabilities (zero day) and tools that can be used to exploit systems. Malware writers want their creations to stay undetected so that they can continue siphoning off data and remain under their control. Malware automates the exploitation of vulnerabilities through software that simplifies the process of infection and privilege escalation on the endpoint. The goal is to "own" the endpoint so that it can be used for spam, attacking websites, stealing private information, or other activities. The names used to describe various forms of malware come from the manner in which they propagate. The following examples of malware highlight some of the most common variants, but it's by no means a complete list. Auditors should constantly read and learn about new variants as they arrive on the scene. Only through education and vigilance can malware be defended against.

- The *virus* is the best known form of malware and refers to a computer program that has the capability to compromise a computer by overwriting or altering executable and system files as a means to spread itself from system to system. A virus can infect a computer in many ways, from e-mail attachments to USB memory drives shared between users. Viruses can also be attached to executable files, document files on network shares, and pictures.

- A *worm* is a piece of malware designed to replicate across the network by compromising vulnerabilities on remote systems to install itself. The worm is best known for its capability to infect a computer without the user having to do anything but be connected to the network. Simply having the vulnerability is enough as the worm is programmed to attempt to exploit any computer it can reach. After a system is compromised, the computer searches for other systems on the network to infect, which results in rapid infection rates for interconnected computers.

- A *Trojan* operates by pretending to be a legitimate executable file or a document that just happens to have malicious code attached. The way a Trojan works is by tricking the user into executing it to compromise the machine and load itself somewhere in the operating system file structure so that it can survive a reboot of the computer. Trojans are often sent through e-mail in the hopes that the user operates with administrative privileges when reading e-mail, allowing the Trojan to gain control.

- *Spyware* is a class of malware whose intention is to report on web browsing habits and other personal information that can be used for tracking which sites a user visits. Spyware can also be used to force users to certain websites in the hopes of selling them products. These programs operate like Trojans and often are loaded as toolbars or other "helper" applications in web browsers.

- A *botnet* is a group of compromised systems that are controlled by a single entity. Botnets can be controlled through web services such as Twitter, IRC, and IM, and they use encrypted protocols to hide their traffic. A botnet can consist of hundreds of computers, and some botnets have been reported to be in the millions of compromised devices. Botnets can be used for sending spam, infecting websites, sniffing network traffic, identity theft, pay-per-click advertisement fraud, or be part of a distributed denial of service attack. Their services can be rented for the right price.

■ *Key loggers* are a class of malware that can record keys pressed on the keyboard in the hopes of snagging passwords, credit card numbers, Social Security numbers, or any other piece of information that can be used for identity theft or credit card fraud. Keystroke loggers can be software-based or hardware-based, and most users never know they are installed. Key loggers are often included as part of a malware package but can also be used by themselves. Internet kiosks and cafes are common targets for this type of malware, but targeted attacks against banking sites are often including key loggers to grab user credentials.

■ *Scareware* is a class of malware that attempts to trick users into believing that they have become infected by viruses and worms in the hopes of frightening them into purchasing virus removal software. The software is usually either freeware antivirus software that the scareware advertiser sells as a commercial package or malicious software that does nothing to prevent malware but introduces it to the computer. Some scareware actually compromises the computer and loads a "security" product that can't be removed unless the user pays a licensing fee for the application.

Web-Based Threats

The web browser has become the hottest battleground in the fight against malware. Websites are a common source of endpoint infection, taking advantage of browser vulnerabilities, plugins from third parties, and inherent weaknesses that exist in web technologies to compromise endpoints at an alarming rate. During the last few years, criminals have learned how to make money by compromising as many machines as possible and using them for various illegal purposes, such as sending spam or stealing credit card information. The more devices criminals can exploit, the more money they can potentially make. In the past, users were at risk if they went to dubious websites looking for some of the Internet's less wholesome content, but much of this has changed as attackers have figured out ways to exploit trust boundaries in the browser and force users to run malicious code hosted on servers whose sole purpose is to deliver malware. If a popular website or blog is compromised and malicious code is injected on its pages, the criminal might have the ability to infect hundreds of thousands of users. These kinds of numbers are simply irresistible to individuals looking to make money with the dark arts of the web.

One of the fundamental problems in protecting users while surfing the web comes from the fact that websites are really just a collection of content that can originate from hundreds of different sources, many of which are not under the control of the owners of the primary website. Users might think they are browsing to CNN to view the latest news, but in reality they make connections to all of CNN's advertisers, affiliates, video providers, and other services, all of which make up the web page. This aggregation and outsourcing of content is where attackers can inject links to malicious sites to which most users have no clue they are connecting. This type of attack is called a "drive-by download" and alludes to the fact that the user is simply browsing the wrong website at the wrong time and was compromised by malicious code while viewing a legitimate and normally safe website that attackers found a weakness on and exploited. The techniques used to perpetuate these attacks are often not vulnerabilities in the web browser or server, but simply take advantage of how HTML works.

A common example that highlights a way to abuse HTML for evil purposes is found in the use of iframes or inline frames. As HTML has evolved, so has the ability to use sophisticated layout and design functions to better format and display text and images. Formatting is accomplished through multiple objects called tags that allow images to be displayed, scripts to be called, or input to be gathered from the user. Iframes are used in HTML to tie together multiple HTML documents or scripts for the layout of webpages so that content that changes on a regular basis can be separated from content that doesn't change, such as headers, footers, and sidebars. Iframes are a method for nesting frames and are a convenient and legitimate way to dynamically load lots of content, such as ads and news feeds, into a webpage. The problem with iframes is when this HTML function is used for attacking users through websites by inserting malicious code into the iframe that loads content from a website hosting malware and making the iframe invisible through setting the pixel size to 1x1. The following example shows an iframe with a width of one and a height of one and visibility that is hidden:

```
[iframe src= www.badsite.com/ width=1 height=1 style=visibility:
hidden;][/iframe]
```

Cross-site scripting (XSS) is a common web attack targeted at scripts on a webpage that are intended to run on the endpoint browser and takes advantage of weaknesses in the fundamental security trust mechanisms used in browsers. XSS works by inserting malicious scripts onto a website or appended to a link for a website that doesn't properly check user input, allowing the scripts to be run on the client side. Browsers rely on a concept called "same origin policy" to provide security for webpages. The principle behind the same origin policy is to prevent a script or code from one web domain (www.evil.com) to be run from another domain (www.yoursite.com). The same origin policy uses the domain name, application protocol, and TCP port number of the HTML document that called the script to determine whther a script should be run. To get XSS to work, you simply need to find part of a website that allows a user to post content that isn't validated, or find a web page that generates content based on a users input (like a search page). The evil script appears to be called from the legitimate website, and the browser happily executes it with the same permissions, giving the evil script access to session IDs and variables run on the legitimate website. This allows the attacker to gather a user's session information, cookie data, and keystrokes directly through the browser. There are literally hundreds of variations of this type of attack, and a large number of websites simply don't check user input properly.

Another wide spread method used to attack endpoints is called Cross Site Request Forgery (CSRF). This type of attack can take advantage of a user logged into a web application by forging commands and requests that the endpoint browser executes. Any web-based application such as a banking site, social networking site, or hosted web service can be vulnerable to these types of attacks. Websites typically use cookies and session IDs to identify authenticated users, and these cookies are stored temporarily on the endpoint browser while the user is connected. The URLs used to interact with the applications are typically static, and they can be mapped by an attacker with access to the application. The attacker simply needs to get the user to click on a link that runs the commands the attacker wants the user to execute in the application, such as transfer money. As long as the user is authenticated (or uses a stored login credential) to the application at the time he clicks the forged requests, the browser happily submits the requests and neither the user nor the server can tell that anything malicious happened. These forged requests can be hidden in iframes, images, and scripts on websites or sent as HTML e-mails.

Browsers are often targeted for attack because browsers act as a framework that is extendable with new capabilities through browser helper objects. Browser helper objects extend the functionality of the browser by allowing third-party applications and toolbars to operate in the browser. Malware creators use these components to introduce malicious applications such as spyware and keystroke loggers to end-user computers. Two of the most popular web applications, Acrobat Reader and Flash, are produced by Adobe and offered as plugins. Browsers can dynamically call these two applications through web pages, which allow maliciously created PDFs and Flash videos to gain control of the browser and potentially the underlying operating system. The massive installation base of Flash and Acrobat Reader makes them a tempting target for attackers because of their ubiquity. Software vendors such as Google and other third parties pay software providers to insert their toolbars into their applications, and many users are not aware that they are being loaded into their computers, providing yet another target for attackers to exploit.

Java is a programming language that can be used to create programs that dramatically improve the user's web experience. The power of Java is in its portability between any operating system and browser. This ubiquitous nature makes Java an ideal target for attackers looking to slip malware onto a user's machine. Vulnerabilities that exist in these applications have been the source of a wide range of exploits over the years. These applications must be updated individually and are typically not automatically updated with operating system updates, creating a potential lag in getting fixed code to users.

ActiveX is similar to Java, but it runs only on Microsoft operating systems. It provides programming interfaces for web designers to build interactive applications that subsequently provide deep integration into the web browser and operating system itself. There has been a significant amount of malicious code written to exploit security weakness in this programming language, and Microsoft has done a much better job in current versions of their browser and operating system to limit exposure. Just like Java, ActiveX has many of the same problems, and because Windows is the dominant operating system, it continues to be a target for attackers.

Javascript and VBscript are two of the most common scripting languages in use today on the Internet. Java and Javascript share part of their names, but are implemented differently. Java is a programming language like C++ and allows for the creation of cross-platform applications. Javascript is used to extend the functionality of websites through client-side scripting. Javascript and VBscript both allow client-side commands for the purposes of creating web interfaces and better user experiences. These scripting languages are also used as a vehicle for injecting malicious code onto websites and exploiting vulnerabilities in client browsers. A common defense against malicious scripting is to run programs like NoScript (noscript.net) to limit script execution to specific sites. The technical complexity makes it difficult to recommend to the average user, and barring the disabling of all scripting, there is really no way to adequately defend against malicious scripts on the client side alone. Modern browsers have started to implement some of this functionality but it is rudimentary. Cisco offers the Web Services API (WSA) platform to provide this protection by looking for malicious code and using website reputation scores to monitor and deny external site requests to sites that host malicious code before it ever reaches the browser.

Browser vulnerabilities are still one of the most common methods for gaining control of remote systems; researchers have discovered hundreds of vulnerabilities in all the major Internet browsers in use today. Early browsers thought little of security and provided direct access to the operating system that could be exploited and allow an attacker to fully control the machine. Modern browsers have added many new security features to harden the browser against attack, but they're not perfect. It also doesn't matter which browser you use, because they all have been shown to contain critical bugs that have needed patching. Unpatched browsers pose a significant risk to being attacked without the user knowing anything happened.

Social Networking and Web 2.0

The term Web 2.0 is used to describe the collaborative multiuser web applications written today. The user is now the center of focus for web design and has changed the way individuals interact with colleagues and friends. The ability to collaborate on projects and leverage the many pockets of information and talent in an organization can greatly improve the productivity and efficiency of business processes. Files and data are no longer locked on individual computers, but can be shared for cross collaboration. Through hosted web applications, teams can work on a project virtually, with individual members residing anywhere in the world. Problems with the new collaborative paradigm come from the trust that users place in these applications, and the security that they afford them for privacy and protection of shared content. This is especially of concern when the hosted applications reside on third-party networks where the organization has no control over how the data is protected.

Social networking has exploded over the past few years with services such as Twitter and Facebook as clear leaders in this method of connecting people and groups. Many employees are part of social networking sites with their colleagues and peers in their various industries. For the criminally minded, social networking can provide opportunities for social engineering at its finest, and online scams increasingly use these applications as a vehicle. The attacker just needs to get the user to click on a link or view a video to potentially infect the user's machine with malware. The ability for an attacker to selectively target members of an organization is now much easier with social networking, because finding specific individuals employed at a company requires a simple search. Targeting an employee or her friends can be an effective way of gaining access that would normally require significant risk in attacking corporate boundaries. Tricking the user into clicking a tiny URL that hides the fact that it links to a malicious website can allow the attacker to create a backdoor into the corporate network.

Koobface is an example of a social networking worm that's been attacking users of Facebook by sending messages to users asking them to look at a funny video. When users go to click on the link, they are presented with a video and a worm. After a user's machine is infected, it then sends out status updates to all of that user's friends on Facebook to trick them into becoming infected and ultimately spreading the worm. This is just one example of many that highlight some of the risk associated with social networking.

E-Mail Threats

In today's social networking and tweet-filled world, e-mail is still one of the most widely used applications on the Internet. Most people spend a good portion of their day reading and responding to e-mails in a corporate environment, and users have come to rely on it as much as they do their telephone. From a security standpoint, the problem with e-mail is how easy it is to anonymously spread malware, spam, and other malicious content. Most organizations realize that e-mail is a necessary evil, but they must take precautions to minimize the risk that e-mail can pose.

E-mail is a common method for delivering malware. Viruses and Trojans can be sent as attachments, just waiting for users to open the file and execute it. Malware can reside in pictures, documents, spreadsheets, PDFs, screensavers, or any other type of application that can be sent in an e-mail. All the user has to do is launch the file and the computer can become infected.

E-mail applications also have browser functionality, opening them up to the web-based attacks discussed in the previous section. The preview pane allows for the immediate viewing of an e-mail in HTML, which can cause the execution of malicious software without the user having to do anything but select the e-mail message.

Phishing is an attempt to get a user to divulge personal or financial information for the purposes of theft or identity fraud. Early phishing attempts were easy to spot due to poor grammar and other mistakes that tipped a user off to the fact that something was not right. Phishing has since become much more sophisticated and in many cases, a trained professional would find it difficult to spot a phishing site versus the real site. One of the most popular phishing techniques is to trick a user by sending an e-mail pretending to be from a bank or other institution and asking the user to update his account settings for security purposes. When the user clicks on the link to update his account, he is taken to the attacker's website and all his information is then recorded.

Spam is unsolicited e-mail designed to get you to buy something you probably don't want or need and definitely did not ask for. Spam can range from extremely annoying to down-right offensive, and not a day goes by that organizations don't have to deal with a rash of spam trying to sell the latest in male enhancement products and other pharmaceuticals. The problem is so severe that roughly 90 percent of all e-mail sent on the Internet today is spam. Botnets are often tasked in the delivery of spam, which makes it hard to stop, and it is often like an electronic version of whack-a-mole. The minute that one source of spam is stopped another appears to take its place. Spam is often a delivery vehicle for malware, phishing, and online scams as well.

The biggest threat to e-mail security is loss of confidentiality, because e-mail is typically sent in plain text meaning that anyone that places a sniffer on the network can potentially gain access. Utilization of encryption techniques and secure deliver applications for e-mail can reduce this threat, but are not widespread enough. The Cisco Ironport e-mail appliance has the capability to stop spam, the spread of malware, and can be configured to encrypt e-mail through a service that can address many of these risks.

Data Loss Threats

If data stayed in just one place on the network, it would be so much easier to protect. Unfortunately, with the explosion of mobile computing and devices, data can be strung all over the globe and becomes difficult for organizations to secure. Unauthorized or accidental data disclosure is one of the most severe threats to organizations today; it can result in the loss of customer confidence or hefty fines, not to mention the monetary losses associated with the disclosure of intellectual property or other valuable data.

Data typically exists in three states:

- **In process:** Data the user works with at a given point in time

- **In motion:** Data that is transmitted between applications or to and from the client

- **At rest:** Data that is in storage either locally or centralized

Data can leave the network in several ways:

- **E-mail:** Webmail and thick clients represent the most common sources of data loss that usually occurs by mailing confidential documents either accidentally or intentionally. Those documents up in the hands of competitors.

- **IM:** Most instant messenger applications have file-sharing features, enabling users to send documents to each other.

- **FTP:** FTP clients are built in to most browsers and command-line versions reside in operating systems.

- **Web Forms:** Posting confidential data onto web applications through web forms enables quick HTTP file uploads without the need for anything but point and click.

- **Peer2peer (P2P) applications:** P2P is used to share files and applications and if improperly configured, it can accidently share sensitive document directories to the world.

Accidental disclosure can be as bad as intentional disclosure and sometimes even harder to identify. Companies have individuals responsible for press releases due to the sensitivity of timing and legal aspects that can arise with public announcements. With the popularity of social networking sites, such as Twitter and Facebook, companies have started experiencing problems with premature announcements and information leaks at a significantly higher rate. Employees who engage in social networking increase the risk of disclosing sensitive information, such as new products, customer information, or other day-to-day activities they choose to share.

Document classification is essential to determine what is sensitive and what is free to share with the public. Companies that don't spend the time to classify their data in a simple-to-understand scheme are at risk of having employees mishandle the information, resulting in data loss.

Removable media such as USB thumb drives is available in capacities of up to 256 GB and is increasing in size every year, which enables massive amounts of storage in an extremely small package. These devices are handy for copying files and sharing documents; they are also easy to lose. Smart phones are also used extensively for e-mail and storage of corporate information; they represent a data loss risk, too.

Unauthorized applications loaded on corporate devices can represent not only a data loss opportunity, but can also be a source of malware. In many cases, users treat their corporate laptops and devices as personal and have no qualms about loading new software.

A lack of data loss awareness training can also be a significant risk to organizations because users might not know that their activities can put their company at risk.

Policy Review

Writing policies that detail what a user can and cannot do while utilizing business resources that interact with the Internet can be difficult. Policies do not often keep up with technologies, and one fact of life with users is that they find a way to leverage new technologies in the most creative and unexpected ways. Important policy considerations for endpoint protection include the following:

- **Acceptable use:** Acceptable use policies are the catchall policy for defining what a user is allowed to do with company equipment. Businesses buy laptops for users to perform business activities, not for surfing the Internet and playing fantasy football. The acceptable use policy is the primary policy used for disciplining employees who violate the rules of conduct with corporate equipment.

- **Minimum access policy:** The minimum access policy should require that updates be applied to both the operating system and applications for access to be granted to the network. Enforcing this through policy and technical controls can ensure that endpoint vulnerabilities are patched as quickly as possible before a user is allowed to interact with the network.

- **Risk assessment:** A risk assessment policy should also be present to ensure that the organization is continually reviewing current threats and vulnerabilities to key systems and developing countermeasures and processes to mitigate risk.

- **Data classification policy:** Data classification is not an easy process, but for data loss prevention technologies to work effectively, all data and assets should be tagged by their confidentiality levels. Placing these tags on and in documents makes scanning for potential loss much easier, and users have an immediate and visible way to know what actions are allowed with the document they are viewing.

- **Right to monitor:** All organizations need a right-to-monitor clause in their policies to allow for the utilization of security technologies and the inspection of e-mail and web traffic.

- **Approved software:** Organizations should have a policy prohibiting unapproved applications from being installed on company owned assets. Updates of known applications and monitoring for known vulnerabilities are much easier when staff knows what applications users have installed.

- **Internet policies:** Internet policy (often a part of the acceptable use policy) should detail the types of websites and web applications users can engage with when at work. URL filtering technologies can help to automate the enforcement of these policies, but it must be defined in the policy for violations to be actionable.

- **Social networking policy:** Social networking is a relatively recent phenomenon that has left many organizations ill prepared for the amount of time users spend tweeting, blogging, and catching up on Facebook. The benefits of these tools are well known, because they allow for interaction between customers and clients, but the risk of inadvertent disclosure of sensitive information and inappropriate comments can directly impact an organization. Every employee with a social networking account has the potential of becoming an unofficial spokesperson for the business. A well written and public policy can help to minimize these types of costly and embarrassing mistakes.

- **Data loss prevention policy:** Data loss prevention policies should detail requirements for protecting data in motion, at rest, and data on the endpoint.

- **E-mail policies:** E-mail policies should identify the types of interactions permissible and the types of information and files allowed to be shared through e-mail. Sensitive information should never be discussed or sent over unsecured e-mail; encryption should be employed for private conversations or sensitive information. Providing detailed lists of the types of information that are prohibited, such as Social Security numbers and credit card information, should be part of the policy. Scanning of all attachments for malware should also be required.

- **Malware polices:** Polices that address antimalware controls provide guidance for both network architects and users. These policies should prohibit the disabling or circumventing of security technologies and require scanning of all incoming and out-going e-mail. Antimalware web gateways are also recommended for prevention of drive by downloads and attacks from malicious websites. Scanning for malware should be conducted on all media connected to the system including DVDs, CD-ROMs, USB memory sticks, and external hard drives because they can pose a risk of introducing malware.

Endpoint Protection Operational Control Review

An endpoint operational control review assesses the businesses processes for identifying threats and performing proactive management of endpoint devices. The auditor assesses the following:

- Threat intelligence gathering

- Vulnerability management

- Patch management

- Software inventory management

- Monitoring and incident handling

- User awareness programs

Current Threat Intelligence

IT needs to be aware of new threats and vulnerabilities to protect endpoints from attack. Information about the latest threats can be gathered from a number of locations on the Internet and through subscription services that specialize in distilling threat data into actionable items. Auditors should determine how the organization under review stays aware of current attack trends, threats, and vulnerabilities. The following are some methods organizations (and auditors) can use to stay current.

- **Cisco Security Intelligence Operations (SIO):** Cisco provides this excellent web resource. Cisco SIO is powered by IntelliShield, which is the Cisco threat and vulnerability research division. This website provides an enormous amount of information including current threat activities around the globe, plus vulnerabilities identified in Cisco and third-party products and services. Cisco even provides a free iPhone application that can be downloaded for syncing with the SIO service and providing automated feeds of new information. Figure 11-1 shows the Cisco SIO home page.

- **Cisco Ironport Senderbase:** This is another source for current threat information regarding spam and virus outbreaks. It shows a global map of the top threats, locations, and IP addresses of confirmed malware sources. There is detailed analysis of worms and viruses for staff to better understand how malware is propagating and how to identify potential infections. The Cisco Ironport Senderbase web portal is

Figure 11-1   *Cisco SIO Home Page*

shown in Figure 11-2.

- **SANS Internet Storm Center:** The SANS Institute offers a free service called the internet Storm Center that is staffed by knowledgeable volunteers who analyze current attacks and write about their findings in an online blog. Many of the researchers (called handlers) are top SANS instructors and offer good insight on new attacks and Internet events. Figure 11-3 shows an example of a SANS Internet Storm Center Handler's Diary.

There is also a wealth of information from bloggers and other information sources that can be combined and tracked via RSS feeds. RSS feeds allow automated retrieval and searching capabilities across all of the websites and blogs that a user subscribes too. RSS is a great way to keep up to date. It provides a single location to review that is much easier than going to each individual website.

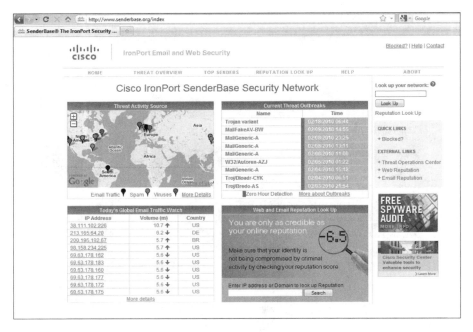

Figure 11-2   *Cisco Ironport Senderbase Web Portal*

Figure 11-3   *SANS Internet Storm Center Handler's Diary*

Vulnerability and Patch Management

Software inventory management is the cornerstone of a vulnerability and patch management program. A solid application inventory is important for identifying the applications that users have loaded on their computers and for developing an update strategy for addressing any identified vulnerabilities. Protecting endpoints also requires finding unapproved software that might be installed such as peer-to-peer file-sharing applications, instant messaging, and noncorporate e-mail applications.

Vulnerability management is a practice required for all organizations and is a critical aspect of reducing the risk of infection from malware. A solid inventory of all software versions and tools that compare them with newly released vulnerabilities can help to prioritize patching processes and ensure that the most critical systems and applications are addressed first. All businesses need a well defined and documented vulnerability management process, and companies should perform vulnerability scans using scanning tools like Qualys or Nessus to automate the process and quickly identify vulnerable systems.

Patch management is an essential part of protecting the endpoint; it is the process of plugging vulnerabilities as quickly as possible after they are identified. Patching should be conducted in an automated fashion to ensure that patches are consistently applied and reports are generated to detail patching failures and successes. Applications and operating systems both need to be patched, which is why it is important to have accurate software inventories to know what applications (and which versions) are being used. The patch management process should be documented, and the business should be able to produce patching reports and software inventory lists for the auditor to review. NIST 800-42 can provide guidance on setting up a vulnerability and patch management program and metrics to measure its success.

Monitoring and Incident Handling

The identification of malware is largely handled by technology, but staff must monitor alerts and review logs to determine the state of protection technologies and endpoint devices. Log reviews should be conducted on a regular schedule and be implemented as a routine part of daily management of security. Identification of malware early is important to minimize potential loss.

After a security incident has been identified, the system or service should be quarantined and logically or physically separate from other devices. This can reduce the risk of malware spreading or allowing the infected device to launch attacks against other internal resources. The organization should have a well documented quarantine process and be able to quickly segment infected devices remotely. Security management products can automate this process and Cisco MARS has a feature that allows administrators the ability to shutdown switch ports of infected devices.

Remediation of a compromise restores the system to a pre-infection state and patches the vulnerabilities that were exploited. Many viruses and worms being spread today are difficult to completely eradicate, so it is usually recommended to completely reload the operating system. You can never be sure you removed all the affected files, or that a seldom used application was not compromised, just waiting for the user to execute the program and reinfect the machine. IT staff should have software images available for rapid restore and a process for implementing recovery operations.

Security Awareness Program

All companies should have an active user security awareness program to inform users of security threats and to constantly remind them of appropriate acceptable use of corporate resources. Information protection training should include safe computing education and should be conducted, at minimum, on a yearly basis. This training should include the following points:

■ **Safe e-mail practices:** Users should be aware of safe e-mail practices and learn to be suspicious of all e-mail attachments, especially executable files.

■ **Phishing:** They should also be made aware of common scams, spam, and phishing tactics prevalent on the Internet. Users should be clear that IT does not send them e-mails asking for personal or financial information and that they should never reply to those attempts.

■ **Security features:** Users need to be reminded that disabling security features puts them at serious risk to attack and malware infection. They should also be asked to review policies requiring security software as a minimum standard for access to the network.

■ **Passwords:** Passwords should never be recycled or used for multiple logins. It's not uncommon for users to use their corporate passwords for social networks or other websites.

■ **Social networking:** User should be made aware of policies regarding the acceptable use of social media, and what types of information they are allowed to post or communicate about. Many users are unaware of the various privacy settings that must be configured on social networking sites to protect private information. It's a good idea for organizations to have safe social networking training programs to teach users how to safely use applications such as Facebook and Twitter.

Current threats should also be disseminated to the organization as they arise to ensure users are aware of potential scams and attacks that could compromise their personal identity and affect the organization as a whole.

Endpoint Architecture Review

Auditing endpoint protection requires the auditor to take a holistic view of how data travels through the network, and the threats and risk associated with the way endpoints interact with internal and external resources. The typical assessment starts with a policy review to identify corporate standards, and then continues with a review of key processes that should be in place, and is then followed by a technical architecture review that examines controls and tests their ability to identify and respond to threats.

Cisco Security Intelligence Operations

Any discussion of Cisco endpoint security controls must include an overview of Cisco security intelligence operations, which are the core of Cisco security architecture. The Cisco SIO consists of three components that work together to make Cisco security products provide a strong security response and protection for evolving threats. These components consist of Cisco SensorBase, Cisco Threat Operations Center, and dynamic updates. Cisco SIO architectural components are shown in Figure 11-4.

Figure 11-4   *Cisco SIO Architecture Components*

SensorBase

The first component of SIO is the Cisco SensorBase, which consists of the world's largest threat-monitoring network and vulnerability database. SensorBase has more than 40,000 historical threats and dynamically adds new threat data as soon as it is detected through a network of thousands of devices spread across the globe. Cisco receives this information from IPS, e-mail, and web security appliances and analyzes more than 500 GB of raw threat data per day. Cisco also receives more than 500 third-party feeds and 100 security event newsfeeds through open source and vendor partnerships. All this information is used to understand the vulnerabilities and exploit technologies as they arrive on the scene. Because this information crosses many different vectors of attack, blended attacks and threats that use multiple attack methods can be better analyzed and protected against.

Cisco Threat Operations Center

The Cisco Threat Operations Center consists of a global team of security analysts and automated technologies that gather and extract actionable security responses based on security information generated through SensorBase. Cisco employs a team of more than 500 security analysts and white hat engineers to analyze the data on the latest malware and vulnerabilities that customers face. These engineers are responsible for validating new threats and identifying workarounds and good practices to protect against those threats.

The Threat Operations Center is also responsible for generating IPS signatures and the correlation and validation of reputation information. Cisco uses reputation data to identify sources of malicious data and attacks and uses reputation as a means to stop subsequent attacks by blocking traffic from sites that have been identified as hosting malware. Reputation is a huge differentiator for Cisco products because of how effectively it can stop attacks before they have an opportunity to affect endpoints. In a similar manner to how a person would know to avoid the bad parts of town, when malware-infected sites are identified, the addresses and DNS entries can be stored in the reputation database and given a low reputation score. This low score can cause Cisco security products to automatically respond more aggressively to packets sent from these locations and effectively neutralize their threat. This contextual awareness of current threats is accomplished by focusing on who distributes the threat, how the threat evolves and propagates, what the threat targets, and how it moves across the Internet.

Dynamic Update Function

The dynamic update function is implemented for Cisco security devices as a mechanism to automatically deliver IPS signatures and software updates on a regular basis. As new threats are identified, reputation data can also be sent to Cisco security devices, allowing for a fast and automated response to attacks. Cisco also offers a wealth of free security intelligence information, which is provided as a service to security community and includes reports, publications, and podcasts on the latest threats, in a vendor-neutral fashion. The IntelliShield service provides real-time security threat information and workarounds for security vulnerabilities and threats.

Web Controls

Web controls offer policy enforcement and protection against threats that use the web as a means of attack. Cisco Web controls include the Cisco Ironport Web Security Appliance, Cisco ASA Firewall, Cisco Intrusion Prevention System, and Cisco Security Agent.

Web Security Appliance

The Cisco Ironport S-series Web Security Appliance (WSA) combines web reputation-based filtering, antimalware scanning, layer 4 traffic monitoring, and data protection features in a single platform. Senderbase is used to rank the reputation of websites based on identified malware and malicious behavior. The ranking system for reputation is from -10 to +10; this system more effectively ranks websites based on the level of risk that each individual company is willing to accept. With reputation, there are no easy black and white answers to differentiate good websites from bad. However, Senderbase tracks 200+ different parameters; some of the most important are:

- Domain
- Network owners

- Dynamic IP address

- Compromised host lists

- Known threat URLs

- Web crawler data

- Global volume data

- Company and website history

- URL behavior

- HTML content data

- Spam links

Individual pages of websites receive scores as well, because web pages are rarely self-contained and might have links to hundreds of other sites or services. These scores are calculated with a bad score meaning malware, phishing, or fraud is present, and a good score means that the page is safe and uncompromised.

Acceptable use policy enforcement is an important control for most organizations. The WSA operates as a web proxy that users can connect through before accessing the Internet, allowing for deep content inspection and caching of Web content. The WSA performs URL filtering to ensure policy compliance with Internet acceptable use policies. Ironport web usage controls contain 65 categories of websites built into the platform, with unlimited support for custom groups. Policies can be configured by time, allowing, for example, different levels of Internet access outside of working hours. Web usage controls use the dynamic content analysis engine to assess content on-the-fly and categorize web pages based on what types of material are present. Based on this analysis, the DCA engine can monitor (log and report), warn the user, or block nonwork-related or questionable content. Figure 11-5 shows some of the URL-filtering categories available.

The WSA can be configured to decrypt HTTPS traffic on the fly in accordance with configured security policies. This allows the WSA to inspect encrypted traffic for malware and security policy violations on a risk basis. If a website using HTTPS has a low reputation score, the WSA can be configured to automatically decrypt and inspect communication to that site, whereas a site with a good repetition score might not need to be inspected based on policy and risk. This is not only good for performance, but allows the device to spend its time inspecting suspicious traffic instead of lower risk traffic.

Malware scanning and detection at the gateway stop malicious code before it reaches the endpoint. The WSA utilizes two different scanning engines, one from McAfee and the other from Webroot. The two scanning engines can be used separately or together to improve the effectiveness of malware detection. The McAfee engine provides scanning for malware and virus signatures and can be configured for heuristic and signature-based scanning. The Webroot engine provides antivirus and antispyware detection capabilities as well using different scanning technologies. The WSA is able to utilize the two scanning engines by leveraging the dynamic vectoring and streaming (DVS) engine, which is custom-made to provide extremely fast parsing and scanning of malware. Having two scanning engines improves the detection rate.

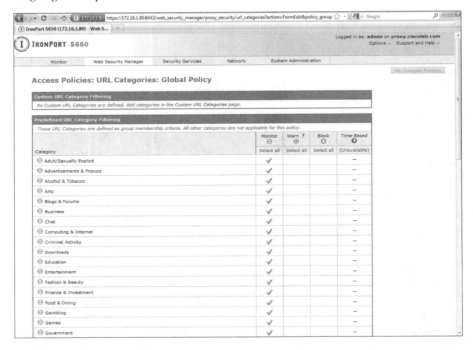

Figure 11-5   *URL Filtering Categories*

Layer 4 Traffic Monitor (L4TM) is designed to scan all 65,535 ports looking for malware activity that might be trying to hide in the network by using non-standard ports or tunneling through commonly-permitted internet services like HTTP. One of the most useful features of L4TM is the ability to detect botnet traffic while communicating out onto the Internet when it "phones home" to the botnet control point. This inspection capability also allows for easy identification of bot infected hosts on the internal network by IP and or user name of the infected host. L4TM also looks for IM and P2P sessions that are trying to circumvent access controls by tunneling through authorized protocols.

ASA

The Cisco ASA, as of the 8.3 release, now includes a licensed feature called Botnet Traffic Filter. This feature leverages global correlation data from Sensorbase to be able to identify the presence of phone home traffic passing through the firewall on any port. The ASA downloads this database as new updates are made available. The current functionality of Botnet Traffic Filter enables automatic response and reporting of potential botnet infections within the network. It operates in a similar manner as L4TM on the WSA, but at the firewall level. This feature is useful for providing IT staff with the IP address information of infected hosts inside the network for quick cleanup of an infection. Figure 11-6 shows how the ASA identifies botnet traffic in the network.

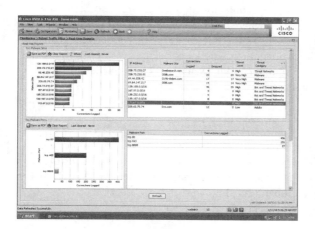

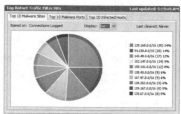

Live Dashboard

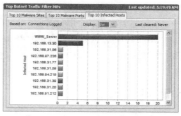

Integrated Reporting

Monitoring

Figure 11-6 *ASA Botnet Traffic Monitoring*

The ASA has support for optional Security Services Modules to add additional function-ality to the firewall. In addition to the IPS SSM, Cisco also offers the Cisco Content Security and Control services module (CSC). The CSC leverages Trend Micro virus wall technology to integrate antivirus, antispyware, antispam, URL blocking and filtering, and content filtering on a single module that plugs into the services module slot on the ASA firewall. This module is designed for small to medium businesses and remote offices with less than 1000 users. The CSC module offers:

- Malware protection using trend micro is antivirus and antispyware technologies.

- Signature-based antispam and antiphishing.

- Integrated URL Filtering with categories, scheduling and caching to block employee access to inappropriate or nonwork-related websites.

- Content filtering for policy for acceptable user policy enforcement.

IPS

The Cisco Intrusion Prevention System, available as an appliance and a module for the ASA, provides a number of important Web security protection features, including virus, worm, spyware, and botnet traffic detection signatures. An IPS is an important control for stopping and detection infected hosts and acts as an alarm system for the network. Chapter 9, "Access Control," covers the IPS in detail.

IPS global correlation is available in IPS version 7.0 and includes the ability for the IPS to modify risk rating of traffic by reputation scores downloaded from Sensorbase. This enables the IPS to block traffic based on where it is coming from and if that location is a known source of attacks or malware. This feature increases the IPS effectiveness at stopping known and unknown attacks exponentially. Global correlation also enables the IPS to report back to the Cisco SIO the source IP address any malicious traffic detected further populating the reputation database.

CSA

Cisco Security Agent provides host, behavior-based malware defense, to protect endpoints from locally run and network malware. CSA offers complete policy control and enforcement on the desktop including acceptable use policy enforcement. Antivirus scanning is also included to identify and quarantine known malware.

E-Mail Controls

The Cisco Ironport E-mail Security Appliance (ESA) is designed to block spam, phishing, and e-mail-borne malware and to enforce corporate e-mail policy. The ESA runs a hardened operating system known as AsyncOS that is custom built to provide high performance and efficiency. The ESA operates as a mail transfer agent (MTA) sitting between the Internet and internal groupware servers like Microsoft Exchange. The MTA's role is to route e-mail messages to recipients on the Internet and receive e-mail on behalf of the organization's users.

The most powerful feature of the ESA is the reputation filtering capability enabled by Senderbase. When reputation filtering is enabled, the ESA can block e-mail from the addresses of known spammers automatically with an extremely high success rate. Senders that have no reputation score or questionable reputation can then be sent to the antispam scanning engine for further analysis. Senderbase rates e-mail senders by their history of sending spam, allowing for profiling of spammers that can block as much as 90 percent of typical spam. The Senderbase database is fed from more than 120,000 businesses, universities, and ISPs around the globe.

Malware scanning is accomplished through antivirus technologies from McAfee and Sophos. When scanning incoming e-mails and files, the two scanning engines can work simultaneously to identify the type of file and scan for threats. Multiple scanning engines are used to increase the effectiveness and catch rate of malware. Each engine has different technologies for detecting viruses and spyware allowing for much better detection rates than one scanning engine alone. If malware is detected, it can be discarded or quarantined.

Having antivirus signature stops known malware, but it does not help with brand-new variants or day zero attacks. This is where the ESA virus outbreak filters come in to play, using Senderbase information to detect virus-like behavior. This engine uses a rule-based technology to identify suspicious messages and quarantine them until antivirus signatures are updated to detect the new threat. After signatures are updated, messages in quarantine are then rescanned, and if clean are then sent directly to the delivery queue

E-Mail Policy Enforcement

Policy enforcement is performed by the ESA in a number of ways. The ESA can enforce e-mail attachment control that can prevent attachment of certain types of documents to be sent inbound or outbound, or e-mails greater than a certain size. The filter can, for example, be set to strip an incoming e-mail of MP3 files and alert the user that MP3 was removed due to policy. Another policy enforcement capability is the inclusion of basic rules on typed of information in the e-mail text. An outbound filter can also be configured to look for keywords or credit card numbers, and any message that matches would be quarantined and human resources alerted. Content filter configuration enables direct enforcement of acceptable use policies and helps to prevent violations through direct feedback to the user.

E-mails originating from a company should include disclaimers and legal notices that inform the user that the message is private and confidential. Some countries even require that all e-mails from a company include business address and registration numbers on all correspondence. These can be automatically applied to outgoing messages with a simple rule configuration on the ESA.

Ironport Image Analysis is a policy enforcement feature that can be used to prevent the sending of inappropriate images with sexual content through e-mail. Harassment in the workplace is a serious matter, and businesses can be held legally responsible if they do not take precautions to provide protection for employees. Image Analysis can help to reduce the risk of inappropriate images being sent that employees might find offensive. Image analysis filters scan all messages, both outbound and inbound, looking for image files or links to images. If the message has no images, it is considered clean and passed on. A suspect image is sent to the image analysis algorithm where any jpeg, bmp, png, tiff, gif, tga, ico, or pcx file can be scanned. The image analysis feature can also address images embedded in other files such as Word, Excel, and PowerPoint. If an image is found to be inappropriate it is quarantined.

Image Analysis works by looking for skin tone and body parts in images and running the image through an algorithm that determines if the image is pornographic. This process typically results in 70 percent accuracy with 1 percent false positive. There are three potential rankings for an image; inappropriate, suspect, and clean on a scale of 0 to 100. The recommended settings and enforcement are as follows:

- Inappropriate (75–100): quarantine and notify

- Suspect (50–74): tag if inbound, notify if outbound

- Clean (0–49): no action

E-Mail Authentication

Sending an e-mail has often been often described as being similar to sending a postcard, in that there is no easy way to prove who really sent the message. Spammers and phishing attacks often create spoofed e-mails to pretend to be from legitimate companies. Because the message is forged, it is impossible to find out where the spam originated from. To combat spoofed e-mails, a number of the authentication mechanisms have been created:

- **Sender Policy Framework (SPF):** SPF allows the business to use a special DNS record to identify and publish which addresses can be used to send e-mail messages on behalf of the company's domain. SPF validates the senders e-mail domain and mail from address (or return path), otherwise known as the envelope layer in SMTP. When an e-mail arrives, a mail system can check SPF to determine whether the sending IP address is authorized. If it's not, the mail system can drop or quarantine the message. Of course this only works for spoofed addresses and doesn't help if an endpoint within the company is compromised and its e-mail facilities are used. Publishing an SPF record in DNS can also have the secondary benefit of making a company's domain less attractive for spammers to use to forge their e-mails. Spammers realize that if a company uses SPF, its messages are more than likely be dropped and won't bother with trying to spoof that domain. Before the addition of a specific SPF DNS type 99 entry that you can select as a DNS type, you had to create a text file in DNS and include the SPF policies there. Although this text file record approach for inserting SPF information into DNS servers is considered deprecated, some DNS registrars still use it.

- **SenderID:** Sender ID was created by Microsoft and based on SPF. Sender ID includes an SPF version tag in its syntax, which has caused confusion because Sender ID is not version 2 of SPF. They are completely different protocols and authenticate different parts of the e-mail message. Although SPF looks at the e-mail header, Sender ID can additionally use an algorithm called Purported Responsible Address (PRA) to attempt to identify which e-mail header is responsible for sending the e-mail message. PRA analyzes from, sender, resent-from, and resent-sender header fields. Using PRA is a way to identify which domain the e-mail is claiming was the source. In the case of mailing lists and users resending e-mails received from others, just looking at the mail from address does not tell you if the original message was legitimate, only that it was from the last e-mail domain to receive it. This information is then used by Sender ID to check to see if the e-mail source is authorized to send e-mail on behalf of any other domains found in the e-mail headers. Sender ID's extensions on SPF can assist with identifying phishing attacks because they are often crafted in this manner.

- **Domain keys identified mail (DKIM):** DKIM is an open standard that combines Yahoo's Domain Keys and Cisco Identified Internet Mail specifications for e-mail authentication. Whereas SPF and SenderID only use the e-mail domain to authenticate outbound e-mail, DKIM uses public key cryptography to authenticate the source e-mail domain through digital signatures. DKIM digitally signs all outbound messages so receivers can verify that they came from your site and prove that the company's gateway actually sent the message and the sender's address was not spoofed. DKIM can optionally verify that the message was not altered with checksums that are signed by the mail gateways private key, which can help to reduce e-mail fraud. DKIM works by adding a header field to an e-mail named DKIM-Signature that holds the digital signature of the entire e-mail message. When a receiving e-mail server processes a DKIM-signed e-mail, it uses the domain name the message is claiming to be from to look up the domain's public key in DNS. The mail server uses the public key to decrypt the hash values and checks the results. Successful decryption of the message verifies that the e-mail was legitimately sent from the domain it is claiming to come from. Just like the previous authentication frameworks, DKIM is also implemented within DNS records through the addition of a text file.

E-mail authentication has the benefits of helping to reduce spam and spoofed messages and can help protect brand and reputation by reducing forged messages sent to end users. Although e-mail authentication technologies are not perfect, they do add value and should be standard practices for organization to implement. The following links can help with the creation of Sender ID and DKIM DNS text files to implement these features on mail gateways like the ESA.

- Sender ID Record creation wizard, http://www.microsoft.com/mscorp/safety/content/technologies/senderid/wizard/

- DKIM DNS record creation wizard, http://www.port25.com/support/support_dkwz.php

Data Loss Prevention

Cisco data loss prevention (DLP) technologies primarily address data in motion. Web e-mail DLP controls are addressed with the WSA, e-mail DLP controls on the ESA, and Cisco Security Agent includes DLP scanning features on the endpoint. Cisco partners with RSA to address DLP concerns for data on servers and in storage. This section covers network-focused DLP controls.

Web

The DLP capabilities built into the WSA allow for policy enforcement of any web-based application. For example, it is possible to configure policy on the WSA to selectively prevent the uploading of Excel documents greater than a certain size or files with predefined keywords in them to web applications and social networking sites. The platform allows granular control of policy enforcement and includes the ability to apply policy differently to specific users or groups and control their abilities to connect to web mail, social networking sites, FTP, blogs, or any other destination that could be a potential vector of data disclosure. Policies are constructed by analyzing:

- **Who:** Each user or group of users has different levels of access to sensitive data requiring specific policies.

- **What:** The types of files or presence of keywords can make a simple e-mail a potential loss.

■   **Where:** The reputation of the site they are connected to; uploading files is taken into account.

Based on these criteria, the policy can be applied and enforced. The Cisco WSA can also integrate with third-party DLP vendors for deeper analysis of content through the ICAP protocol.

E-Mail

Data loss prevention can be accomplished for e-mail by automatically blocking sensitive data such as credit card account number, bank routing numbers, and Social Security numbers. The ESA has built-in smart identifiers to look for this type of information and allows for the creation of custom dictionary files that can search for business specific information such as account numbers or customer ids. The system can have multiple responses to the presence of this type of data, including the following:

■   **Encrypt:** Require encryption of e-mails from specific users or groups.

■   **Quarantine:** Store potential policy violations for administrator approval.

■   **Drop:** Do not send the message and discard it.

■   **Bounce:** Return the message to the user as undeliverable based on policy violation.

■   **BCC:** Blind carbon copy to a specific e-mail address to maintain a record.

■   **Strip content:** Remove the DLP violating data from the message.

In addition to its built-in capabilities, the ESA allows customers to use RSA DLP scanning technology for advanced identification and classification and policy enforcement of confidential information. This licensed feature enables more than 100 predefined templates that can be used to address the requirements in acts such as HIPAA, SOX, GLBA, and PCI Custom policies can also be created for special use cases that businesses might run into. The RSA DLP features are integrated into the ESA and managed through the same interface.

E-mail encryption for sensitive information is not only a good idea, but many states require it, with hefty fines if a violation is reported. ESA supports two methods for e-mail encryption: Transport Layer Security (TLS) and Cisco E-mail Encryption Service.

TLS allows for the creation of an encrypted tunnel between mail transfer agents. This is useful for encrypting e-mail between companies with a business relationship or among government agencies. Mail TLS capabilities require that both sides be configured to support encryption and is not used for end-user encryption needs.

To address individual recipient encryption, Cisco offers an encryption service that allows the ESA to register e-mail keys with Cisco allowing recipients to view encrypted e-mails on their machines securely without having to run special software or clients. Cisco doesn't store the actual message, but instead brokers the key exchange between the end-user and the ESA, similar to how public key cryptography works with certificate authorities. When the user receives an e-mail there is a link to the Cisco registered e-mail service. The user can then click on the link and view the encrypted message. The sender can track the deliver and receipt of messages and recall messages through the service. This service works with any e-mail client including web-based e-mail. Figure 11-7 shows the Cisco E-mail Encryption Service.

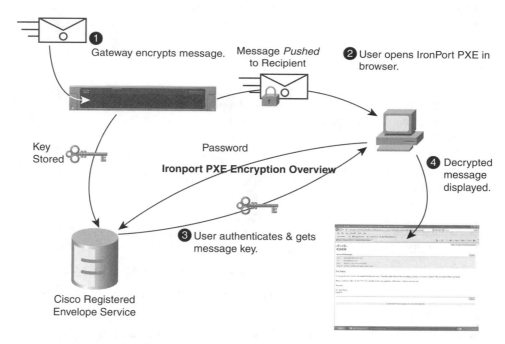

Figure 11-7   *Cisco E-mail Encryption Service*

Client

Client controls can be used to enforce DLP policy directly at the user's machine. Cisco Security Agent includes DLP features that can be used to inspect an endpoint for locally stored data of a sensitive nature, such as credit card and Social Security numbers. Finding and preventing sensitive data from being stored locally can reduce its potential for loss.

Patch Management

Cisco can help enforce and automate patch management through network admission control (NAC) by performing posture assessments on client machines before they are allowed direct access to the rest of the network. NAC can also assist with remediation of unpatched machines by initiating update services or providing links to download specific patches. Strong patch management controls are crucial for reducing endpoint vulnerabilities that can lead to compromises. Chapter 9 covered NAC in detail.

Monitoring

Monitoring controls provide visibility into the organizations defensive capabilities. Monitoring for endpoint protection is accomplished through the following built-in tools and products.

Web

The WSA has built-in reporting that allows administrators to view real-time and historical information on web activities, malware detection, and reputation information. The WSA reporting categories are:

- **Overview:** General WSA performance, top URL categories, top malware, L4 Traffic Monitor

- **L4 Traffic Monitor:** Malware ports detected; malware sites detected

- **Client Web Activity:** Individual user web activity information including bandwidth used, URL categories visited, malware identified

- **Client Malware Risk:** Clients with detected malware by name and IP

- **Website Activities:** Top sites by high-risk transactions and top sites with malware; includes site details by site name

- **Antimalware Detection:** Malware categories detected; malware threats detected

- **URL Categrories:** Top URL categories detected and blocked, detailed URL categories identified

- **Web Reputation Filters:** Web reputation actions block; scan further malware detected, scan further clean, allow

More detailed monitoring of the WSA is accomplished using Sawmill for Ironport. Sawmill is a log management and reporting tool that has been implemented as a special edition custom built with predefined reports for the WSA. There are three profiles defined for Sawmill for Ironport, and each profile is developed to provide information for different classes of users.

- The *HR profile* is tailored for individuals analyzing acceptable business use of Internet resources and detection of potential legal liabilities.

- *SecOps* includes information more pertinent for security operations personnel analyzing malware trends and potential compromises of corporate resources.

- The *L4TM profile* is useful in identifying the day zero attacks and potential bot net infections within the organization.

Figure 11-8 shows Sawmill's top URL reporting for Ironport WSA.

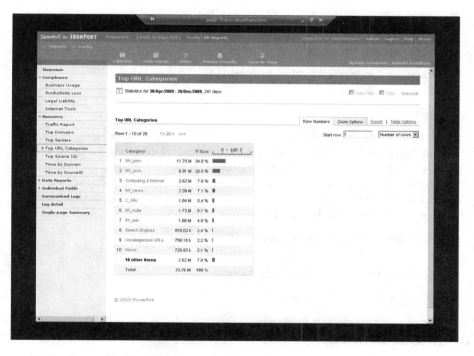

Figure 11-8 *Sawmill's Top URL Reporting for WSA*

E-Mail

Monitoring e-mail security events is accomplished with the ESA's built-in reporting features. Some the most important reports for auditors include:

- **Overview status:** System quarantine, what the system did with incoming mail and outgoing mail processing results

- **DLP incidents:** Any detected DLP events identified by the ESA

- **Content filters:** Any content filter actions performed by the ESA based on preconfigured content rules

- **Virus outbreaks:** Identified virus outbreaks and the system the involved

- **Virus types:** List of detected virus types by name

- **TLS connections:** TLS connections made attempted or rejected based on destination for compliance reporting

- **Quarantines:** Messages sitting in quarantine

MARS

Cisco Monitoring and Analysis Response System (MARS) is used to analyze logging information from Cisco security devices. MARS receives data from the network infrastructure, firewalls, intrusion prevention systems, network admission control, and Cisco security agent. These events are then correlated to determine whether a security incident has occurred. MARS is an essential component of monitoring Cisco network and provides great visibility into the security posture of the organization.

Key endpoint protection report categories for MARS are:

- Client Exploits, Virus, Worm, and Malware

- Security Posture Compliance (NAC)

Technical Testing

Technical testing for endpoint security controls validates that policy is enforced by the technical controls deployed. The following areas should be tested to identify any weaknesses, misconfiguration, or missing controls.

Acceptable Use Enforcement

Acceptable use policies provide guidance about what activities that can be conducted with corporate resources are permissible. URL filtering is a technical control designed to help the organization better manage employee Internet usage. Auditors should test to make sure that URL filtering operates as expected by testing various classes of websites that are being filtered or monitored. Attempting to connect to unapproved websites should result in the URL filtering device blocking access, or warning the user that the actions are reported (which in many cases is just as effective as blocking). Most proxy devices require the configuration of proxy settings in the browsers to point the browser to the proxy's IP address and port numbers. Of course, this is easy for most users to bypass by simply deselecting the proxy in the configuration tabs of their browsers. Auditors should test for firewall rules blocking direct port 80 and HTTPS access to the Internet to prevent this circumvention of web filtering. If transparent proxy is enabled, WCCP forces the appropriate web ports directly to the WSA without anything being configured in the user's browser. L4TM also detects attempts to bypass the proxy, but does not stop users.

Other proxy bypass methods that should be tested for include:

- **Google cache:** Google caches web pages on its servers, allowing users to view these sites without actually going to them. Make sure that this is blocked as well.

- **Google translation:** Google has the capability to translate from one language to another, but can also be asked to translate English to English, which forces Google to retrieve the banned website for the user.

- **SSH:** SSH can be used to create a VPN tunnel that allows users to bypass URL filters. SSH to outside network locations should have specific business needs; otherwise, block it from user segments on the firewall.

- **SSL:** SSL VPNs can be used to bypass URL filters so the WSA should be configured to intercept SSL traffic to unknown or low reputation websites, allowing for inspection.

- **IPsec:** IPsec tunnels should not be allowed from user segments without a specific business case. Most organizations block IPsec at the firewall to prevent outbound tunnels.

Corporate policies on outside e-mail accounts should be tested as well as direct SMTP access. Many organizations prohibit personal e-mail at work, and the WSA prevents users from accessing webmail, such as Gmail or Hotmail. SMTP should be allowed only from the business's approved MTAs, and never from an end user's client machine. Malware uses SMTP as a way to send spam, and it is easy to prevent by blocking outbound SMTP at the firewall to prevent SPAM from being sourced from the internal network.

Acceptable use of instant messaging (IM) can be tested by initiating a chat session from within the corporate network. Approved IM servers should be allowed, but others should be blocked. The WSA, ASA, and IPS can block tunneled IM traffic.

Malware Detection and Quarantine

Testing e-mail malware detection capabilities are made simple by using an Eicars file, which is a simple (and harmless) string of text that all antivirus vendors should be able to recognize and report on. To test, simply e-mail the file to a test user account and verify that the ESA inspected and quarantined the file. The goal of this type of testing is to ensure that inspection policies are configured properly and that the quarantine functions work as expected.

SPAM, Phishing, and E-Mail Fraud

Authentication of e-mail is an important tool to help combat spam and e-mail fraud. A useful tool to test e-mail authentication mechanisms is built into the ESA and is called Trace. E-mail authentications should be tested both outbound and inbound to the MTA.

Another way to test proper configuration of outbound e-mail authentication is to use the free reflector located at check-auth@verifier.port25.com. Sending an e-mail from the domain under review provides checks against SPF, SenderID, and DKIM. The results of the test and subsequent analysis are retuned as an e-mail. Any misconfiguration or deficiencies are detailed in the results.

Inbound e-mail authentication can be tested with the ESA trace tool. Alternatively, the auditor can generate spoofed e-mails and send them directly to the ESA to test real-world handling of spoofed e-mails.

Encryption

Running the TLS report on the ESA can assess TLS encryption between configured sites. This report details the number of messages sent, received, and any errors encountered. The auditor can send a message to one of the TLS-enabled peers and test to ensure that it is sent via the TLS process.

Testing Cisco Secure envelope service can be conducted for organizations that require encrypted e-mails be sent when transferring confidential information. Sending a test message to an external account and retrieving it verifies that the service works as expected.

Patch Management and Enforcement

The auditor should inspect patch management controls to ensure that the patch management system functions as expected. A multitude of patch management vendors addresses both application and operating system patching. Microsoft also offers a free Windows update service that can be enabled in an MS environment to handle patching Microsoft OS and applications.

If NAC is implemented on the network, an auditor should also test NAC posture assessment capabilities to determine whether unpatched machines are quarantined before being given access to the network. This can prevent a machine with a vulnerability that might be compromised from interacting with the rest of the network until all patches are up to date. Testing these features can be conducted by removing a required patch and trying to connect to the network. NAC would detect the missing patch and quarantine the system, and then offer remediation options to address the missing patch.

Data Loss Prevention Testing

Data loss prevention policies can be detailed, and organizations that use this technology need to have a strong DLP program that has properly classified types of data and the information sensitivity. The role of the auditor is to test the applied policies to determine whether they actively protect the organization from loss.

Policy testing should include review of web and e-mail controls to prevent sensitive information from leaving the network. Testing these controls can be accomplished by e-mailing or uploading test files that simulate confidential information. Auditors should test for the detection of account numbers, credit card numbers, and Social Security numbers along with any other organization-specific private information.

Logging in as a user and attempting to upload a test file to a social networking site is a good test of web acceptable use policies that control the upload of files and documents.

Detection and Response

Preventative technical controls work in conjunction with detection and response. All the testing performed during the audit should generate a significant number of log and security alerts. These should be reviewed to make sure that all attempts at circumventing controls and other security events are properly reported. This is also a good time to review the organization's processes for handling endpoint and DLP-related incidents.

Checklist

Assessment Area	Assessment Technique
People	
Has an endpoint risk assessment been conducted?	Review endpoint risk assessment documentation and determine whether appropriate threats and vulnerabilities have been identified.
Are endpoint protection policies adequate for the organization's level of risk?	Review applicable endpoint protection policies: acceptable use, minimum access policy, data classification, right to monitor, social networking, data loss prevention, e-mail, web access, and malware.

continues

Assessment Area	Assessment Technique	*(continued)*
Have endpoint client security controls and standards been created?	Review documentation of required endpoint security controls for minimum access, standards security applications, and personal firewall rules.	
Has a social networking policy been implemented?	Review social network policies and standards for approved social networking activities and conduct. Ensure that users have been made aware of threats and risks of social networks.	
Has document classification been conducted?	Review document and data classification standards. Analyze data for appropriate classification tags.	
Have employees signed and acknowledged the employer's right to monitor e-mail and web traffic?	Review employee signed documentation or click to accept logs.	
Are web acceptable use polices implemented?	Review web acceptable use standards. Standards should include URL filtering and appropriate use control requirements.	
Are e-mail acceptable use policies implemented?	Review e-mail acceptable use policies and standards. Standards should include e-mail malware, spam, and phishing protection.	
Process		
Does the organization seek information about new threats and attacks?	Review information-gathering processes for security specialists to update themselves and the organization on new threats.	
Is there a vulnerability management process?	Review vulnerability management and detection processes to determine whether the organization is actively scanning and detecting new endpoint vulnerabilities.	
Is patching of OS and applications centralized and managed?	Review patch-management process for automated delivery of operating system and application updates.	
Is an endpoint monitoring and incident handling process in place?	Review endpoint security event monitoring and incident handling process. Review endpoint security detection and remediation.	
Is user security awareness training conducted and users updated on breaking threats?	Review security awareness training program. Education should include acceptable use, password management, e-mail security, and social networking security.	

continues

Assessment Area	Assessment Technique	*(continued)*
Technical Architecture Review		
Web Controls		
Are web acceptable use policies enforced?	Confirm the presence and functionality of acceptable use controls for web access including: URL filtering, IM, webmail, and other applications.	
Is malware scanned at the gateway for all web traffic?	Ensure that web traffic is scanned for malware at the Internet gateway.	
Is SSL based web traffic inspected and tunneled http traffic prohibited?	Review web controls to ensure that SSL traffic can be inspected for malware and policy violations. Inspect IPS and FW configuration for identification and blocking of HTTP traffic tunnel through other ports.	
Are risky protocols blocked at the firewall for internal users?	Inspect the configuration of firewall for blocking of SMTP, IM, P2P, and other protocols prohibited by policy.	
Are intrusion prevention products configured for malware detection?	Inspect IPS configuration for malware signature detection and automatic response.	
E-mail Controls		
Is spam and phishing blocking preformed by the e-mail gateway?	Spam and phishing attempts should be blocked at the gateway. Confirm controls are in place.	
Is e-mail malware scanning preformed at the gateway?	Malware scanning for e-mail should be configured to detect and quarantine malware and suspicious files.	
Are e-mail acceptable use policies implemented?	Inspect e-mail controls for attachment control, presence of disclaimers and legal, and image analysis	
Are inbound and outbound e-mails authenticated?	Confirm configuration in DNS of Spf, senderid, and dkim to authenticate outbound e-mail. Confirm configuration of authentication checks on incoming e-mail.	
Data Loss Prevention Review		
Are DLP controls in place to limit posting of data to web applications?	Confirm configuration of DLP controls for web applications. Scan for tagged documents and transferring of prohibited document types.	

continues

Assessment Area	Assessment Technique *(continued)*
Are DLP controls in place to detect and remove sensitive information from e-mail?	Confirm detection and analysis of e-mail messages for sensitive information such as credit cards, Social Security numbers, and any other personal or company confidential information.
Is TLS encryption configured for business partners and third parties that require confidentiality?	Ensure that encryption is configured for sending e-mail confidentially between business partners and peer agencies.
Are recipient encryption technologies used to comply with confidentiality laws?	Confirm configuration of encrypted e-mail delivery for transmission of private and protected private information to customers.
Are client DLP technologies in place to discover confidential information residing on endpoint systems?	Review endpoint DLP controls to discover confidential information that might be on endpoint devices.
Patch Management Review	
Are Patch management technologies in place to automate OS and application patching?	Inspect the configuration of patch management applications and patch delivery methods.
Is NAC posture assessment in place to reduce the risk of vulnerable endpoints?	Inspect the configuration of NAC to ensure posture assessments are conducted to determine whether endpoints are patched and anti-malware enabled.
Monitoring and Incident Handling Review	
Does the organization review log data for web and e-mail acceptable use violations?	Inspect log data and review process for acceptable use violations.
Does the organization review logs for detected malware or infected hosts?	Inspect malware detection logs for anomalies and review malware detection process.
Is firewall, IPS, and host security technologies reviewed for security incidents?	Inspect firewall, IPS, and host security log data for anomalies. Review security incident analysis process.
Is there a defined process for handling endpoint security incidents?	Review incident handling process and procedures.
Technical Endpoint Control Testing	
Do acceptable use controls enforce policy?	Test acceptable use controls by performing prohibited actions identified by policy. Test web and e-mail for policy enforcement.

continues

Assessment Area	Assessment Technique *(continued)*
Are anti malware technologies scanning web and e-mail traffic for malicious code?	Test antimalware scanning and detection using Eicars file to confirm that virus scanning is configured and functional.
Is e-mail authentication functional for outbound and inbound e-mail messages?	Test e-mail authentication with outbound proxy for proper SDF, SenderID, and DKIM configuration. Use ESA trace to test inbound e-mail configuration.
Is TLS operating as expected for encrypting e-mail transport between business partners or agencies?	Review ESA logs for TLS to determine whether TLS is required for business partners and agencies.
Is phishing and spam prevention configured and working?	Test spam capabilities by sending unsolicited e-mail directly to the ESA. Review logs and quarantine of messages.
Are patch management technologies updating OS and Applications as expected?	Test patch management applications to ensure that the latest patches are being deployed and patch fail rate is not excess for endpoints.
Is NAC configured to quarantine and remediate vulnerable machines before being given access to the network?	Test NAC posture assessment with an unpatched endpoint. Make sure that client is quarantined and that remediation options are presented.
Are DLP technologies scanning, identify, and blocking confidential data?	Test DLP technologies for detection of sensitive data being transmitted through e-mail or web. Test tagging and detection of multiple file types.
Is botnet traffic monitoring configured to detect phone home traffic and identify compromised hosts inside the organization?	Test botnet traffic detection capabilities on ASA and WSA L4TM. Review logs for identified botnet hosts.
Did the organization detect technical testing of controls?	Review logs and detection technologies to confirm detection of testing traffic and activities.

Summary

Endpoint protection is one of the hottest battlegrounds that security professionals face today. With the explosion of Web 2.0 programming techniques and social networking, endpoint attacks are becoming more predominantly web-based. Malware has gotten much smarter and harder to detect, resulting in a shift away from relying on signatures alone to detect what is bad. This chapter focused on the threats and risks that organization face utilizing the Internet and the technical controls that Cisco offers to help reduce those risks for endpoint systems. In summary:

- The loss of sensitive data, reputation, and financial fraud are significant risks for businesses, which is why it is so important for organization to conduct risk assessments on endpoint security controls where the greatest threats are targeted.

- Web threats target the most common applications and plugins, making everyone that uses the web a potential victim. Organizations must deploy controls that protect their endpoints from drive by malware infection and other client exploits.

- E-mail is essential for communicating with customers and employees, but is also a significant source for the spread of malware and fraud. With spam accounting for almost 90 percent of global e-mail volume, controls that protect users from this vector of attack are required.

- Data loss prevention strategies and controls help a business keep private information private. For DLP to be effective it requires data to be classified and tagged and it requires the appropriate polices to be in place.

- Testing endpoint controls are essential for validating that they are properly configured and actively protecting the organization from threats.

References in This Chapter

Cisco 2009 Annual Security Report, www.cisco.com/web/go/securityreport

The Open Web Application Security Project, www.owasp.org

www.enisa.europa.eu:

- ENISA Web 2.0 Security and Privacy

- ENISA Botnets—The Silent Threat

- ENISA Security Issues and Recommendations for Online Social Networks

NIST 800-40v2 Creating a Patch and Vulnerability Management Program, csrc.nist.gov/publications/nistpubs/800-40-Ver2/SP800-40v2.pdf

Chapter 12

Unified Communications

Over the past ten years, Unified Communications (UC) deployments have grown exponentially as VoIP technologies have matured. Businesses have come to realize the cost
savings of a converged network and the advantages of integrating the phone system with
customer-focused applications. Voice and video traffic routinely use the same network as
data, which results in a consolidation of services and resources. Voice is now simply
another service, part of an integrated suite of applications that have their own unique
properties, which users expect to deliver the quality and reliability of their legacy phone
system. The challenge of securing a UC system requires organizations to maintain the
confidentiality, integrity, and availability of this service while providing access to a wide
array of mobile handheld devices and applications. Security has become much easier
since the early days of VoIP, but VoIP in general is still a complex technology with many
components that require special handling and protection. Auditing a voice network for
good security practices can help reduce the risks associated with VoIP and create a solid
foundation on which businesses can rely. This chapter covers the building blocks of that
foundation and the areas that auditors should review when assessing Cisco UC security.

Unified Communications Risks

Deploying UC can expose a business to many of the same risks prevalent in a traditional
data network and legacy PBX combined. The functions and components of the legacy
PBX have been decoupled and moved as services to various parts of an IP network. This
evolution from proprietary systems to open and interconnected devices is not unlike how
mainframes and terminals were replaced by multipurpose PCs. Instead of a single piece
of hardware that needs to be secured, businesses now must consider the component
parts individually and plan protective strategies according to the risks that each component faces. As Figure12-1 highlights, it is easy to map PBX functions to network devices,
allowing for the identification of key assets, which is the first part of assessing risk.

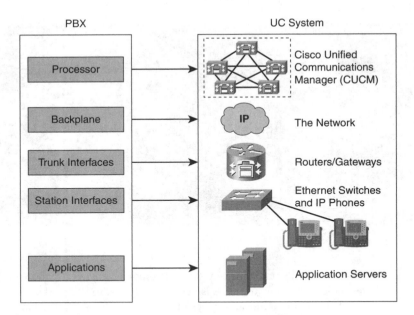

Figure 12-1 *PBX to UC Functions*

Risk in a UC environment is generally categorized by its impact to the business. Potential areas of loss from an insecure UC deployment include the following:

■ **Business disruption:** Business customers are accustomed to picking up their phones and hearing a dial tone every time they place a call. There is also an expectation of a high level of voice quality that a VoIP environment is expected to maintain. UC networks are sensitive to packet delay and inconsistent delivery. Any of these issues can directly impact a business's capability to communicate with clients, which can cost the company significant money in missed opportunities and lost customers. Service interruptions of any kind are typically not tolerated well by businesses of any size.

■ **Unauthorized disclosure of confidential information:** Users expect their private phone conversations to stay private. Conducting business in a poorly configured VoIP environment can result in the potential for unauthorized disclosure of sensitive information. Although tapping a hardwired phone is actually easier than eavesdropping on a VoIP call (if you have the right equipment), many of the tools and techniques for tapping VoIP systems are free and widely available on the Internet.

■ **Loss of reputation:** Reputation equals trust in the eyes of customers; it can take years to build, but it can be ruined in an instant. The phone system represents a business's capability to communicate with and service the needs of the customer. If an attacker is able to impersonate the company by using its phone system, the resulting impression left with the customer is anything but positive.

- **Fraud:** Theft of long distance is nothing new in the PBX world. With hardwired connections, an attacker would need to physically tap into the company's phone connections. In a VoIP environment, the possibilities of remotely hijacking a business's long-distance services is real, especially as IP phone service through Session Initiation Protocol (SIP) becomes more popular.

- **Noncompliance with regulations:** Regulatory requirements for ensuring the privacy of credit card and personal information must be addressed with UC to protect client and business partner confidentiality. A business that does not adequately protect its VoIP system can look forward to fines and legal headaches that can result in significant damages.

These risks, while sobering to think about, can be mitigated with a thorough understanding of the threats that face a UC system and the deployment of controls to address each threat. The next section provides some examples of how attackers can compromise the confidentiality, integrity, and availability of UC.

VoIP Threats

Threats to a UC deployment can target vulnerabilities in a number of areas, including protocol weaknesses, social engineering, and misconfiguration. Regardless of the specific method, the intended purpose of the attack generally falls within one of the following categories:

- Denial of Service (DoS)

- Confidentiality

- Fraud

Because there are a wide array of protocols and deployment mechanisms associated with VoIP and UC, security researchers have found many vulnerabilities, and subsequently, they have developed an extensive list of tools intended to abuse poorly designed and configured VoIP networks. These threats can be defended against if taken into consideration during the design phase, and those defenses are implemented during deployment. Understanding these threats can help an auditor identify the various design, configuration, and control weaknesses that can result in compromise of the integrity of a UC system.

Denial of Service

DoS is one of the oldest threats to networked communications, and it is alive and well in a UC environment. What started as pranks played on coworkers to force their computers to reboot has turned into a tool that can be used to stifle competition and silence dissenting voices. DoS takes on a new meaning when a business's phones stop ringing (or they all ring at the same time) and orders cannot be placed or shipped. Downtime for a phone system can be devastating in terms of lost productivity and revenue. The protocols that enable VoIP to operate are sensitive to packet loss and delay, making DoS attacks particularly useful in shutting down an IP phone system if not properly protected. The good thing about VoIP is that redundancy and failover mechanisms are more robust than a legacy PBX system, providing more methods to protect its availability due to the decentralized nature of UC. Following are some examples of attacks that can result with DoS:

- **Power outages:** Although not generally considered part of an attack, power outages play a direct role in DoS. UC phones are usually powered by an Ethernet switch or a power pack plugged into the wall, leaving them vulnerable to local power disruptions at the switch or through someone accidentally disconnecting the power pack. Legacy PBX phones were usually line-powered, and the PBX itself had integrated batteries that enabled the phones to continue to work without external power for hours. In a UC environment, this is achieved through the use of uninterrupted power supplies (UPS) in the wiring closet where the switches are located and in the datacenter that houses the UC servers. Poor or inadequate backup power can result in a shutdown of the business's phone system in an emergency and can cause sporadic phone reboots that can cause a delay as the phone reconnects after power is restored.

- **Call flooding:** VoIP is sensitive to packet delay and requires less than 150 ms total travel time between endpoints to maintain good voice quality. Anything over the 150 ms threshold creates a noticeable lag when talking to someone on the phone. VoIP trunks across the Internet are a common mechanism for connecting remote offices, which means that packet flooding attacks targeted at edge routers can cause voice quality to suffer or the trunk to be completely unusable. VoIP doesn't handle lost packets well either, which results in clipped voice conversations and other unpleasant experiences. As little as 6 percent packet loss can impact a VoIP conversation. Attackers can use this sensitivity to network conditions as a way to disrupt a business's communication capabilities.

- **Call control attacks:** If an attacker can send packets to a voice network that is unprotected by firewalls and IPS, he can usually find a method to disrupt services. Phone registration, call request, call control, and service flooding are commonly used to prevent phones from being able to communicate to each other or to call control services.

- **Protocol attacks:** Manipulating protocols to create packets that do not conform to standards can cause increased processing time and potentially disable the service entirely. *Fuzzing* is a technique used to test protocol robustness by generating random or improperly formatted data as input, usually to find programming defects during quality assurance testing. Fuzzing techniques can be used by attackers to find vulnerabilities in protocols that they can leverage for privilege escalation attacks. Fuzzing can also be an effective way of disabling call control by crashing a service or application necessary for communication setup.

Confidentiality

The privacy of UC is of great concern for businesses because of the potential loss of proprietary information and the legal ramification of unauthorized disclosure to a third party. Following are a few of the privacy threats that should be considered when assessing a UC network.

- **Eavesdropping:** The default configuration of VoIP does not utilize encryption, which results in the media stream that carries the conversation being susceptible to packet capture and replay. Many free tools have been developed that make eavesdropping on VoIP conversations a trivial process. To listen to someone else's conversation, the attacker must have a means of gaining access to the voice media stream. This can be accomplished when there is a lack of voice and data network separation, or through techniques that allow the attacker to gain access to an undefended voice VLAN. When the attackers can monitor voice traffic, they have the ability to reconstruct any conversation they choose.

- **Call pattern tracking:** This is an information-mining attack used to identify patterns in all the ingoing and outgoing calls that employees make. An attacker can learn a great deal about a target company by monitoring who is called and when. This can be useful for determining business relationships, clients, and it can be used for social engineering.

- **Fax capture:** The T.38 Fax relay standard brought fax capabilities into the VoIP world. Faxes follow the same path as voice traffic in a UC environment and can be captured and reconstructed just like voice conversations. The fax machine is still an integral part of business communications, and many companies use faxing as a mechanism for receiving and placing orders. Faxes might include private information such as credit card numbers or personal information that should be protected.

- **Video capture:** Video has become a method for facilitating virtual meetings without the need to travel. Video use has increased exponentially within companies as a means to rein in travel budgets and provide more efficient and timely interactions with customers. Video is an integrated part of Cisco UC, and as such it faces the threat of unauthorized capture and reconstruction.

Fraud

Fraud is defined as intentional deception for personal gain, and in the case of fraud perpetrated against VoIP systems, personal gain is definitely a strong motivation. Attackers look for ways to make money at the expense of others, and hijacking another business's phone services enables a wide range of money-making schemes. Open source IP phone software is free and easily attainable, and with a little technical knowledge, it can be pointed at a compromised voice system and take advantage of its services. The following are a few examples of types of phone system fraud:

- **Toll fraud:** Stealing long-distance service can occur from within a company or from a third party taking advantage of a telephone system's security weakness. The net result is unauthorized access to a company's telecommunications equipment to place long-distance calls. For example, an employee can call forward a phone to a long-distance number, redirecting all calls, creating a free "hotline" for friends to use. An attacker can also compromise an insecure voice media gateway, enabling full control of a company's incoming and outgoing calls that can then be used for a number of illegal activities, such as reselling voice services to others.

- **Voice phishing:** A *voice phishing attack* (also know as vishing) is when an attacker uses VoIP to target customers of a company or bank by dialing their number and leaving an urgent message asking them to call a specific number regarding their account or credit card. After the customer calls the number, the attacker pretends to be a representative of a legitimate company in the hopes of tricking someone into divulging personal information such as account numbers or other personal information. These attacks can be fairly sophisticated and include Interactive Voice Response systems for automated recording of account information that mimic the way legitimate businesses provide account lookup services. Customers are familiar with these types of systems and think nothing of entering their private data, exposing them to identity theft and financial loss. Using a company's own phone system to perpetrate these types of attacks lends credibility to the attack and makes it hard for a customer to recognize the difference.

- **Call redirection:** When you dial a business's phone number, your call can be routed anywhere in the world before it rings the phone of a live person. With technologies such as single number reach (SNR), calls can follow us no matter where we are. A call redirection attack takes advantage of this routing technology by manipulating call routing to redirect calls to another location where the attacker is able to control the conversation and trick the user into divulging private information.

- **Call hijacking:** If VoIP uses unencrypted and unauthenticated protocols, there is a potential for an attacker to insert himself into an active call, allowing him to take over the conversation. If this is done as soon as a customer calls in and before the customer speaks to a live person, he would never know what happened. This attack can target internal call control systems or IP trunk lines.

- **Spam over IP Telephony (SPIT):** *SPIT* is a technique that operates in a similar fashion to e-mail-based spam. Instead of receiving an e-mail that attempts to sell some pharmaceuticals or male enhancement products, the victim receives an automated phone call pitching the product. If an attacker can compromise a business's voice gateway, he can use it to automatically call customers and impersonate the business, which can impact reputation and trust.

UC Policy and Standards Review

The strategy and tactics used to protect a UC environment are defined through policies that describe acceptable use of the phone system and written standards for security controls. Policies and standards are written as a result of risk assessments to reduce risk and maintain confidentiality, integrity, and availability. Auditors should review the following policy and standards areas:

- **Acceptable use of UC:** The acceptable uses of UC systems include policies on types of activities employees can engage in when using the phone system. The policy should state that the system is intended for business purposes only and have restrictions in place on personal use. Disciplinary actions should be noted regarding failure to comply. Contractors, guests, and other third-party usages of the UC system should be addressed along with any restrictions.

- **Password and PIN polices:** UC services such as voicemail, conferencing, and soft phones require user authentication and must follow the same password management and protection standards as any other corporate application. This policy should detail password and PIN complexity requirements and password change frequency.

- **Remote access policies:** Voice has become a highly mobile application through both soft phones on PCs and the use of mobility clients on smart phones. Many companies also allow employees to take IP phones home and provide a business extension that connects over the Internet. These deployments should use encryption and secure credentials to reduce the chance of compromise. This policy details the requirements for obtaining UC remote access services and the protective measures required.

- **Business partner connection policies:** Enabling direct VoIP communications with business partners through IP trunking is a good way to enable cost-effective voice capabilities. Policies should be in place to address security requirements necessary for protecting those connections. Firewall and monitoring requirements should be listed, too.

- **Long-distance policy:** Long-distance service can be costly and should be monitored for fraud and excessive use by employees. This policy can include requirements for account billing codes and monitoring of call detail records that can expose improper phone use. A long-distance policy provides guidance about who is authorized to make long-distance calls and how they are accounted for.

Standards work in conjunction with policies to address the specifics of how a policy should be enforced. The following standards are examples of good practices that auditors should look for:

- Physical access to UC system components such as servers and switches should be restricted to administrative personnel only. Handsets should be physically secured when possible, and all configuration access should be disabled on the handset.

Common area handsets should be mounted on a tamper-resistant bracket or secured with a lock.

■   VLAN segregation of voice and data traffic is an essential component of voice security. The configuration of a voice VLAN should be standard practice for all UC deployments. All traffic between the voice and data network should go through a firewall to add access control and policy enforcement at the network boundary. Businesses should also consider intrusion preventions systems to prevent and detect network attacks against voice services.

■   Standards for access control and authentication of IP phones should be in place, and the use of 802.1x for secure authentication is recommended. Unique digital certificates are available on each phone that can be used to identify approved devices to the network before access is granted.

■   The use of encryption can reduce the risk to confidentiality that sniffing voice traffic can present. Encryption is possible for both the media stream and call control and setup. Standardizing classes of users who can benefit from encryption due to the sensitivity of their positions and risk is a good way to minimize the challenges of deploying encrypted VoIP throughout the organization.

UC Operational Control Review

Operational management and controls of UC are necessary for detecting fraud and reducing misconfiguration that can result in compromise. Documented procedures for addressing security in UC systems are necessary for the consistent enforcement of policy. The following areas should be reviewed by the auditor:

■   User and phone provisioning

■   Change management

■   Asset management

■   Call detail record review

■   Administrative access

■   Vulnerability management

■   Security event monitoring and log review

User and Phone Provisioning

The process used for provisioning users and phones in a UC system includes the assignment of hardware and the appropriate accounts and access each user is granted. Usernames are used for logging into the Communications Manager for administering phone features, services, and credentials for soft phone. Pins can also be used for voicemail access and features that can be interacted with by dialing into the business's pilot number. Password assignment and initial setup should include a secure mechanism for assigning passwords that comply with complexity policies and passwords history requirements. Cisco Communications Manager also enables integration with LDAP and Active Directory, enabling Windows domain passwords and single sign-on.

Each class of user represents a different level of risk and should require a different level of service. Organizations should have well documented user service requirements and required security features. At a minimum, each profile should include the following:

- **Dial plan restrictions:** What types of number the user can dial, such as emergency, local, long distance, and international

- **Hours:** Hours the user is allowed to use voice services

- **Soft phone:** Whether or not the user is allowed soft phone privileges

- **Conferencing:** Conference access requirements and restrictions

- **Video:** Video access requirements and restrictions

- **Remote access:** Whether or not the user is allowed home office access for a remote line appearance

- **Encryption:** Encryptions requirements for voice media and signaling

- **Services:** Any UC application access privileges

A user classification profile helps with consistent privilege assignment and feature requirements.

Change Management

Auditors should review the organization's change management procedures, which are critical for reducing the risk of UC misconfiguration. During the change management process, you define specific steps necessary for initiating the change and an approval process that checks for errors before any changes are actually performed. There should also be a log kept of all changes that detail who, when, and why a change occurred. Obviously, a software management system is recommended to ease the administrative burden of change control.

Asset Management

One of the benefits of VoIP is that moving an IP phone does not require someone physically going to a wiring closet with a punch-down tool to make a new extension. A phone can be picked up and moved to an available switch port easily. This can, however, make keeping track of where UC system assets are located more difficult. Cisco provides a management application to ease the burden of inventory and provisioning of phones called Cisco Unified Provisioning Manager. At a minimum, the organization should be able to produce records of the following:

- **Asset information:** MAC address and type of phone

- **Owner:** User or users assigned privileges for the phone
- **Location:** Physical location of the asset

Call Detail Record Review

The organization should regularly review Call Detail Records (CDR) to identify odd calling behavior or sudden spikes in utilization. Cisco provides a reporting tool that is integrated into Communications Manager called CDR Analysis and Reporting that can provide reports on demand or automatically generated, by criteria like top users, by cost, number of calls, and duration. Organizations should have a process for reviewing the records on a quarterly basis at minimum. This review should look for:

- Large numbers of unauthorized calls
- Unusual call destinations
- Long duration calls
- Large numbers of calls to the same destination
- Calls outside of business hours
- Dropped calls

Administrative Access

UC administration should be conducted in a secure fashion, leveraging individual administrator accounts and secure management protocols such as HTTPS and SSH. Administration of the UC network gateways should be conducted from secure management VLANS where possible, following good change control processes. In addition, multilevel administration should be required for larger organizations with decentralized support. Multilevel administration is a feature in Communications Manager that can give support personnel different levels of access based on their role. A helpdesk person, for example, might have the ability to look at basic configuration and change phone settings but not anything that might impact multiple users or Communications Manager enterprise settings.

Vulnerability Management

Cisco provides news feeds and alert services that inform customers of any vulnerability identified and the patches required for UC systems. The organization should subscribe to these services and review them on a regular basis. All patches should be deployed as soon as possible during maintenance windows to remove vulnerabilities. The UC system is distributed across multiple devices, and each component must be reviewed for vulnerable code.

Software-level inventories should be maintained and reviewed for the following UC components:

- Communications Manager
- Call gateways
- Switches
- IP phones
- Soft phones
- UC applications

Cisco offers multiple methods for automatically receiving updates on vulnerabilities pertaining to UC systems:

- **Cisco Notification Service:** Enables a user to choose the class of technology (UC, for example) and receive, through e-mail or RSS feeds, the latest field notices on product deployment workarounds and security advisories. This service is found at www.cisco.com/cisco.support/notifications.html.

- **Cisco PSIRT:** Administrators can subscribe through RSS to Product Security Incident Response Team (PSIRT) announcements directly for new vulnerabilities in Cisco products with workarounds.

- **IntelliShield:** IntelliShield provides holistic security announcements that deal with Cisco and other vendors' products. A free version of the service is available through the Cisco Security Intelligence Operations Center, which is available at www.cisco.com/go/sio.

Security Event Monitoring and Log Review

Security events generated by the UC system and network hardware should be reviewed regularly, and a process should be in place to follow up on suspicious activity. As mentioned previously, CDR is an important logging mechanism for looking at call histories, which are useful for fraud detection. Because UC relies so heavily on a networked architecture, the same security-monitoring tools that are used to defend the network against attack are also used for monitoring security events that impact the voice network. Special attention should be given to any security-related events at the gateway due to its attractiveness as a target. Numerous invalid login attempts for soft phone, for example, can be an indication of password guessing. Sudden service degradation through increased delay or lost packets can also be an indicator of hacking attempts. It is essential for businesses to understand their voice networks and have good baselines to better identify the anomalies that might be warning signs of an active attack.

Disaster Recovery

The resiliency capabilities of UC are extensive with multiple levels of redundancy and the inherent survivability of an IP network. Proper planning and design are vital for high levels of availability, even when unforeseen circumstances arise. A disaster recovery plan should be developed to address what-if scenarios that can potentially disable the voice network. This plan should be reviewed at least quarterly, and it is recommended that tests of the plan be performed during maintenance windows. Auditors should review this plan for the following elements:

- Power backup and recovery strategy providing at least 30 minutes of emergency access to the phone system.

- Public Switched Telephone Network (PSTN) trunk redundancy and recovery. SIP backups or additional hardwired PSTN connections are useful as redundant connections. If SIP is used as the primary connection for external calls, plans should be in place for a SIP trunk backup through the PSTN in the event that an Internet connection providing the SIP trunk is out of service.

- Gateway redundancy in case of failure. Multiple gateways configured in Communications Manager to automatically take over for a failed router are recommended.

- Communications Manager redundancy in case of failure. Phones can be configured to connect to three Communications Managers for failover.

- Communications Manager Backup and recovery procedures for software failure.

UC Architecture Review

UC deployments can range from a small business running a UC500 for five phones in one location, to a multicluster Cisco UC Manager with hundreds of thousands of phones spanning the globe. As the size of a UC installation increases, scale definitely adds to the complexity of an assessment, but understanding the fundamentals of the technology can help breakdown the system into component parts. A UC system consists of the following components, each of which are described in more detail in the following:

- **Call Control:** Communications Manager or Communications Manager Express/Survivable Remote Site Telephony (SRST)

- **Protocols for VoIP:** H.323, Skinny Call Control Protocol, Session Initiation Protocol, Media Gateway Control Protocol, Real Time Protocol, d aSecure Real Time Protocol

- **IP network:** Transport for UC

- **Routers/gateways:** Terminated connections to the PSTN

- **Switches:** Network connectivity for voice endpoints

- **Firewalls and IPS:** Access controls, policy enforcement, and security event detection

- **Voice endpoints:** IP phones, soft phones, and conferencing systems

- **Application servers:** Contact Center, Unity voicemail, Presence, mobility, and third-party software integration to UC

Figure 12-2 shows how these components work together to provide UC services.

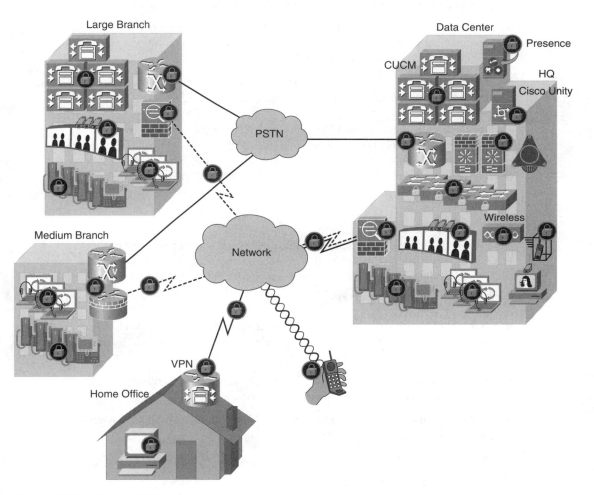

Figure 12-2 *Secure UC Deployment*

Unified Communications Fundamentals

VoIP technology employs a wide array of protocols and services to deliver voice across an IP network. Auditors need to be aware of the basics of how a call is constructed and the devices that are used for handling and transporting the call to its ultimate destination.

Cisco IP Telephony makes use of the following four primary protocols for signaling and call setup:

- **H.323:** H.323 is a standards-based suite of protocols that provides audio and video communications across an IP network.

- **MGCP:** Media Gateway Control Protocol (MGCP) is a protocol designed for gateway communications and utilization of voice ports connecting to the PSTN.

- **SCCP:** Skinny Client Control Protocol (SCCP) is a Cisco-developed protocol for communication between Cisco IP Phones and Cisco Communications Manager to set up calls between endpoints and the PSTN.

- **SIP:** Session Initiation Protocol (SIP) is a standards-based communication protocol that handles signaling and call setup between endpoints.

Each of these protocols uses Real Time Protocol (RTP) or the encrypted version Secure Real Time Protocol (SRTP) for the voice conversation portion of the call. Together, these protocols are the building blocks of a voice network. The following covers the key concepts of these protocols that auditors find useful when analyzing the security of UC.

H.323

H.323 is an ITU standard for voice and video communications across an IP network. H.323 is a framework that includes other protocols that handle all the details of call encoding/decoding, setup, teardown, and security for multimedia. The following are the primary sub protocols for H.323:

- **H.225/Q931:** Responsible for establishing connections between two H.323 endpoints, H.225/Q931 handles registration, admission control, bandwidth requirements, status, and teardown procedures for calls.

- **H.245 Control Signaling:** Used to manage the capabilities of codecs, ports used, and flow information for H.323 communications.

- **H.235:** Defines authentication, integrity, and encryption for H.323. There are three primary security profiles detailed:

  - **Annex D:** Baseline Security, voice encryption, and authentication.

  - **Annex E:** Signature Security, digital signatures for control messages.

  - **Annex F:** Hybrid Security, combined security features from Annex D and E and relies on PKI.

- **Audio codecs:** Used to encode and decode digital audio codecs. Commonly used codecs for Cisco voice are g.711 (64 kbps) and g729 (8 kbps).

- **Video codecs:** Handles video encoding and decoding for H.323.

The logical components used to enable H.323 communications include terminals, gateways, gatekeepers, and Multi-point Control Units (MCU). These functions can exist on a single device or as discreet components distributed throughout the network.

- **Terminals:** Endpoints in H.323 refer to receiving and transmitting stations such as phones and video conference units.

- **Gateways (GW):** Connect to the public switched telephone network (PSTN).

- **Gatekeepers (GK):** Responsible for call admission control, registration, and translations services for endpoints. Gatekeepers are typically used to control bandwidth and call volume across wide-area network (WAN) connections between branches or separate organizations.

- **MCU:** Multipoint conference units are used to connect two or more H.323 devices (terminal or gateways) together in a conference.

Figure 12-3 shows how these components are used in H.323.

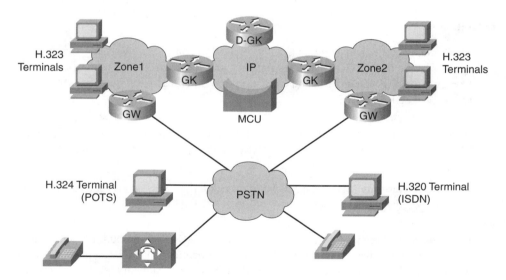

Figure 12-3   *H.323 Logical Components*

Basic H.323 call setup and flow uses H.225 for initial setup, and then H.245 for capabilities exchange and port setup for media transport. RTP is then used between endpoints for voice transport. Figure 12-4 shows a basic H.323 session between two gateways.

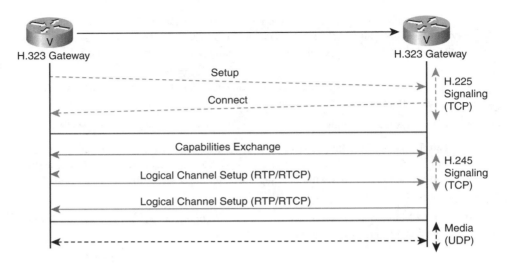

Figure 12-4   *H.323 Between Two Gateways*

MGCP

Media Gateway Control Protocol (MGCP) is used to control gateways connecting VoIP systems to the PSTN. MGCP handles signaling and call control while relying on Communications Manager to handle call state and other high-level functions. MGCP has two logical components:

- **Media Gateway Controller (MGC):** Also known as a call agent, MGC is responsible for control of the MGCP gateway. This function typically resides within Communications Manager.

- **MGCP Gateway (MG):** The MG interfaces with the PSTN and is used to terminate voice media traffic.

RTP is used for voice media transmission for MGCP. MGCP has no built-in security features and requires the configuration of IPsec for authentication and encryption. Figure 12-5 shows MGCP call setup between two media gateways and a media gateway controller.

SCCP

Cisco Skinny Client Control Protocol (SCCP) is a proprietary signaling technology for endpoint call control and setup. Skinny was designed to be a lightweight protocol for use with Communications Manager. When a call is placed, the IP phone uses SCCP to signal to Communications Manager to setup the call and signal the dialed endpoint to setup the media stream. SCCP signaling can be encrypted and authenticated to Communications Manager through Transport Layer Security (TLS).

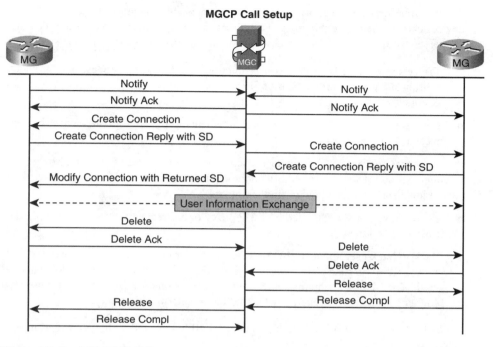

Figure 12-5   *MGCP Call Setup*

SIP

SIP is widely viewed as the standard protocol for voice, video, instant message, and presence. Based on HTTP and SMTP, SIP is text-based and sent in the clear over TCP or UDP port 5060. Encryption can be enabled for SIP with TLS on TCP port 5061. SIP handles only call control, leaving RTP to provide media transport. SIP has a number of logical elements that govern how the protocol operates; the primary elements of SIP are as follows:

- **User Agent (UA):** A SIP endpoint that creates or receives SIP messages, it can act as a client or server in a SIP conversation depending on whether it is initiating or receiving the session.

- **User agent client (UAC):** The UAC is the initiator for SIP and can be a user initialing a call or a proxy starting a session on behalf of a user.

- **User agent server (UAS):** The UAS is the receiving SIP entity and responds to SIP requests.

SIP endpoints consist of phones that can act as either a UAC or a UAS, depending on whether or not they are sending or receiving a call, and gateways that provide call control and translations to other services like H.323. SIP gateways and phones are fully supported by Communications Manager and can be used natively.

SIP uses four logical server entities to facilitate the establishment of SIP calls. While SIP devices can communicate directly to each other in a peer-to-peer fashion, the following SIP servers automate location services and communications to other domains.

■ **Proxy server (PS):** The proxy server function in SIP forwards requests and provides routing and policy enforcement of SIP sessions. Authentication of users and devices occurs here.

■ **Redirect server (RED):** Used to point SIP clients to the appropriate devices to complete a connection.

■ **Registrar server (REG):** A special case of the UAS that receives SIP Register requests and stores registered SIP endpoints in a database so that proxy servers and redirect servers know how to find endpoints.

■ **Location server (LOC):** Used by a SIP proxy or redirect server to query for SIP destination IP addresses.

■ **Back to back user agent (B2BUA):** Responsible for processing SIP requests and responses and can send those requests on to other domains outside of the local network. The B2BUA maintains control of the SIP session during the call and is used to connect SIP networks together while hiding the internal topologies.

Figure 12-6 shows how a call is set up between an IP phone and a SIP gateway using a proxy, location, and redirect server.

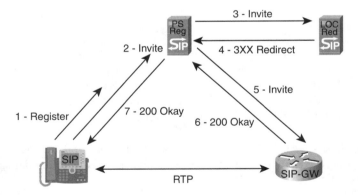

Figure 12-6   *SIP Call Setup to a Gateway*

Every device in a SIP network makes use of a Uniform Resource Identifier (URI) to identify user agents (endpoints) and is based on standard Internet addressing used in e-mail and web services. A URI is typically constructed as follows:

`sip:username:password.`

TLS encryption can be specified with SIPs. The URI is used in the invite message to initiate a call. The invite message is sent to the proxy server to locate the called party.

After the called party is located, the proxy server sends the invite to the called party and attempts to make a connection. After the user picks up, the call is acknowledged and an RTP stream is created for voice media. Figure 12-7 shows how a SIP call with a proxy is set up.

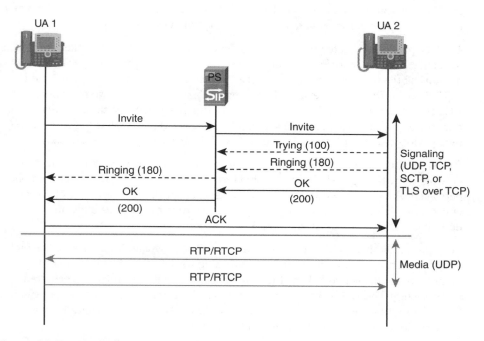

Figure 12-7 *SIP Call Setup with a Proxy*

Session Border Controller

Session Border Controller (SBC) is a logical demarcation point between two voice networks used for interconnecting and translating protocols. An SBC can support SIP, H.323, and MGCP signaling and is most commonly used with IP PSTN SIP trunks for interoperability and security. With SIP, an SBC operates as a B2BUA and controls signaling and media traffic. Cisco offers SBC services through Cisco Unified Border Elements as a software feature for gateway routers. An SBC can provide the following services:

- DoS Defense
- Internal topology hiding
- NAT and firewall traversal
- Protocol translation (codec and TLS)
- Quality of service

RTP and SRTP

RTP and RTCP (real-time control protocol) are VoIP media transmission protocols, and they run on top of UDP. RTP is responsible for voice transport across the network and is used between two devices (such as phones or a gateway) after the call has been set up by the Communications Manager. RTCP is used to embed RTP status messages to help monitor the voice stream for network traffic issues or error messages.

The RTP payload is created through codecs (coder/decoder) that sample audio and video to encode it for transmission. Digital signal processing is preformed on the voice endpoint using the G series standards from the International Telecommunications Union (ITU). Many different codecs provide varying levels of quality. The two most popular for UC networks are G.711 and G.729. The primary difference between the two codecs is in total packet size and sampling rate with G.711 using 64 Kbps sampling, resulting in 160-byte payloads, and G.729, which samples at 8 Kbps, generating 20-byte payloads.

RTP is sensitive to packet delay greater than 150 ms. Transmission of voice on an IP network must be kept below that threshold to prevent obvious lag times between one person speaking and the other person responding on a call. All processing of packets either through encryption or just passing from one router to another adds time to the delay budget.

Jitter can be another problem experienced by a UC deployment. Jitter refers to the problem of packets arriving at different times, affecting voice traffic reconstruction. Without proper QoS on the network, large file transfers can cause RTP traffic to be delivered inconsistently. This is usually compensated through buffering on the endpoint or gateway. RTCP uses timestamps on each voice packet, allowing the IOS to dynamically increase or decrease jitter buffering based on current conditions.

Voice communication doesn't tolerate RTP packet loss greater than 6 percent, which causes noticeable call quality degradation. Packet loss can occur when links are saturated or network devices are operating at high CPU levels. Network devices must have sufficient processor and memory reserves to adequately perform the task.

RTP does not provide any confidentiality or authentication functions natively, which leads to the development of Secure RTP (SRTP) as a mechanism to secure voice media transport in an IP network. To set up a secure call between two VoIP endpoints, media encryptions keys used to secure the voice media session are transmitted through signaling, which is also not natively encrypted. Because it doesn't provide much value to encrypt RTP just to send the encryption keys unencrypted, IPsec or TLS is used to secure the signaling path back to the Communications Manager or to gateways.

Call Processing

The VoIP protocols that you have been introduced to are the underlying technology that enables Unified Communications to work. IP phones typically use SCCP or Skinny for signaling and RTP for voice media. Communications Manager handles signaling to gateways for PSTN calls through SIP, H.323, or MGCP. From a high level, call processing operates in the same manner regardless of the protocols used in the network.

When users wants to make a phone call, they pick up the handset and initiate a process that uses a number of different protocols to set up the call and connect the IP phone to the destination party. Communications Manager is in the middle of this process and provides the intelligence for call routing and service connection. When a user picks up the handset, an off hook signal is sent to the Communications Manager to open a channel for sending the dialed digits. The user then dials the number he is trying to reach, and those digits are sent to Communications Manager. The dialed digits are compared to the dial plan, and if the digits match a destination, the call is processed further; if not, the user hears the reorder tone in the handset. After the call is matched to a destination, an alert signal to ring is sent to the called phone and a ringback tone is sent to the calling phone. After the called phone goes off hook, it signals Communications Manager to make the media connection. Communications Manager selects the ports and codecs and passes that information to the phones so that they can set up the RTP stream for communication. Figure 12-8 shows the communication process used for making a call between two IP phones.

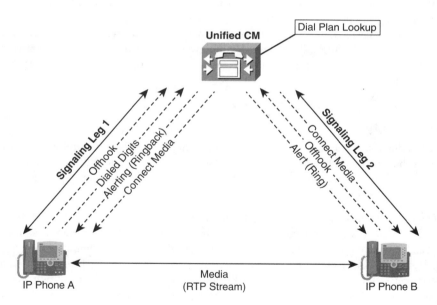

Figure 12-8   *Phone-to-Phone Call Setup*

Call setup to a gateway for connection to the PSTN operates in much the same way as between phones. Communications Manager brokers the call setup and handles all signaling between the phone and the gateway. The phone and the gateway communicate directly through RTP streams on the ports and codecs supplied through Communications Manager. Figure 12-9 shows a call setup to a gateway.

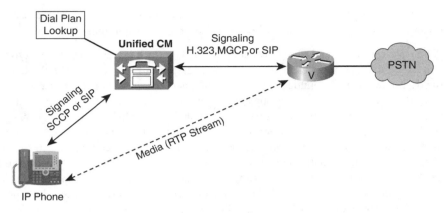

Figure 12-9   *Call Setup to Gateway*

Infrastructure Controls

Protecting the network infrastructure is the foundation of secure UC. Without strong controls to prevent network-based attacks, voice services can be compromised and confidential information exposed. Infrastructure controls involve switch security, access control lists (ACL) and firewalls, and intrusion prevention. Much of these topics are covered in detail in Chapter 7, "Infrastructure Security," but due to their criticality for secure voice, they are covered here with a UC focus.

Switch Security

Protecting the UC infrastructure starts at the switch level. Cisco has multiple security features that can be leveraged in the catalyst switch line that provides protection for the most common network-based security threats. The following features represent security best practices for voice networks.

The first general security requirement is to separate voice and data networks through VLAN segmentation. Separating voice and data networks creates different broadcast domains, which prevent users on the data network from directly communicating to voice infrastructure devices. This separation also allows for the insertion of firewalls and intrusion prevention systems to identify and stop malicious activity. Care must be taken to prevent *VLAN hopping*, which allows an attacker to gain access to the voice VLAN by leveraging an 802.1q trunk to communicate through the phone or natively on a trunk-enabled switch port. Figure 12-10 shows a switch configured with a voice and data VLAN and 802.1q pass-through disabled on the phone.

Disabling VLAN trunk capabilities on nontrunk ports is recommended for all direct access user-facing data connections to prevent someone from configuring her laptop for 802.1Q and attaching to any VLAN she chooses. Cisco IP phones use CDP to dynamically create an 802.1Q trunk for access to the voice/data VLANs, preventing the need to configure a static trunk.

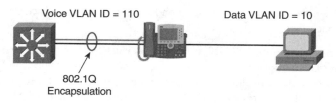

Figure 12-10   *VLAN Segmentation with 802.1Q*

Spanning tree is the mechanism that switches use to learn where to forward traffic to and create a loop-free Layer 2 network. Protecting spanning tree prevents an attacker from manipulating that topology and prevents topology changes that might cause an attacker to become the spanning tree root, thereby causing all voice traffic to be forwarded for capture. Cisco provides two powerful features, BPDU Guard and Root Guard, for protecting spanning tree and should be enabled to defend against these attacks:

- **BPDU Guard:** BPDU Guard prevents the switch from accepting BPDUs from user ports by automatically shutting them down. BPDUs are used to calculate the root bridge in a spanning tree and can be manipulated to reconfigure the forwarding topology of a VLAN.

- **Root Guard:** Root Guard prevents the root bridge from changing to an unapproved root bridge port. This feature enables the use of BPDUs to prevent loops at the port level while protecting the spanning tree root bridge path.

MAC flooding is another common attack used to force packet capture on a switch. The attacker floods the switch with bogus MAC addresses, filling up its address table databases. After the tables are exhausted, the switch forwards all packets to every port (instead of the ones that the traffic is destined for). In a voice network, this can be used to enable the capture and reconstruction of any conversation on that voice VLAN segment. Cisco helps address this problem through a switch feature called Dynamic Port Security. Dynamic Port Security configures the switch to learn a specified number of MAC addresses, limiting how many devices can communicate on the port and prevent the MAC address from port mapping table exhaustion. Setting the switch to only accept two MAC addresses provides access for the phone and a PC. On some older switches that do not use Cisco Discovery Protocol to dynamically configure the voice and data VLANs, a maximum of three MAC addresses need to be configured.

DHCP is an essential service in a UC environment that phones use both to learn how to communicate to the UC network and to pull down configuration and software image files from Communications Manager. An attacker can set up a rogue DHCP server closer to the requesting endpoints on the network (in the same VLAN) and beat the real DHCP server in responding to DHCP requests. This enables the attacker to control where a phone pulls its configuration files from, which gives the attacker the ability to ultimately control the phone itself. DHCP snooping is a switch feature that monitors DHCP requests and replies to map IP addresses assigned to the appropriate switch ports. It can also block rogue DHCP servers from responding to phone requests on the network, stopping these types of attacks.

Address Resolution Protocol (ARP) is used for devices to query the network for IP-to-MAC address resolution. In typical network communications, devices reply to ARPs, but devices also have the capability to announce their MAC address through an unsolicited ARP, aptly named *Gratuitous ARP (GARP)*. An attacker can send a GARP packet claiming to have the IP address of another endpoint (such as a phone) on the voice VLAN. The default behavior in TCP/IP is for all devices that receive the GARP to change their ARP tables with the newly learned IP-to-MAC address. Any traffic destined for the spoofed system flows to the attacker, allowing for sniffing or other mischief. This technique is often used for man-in-the-middle attacks. To combat this, Dynamic ARP Inspection can be configured on a Cisco switch to operate in conjunction with DHCP snooping to record the IP and MAC addresses of devices that receive IPs from a DHCP server. If an attacker attempts to send a GARP pretending to be another device, it is blocked by the switch because it does not match what the switch has recorded.

Spoofing an IP address is as easy as typing the address in the configuration settings on a network interface card. To prevent this, IP Source Guard can be configured to filter IP traffic based on addresses and MACs learned through DHCP snooping, and as manually configured addresses. Any attempt to communicate on the network with an address not learned from an approved DHCP server is blocked, which prevents an attacker from spoofing a legitimate endpoint.

Quality of service (QoS) features in Cisco switches help voice networks give voice traffic preference over data traffic to deliver consistent and predictable service. QoS is also useful for protecting voice from DoS attacks that flood the network in an attempt to starve voice traffic of bandwidth. Cisco switches have the AutoQoS and Smartports feature that dramatically simplifies configuration of QoS parameters for indentifying and queuing voice. Auto QOS limits signaling traffic to 36 k and media traffic to 320 k per port preventing a flooding attack against these services.

The best way to prevent attackers from getting on the voice VLAN without authorization is through 802.1x. 802.1x is supported on new IP phones and many of the generation 2 phones, and it provides port-level authentication and authorization through certificates installed on the IP phone. Current model Cisco switches support multiple domain authentication, allowing 802.1x to authenticate and authorize both the voice VLAN and the PC port separately. With 802.1x configured for the voice VLAN, attackers cannot communicate without valid credentials.

ACLs and Firewalling

ACLs can be enabled on switch VLANs to control endpoint communication in the Voice VLAN itself. Creating static ACLs for UC is not for the faint of heart and can be difficult to manage at the endpoint level. UC use a wide range of protocols that open dynamic port ranges for call signaling and media transport. Protecting these systems by limiting access to only those ports and services required for communication is an important security practice but can be challenging without intelligent firewalls. ACLs can be used to limit access to specific ports, but in the case of voice audio transport, the range of ports used can be from port 16384–32767, which would be a large range to leave open with static ACLs. These ports can change somewhat between software releases, so auditors should review the required ports whenever assessing ACLs for UC.

Cisco provides a list of the ports used by UC systems that auditors might find useful in the analysis of ACLs, which can be found at http://www.cisco.com/en/US/products/sw/voicesw/ps556/prod_maintenance_guides_list.html.

An easier way to manage an access control solution is to use UC-aware firewalls to protect the UC environment. Firewalls used for UC need to understand signaling and voice protocols to dynamically open and close ports as needed. Cisco offers these application layer gateway features in the ASA, FWSM, and IOS firewall, and they are recommended for protecting call control and voice VLAN communications.

Cisco firewall platforms understand UC protocols and can enforce protocol conformance to prevent fuzzing attacks that send malformed VoIP packets aimed at disrupting call control and signaling. SIP and SCCP inspection can drop these types of attacks at the firewall before it has a chance to impact call setup and control on the Communications Manager. DoS protection is also available in Cisco firewalls by setting limits on the number and speed of registrations.

Regardless of the use of ACLs or firewalls, the following access rules for Voice VLAN communications should be in place to protect the UC environment:

■ Permit phone-to-phone communication via UDP (16384-32767).

■ Block nonessential communication to the voice VLAN from the nonvoice network.

■ Block nonvoice traffic to a UC gateway except for management traffic from approved networks and hosts.

■ Permit DHCP, DNS, and TFTP to approved addresses only.

■ Permit web access to and from phones to Call Manager and required applications only.

■ Permit ICMP to phone, gateway, and network management stations only.

IPS

Cisco IPS technologies can be deployed through the network to gain visibility into malicious behavior. Using IPS to protect the voice network provides instant defense against multilayer attacks that target the voice gateway infrastructure and the servers that manage call control and registration. Cisco IPS has UC-specific signatures in addition to a wide range of LAN, application, and malware attack signatures. Some of the defensive capabilities present in the platform are as follows:

■ SIP attacks

- Communications Manager DoS attacks

- Failed login attempts

- CTL overflow attempts

Gateway Protection

The gateway is one of the most important parts of a UC network. If an attacker can gain control of the gateway, he can directly interface with all of the company's inbound and outbound phone conversations. Defending the gateway from these types of attacks is relatively straight forward, if the network is segmented properly and the gateway is in a trusted part of the network. A UC gateway is also a router, which means that good security practices for routers apply, such as using only secure protocols for management. Additionally, the gateway should be protected by a firewall, either integrated with the router or at the demarcation between the voice network and the data network.

Firewall protection of the gateway can be deployed in two ways, with both voice media and signaling flowing through the firewall (gateway behind the firewall), or the firewall just protecting signaling between the gateway and Communications Manager leaving the voice media traffic to flow from the endpoints to the gateway directly bypassing the firewall.

If the gateway is behind a firewall, all phones need to communicate through the firewall, increasing processing load on the firewall, but this does enable DoS prevention of voice media traffic and protection against signaling attacks. Because the firewall has to monitor all voice communications, care must be taken to keep CPU usage below a recommended value of 60 percent.

Firewalls protecting Communications Manager and signaling to the gateway protects only the signaling flow and does not monitor the voice RTP streams. This can reduce the load on the firewall, but it gives up some of the protection afforded by the firewall's inspection capabilities. If this design is used, the switched infrastructure must use QoS to rate limit signaling per port to prevent media processing DoS attacks against the gateway.

Voice protocols should be blocked from direct access to the data side of the network whenever possible. For soft phone or phone access requirements that don't allow for voice VLAN access, utilization of phone proxy is recommended.

Site to Site

UC networks spanning multiple sites must provide for secure transport of media traffic and signaling between telephone networks. Encryption and authentication allows this traffic to traverse the Internet in a secure fashion. Chapter 10, "Secure Remote Access," covered VPN technologies in depth and can be used as a reference for auditors to ensure that confidentiality and authentication are enabled.

Wireless

Voice over wireless adds mobility to VoIP and inherits all of the security concerns of providing secure data communication across a wireless LAN. The same threats that exist for wired data communications are also present for wireless, but without the requirement for an attacker to find a physical data port to connect to the network. Any attacker with a good antenna can attempt to compromise a wireless LAN from significant distance away. Security capabilities in Cisco wireless LANs can greatly reduce the risk of compromise if properly implemented. Chapter 7 covers wireless security features in more detail. When assessing voice over wireless solutions, an auditor should review the implementation for the following good security practices:

- Voice VLAN bridged to voice only Service Set Identifier (SSID).

- Data VLAN used for user traffic.

- Wired Equivalent Protocol (WEP) is not used.

- Uses WiFi Protected Access (WPA) 2 with Advanced Encryption Standard (AES) encryption.

- Authentication Authorization and Accounting (AAA) is enabled.

- 802.1x is enabled for authentication and setup of encryption keys.

- EAP-fast, EAP-TLS, and PEAP are all Extensible Authentication Protocol (EAP) types that can be used for 802.1x on VoWLAN. EAP-TLS is the preferred protection mechanism.

- Firewalling or access control lists are present to limit voice VLAN access from wireless clients.

- IPS is used to monitor wireless voice networks for malicious activities.

Call Control Protection

Call control is like the central nervous system of a UC deployment. Cisco offers two platforms that provide call control: Cisco Unified Communications Manager (CUCM) and Communications Manager Express (CME). CUCM is meant to provide highly scalable UC call control with multiple levels of redundancy and includes the latest UC features. CME is positioned for the small-to-medium enterprise or branch and has a subset of the features available in CUCM. CME operates as a software feature on a router and can include gateway functionality. This section covers security requirements for both platforms.

Communications Manager Hardening

The first areas to assess are hardening features of CUCM and CME. Table 12-1 outlines the security practices that you should follow to protect the call control platforms.

Table 12-1   *Communications Manager Security Practices*

CUCM Security Practices	CME Security Practices
Use built-in firewall to prevent access to unused services.	SSH.
Use CSA on windows platforms (installed by default on Linux appliances).	HTTPS for management.
Ensure that the latest patches are applied.	Disable CDP.
Automatic phone registration is disabled.	Enable FW features for nonvoice ports.
Use appliance mode on Windows platforms.	IOS image is free from known vulnerabilities.
	Automatic phone registration is disabled.

Authentication, Integrity, and Encryption

Enforcing endpoint authentication, integrity, and encryption is an important aspect of providing secure UC. All businesses should be concerned with the loss of phone conversation confidentiality and need to integrate controls to reduce exposure. Authentication and encryption can add another layer of complexity to the voice deployment that many organizations avoid for fear of increased difficulty in troubleshooting and the overhead encryption places on the UC infrastructure. Cisco has made great strides in simplifying the configuration of encryption, making it a recommended practice for highly sensitive job roles.

Cisco uses TLS and SRTP to authenticate, provide integrity, and encrypt voice in a UC environment. TLS is used to protect the signaling component and authenticate the phone to Communications Manager, whereas SRTP is used to protect the voice media transmission. The two working together can provide end-to-end encryption and authentication services for all voice endpoints in the network that support it.

For authentication, Cisco uses X.509v3 digital certificates for phones to prove their identity when registering to Communications Manager Services. These certificates come in two forms:

- **Manufacturer Installed Certificates (MIC):** Loaded on phones at the factory by Cisco, MICs provide each phone a unique preloaded identity. These certificates are validated by Cisco root certificates and are stored in a protected, unerasable portion of storage on the phone.

- **Locally Significant Certificates (LSC):** Installed by organizations wanting the use of their own certificate authorities to authenticate individual devices or users. Certificate Authority Proxy Function (CAPF) is an optional service that is enabled on the Communications Manager to provide LSC certificates to phones.

Phones also need to know what devices and certificates they should trust in the network. To accomplish this, phones utilize a Certificate Trust List (CTL), which is a preconfigured file that lists all of the certificates for the devices the phone should trust. This list includes Communications Manager, TFTP server for configuration files, CAPF, Unity Voice Mail, Gateways, and other services. The CTL file is created by a utility that is run on the administrative workstation and then delivered to the phone during boot up through TFTP. All phones in a Communications Manager cluster have the same CTL file.

For secure signaling between the Communications Manager and IP phones, TLS is used. TLS relies on the phone and Communications Manager certificates to mutually authenticate both devices and create an encrypted tunnel between the two devices. HMAC-SHA-1 is used to authenticate and provide integrity for the session. AES-128-CBC encryption delivers protection for session keys, DTMF tones, and other call setup and feature data exchanges.

Media encryption is handled through SRTP, which enables the encryption and authentication of voice communications. Just like TLS, SRTP uses HMAC-SHA-1 for authentication and integrity and AES-128-CM for encryption. The keys used for encrypting the RTP streams are generated by Communications Manager and sent to the phones through signaling, which should be protected by TLS. It is possible to configure SRTP without signaling encryption, which enables an unencrypted view of the keys used for media encryption if an attacker had a sniffer on the LAN segment. This enables an attacker the ability to decrypt the media stream because he would have access to the keys.

SRTP is used for encrypting voice traffic to gateways, which ensures that outbound calls are encrypted as voice traffic makes its way to the PSTN. CUCM sends SRTP session keys in clear text to MGCP and H.323 gateways and does not use TLS, so it is recommended you enable IPsec encryption to protect the signaling path to gateways to prevent the compromise of session keys. The three scenarios where IPsec encryption is recommended are as follows:

- Intracluster signaling between Communications Managers

- Intercluster signaling between multiple Communications Manager clusters to communicate to each other

- Signaling to MGCP and H.323 gateways

IPsec can be configured natively on Communications Manager to secure signaling to gateways, but this is performed in software and impact performance of the Communications Manager. Communications Manager can use certificates or preshared keys for IPsec authentication. Where Communications Manager performance is a concern, it is recommended you utilize a separate router or firewall to perform IPsec so that Communications Manager can devote resources to handling calls.

TLS proxy enables the addition of the ASA firewall to a phone's CTL, which allows the phone to create a TLS session for signaling directly with the ASA. The ASA creates a TLS session to the call manager for the phone completing the connection and sits in the middle of the connection. This enables the ASA to inspect encrypted signaling to enforce policy and protect the UC environment from attacks. TLS proxy is only for decrypting TLS-encrypted signaling; SRTP is not terminated at the ASA but passed on to the endpoint directly without inspection.

Phone Proxy

Phone Proxy is an ASA firewall feature that is designed to support remote access for IP phones and soft phones by leveraging TLS/SRTP to create a secure connection directly to the ASA. With Phone Proxy there is no need to provision a router or other VPN device at the phone's location to provide a secure phone extension across the Internet. Users can plug their phones into any broadband connection and access the corporate Communications Manager as if they were sitting in the office. All media and signaling is sent to the ASA and forwarded back to the UC network. Certificates can be used for authentication making the connection to the ASA automatic and transparent to users.

Secure SIP Trunking

The term *trunk* refers to the connection between a UC system and the PSTN or the direct interconnection between UC systems. Trunking has changed dramatically from the days when organization pulled large bundles of wires into their facilities, to today's use of IP across the same network that data travels over. SIP has taken off over the last few years and become the open standard for interconnecting different vendors' phone systems over IP and an alternative method for provisioning PSTN phone service. Why pull separate wires and spend more money for a physical connection when you can use IP to deliver your phone service? In the same manner in which VoIP has had to develop solutions for security, SIP has had to address vulnerabilities in its deliver mechanism.

The following are a few general SIP trunk security practices:

■ Don't terminate SIP trunks directly to Communications Manager if at all possible because it might be exposed to attack. If using CME, configure IOS firewall to protect against SIP attacks.

■ All SIP trunks should terminate to a Session Border Controller, provided on a Cisco network through Cisco Unified Border Element (CUBE).

■ Hide internal topology to prevent data leakage. With CUBE, calls appear to originate and terminate from the router hiding the internal topology of the UC network. NAT alone does not do this because of addressing information inside the SIP messages.

■ Configure access control features to prevent access from unexpected sources and application layer firewalling to dynamically open ports for the duration of a call and closing them on call completion.

■ Secure authentication of SIP through Digest Authentication to prevent unauthorized users from using the SIP trunk service.

- Use TLS encryption of SIP signaling and SRTP encryption of media.

SIP can be a cost-effective way for an organization to provide PSTN access in a secure manner with the appropriate safeguards in place. Two of the most common controls for protecting a SIP trunk connection are firewalling and the CUBE IOS feature.

ASA and IOS Firewalls

A firewall is necessary for SIP to enforce policy and protect the SIP connection from attack. The ASA firewall can inspect a SIP connection for policy violations and block unapproved actions. The IOS firewall software is available as a licensed feature on Cisco IOS routers and provides many of the same inspection and application layer gateway functions available in the ASA firewall. The following are some of the capabilities for enforcing policy available in the ASA and IOS firewall:

- Restricts malicious traffic

- Enforces header fields

- Restricts forbidden headers

- Checks header parameters

- Discards nonSIP traffic on SIP ports

- Provides logging of SIP communication

- Protects against DoS attacks through rate limiting SIP INVITE and REGISTER messages

- Limits the number of active calls

- Blacklists and whitelists callers and those called

- SIP command filtering

- SIP URI filtering

- SIP version filtering

- SIP header fields

- Hides endpoint software versions

- Checks for buffer overflow attacks in SIP messages

- Blocks SIP IM activity

CUBE

Cisco Unified Border Element is a licensed feature that is designed to act as a *Session Border Control* in SIP. A Session Border Control is a demarcation between two networks and acts as an interconnection between an organization and telephony service providers.

CUBE provides a number of features for protecting SIP and the UC environment. The following list highlights some of the key features:

- H.323-to-SIP transcoding

- IP address and UC topology hiding

- Secure call connectivity between organizations

- Terminates the SIP trunk from the service provider

- Call Admission Control

- Protocol normalization (enforce protocol standards)

- SIP registration

- SIP Message Digest Authentication

- DoS protection

Toll Fraud Prevention

Toll fraud can cost a company a lot of money and is difficult to prevent without the appropriate controls in place. There are many methods used to perpetrate toll fraud and can occur inside the company or outside. The good news is that most toll fraud can be prevented by configuring the phone systems to block the most common attack methods. Some examples of toll fraud techniques are:

- **Transfer from Voicemail:** Many businesses provide an external phone number employees can dial to check voicemail when on the road or at home. If the voicemail system is configured to allow the transfer of a call externally, then the user could be presented with a dial tone and be able to make long-distance calls to other parties.

- **Call Forward All:** The Call Forward All setting on the phone allows for the redirection of phone calls to a specific number, such as a cell phone or other number the user would more likely be at. If a phone system is configured to allow call forwarding to long-distance numbers, any call that comes in to the extension is forwarded to the toll number.

- **Social engineering:** Scams and social engineering are always an issue, and phone scams have been around for many years. Tricking a user or an admin into transferring a call to a specific number, such as extension 901, causes the phone system to transfer the caller to an outside line where he can dial any number he chooses.

- **Insider facilitation:** Sometimes employees make poor decisions about corporate resources and allow friends and family to take advantage of the company's telephone service by transferring a friend's call to a long-distance number.

Reducing the risk of toll fraud is something every auditor should assess when analyzing the security of a UC system. The following toll fraud prevention controls for

Communications Manager, gateways, and voicemail should be implemented whenever possible.

Communications Manager

CUCM has three primary methods for controlling the numbers a user can dial:

- **Route pattern:** A route pattern is used to map dialed numbers to gateways for access to the PSTN. A route pattern filter is configured to deny specific digit patterns from being sent to a gateway.

- **Partition:** Used to logically separate route patterns by location and call type. For example, calls matching the area code 941 can be handled by the Sarasota, FL, partition. Partitions can also define time restrictions.

- **Calling search space:** Comprised of the various route patterns that apply to a specific gateway or service such as voicemail, handling calls for that partition of dialed numbers.

These mechanisms are used to define what services can be dialed, what gateways can be used, and when they can be used, as well as preventing specific numbers from being dialed. The following are good security practices for using these controls in CUCM:

- **Call Forward All Calling Search Space:** This calling search space controls the numbers to which a phone extension can be forwarded.

- **Restrict Applications Calling Search Space:** Many applications that interoperate with Communications Manager have the capability to forward calls. Limit the capability for applications to transfer or forward to unapproved numbers.

- **Restrict Voice Mail Calling Search Space:** Can be used to restrict where a voicemail call can be forwarded to through Communications Manager.

- **Route Pattern Filtering:** List of digits that can be blocked. For example, this can stop 900/976 calls and accidental dialing of international exchanges to the Caribbean (649, 809, 284, and 876).

- **After Hours Restrictions:** Partitions can be configured to have different outgoing dialing capabilities based on the time of day, also known as time of day routing. During business hours, calls can be routed to the PSTN; after hours, they are blocked.

- **Restrict External Transfers:** Restricting external transfers prevents users from forwarding a call to external parties. Some organizations might want to enable users to forward a call to a cell phone or other local location, but prevent forwarding to long distance or international numbers.

- **Conferencing Restrictions:** Communications Manager can be configured to drop conference calls after the individual that set up the call has disconnected from the meeting. This can help to prevent external conference attendees from staying on the conference bridge after the call has ended, tying up resources.

Client Matter Code (CMC) and Forced Authorization Code (FAC) are other mechanisms that are useful for controlling long-distance dialing and identifying toll fraud.

- **Client Matter Codes:** The CMC is configured through route patterns to create a record of calls through the use of billing codes for specific number patterns, such as when a lawyer calls a client and needs to track the length of the call for billing purposes. When the user dials a matching number, he is prompted for a code that is assigned to call categories, groups, departments, or individual users. This is useful for internal tracking of the number called, the length of the call, both for billing purposes and to monitor individual user calling habits.

- **Forced Authorization Codes:** Users must enter an authorization code to dial specific number patterns (such as long distance numbers). The authorization code can be useful for identifying individual users and allows for reporting by code for toll fraud detection. When the code entered is invalid, the information is recorded in CDR, creating a record of potential code guessing attempts.

Communications Manager Express toll fraud prevention follows the same concepts as CUCM and makes use of features in IOS to manage where, when, and how users can make calls. Following is a list of good CME toll fraud prevention controls:

- **After Hours Restrictions:** CME can be configured to prevent after-hours calling to restricted numbers.

- **Transfer Pattern:** Blocks digits that can be used for transferring calls to prevent dialing of 900 numbers and other prohibited calling destinations.

- **Call Forward Max Length:** This control specifies the maximum number of dialed digits to which a call can be forwarded.

- **No Auto-Reg-Ephone:** By default, CME auto registers any phone that it connects to. Configuring No Auto-Reg-Ephone prevents this function and reduces the risk of automatically adding rogue extensions.

- **Call Activity Monitoring and History Logging:** This can be configured to record information on all calls placed and received by CME. This feature works in conjunction with Cisco unity express and is useful for spotting suspicious phone calls.

- **Translation Rules:** Controls should be configured to block unapproved calling patterns.

Gateways

CME and IOS gateways share a common heritage and inherit many of the same configuration capabilities for preventing toll fraud. For small environments, CME handles call control and gateway functionality in the same device. The following features apply to both uses:

- Class of restriction is used on gateways and CME to control the types of numbers a user can dial for a given port or ports connecting to the PSTN. Each user is assigned a specific class of restriction list, or corlist, depending on the approved dialing capabilities. For instance, a manager can dial local numbers, 911, 800 numbers, and long distance, but office personnel can only dial 911, 800 numbers, and local calls. Each user's phone is configured with a corlist that includes dialing rights. Dialpeers are how gateways know which port or destination to send a particular call based on the digits dialed. The corlist is then applied to a dialpeer, which matches the numbers that the user is trying to call. If the dialpeer corlist includes the user's group, then the user is allowed to make the call, if not the call is blocked.

- Disable Secondary dial tone on voice ports.

- Use ACLS to allow only authorized devices to connect to the gateway through H.323 or SIP.

- Configure explicit permitted destination patterns and not wildcards.

Voice Mail

Cisco offers Unity Voice Mail for enterprise voicemail and Unity Express for smaller CME deployments. Toll fraud is possible through voicemail if not configured to prevent exploitation. The following are good practices for preventing Unity and CUE Toll Fraud:

- Configure call restriction tables to block calls to the international operator.

- Block international and long-distance access for those users in the organization who are not allowed to make these types of calls.

- Restrict numbers that can be dialed through the system transfer feature.

Unity Voice Mail security practices include the following:

- Don't allow external transfers in auto attendant scripts or limit the numbers to which auto attendant is allowed to transfer.

- Configure CUE restriction tables to define the call patterns that are allowed or denied for the following services:

  - Fax

  - Cue live reply

  - Message notification

  - Nonsubscriber message delivery

Application Controls

Integration of applications that extend services to Cisco UC technologies is one of the reasons customers invest in Cisco. Cisco also produces applications for UC-like presence, mobility, and the contact center. Each application can be run on different platforms and integrates with the telephony solution in a multitude of ways. There simply is not enough room to cover each of the applications in detail. However, a few good practices apply to every application that is integrated with UC to maintain a strong security posture:

■   Use of encrypted signaling and media transport should be implemented whenever possible. This sometimes breaks applications that were not designed for encrypted media, or as in the case of call monitoring applications, might not be possible to encrypt. Compensating controls should be in place in these instances to reduce the risk of eavesdropping.

■   Each application should use HTTPS for management and user interaction where possible.

■   Use LDAP for user authentication and strong passwords or pins whenever possible.

■   Harden application servers by removing unneeded services, using host firewalls, and making sure all patches are properly applied.

■   Use hardware firewalls and intrusion prevention technologies to monitor and stop attacks against the application when possible. Cisco provides guidance on firewall requirements for each application and includes required port numbers for firewall rules.

Voice Endpoint Controls

Cisco phones are advanced devices that operate like a PC with the ability to browse the web and interactive with application servers. The phone also operates like a switch for automatic VLAN separation through 802.1q. Phones have a number of security enhancements to reduce the risk of the phone being compromised. Auditors should assess phone configuration to determine whether these features have been enabled.

■   Isolation of the voice VLAN from data VLAN on the phone to prevent VLAN hopping attacks on the PC port.

■   Ensure that PC port monitoring on the phone for voice traffic is disabled.

■   Disable unused PC ports on the phone to prevent unauthorized access, especially in public areas such as lobbies.

■   Enable gratuitous ARP protection to prevent the phone from updating its ARP tables automatically. This is often used for man-in-the-middle attacks.

■   Disable the internal phone web server if XML push applications are not used.

■   Create VLAN ACLS to restrict access to the internal phone web server to authorized addresses only form applications that require access.

■   Configure the phone to not allow users to access the network settings configuration page on the phone so that topology information and addresses are not disclosed.

■   Ensure signed phone software images and signed configuration files are enabled on Communications Manager.

- Authenticate and authorize phones through digital certificates and 802.1x when possible.

- Enable encryption where feasible to prevent eavesdropping for signaling through TLS, and SRTP media encryption of the voice conversation.

- Remote Access of phones should use phone proxy for encrypted service and certificate based authentication to the ASA firewall.

Monitoring and Management

Monitoring and management of UC is an important aspect of security to ensure uptime and spot anomalies that might be the result of an attacker trying to compromise the voice system. Cisco offers a suite of products to assist with administration and operations.

CDR Analysis and Reporting (CAR) can be used to run reports on quality of service, traffic utilization, user call volume, billing information from FAC and CMC, and gateway utilization. CDR is a great tool for detecting toll fraud and abnormal calling patterns. The following reports are available through CAR:

- Top phone usage by charge code or duration

- Top phone usage by number of calls

- Gateway usage summary

- Gateway usage detail

- Conference bridge usage

- Voice mail usage

Real Time Monitoring Tool is a performance and troubleshooting tool offered for free as a client for CUCM. Although its primary function is to monitor the health of the UC environment, it offers reporting capabilities that can be useful in monitoring security events.

- Integrated trace and Syslog viewer

- OS monitoring CPU, memory, and services

- Failed authentications

- Malicious call trace

- Number of registered devices increased

- Number of registered gateways increased

The Cisco UC Management Suite is a comprehensive management package for all aspects of UC operations, deployment, and maintenance. This suite consists of the following:

- Provisioning Manger

  - Provisions users and services through single interface

- Initial deployment through templates and bulk import

- Policy-based workflow for management

- Multiple levels of access for admins

- Audit and track changes for policy adherence

- Operations Manager

  - Real-time monitoring of all UC devices, endpoints, and links

  - Graphical view for fault isolation

  - Automatic notification through e-mail, pager, and SMS

  - Filters and thresholds for critical events

- Service Manager

  - Voice quality measurements and reporting

  - Alerting on MOS, Codec, endpoint, and phone type

- Service Monitor

  - Historical reporting of trunk, feature, and call volume

  - Reporting on service quality, and availability

MARS can also provide correlation of voice network security events form firewalls, IPS, routers, and switches.

Technical Testing

There are literally hundreds of VoIP security testing and hacking tools available for free on the Internet, which makes this section more about the aspects of VoIP security testing that auditors should be focused on as opposed to a review of specific tools. A number of books cover fuzzing and advanced attack techniques and provide detail on protocol weaknesses used to exploit voice networks. This section is intended to cover some of the key areas where technical testing should be conducted when assessing a voice network.

VLAN Separation

If attackers can't connect to the voice VLAN, then they are significantly limited in their abilities to attack the voice infrastructure and call control functions. Auditors should test whether or not the voice and data VLANs are adequately separated.

Using simple ping testing and NMAP scans, the auditor can test to see if the data network can directly interact with the voice network. The boundaries between the voice and data VLANs should be firewalled, with access granted only to applications with which users are authorized to interact. Voicemail and user-configurable phone parameters on

Communications Manager might be reachable from the data VLAN and should use HTTPS when possible.

One of the easiest ways to test for voice VLAN separation is to simply plug a laptop into the back of a phone and determine whether the assigned VLAN is separate from the one used by the IP phone. This might seem unnecessary, but a surprising number of voice deployments have segments that do not use voice VLANs, leaving phones and users directly connected.

If the voice VLAN is deployed, auditors should then check if the phones have been configured to prevent VLAN hopping, by sending 802.1q tagged packets directly to the phone pc port destined for the voice VLAN. The phone should drop the packets and prevent access to the voice VLAN.

Another test that the auditors should perform is to assess switch port security by unplugging the IP phone and connecting the laptop to the port instead. Again, using 802.1q, the auditor should test to see if they can communicate to the voice VLAN with standard 802.1q trunking. The port should not allow non-phones to create 802.1q connections directly. Phones use CDP to auto-configure the voice and data VLAN when they connect. If the attacker can craft CDP packets, then there is a potential that they can gain access to the voice VLAN by simulating a phone's auto-configuration process. IOS software, which runs on catalyst switches, has been updated to use other characteristics in addition to CDP as a mechanism for determining if a phone is present. A switch can look for the presence of in-line power and full duplex port settings to better identify whether or not a legitimate IP phone is connecting. A useful tool for testing this protective functionality, VoIP Hopper, simulates a number of Cisco IP phones and can automatically configure the laptop to attach to a voice VLAN by spoofing CDP and the Mac address of a phone. If successful, the auditor is placed into the voice VLAN in the same manner the phone would and have full access to the voice network. Figure 12-11 shows VoIP hopper gaining access to an unprotected Voice VLAN by spoofing a Cisco IP phone.

The best method for preventing unauthorized access to the switch port is the use of 802.1x to authenticate the IP phone to the switch. If a phone is using 802.1x, a legitimate certificate must be presented before the device is given access to the voice VLAN. Xtest is a tool useful for testing 802.1x authentications in VoIP environments and can be used to assess certificate strength and mutual authentication between Communications Manager and the IP phone.

Soft phones might be deployed on laptops or desktops and need access from the data side of the network to the voice side. This type of connection should always be encrypted, and an ASA phone proxy to protect and terminate voice traffic should be present. Auditors should ensure that soft phones are securely configured.

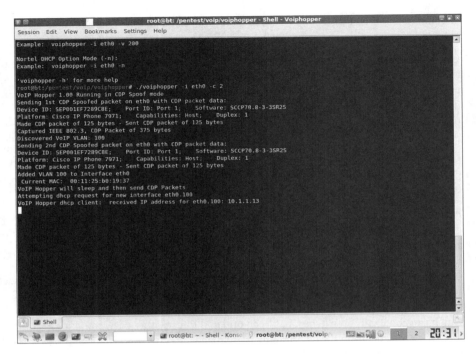

Figure 12-11 *VoIP Hopper Testing Voice VLAN Protection*

Other areas of consideration include the following:

- Switch management access (span ports)

- Spanning tree topology modification

- MITM mitigation

- DHCP server protection

- TFTP server protection

Eavesdropping

The best mechanism for preventing eavesdropping is to encrypt signaling and voice media streams. The auditor should check to see that voice encryption is enabled for sensitive employee roles and executives. An easy way to test for enabled encryption is to examine the phone and look for the Shield or Lock icon displayed during an encrypted call. The Shield icon tells the user that signaling is encrypted and authenticated, but the media stream is not. The Lock icon tells the user that both signaling and media encryption are enabled.

Without encryption, soft phone clients are vulnerable to eavesdropping. All soft phone users should use encryption and preferably terminate to an ASA running phone proxy.

Voice sniffing can be accomplished with Wireshark through simple packet capture of voice streams. Wireshark even provides an integrated facility for saving the captured voice stream as a wave file for easy playback. Tools such as Cain and Abel can record voice calls and have the capability to perform MAC flooding attacks on switches to allow for the sniffing of other users on the same VLAN. Cisco provides protection against these types of attacks through port security features that limit the number of MAC addresses that can be learned through a single port. The auditor should test that this feature is enabled and can error disable the port if MAC flooding is attempted.

UCSniff is an all-in-one tool that greatly simplifies the testing of eavesdropping prevention controls and allows for the recording and playback of both voice and video in a UC environment. Not only does the tool sniff voice and video, but it also automates VLAN hopping and VLAN discovery. Some the capabilities of this tool are:

- Support for all major voice codecs

- Support for H.264 video

- GARP attacks

- TFTP man-in-the-middle attacks

UCSniff is shown in Figure 12-12 gaining access to a voice VLAN, performing ARP spoofing, and recording a live VoIP conversation. This application can test all aspects of endpoint security and should definitely be part of an auditor's tool kit.

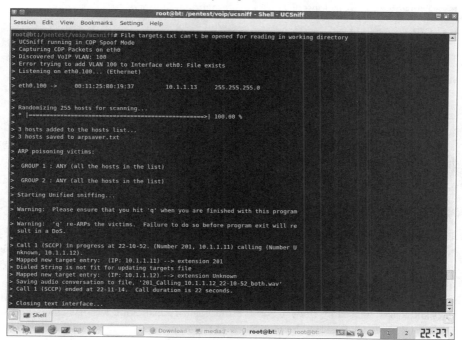

Figure 12-12 *UCSniff Testing Eavesdropping Protection Controls*

Gateway

Gateways to the PSTN should be protected, with restrictions on the devices to which they allow connections. Running MAP on a gateway can indicate what ports are available and help identify mistakes in hardening the gateway from attack. After the services have been mapped, auditors should attempt to make direct calls through SIP or H.323 to see whether the gateway allows it through. IPsec should be configured on the gateway for signaling that would prevent direct connection without the appropriate authentication methods. With SIP, UDP port 5060 is commonly used. Auditors should check to see whether message digest authentication has been configured. There are numerous methods for attacking SIP, but proper authentication and access rules can reduce the risk of unauthorized use of PSTN connections.

Toll Fraud

Testing toll fraud controls involves reviewing and assessing dial plans and calling restrictions for different classes of users. Auditors should review dial plan configuration for adherence to phone usage policies. Auditors should test the following controls:

■   Trunk-to-trunk transfers

■   Call Forward All to unapproved numbers

■   Transfers of calls to long distance or international numbers

■   IVR Script External Transfer capabilities

■   Voicemail transfer to long distance or international numbers

■   Prevention of commonly abused area codes and pay services such as 900 numbers and 809 scams

If forced authorization codes are used, they should not be easily guessed or sequential and should have a sufficient number of digits to prevent brute forcing. A user's or group's FAC should be changed on a regular basis and be treated like any other password.

Monitoring and Incident Detection

Detecting attacks against UC requires a combination of typical network security-monitoring tools and techniques and voice-specific monitoring applications. While performing testing of the various security controls, logs should have been generated for invalid login attempts and port security features used to detect VLAN hopping. Security Incident Management products such as MARS play an important role in consolidating the various logs and alerts created by firewall and IPS that identify malicious activity against the UC. On the UC side, CDR should be monitored to track call usage and display any invalid FAC attempts. Monitoring service levels and packet delay are ways to find problem areas that could be related to attack attempts. Invalid registration or denied attempts to connect to UC resources from areas of the network that have no need to directly connect should be investigated. Auditors should review documented incident-handling procedures for suspected voice attacks.

Checklist

Assessment Area	Assessment Technique
People	
Are UC policies adequate for the organizations level of risk?	Review applicable UC policies, such as acceptable use, pin and access credentials, remote voice access, long-distance service, voice mail, and video.
Has a UC risk assessment been conducted?	Review UC risk assessment documentation to determine whether appropriate threats and vulnerabilities have been identified.
Have UC security controls and standards been selected?	Review documentation of required UC security controls for firewalls, VLAN separation, access control, security monitoring, encryption, gateways, voice trunking, and remote access.
Process	
Have user roles been classified by security and service requirements?	Review role classifications to determine whether appropriate security measures are applied (such as CEOs and finance officers who require encryption on all calls). Review user service authorization (long distance, video, conferencing, and applications).
Are change-management procedures followed for moves, adds, and changes?	Review change-management procedures and documentation. Change reports should include who made the change, why the change was made, and any required authorization.
Has a complete inventory of IP phones been conducted?	Review documentation of voice assets for MAC addresses, locations, and user assigned inventory.
Are call detail records reviewed for potential toll fraud?	The organization should have a procedure for reviewing call detail records to spot a suspicious call destination, duration, unauthorized calls, and calls outside of business hours.
Is there a vulnerability management process for the UC system?	Review vulnerability management and detection processes to determine whether the organization is actively scanning and detecting new UC vulnerabilities.

continues

Assessment Area	Assessment Technique	*(continued)*
Is UC patch management performed?	Patch management of UC systems should include Communications Manager, gateways, voice endpoints, soft phones, and network infrastructure.	
Are UC monitoring and incident-handling procedures in place?	Review endpoint security event monitoring and incident-handling process. Review endpoint security detection and remediation procedures.	

Technology

Technical Architecture Review

Are voice and data VLANs segmented?	Review UC network design to ensure that voice and data VLANs are separated and voice VLANs use private, RFC 1918, addressing.	
Are layer 2 switch controls implemented?	Confirm that the following features are enabled: DHCP snooping, Dynamic ARP inspection, IP Source Guard, and Port Security with a maximum of three learned MAC addresses.	
Are good switch security practices followed?	Confirm that unused ports are disabled and placed into a nonrouted VLAN. Confirm that VLAN trunks are not enabled on user ports and statically defined VLAN trunks are not used for phone access.	
Is Spanning Tree protected?	Review switch configuration for Spanning Tree protection features BPDU Guard and Root Guard to prevent attackers from changing the Spanning Tree topology.	
Is QoS and rate limiting enabled for voice protocols in the voice VLAN?	Review switch configuration for smart ports and Autoqos.	
Are VLAN access control lists used to control endpoint traffic within the voice VLAN?	Inspect switch configuration for VLAN access control lists to ensure that unnecessary protocols and traffic are blocked.	
Are firewalls used to protect network boundaries between voice and data VLANs?	UC design should include the use of firewalls as access control devices between voice and data networks.	

continues

Assessment Area	Assessment Technique	*(continued)*
Is an IPS used to monitor and block malicious traffic entering the UC network?	UC design should have IPS placed at the network entry points to the voice network to monitor and defend it against malicious traffic.	
Are voice gateways protected from unauthorized access?	Voice gateways should be configured to block access to voice ports from unapproved address ranges. Firewall protection is recommended through integrated IOS firewall or ASA.	
Is encryption used to secure voice trunks to remote sites?	IPsec should be leveraged to encrypt and authenticate UC trunks to remote branches.	
Are wireless IP phones secured from attack?	Wireless IP phones should use the AES encryption and 802.1x authentication to the voice network. Dedicated SSIDs for wireless IP phones should be used with firewalling and IPS to monitor for unauthorized access attempts.	
Call Management Controls		
Have basic security practices been implemented for CUCM and CME?	Each platform should be hardened to reduce the risk of vulnerabilities following Cisco security guidelines.	
Has phone auto registration been disabled for Communications Manager?	After initial installation, auto registration of IP phones should be disabled for CUCM and CME.	
Is encryption and authentication of Signaling enabled between Communications Manager and endpoints?	Signaling authentication and encryption is recommended to protect from signaling attacks and calling pattern disclosure or denial of service.	
Is Voice media encryption enabled?	Secure RTP is recommended to prevent attackers from eavesdropping or manipulating phone conversations.	
Is IPsec configured to protect signaling between Communications Manager and gateways?	IPsec is recommended for encryption and authentication between Communications Manager and MGCP or H.323 gateways.	
Is IPsec configured for inter and intra cluster traffic between Communications Managers?	IPsec encryption is recommended for traffic between Communications Managers.	
Is Phone Proxy used to protect soft phone and remote IP phones?	ASA Phone Proxy provides encryption and authentication for voice endpoints that are mobile or remotely provisioned.	

continues

Assessment Area	Assessment Technique _(continued)_
Are SIP trunks protected from Internet attacks?	SIP PSTN access should be protected from attack through firewalls and CUBE.
Do SIP trunks use Message Digest Authentication?	Message Digest Authentication can prevent the hijacking of IP PSTN services and can protect the disclosure of authentication credentials.
Toll Fraud Prevention	
Are calling search space restrictions in place for common toll fraud methods?	Call forward all, application, and voicemail calling search space should be configured to prevent long-distance dialing.
Are route patterns configured to prevent toll dialing where applicable?	Route patterns should be configured to block call attempts to 900/976 numbers and international exchanges that use North American area codes (for example, 649, 809, 284, and 876).
Are after hours calling restrictions in place?	After hours calling restrictions can prevent unauthorized calls outside of business hours.
Are call accounting features enabled to monitor call usage?	Call monitoring can help identify toll fraud and abuse through CDR records and should be enabled.
Are forced authorization codes (FAC) used to authorize long distance calls?	FAC codes can be an effective way to prevent unauthorized long distance. FAC codes also attribute calls to individuals to better facilitate reporting and usage monitoring.
Are external transfers of calls blocked?	Transferring an incoming call to an external long-distance number is a common toll fraud method. Blocking this feature or restricting it to local destinations is recommended.
Are voice conferencing services configured to end the conference after the host has dropped?	Conference services should be configured to immediately drop a conference call after the host has left. This prevents conference attendees from staying on the bridge after the call has ended.
Are IVR scripts and auto attendant configured to prevent external transfers?	Preventing external transfers can stop an outside caller from dialing back out through the phone system.
Application Controls Review	
Are encrypted signaling and media used for voice applications?	The use of encrypted signaling should extend to applications if possible.

continues

Assessment Area	Assessment Technique	*(continued)*
Are voice application protocols authenticated?	Application protocols should be authenticated in a secure fashion.	
Are firewalls used to protect application access?	UC applications should be protected like any other application on the network.	
Voice Endpoint Protection Review		
Are phone configuration functions protected?	IP phone configuration features should be disabled or protected with an access code.	
Is gratuitous ARP response disabled?	Disabling gratuitous ARP on the phone prevents it from updating MAC to IP tables with bogus information.	
Is voice VLAN access disabled through the phone?	Phones should be configured to prevent access to the voice VLAN from the PC data port.	
Are signed software images and configuration files used?	Phones that use signed images and config files prevent attackers from being able to supply hacked boot images or modified configuration files.	
Are unused phone PC ports disabled?	PC ports should be disabled on common area and lobby phones to prevent unauthorized data access.	
Monitoring and Management Controls		
Is multi-level administration used for Unified Communications Manager?	Mutli-level administration should be configured to enable different levels of configuration access by user or by group.	
Is MARS used to monitor security products protecting voice assets?	MARS is useful for aggregating security events from multiple devices.	
Is CSM used for consistent policy enforcement on gateways, firewalls, and switches?	CSM provides workflow based configuration of network security products for consistent policy enforcement.	
Technical Control Testing		
Can the data network directly access the voice network?	Attempt to gain access to the voice VLAN from the data side of the network and map any services exposed.	
Are Voice VLAN segmentation controls operating?	Test 802.1q trunking with VoIP Hopper to simulate an IP phone.	

continues

Assessment Area	Assessment Technique	*(continued)*
Are firewalls blocking voice ports from the data portion of the network?	Test firewall functionality to ensure that voice and management ports are blocked from the data side of the network.	
Are switch security features protecting the voice VLAN?	Test layer 2 security features of switches.	
Is voice traffic sent unencrypted?	Use UCSniff to record any unencrypted voice traffic found on the data network or after gaining access to the voice VLAN.	
Are gateways blocking unauthorized access attempts?	Send call requests directly to the gateway to determine whether it allows access from unauthorized sources.	
Are toll fraud protection configurations operating as expected?	Test toll fraud prevention functions by attempting to dial number sequences that should be blocked.	
Was security testing detected by monitoring systems?	Review Security Monitoring tools for logs of testing activity. Review CDR records for unauthorized calls.	

Summary

UC has changed the way in which businesses can interact with customers and employees, by taking a separate hardwired technology and turning it into a service that can be offered across a common network backbone. The ability to integrate UC into business processes provides brand-new tools to better serve the needs of customers but also opens new vectors of attack that need to be defended against. This chapter is focused on ways to ensure the UC is deployed in a safe and flexible manner providing the same level or greater of security expected from legacy phone systems. In summary:

■ Without properly protecting the UC environment businesses face risks to confidentiality, disruption of service, fraud, loss of reputation, and noncompliance with security regulations.

■ There are multitudes of threats facing a VoIP environment, many of which have been inherited from moving to a consolidated network. Threats against UC can be protected against with proper design and utilization of security features.

■ An organization's policies regarding acceptable use of voice resources and standardization of good security practices are essential to protecting UC.

■ Cisco offers a wide range of switch-based security features to defend against common LAN attacks used to gain access to voice traffic.

- Voice VLANs should be segmented and all access from the data side of the network should pass through firewalls to prevent unnecessary access to the UC infrastructure.

- It is essential to defend the Gateway to the PSTN from unauthorized access and protect Internet-based IP PSTN services through session border controllers and firewalls.

- Encryption of voice media and signaling is the most effective way to prevent the possibility of eavesdropping on VoIP calls.

- Soft phones and IP phones can be provisioned securely by leveraging ASA film proxy to terminate encrypted sessions to the UC network, enabling phones to exist anywhere on the Internet.

- Auditors should test LAN security features in common attacks to ensure that security controls are adequately protecting the UC environment.

References in This Chapter

VoIP Security Alliance, http://www.voipsa.org/

NIST 800-58 Security Considerations for Voice Over IP Systems, csrc.nist.gov/publications/nistpubs/800-58/SP800-58-final.pdf

DISA checklist for Internet Protocol Telephony and VoIP STIG, iase.disa.mil/stigs/stig/VoIP-STIG-V2R2.pdf

Cisco Unified Communications SRND Based on Cisco Unified Communications Manager 7.x, http://www.cisco.com/en/US/docs/voice_ip_comm/cucm/srnd/7x/uc7_0.html

Cisco Unified Call Manager Express Solution Reference Network Design Guide, http://www.cisco.com/en/US/docs/voice_ip_comm/cucme/srnd/design/guide/cmesrnd.html

Unified Communications Manager Express Toll Fraud Prevention, https://www.cisco.com/en/US/products/sw/voicesw/ps4625/products_tech_note09186a00809dc487.shtml

Voice Security Primer: Protecting the Voice Infrastructure, http://www.cisco.com/en/US/solutions/collateral/ns339/ns639/ns641/net_implementation_white_paper0900aecd80460724.html

Index

Numbers

A

O

P

W

FREE Online Edition

Your purchase of **Network Security Auditing** includes access to a free online edition for 45 days through the Safari Books Online subscription service. Nearly every Cisco Press book is available online through Safari Books Online, along with more than 5,000 other technical books and videos from publishers such as Addison-Wesley Professional, Exam Cram, IBM Press, O'Reilly, Prentice Hall, Que, and Sams.

SAFARI BOOKS ONLINE allows you to search for a specific answer, cut and paste code, download chapters, and stay current with emerging technologies.

Activate your FREE Online Edition at www.informit.com/safarifree

> **STEP 1:** Enter the coupon code: JQPYYBI.

> **STEP 2:** New Safari users, complete the brief registration form.
> Safari subscribers, just log in.

If you have difficulty registering on Safari or accessing the online edition, please e-mail customer-service@safaribooksonline.com